PENG

SHOW M

Annie Caulfield's work includes collaborations with the comedian Lenny Henry as well as episodes of *This Life*. Her most recent trip to Benin was as adviser and guide to Spice Girl Mel B for her Channel 4 documentary *Mel B Vodou Princess*, also featuring Isidore the taxi-driver.

SHOW ME THE MAGIC

travels round Benin by taxi

ANNIE CAULFIELD

PENGUIN BOOKS

PENGUIN BOOKS

Published by the Penguin Group
Penguin Books Ltd, 80 Strand, London WC2R 0RL, England
Penguin Putnam Inc., 375 Hudson Street, New York, New York 10014, USA
Penguin Books Australia Ltd, 250 Camberwell Road,
Camberwell, Victoria 3124, Australia
Penguin Books Canada Ltd, 10 Alcorn Avenue, Toronto, Ontario, Canada M4V 3B2
Penguin Books India (P) Ltd, 11 Community Centre,
Panchsheel Park, New Delhi – 110 017, India
Penguin Books (NZ) Ltd, Cnr Rosedale and Airborne Roads,
Albany, Auckland, New Zealand
Penguin Books (South Africa) (Pty) Ltd, 24 Sturdee Avenue,
Rosebank 2196, South Africa

Penguin Books Ltd, Registered Offices: 80 Strand, London WC2R 0RL, England

www.penguin.com

First published by Viking 2002
Published in Penguin Books 2003
1

Set in Monotype Bembo
Printed in England by Clays Ltd, St Ives plc

For Mr Patrick – magic always

Acknowledgements

With thanks to: Solomon Abebe; Juliet Burton; Jo and James Caulfield; Sarah Daniels; Jon S. Fink; Eleo Gordon; Anastasia Mousas; Kaisley Phillips; Woodrow Phoenix; Cassandra Struthers; Akum Uwakemu; Mike Walker; Jasmine, Mary and Molly Warwick; Claude Wishick. Special thanks to friends, acquaintances and passers-by in Benin, particularly my friend Isidore Loko and his family.

Contents

I

Careful Who You Slap in the Face

'This is where the politician exploded.' Isidore waved a hand at the town sign. 'Paf! And gone.'

I thought he was talking about a bomb.

Benin had violently changed governments nine times in twelve years during the nervy, bad old days between 1960 and 1972. One political hopeful declared himself president at nine in the morning and was gone by teatime. Running Benin was no job for anyone looking for a good night's sleep, a pension plan or a long life – until President Kérékou came along in 1972 and showed how a tough guy with a heavily scarred face, and no qualms about house smashings or random arrests, could keep himself in charge for a very long time. Yet even under Kérékou's stern regime, coup enthusiasts made sure no more than three years passed without running, shouting, shooting and bleeding outside the presidential palace, right up until the late nineties. So when I heard talk of exploded politicians, a bomb did seem likely.

'Who blew him up?'

Isidore looked at me, then quickly back at the road – in these country towns a chicken or a child could be darting recklessly in front of the car at any moment. 'In fact,' he said. 'He did it himself.'

'An accident?'

Regardless of small darting perils on the road, Isidore had to look at me again. As always, impatience was tempered to a long-suffering weariness, the way the good-natured remind themselves not to snap at the slow-witted – just take a deep breath and try to communicate, yet again.

'How could it be an accident? You know the story?'

'No.'

'No. So how can you talk of an accident when you're hearing this for the first time?'

I said nothing. Isidore drove on a while, composing his thoughts for the storytelling, steeling himself to deal with further treacle-headed incomprehension, bound to spoil things before his punchline if he didn't keep strict control of the conversation.

Apparently some people can do that thing where you hire a taxi driver and you're in charge of things. I'm sure I've done it myself on a number of occasions, but not with Isidore. With Isidore, I paid him, but if I proved to be unable to meet the standards he required of a passenger, I could find myself put out at a roadside anywhere in Benin's 113,000 square kilometres, an area slightly smaller than England but inconveniently hot and unfamiliar for the sudden pedestrian.

Isidore told me what time he'd collect me, where I'd be going, what to learn from the journey and where I'd be staying at its end. He told me what to eat, when to eat it and how much water to drink with and between these meals. If I didn't eat enough, or drink the right gallonage of water, I'd be firmly scolded. And sleep? If I didn't sleep enough, well, that was just pushing Isidore to the limits of his tolerance.

It was no good me insisting that I didn't usually sleep much; Isidore simply wasn't having an ill-rested passenger in his car. He reintroduced me to the concept of the afternoon nap, not something I'd taken since the age of four. It was no use me imagining that now I was closing in on four-zero I might be old enough to know my own sleep requirements. Isidore was as dogmatic on the nap subject as my nap-insisting granny had been – and he didn't even bother bribing me with a Wagon Wheel.

'Listen, we've had a busy morning. There are things to see later, when it's cool, so if you don't sleep now you'll be destroyed for them. I'll be back at six. Wake up at five-thirty, shower and change so you'll be fresh for the next events.'

'But . . .'

After the first defeat over nap time, I still had a spark of rebellion left in me; when Isidore returned on the dot of six, triumphantly crowing that I looked wonderfully refreshed, I told him that I'd not actually slept, just lain on my bed reading. He frowned and sighed. The following day when I was sent to my hotel after lunch, he said: 'And make sure you sleep. Don't read.'

I lied after that, told him I had marvellous deep dreams, cat-on-the-mat luxuriant afternoon sleeps – because you can keep disobeying your granny and she'll forgive you, but Isidore . . . He didn't need to be doing with the likes of me. He could go back to the taxi drivers' off-season state of having no passengers at all; hanging around outside a hotel in Cotonou, Benin's non-official capital, for fareless hours on end, his bills at home mounting up, the family larder running low – anything was better than ferrying about some substandard passenger in his carefully preserved, hand-painted, glowing turquoise 1980 Peugeot.

So, by day five, I knew an exploded-politician story was best left to be told and not interrupted with fool questions from someone who would surely be thinking more clearly had she really had her full nap time as instructed.

'A young politician from the south went north to talk to the people . . . I'm speaking slowly so you understand.'

I nodded. Isidore knew my grasp of French could be wayward. This was one reason why he felt I should have constant stern supervision – a woman who'd come alone to Benin, with such a comically bizarre command of the country's only European language, was obviously not the full franc piece.

'The politician went around telling people they should vote for him. People said yes, yes, of course, the way people do to make a politician go away. But then he went to see a very old man, who said to him: "I don't trust you young people of today." Then the old man turned his back and started smoking his pipe.

'Very angry, the young politician slapped his face – "You listen to me," he said.

'The old man kept on smoking his pipe. "You shouldn't have slapped me," he said.

'The politician laughed. "Ha! You're an old man, what are you going to do about it?" And he slapped him again!

'The old man just said quietly, "You'll be sorry you did that."

'The young politician laughed even harder and drove away in his limousine.

'On his way home, the hand he'd used for slapping started to swell up. Then the whole arm swelled, swelled up like a balloon. Then his other hand and the other arm swelled. Swelled so he couldn't drive any more. Someone from a village had to take him home and all the way back he kept swelling – one leg, two legs, neck, stomach, back . . . all. They took him to the hospital.

'"Ah no," said the doctor. "We can't cure this with hospital medicine. You need a *guérisseur*." Annie, you know *guérisseur*?'

I was alert. I did. *Guérisseur*, traditional healer, practitioner of the shamanic magic arts of *gri-gri*.

'The *guérisseur* came to the hospital and said, "Yes, this is *gri-gri*. But it's too strong for me. Only the person who put this on you can take it away."

'The old man from the north was sent for. He said he would have lifted the *gri-gri* if it was up to him, but it was his father who did it, and his father had died twenty-one years ago. He'd sent the *gri-gri* from beyond the grave. So, there was nothing to be done. The young politician went on swelling – legs, head, back, front . . . He swelled until he died of it, exploded like a balloon all over the hospital.'

I laughed. 'That'll teach him.'

'It teaches him nothing.' Isidore scowled at me. 'He is dead. But us, we should learn from it. Don't be horrible to anyone in this life, slapping them and such, because they might have more power than you think.'

The politician exploded by *gri-gri* was only one verse in Isidore's unabridged head-bible of *gri-gri* stories. Crooked policemen were chased by *gri-gri* bees, bandits were pursued by the lizards of *gri-gri* justice, and politicians . . . It seemed they barely had a moment's peace to enjoy power before entering the records as yet another example of the particular *gri-gri* vulnerability of their profession. Not that they didn't deserve it. One politician, having stolen tax money from many villagers, had been *gri-gri*-ed into flinging himself from a fast-moving car in the prime of his health and was immediately stone-dead in the road. This one sounded like an assassination cover-story to me, but the alleged power of *gri-gri* to strike a politician on behalf of the average Beninois Joe must have been a comfort in a country where 'politician' was a word often interchangeable with 'thief' or 'thug'.

Thieves and thugs had severely disrupted Isidore's childhood. His father, a respected healer and *gri-gri* practitioner, had been forced to spend years away from the family village, hiding from political whim that could have resulted in his imprisonment or execution.

In the early seventies, the newly installed young Marxist-Leninist dictator, Mathieu Kérékou, decided to shake up the power that the magic men held in rural communities. There were harassments, arrests, shrine desecrations . . . Benin would be sort of Chinese, Cuban, North Korean and, a bit made up by Kérékou, socialist modern. Benin would also be Benin; because, until 1975, it had been something else.

When people asked me where I was talking about, where I was going on my travels with Isidore, I had to remember that the state I was trying to know was not well known, nor was it the place that people who thought they knew, knew.

'The little thin place here on the map between Togo and

Nigeria,' I'd tell the completely Benin blank-minded, finding the atlas page for them.

'It's shaped like a willy,' they'd say.

'Well, there's nothing I can do about that,' I'd say.

And I couldn't do a great deal for the more well informed, who'd start talking about ancient African empires and fantastic Benin bronzes in the British Museum . . . I had to cut them short – tell them they were talking about the wrong place.

That Benin, the fantastic-bronzes Benin, was a fifteenth-century Yoruba Empire adjacent to present-day Benin. Some of present-day Benin used to be the Kingdom of Danhome, until the French came and misheard the name as 'Dahomey'. The French then added several neighbouring states in the country they colonized and called Dahomey for decades.

Kérékou changed the name from Dahomey to announce his restart programme for the country; they would rise from the debris of colonialism and coups to be a shiny new nation, as magnificent as the Benin that used to be next door. Also, as the name Danhome/Dahomey properly belonged only to some of the south of the country, and Kérékou came from the north – an area scattered with peoples, like his own, once at war with old Danhome/Dahomey – the name Dahomey just had to go. Kérékou tore up the old maps and declared the People's Republic of Benin open for a new socialist future.

Kérékou's socialism soon evolved into the sort of totalitarian, bureaucratic, corrupt, disastrously inefficient socialism that the people of Eastern Europe found so pleasing until the late 1980s. Also following the Eastern European trend, the people of Kérékou's people's republic got rid of him, in 1991. Possibly with some American communism-fearing assistance, but who am I to say what the CIA may or may not have done. It can't have delighted them, involved or not, when, six years later, Kérékou returned, was voted back in, promising to behave like a calmed-down democrat – which, as elected president of the now plain Republic of Benin, he did. Sort of.

Happily for me, Isidore and everyone, Kérékou's new millennium

Benin was corrupt, inefficient and poverty stricken – but it was calm. And no one got arrested for saying 'Kérékou' in a disapproving tone of voice or for spitting near his soldiers.

What the whole power-shifting, border-shifting, name-changing mashabout of a past meant was that Benin became rich with fragments of several cultures and histories, contained in a conveniently small, if unfortunately penile, place. My aimless, over-rested wanderings were full of revelations about what happened in Africa, what is happening and what may have happened – depending on how much you believe that the world is full of ruthless international conspirators, magic and inexplicable wonders.

Believer and maker of inexplicable wonders Isidore's father was back in his village now, three wives on from Isidore's mother, untroubled by the new, relaxed-style regime, and not only pursuing his traditional role as *guérisseur* and magic-working priest, but also practising his craft as the village blacksmith.

Isidore's father concentrated on the benign kind of magic, warding off evil for his neighbours, alerting them to evidence of bedevilment and witchcraft in their lives. But where his powers excelled was in helping women with their troubles. Too many children? No children? Heavy periods? No periods? Untoward periods? Sickly pregnancy? Troubled labour? The blacksmith had the cure.

Blacksmiths work with elemental forces – iron, fire and earth. Mythologies all over the world credit blacksmiths with supernatural powers, but to me a big, anvil-bashing, iron-bending man didn't seem the obvious choice for the role of confidant in women's more delicate problems.

'I don't know. It's just how it is,' Isidore said when I asked him what the gynaecology connection was. 'My father can cure women's problems very well.'

I had cynical thoughts about how a healthy blacksmith might cure a seemingly infertile woman with a feeble husband, but period pains?

I had suspicious thoughts about why, very soon after first meeting me, Isidore continually emphasized the blessings that could be bestowed on women who got themselves involved with a Beninois man who had easy access to gynaecological *gri-gri*. White women, that is. Story after story of lonely white women of a certain age, saved by a combination of *gri-gri* and youthful Beninois male vigour. The white woman was always rich; the man strong, handsome and desperately poor. A bit like Isidore.

Isidore's favourite white-woman story was definitely a thing of inexplicable wonder. There was a French woman, forty years old. Her husband had died after twenty years of marriage to her; they had no children and her heart was broken. When she came to Benin on holiday she seldom went on excursions with her friends, just sat alone on the beach reading magazines. A young man saw her there every day. He was very young, just eighteen. He asked her why she was always sad and she told him her story – told him how her situation wouldn't be so miserable if she'd been able to have a child, but she'd had two miscarriages and her doctors said childbearing was impossible for her now. The young man talked to her at length and promised her that, if she had a baby with him, they could go to his uncle who did *gri-gri* and the baby would be fine. The French woman liked the young man and decided to take the risk. The uncle gave her an infusion to drink before sex with the young man. She did what she was asked and she became pregnant. The woman had to remain in Benin in the constant care of the *gri-gri* uncle; he gave her infusions to drink and potions to wash with during every day of her pregnancy. The baby was born healthy. She went back to France, taking with her her thriving child and the young man. It turned out, she wasn't just quite a rich woman – she was a member of the Peugeot family and *incredibly* rich. The young man never had to do a stroke of work again, sent presents to all his family and returned to Benin only for holidays, staying in the Sheraton Hotel with the millionaires.

'They are both happy,' Isidore concluded. 'Through sheer luck, both have what they wanted, both are happy.'

I think Isidore told me these stories hoping that I'd spread the word to single white females back home, having quickly established that I wasn't up for participation in such happiness myself. He'd offered it to me within thirty seconds, jumping out of his car when he saw me sitting on a hotel terrace in Cotonou. Not the Sheraton Hotel for millionaires; a government-run collapse of a place on the beach front. Very Graham Greene; very hard to get a drinkable cup of coffee. Very few nights when the water or the electricity weren't cut; very few mornings when seeing the spray of Atlantic breakers behind coconut palms as I came down the chipped stone stairs to breakfast didn't make me catch my breath with excitement. No day that starts with a chokingly great view can end that badly. No proposal of marriage made within thirty seconds can end well . . .

Isidore had asked me how I liked Benin so far, asked me my age, nationality and if I was travelling alone.

'Alone? Good. I am very interested in European women. English is better for me than French, nicer people. I'm thirty-four, only a bit younger than you. It's ideal, we can marry.'

His medium-height stockiness and military type of hold on himself were contradicted by lash-flickered pretty eyes and perfectly shaped, high-arched brows, like he'd stolen them from Lauren Bacall. His smile was as reassuring as a big, firm handshake. But it wasn't ideal. I invented a live-in, long-standing boyfriend fretting at home.

'I see. You really like him?'

'We'll get married next year.'

'OK. Well, you'll need a taxi driver anyway. Don't speak to any other driver but me. I'm the best.'

As we went on our first short journey around town, to track down where exactly Sabena Airlines and Air Afrique had decided between themselves to send my luggage other than Cotonou, Isidore told me he wasn't seriously expecting marriage. Had just wanted to put forward a future possibility. I suggested that this still wasn't a sensible way to go about things – people needed more time to get to the future-possibility stage.

'But now I know there is no future possibility, that issue is closed, there's no time wasted. Do you want to buy trousers here?'

I was boiling in jeans and couldn't wait till my bags reappeared to find something cooler to wear. Along the main boulevard of Cotonou women used the roadside trees as high, flapping show-rooms for locally made clothes – very cheap and on the noisy edge of cheerful. Isidore bargained some bellowingly loud giraffe-print trousers down out of a tree for me. I decided there was no point paying more for something that looked less clownish when my own quiet trousers should be only a few hours away. Actually they were still in Belgium and, due to some airline-staff determination to keep the old jokes about lost baggage alive and uproarious, they would arrive with me, via Cameroon, in four days' time.

The four days gave me opportunity to decide how I felt about the future possibility of Isidore as a taxi driver to the more remote parts of Benin. By the time I was wearing my own trousers, I knew. As much as you can know if it's wise to put your time in someone else's hands.

As we progressed through the country, Isidore constantly bossing, storytelling and explaining, I was glad he didn't ask me any more about my home life – I could have forgotten details of my made-up fiancé and been caught out. But there was still a worry: what if we bumped into Isidore's father and his metalworking magic sussed me out as a fraud, a free, single woman who, if far from having access to Peugeot-type bank accounts, was still relatively wealthy and going to waste? Scrupulously honest Isidore would certainly have found my big lie to him a sackable offence in a passenger.

Maybe it's not an unembellished truth that he'd have put me out at a remote roadside, a passenger without references, had I failed to comply with his requirements of an employer; but it would have been all too easy to destroy the comfortable dynamic of our relation-ship with more subtle offences than outright lies to him. As with most comfortable things – armchairs, for instance – it could be a small complaint, like a loose tiny wing-nut, that could send every-one sprawling to the floor hurt and embarrassed.

Isidore had created the dynamic. He knew where potential loose tiny wing-nuts could be, so he liked every choice I made to be referred to him. Even my choice of bathroom facility.

'If you really need to go, go, but it's not clean. Better to go in a field later.'

Deciding this was one subject I didn't need discuss with him wouldn't do either.

'You don't piss? It's been three hours. Are you sick?'

'I went in the museum toilets; I just didn't tell you I was going – is that all right?'

'You should tell me, so I don't worry you've got sick.'

Other taxi drivers might have preferred to start and stop their cars as instructed, and not taken the risk of rebuff involved in such minute passenger management. I could have rebuffed – just been the person who paid Isidore to drive, and never found out anything about him and what he knew. He didn't only know the country – its people, its history, food, religions, toilet facilities and dodgy characters to watch out for – he also spoke better French than me, and he spoke five Beninois languages; he knew how to maintain and drive his ancient vehicle in alarming road and traffic conditions; he knew how to protect me from situations where I might be ripped off, be in physical danger, or simply in danger of making a fool of myself.

There were potential dangers in Benin that even Isidore might have found it tricky to extricate me from. Overnight, coup fever might return, blood would spill, and no one would want to marry the white people gadding the streets, because whites about town were usually mercenaries. Benin was a lucrative real-life stomping ground for the Soldier of Fortune likes of Bob Denard and was the inspiration for the mercenary-led coup in the novel *The Dogs of War*.

The governmental salsas in and out of communism had led Benin to be nicknamed 'The Cuba of West Africa'. Many citizens fled. Un-fled young men seemed to have had an allergy to long life and a compulsion to riot in the streets. If this kind of heady atmosphere returned, I could have an untoward Benin experience like Bruce Chatwin's.

In the middle of the interesting old rowdy days, Bruce thought he'd potter around composing a novella. He was assumed to be a mercenary, was roughly arrested and came close to being executed while on his way to a hotel swimming pool on a day when peace came apart in a hail of bullets and bazookas. And if such a day came while I was pottering by the same Cotonou hotel pool, within firing range of the bullet-scarred presidential palace, I'd be needing Isidore to at least vouch for me as a harmless moron in his care.

2

What Kind of Luck Do You Bring?

I found the Virgin Mary at the foot of a rock in central Benin. Just her statue, not her appearing for me in the blue-and-white-frocked person, but she still wasn't the kind of attraction I'd have expected Isidore to swerve off the road for, talking her up as an essential Beninois cultural icon.

Still, why not? She'd been to the trouble of startling a local farmer with her actual presence on the rock in 1972. She could have gone anywhere that evening – busy social calendar, I'm sure – but she picked small-town Benin. I don't know if it's significant that she picked the same year as the secular People's Republic of Benin was launched. And there's no record of whether she was signalling approval or warning against the new regime.

As well as her political opinions, I wondered about her geographical decisions. Why hadn't she chosen to appear twenty miles down the road at the fortuitously named town of Savé? Perhaps she'd been embarrassed by the round and almost identical humps on the horizon behind the town, known as the 'Bosoms of Savé'. In her chosen location, away from sexy hill-curves, at rugged Dassa Zoumé, she was right next door to one of the most ancient and significant vodou shrines in West Africa. Fighting talk, surely.

Chiming in with information gleaned from other sources could end badly with Isidore.

'It says in the guide book there's a very important vodou site here.'

Isidore scowled; my flicks through the guide book were a profound insult. 'I know that. You'll see it. But it's complicated. You can't just go to that one. We'll go when it's the right time. We're doing other things now. So, this is where Blessed Mary came . . .'

Being Irish, I'm fairly well acquainted with the Virgin Mary and her notions to appear on rocks to solitary devotees, usually at dusk or dawn, usually in a remote region with a disastrously meagre source of revenue. But the odd thing about the peaches-and-cream-complexioned Dassa Zoumé Virgin – apart from looking more like she'd say 'Top of the morning' to you than greet you in the local Yoruba dialect – was that she was set in scenery that suddenly looked like northwestern Ireland. Grey rock and green trees around her, while red dust and scrub grass lay outside her immediate radius – the start of the very dry dry season in central and northern Benin.

Driving up from Cotonou and the coast, we had passed through the lush, big-leafed green of the southern rainy-season landscapes. Women sat at roadsides, amid mounds of mangoes high enough to give challenge to the 'Bosoms of Savé'. The women were desperately hoping to sell a basketful for twenty pence to those too lazy to drive on and pick up a few of the million fallen mangoes under trees for themselves.

Isidore said: 'Some of these country people, they're so poor they live on just mangoes and water.'

Mangoes and water sounded like a diet European pop stars would pay a nutritionist a fortune to be put on as a miracle detox and anti-cellulite regime. Actually, the women by the roadside didn't have cellulite – not a pick of superfluous fat on them. But their children, all around them sucking on mangoes, had the pot-bellies of the protein deficient; and the women moved with an all-day exhaustion, listlessly shifting infants who'd got themselves the wrong way up in a mango pile. Unless you needed the women to sell to you. Then they'd fly at the car, finding great hidden wells of strength to haggle vociferously with Isidore for ten minutes, fifteen minutes, never losing the stamina for a new high-volume refusal and counter-attack.

Isidore could talk as loud and as fast as the mango ladies – and had the winning option of walking away. He said they'd see me and lose their minds – they'd think of a number, any number, and triple it. Still, I wondered if we needed to be quite so penny-pinching with the women. It shocked me when I realized he'd haggled a woman with a tiny, gangly baby down to twenty pence.

'That's double what she'd normally get,' he said. 'The first price was her dream.'

A fiver a dream.

Children saw me and lost their minds, not through dreams of riches but just because I was there, a sight as weird as a twin-headed lamb. Passing through villages, if we slowed down for produce purchase or to let me have a stare at people's lives, small children would leap out of mango-crawling lethargy or even sleep, yelling: '*Yovo!*' Whitey! Running like someone had set light to their rear ends. '*Yovo! Yovo!*' they'd yell in our wake, little feet dancing wildly, arms flailing in the air or pointing after us as one child became ten in an instant, more still coming, pelting out of the shade just too late to see a *yovo*.

Yovo spotting was like a sport; points scored for speed of *yovo* announcement, double points if the *yovo* shouted back and a top result if you got the *yovo* to give you a sweet.

At first I worried about tooth-rot-spreading sweet distribution, but in all areas previously *yovo* trodden, kids assumed I came manufactured with sweet-filled pockets as standard, so I gave in.

Isidore had two children of his own; no shouting from a mango pile for them. They could play the more sophisticated game of bragging to their friends about how many *yovos* their father got to know in his line of work. Why, they'd even touched and smelt *yovos*, they'd been this close to them themselves . . . Lucien was ten, Antoine was twelve, and it soon became apparent that all Isidore's work, involving *yovos* or not, was about these two and their future.

Learning about them begged a question about Isidore's status. He told me gruffly that their mother, his wife, had run off five years ago; she'd been difficult from the start and had never understood his belief that two children were quite enough to be fending for on a low income.

'She said she couldn't stand it. She was ridiculed by her family and friends for having so few children. What kind of poor man had she married, a man who could only afford two? So she went. Good riddance.'

Isidore's face told me there was absolutely no need to discuss the matter further.

Although I'd seen Isidore's boys, and didn't quite know how their mother could have abandoned such elegant, gazelle-eyed little faces, it did seem she'd had peculiar ill luck to marry a Beninois man who believed in family planning. Town and country, the earth heaved with children, like they were just bursting out of some spontaneous fertilization of thin air.

I did only have Isidore's side of the story: that he had common sense and she, along with the rest of Benin, hadn't. He could have all manner of faults as a husband. For instance, if he was so bossy with a passenger, what would he be like with a wife?

Whatever, Isidore was a strange one, ploughing his lonely furrow in the world and living in holy terror of African women, in case he was yet again ensnared by their obsessive, ill-considered breeding.

'Caution at all times. One mistake and they'll catch you and trap you with their babies.'

And the cost of wives . . . ? A nightmare. In Cotonou one afternoon we'd come across another taxi driver, an average-sized man, made midget by two gigantic women flanking him – gigantic-wide and gigantic-high. Heels, and tall twists of orange cloth on their heads cheated their height, but their width and depth was all undulating, Rubens's dream female flesh, swathed in robes of red, yellow and orange. There was some greeting between us, some smiling talk about my blue eyes from the women, then the trio swayed away, the man a twig sprouting between majestically moving mountains.

Isidore's farewell smile snapped into a sour grimace. 'See those two? Those are his two wives. I'd hate that, two big wives like that – that's four in food.'

The man hadn't looked troubled; perhaps he didn't dare. He seemed like a mere accessory that the wives had brought with them for the day – a fetching complement to their colour palette in his robe of red and orange patterned with yellow lawnmowers. If he'd had some kind of rebellious turn and appeared in a purple robe he'd chosen for himself, the wives would have been bewildered and indignant – cloth buying was women's territory. In any market the most ferocious bargaining was over lengths of cloth in which to clothe husbands, children, but especially for *pagne*. The *pagne*, strictly speaking, was the cloth that was tied around the hips, but colloquially *pagne* referred to a woman's entire outfit – dress, wraps, head tie – and *pagne* were obsessively accumulated. It would be a shamefully poor woman who didn't have a collection of them squirrelled away; her *pagne* were her achievement, her wealth and something a mother wanted to leave her daughters. Even in the remotest villages, *pagne* salesmen on bicycles struggled round, their shoulders piled high with bales of deep-dyed wax cloth. The patterns were loud or subtle, anything could be on them: patterns of fashionable shoes, perhaps, or a mobile-phone print – this was very popular, as were skyscrapers, electric irons, kettles and radios. Flowers, animals and trees were rare – the preference was abstraction or abstract impressions of modern things. Like lawnmowers. Then there were travelogue prints – Sacré Cœur patterns, Saint Peters, the Statue of Liberty, Big Ben, Arc de Triomphe . . . There were special celebration prints; you could tie the Pope's face round yourself, or Kérékou's, or you could have a run of cloth specially made celebrating your grandfather's

seventieth birthday, or funeral, or your son's graduation, or prais-
ing your candidate for local office. Oranges, reds and yellows
seemed popular in the south; purples, blues and greens in the dry
north.

Two very fancy big wives would be costing the earth in cloth,
never mind food.

Servants were cheaper. Isidore employed a niece from his village
to look after the boys when he was working. He also employed a
university student to give the boys private tuition at weekends
because state schooling could be interrupted for weeks on end
by striking, underpaid staff. If the boys weren't well schooled at
this stage, how would they ever get scholarships to the Jesuit
boarding school in northern Benin? Apparently this was one of
few hopes for poor boys seeking advancement in life. And he
was doggedly determined that his boys would go far beyond a
cab-driving life.

Isidore had desperately wanted to stay in school but family
poverty had forced him to leave at the age of twelve. Most of what
he knew, he'd taught himself, and his head was full of frustrated
yearnings for jobs he might have had if he'd been properly educated.
And it was more than that. He'd once watched me reading a book
and said he wished he could read so easily, relax with a book for
pleasure. In Benin, a poor man with higher education didn't necessarily earn more than a cab driver. It was education for its own sake
that he yearned for; to say to someone, 'Oh yes, I read that book,
I live with my sons in a house full of books.'

On our first long journey out of Cotonou, Isidore wanted to pass
by his home for a last-minute check on the boys before a three-day
absence. And I think he'd promised them a look at his new *yovo*.
We bumped down dirt roads, turning left, turning right, far into
the warren of chicken- and child-run compounds where poorer
Cotonou dwellers rented their homes – one-storey breeze-block
buildings jammed together round communal open rectangles. If
you were poorer than this, you slept on the street. Spick and span,
Isidore's boys emerged from a corrugated-iron door when Papa

sounded the car horn saying to me, 'The house is not tidy. It's better they come out here.'

Both boys were small for their age, but shiningly healthy. In their huge eyes and high cheekbones, I knew I was looking at child mirrors of a beautiful mother; none of Isidore's solid handsomeness showed in them. I've never seen such fine-boned, glamorous little boys; no wonder Isidore wanted to save them from anything like manual labour – a passing stranger would want the same. They were in their school uniforms, short-sleeved khaki suits worn by children all over the country, always made to the same economical three-sizes-too-big design.

Antoine and Lucien looked like twins and spoke in tiny, high-pitched voices to each other, like they'd developed a secret language, barely audible to big people. They fell to silence in front of me and shook my hand with formal gravitas. But their excitement about a *yovo* on the doorstep couldn't be repressed for long. The eldest cracked first; he asked to try on my broad-brimmed straw hat. He preened himself in it, so dancing-legged delighted that I had to say, 'You keep it.'

Isidore insisted Antoine return it, but for once I insisted more forcefully than he did. Lucien watched his older brother in the oversized hat with tangible envy, but said nothing. Both said nothing as I handed them the obligatory sweet ration on departure, too busy rapidly scanning each other's hands to check they had equal shares. They received instructions from Isidore in their own language, then stared, a little mournful, a little worried at their swiftly and cheerfully departing Papa.

A week later, Isidore told me why I'd been wrong about the hat, and why he, as always, had been right.

'This hat of yours . . .' He laughed. 'This wretched hat has been such a drama at home. Antoine kept it on him until he slept and then Lucien was up in the morning early, thinking he'd take it and sneak out to school wearing it, but Antoine caught up with him – there was shouting, pushing, tears . . . The maid had to hide the hat until my return. There were tears again with me. Now we have a compromise: Antoine wears it to school and Lucien is allowed to wear it in the evening for watching television.'

Thoughtlessly unjust hat distribution was a minor *faux pas* compared to the thing I really had to watch out for at the shrine of the Virgin Mary – a proven ability to offend Isidore's religious sensibility. Of all the gods he paid homage to, the Roman Catholic God was of particular importance to him. I'd irritated him considerably, telling him I'd been brought up a Catholic, even had a priest for a brother, but didn't believe any more.

'You'll regret that,' he'd said, with the stern tone of one who's about to have an idiot exploded by *gri-gri*.

When we passed a large, modern Catholic church in Cotonou, he'd said, 'That's where I pray. I go at least twice a week to Mass.'

If he'd been talking about a mosque, or a vodou temple, anything but the old kicked-out, over-familiar faith of my childhood, I might have proceeded with more tact and respect.

'I'd be interested to see how they do Mass here,' I'd said blithely.

'I go to Mass to worship God,' he said. 'If you want to pray, you are welcome; otherwise, not.'

So I approached the Virgin Mary with plenty of cautious respect. Apparently quite a few approaches were made – for a mile around, her craggy rock was fenced by what looked like cattle pens, for holding crowds on pilgrimage, Isidore explained; thousands came from all over Africa and even the Pope had come once. I nodded, working hard to maintain an 'I might be praying' demeanour. I was soon distracted from this as Isidore clambered enthusiastically up the rock and slapped the granite slabs around the Virgin without a shred of divinity-respecting inhibition.

'Look at these! Enormous! Look at these rocks! Look at what God has made here! Take a picture!'

He climbed further; I panted after him. All through the trees was a stony, wandering path, bordered by the stations of the cross. I tried to look at the steep ascent of these numbered metal crosses with reverential piety, but Isidore was dangling above me, hands pressed out against the sides of a cleft in the rock: 'Look! Take a photo! I look like I'm holding these apart before they squash me! Quick, I'm slipping now!'

I took a photo, and that was about it for the Virgin – we didn't even light a candle by her little *yovo* feet.

It was off season for her anyway. Come August, the holding pens would be full of pilgrims, waiting for their chance to light candles and process through the stations of the cross in the manner decreed by the sign at their base: 'GO UP ON YOUR KNEES'.

We passed on quickly, northwest of the Virgin, entering what even the short spell of dry weather had turned into red, dust-bowl territory.

'Now,' Isidore announced. 'We will be typical Beninois. We will go from the Virgin Mary to a very powerful vodou fetish. Ask the fetish what you want – so many requests come true here it's incredible. Incredible.'

Fetish – or *fétiche* – was the French name for a vodou divinity. *Vodou* was the Fon – Isidore's language – word for a divinity and its material representation. So really, he was saying 'divinity' twice when he said 'vodou fetish.' Voodoo, vodu, vodun, or vodou, as Isidore spelt it, were also the various spellings for the system of religious worship traditional in this part of Africa. Literally translated from Fon, in its most academically correct spelling, vodu, '*vo*' meant introspection and '*du*' meant the unknown. So *vodou* meant an actual object, the spirit in the object, a religion, and summarized the motivation behind all the religions of the world.

A locally favoured nickname for Benin was 'The Cradle of Vodou'. The practice went out with the slave trade to Haiti, Brazil, Cuba and North America. It was repressed, disguised, merged with other religions, embellished with beliefs from other African regions and Native American animism and always survived.

People have done years of in-depth study into vodou and related forms of traditional African religion. I'm not doing in-depth here; I'm doing need-to-know as we go along, as the tangle of it became unravelled for me, little by little.

In the vodou districts every village had colourful shrines; every home had statues; every street was roamed on some day of the week by men dressed like kaleidoscopic hedgerows, followed by face-painted boys playing drums, and women in high head-wraps, dancing themselves to the verge of a trance or collapse. From roadside glimpses so far, I'd dismissed all horror-film notions of vodou. It seemed to be a jumping carnival of a religion. So when Isidore drove me miles off the beaten track to pay homage at a powerful shrine, I expected dancing, bright costumes, a bit of a party . . . But this was the kind of vodou shrine that brought to mind Papa Doc Duvalier, zombies, people dying of fright in the darkness . . . One look at it and the blood-drenched downside of vodou took hold of my imagination and froze it stone-still in the middle of the thought: *Get out of here now.*

All I could see around the car were angry clamouring people in burnt, blackened rag-clothes – faces twisted, sweating, hands clawing at the windows. Brueghel monsters in a dark pit. A dead shallow in a red hillside; the squalid dirt basin at the end of the world.

Behind the door-pulling damned was a smoking pyre, about ten feet high. Thick branches protruding from it were hung with the skulls of animals – jaw-bared sheep and goats. There were singed feathers everywhere, a scatter of shattered bones and a stench of boiled fat. In shabby lean-tos around the pyre, skinny women squatted over cooking pots, glowering towards me out of hollow eyes. The thumping on the windows and sides of the car intensified, faces pressed closer. I knew Isidore had made a terrible mistake. These people didn't want me here.

'Hurry up. Out you get.' He grinned at me like we'd arrived at the seaside.

I hesitated.

'Come on.' He opened his door. Hands gripped at him.

'Isidore, is it all right for me to be here?' I asked, not reaching for my door handle.

'Why not?' He grinned again and breezed out into the grimy, pawing crowd.

As I got out I felt the strange, frenzied energy the people were giving off. Women were clutching my arms and pointing to babies at their breasts. Tiny children hugged my legs. I looked a red-eyed man in the red eyes and realized he was laughing. There was a sharp smell cutting through the heavy, fat-laden air. Several of the men brandished bottles of clear liquid. Home-brew rum. Everyone was laughing – what had looked like grimaces were grins. It was all distorted through glass and the desperation to get at me. They weren't angry or violently crazy. They were loony drunk on the gut-rotting, eye-gouging tipple the women were stewing up in the lean-tos, a rum known as *sodadi*. And I was the last thing they'd expected to turn up in the pit that morning.

The spokesman, the middle-aged red-eyed man, as ragged as the crowd around him, began a short, frantic negotiation with Isidore in Fon. Isidore told me to give Red Eye some money – not too much, just a couple of pounds. In return I was handed a rough-hewn wooden stake, sharp at one end, about six inches long; Isidore was given a small bottle of red-palm oil and another smeary little bottle, full of rum.

'This is what you need.' Isidore beamed at me. 'Now it begins.'

Red Eye spoke earnestly to Isidore again, glancing at me as he spoke, passing on instructions for translation.

'Now, Annie, he says you must do exactly as he says, when he says – do you understand? He is the *féticheur*, or priest. The *vodounon*. He is very serious.'

Although I now knew I wasn't heading for a tearing limb from limb, I was in no frame of mind to get the giggles. Inches from my face, a goat skull swung from a bent metal pole. That kept me steady.

We moved nearer to the central mound – I was going to call it a pyre again but there were no embers, nothing was actually burning. On closer examination, the mound was entirely composed of greasy short wooden stakes, like the one I had in my hand. They'd been driven into the ground, one beside the other, until they'd rotted into each other and the earth; then other layers had been pummelled on top of those, stake upon stake, to eventually create the high Guy Fawkes bonfire hillock in front of me.

I wondered if the blackened, greasy surface was from the cooking of animals on the mound; but none of the stakes were charred . . .

'It's not burnt,' Isidore said. 'It's the red-palm oil. In the sun it goes black. The black all around here is only from the oil.'

The red-eyed man, the *vodounon*, handed me a mallet and indicated that I should hammer my stake into the mound.

Isidore told me I had to do this while saying aloud to the stake what I wanted from the *vodou*, telling it what I would give as thanks for my request being granted.

'Promise something like a sheep or a chicken. That's normal. It depends on your circumstances and what you want.'

I decided to go for broke; I wildly pledged a sheep and a big meaty cow if I could get half a million to buy a house in central London, preferably Bloomsbury.

The red-eyed man nodded approval, but I spoke to my stake in English so I don't think he understood what he was approving. Isidore handed me the bottle of palm oil. 'Pour this on the stake and repeat what you said.'

I poured, thinking that for half a million the stake would need a good soaking.

'Not all! Not yet!' Isidore shrieked. 'You need oil for other places.' He snatched the bottle away, exchanged a look of panic relieved with the red-eyed man.

Never mind other places, I wasn't done with my stake yet. I had to take a mouthful of rum and then spit the mouthful on to the stake, somehow managing to repeat my requests and promises at the same time. I spat fast, feeling half my teeth dissolve on contact with the rum – even the short swirl round my mouth was enough to make me feel close to the limb-flailing hysteria of the onlookers. I had to check where my feet were as we moved on, much more rum spitting and they might not be so easy to find.

I knew the metal pole with a blob on the end was meant to be a giant penis. Thrusting out of the ground in front of the stake mound, it was the next object for me to lavish with oil, rum spit and incantations. Giant, up-thrusting penises were everywhere in southern Benin. Sometimes they were attached to a carving of the squatting Legba, bringer of fertility, good fortune and occasional impish tricks when neglected. But often there'd simply be the sticky-up business end of Legba outside a front door, at a crossroads or at the edge of a field, formed from a tree branch, a lump of clay, or a thick metal rod. Not the kind of theological symbol to make you contemplate your mortality, but to come across it unexpectedly could certainly give you a bit of a turn.

Again, I had to say what I wanted and what I'd give, as I judiciously poured out oil and spat rum. Then we moved on to *Les Jumeaux*, The Twins, two identical holes in the ground.

Twins were sacred in vodou, a blessed gift at their birth. Twin children were a frequent feature of paintings and carvings, holding hands, smiling. Twin children could hold their identical hands on a sick person's heart and ease their pain. So special were they, twin children were never said to die; they were said to have disappeared, to be in another village, or gone to play in the forest.

As I wondered what kind of spectacle I'd make to the uninitiated passerby, talking seriously to two holes in the ground, Isidore tapped me on the shoulder, smiling. 'Now you'll see how strong vodou is. I know you'll have your wish.'

He couldn't have heard what I'd been asking for in English – perhaps he might have suggested half a million was pushing it with a small rural shrine; how about settling for a cuddly toy and a teasmade?

It wasn't over yet anyway. Now came the pricey part: to put the seal on my wish package. I had to fold a wad of money – about ten pounds, Isidore suggested, any less would have been mean from a *yovo*. I folded the money as small as possible according to the gesticulations of the *vodounon*, then pushed it in beside my stake, drenched it with the last of the oil and rum and yet again asked for my half-million house-fund and promised a sheep and cow.

'Don't worry,' Isidore said. 'You can send me the money to buy your sacrificial animals and I will bring them here.'

For half a million, I'd have been happy to trouble myself with accompanying a sheep and cow from Gatwick, strapping them into executive class and feeding them clover canapés all the way.

The *vodounon* was agitated. I had more new instructions. This time I had extra lines to say. I had to put my hand on my greasy stake and money, asking the *vodou* to protect me from my enemies.

Not just enemies I knew; there were enemies that I didn't know I had. But the *vodou* knew them, knew all of them. The *vodou* would deal with them.

This made me change my mind about what I was doing. I felt properly serious. I'd been going through the peculiar motions, no idea what was going on, and suddenly here was a splinter of wisdom about how life might be, to take away and examine in my oil-covered hands.

Having politely fallen back while the ceremony was in progress, the women and children of the pit clamoured round me again. Isidore had checked en route that I had pockets full of sweets and small coins for this inevitability. But the red-eyed *vodounon* had to be given a more substantial tip. He also wanted the plastic South Park (don't ask) purse I paid him from.

'Give me that,' he snapped. Suddenly he spoke French.

'Give you the purse?'

'Take the rest of your money out; it's the purse he wants.' Isidore smiled reassuringly at the *vodounon*, who seemed hypnotized by Cartman, Kenny . . .

'Give me that,' he repeated. 'I need that.'

Not wanting to put the damper on half a million for a three-pound knick-knack, I handed it over. The *vodounon* examined the round pink faces of the cartoon characters closely, then, as if deciding they disgusted him, he tossed the purse to a small boy.

The crowd hung back again. Isidore had decided he would do himself some good with the *vodou*, seeing as he was there.

'I've seen the sweet Virgin today. Now I will be typical Beninois – Bible in one hand, fetish in the other.'

He didn't have a long carry-on round holes and penises. Just drove in a stake, folded a small-denomination note beside it, poured on the liquids and muttered in Fon.

As he tipped the *vodounon* considerably less than I had, he said: 'I was here in July. Three months ago. This is just to remind them of me.'

'How long does it usually take to get a request?'

'They say a year. But there are a lot of requests.'

A top-up would probably help, then, push you up the waiting list.

The clamour closed in on us again – grins, pleadings, hands, babies thrust forward . . . The *vodounon* had a last urgent discussion with Isidore before we reversed out of the den, the red dust on our windows once more refracting everyone into Brueghel strangeness.

'He says when I come back, I must bring them *friperie* – second-hand clothes. It's easier to find *friperie* in the city.' Isidore pipped the horn cheerily as we headed downhill.

I wondered how come, if the *vodou* was supposed to be so good, the people hanging around looking after it seemed so dirt-poor and desperate – but, thinking tact would be in order, I asked: 'Isidore, does the *vodou* help these people who live round it?'

He looked at me with despair and amazement. 'Who gets to feast on the sacrificial animals? And do you think they leave the money by the stakes to rot?'

'No. I thought they must take it,' I said meekly. I was only trying to be polite, in case elves came and took it or something.

'Of course they take it. He does, the *vodounon*. He will divide it. There is a village behind there. Looking after the *vodou* is the main livelihood for the entire village.'

I imagined that the money, once it was divided all round, wouldn't amount to that much. Not every supplicant was a nervous *yovo*, eager to hand out fistfuls of cash in case someone got cross with her. But if they spent my money and ate up my animals, did it still all count with the spirits? Isidore sighed at this new stupidity – didn't I know that if you gave out good, good came back and that was that?

I didn't ask him how much good, exactly, in sterling.

A Nigerian friend back home laughed when I told her about asking for a house in London, preferably Bloomsbury.

'You can't ask for that. You're supposed to ask for sons, not houses in Bloomsbury. The spirits won't know what to do with that.'

I imagined stressed, non-English-speaking spirits sorting through piles of overdue requests at the year end, gazing at mine in weary confusion: 'A house in Bloomsbury – what's that?'

'I don't know, she was foreign.'

'Oh. Foreign. Well, give her sons anyway, that's all we've got in the stores. Give her a couple, she did say a cow *and* a sheep.'

There I'd be, standing in a rush-hour bus, maybe even in Bloomsbury, feel a lurch in my stomach and have a sudden surprise of twin boys to explain to the conductor.

Isidore turned on the semi-functioning air conditioner as we closed the windows against the dust. This didn't help much; dust still came in by all kinds of invisible orifices in the car and coated us. He peered over the steering wheel, carefully negotiating what he called *escalier*, stairs – the wind and water formed ridges of earth in the road, broken up by deep potholes, likely to crack axles if hit at the wrong angle. I shared out tissues to try and take some of the oil and dirt off us.

'I suppose I'm not allowed to ask what you asked for?'

'No,' Isidore said. 'And I can't ask you, or it won't work.'

We drove in silence for a while, Isidore frowning thoughtfully. Then he said: 'I've driven tourists before, you know. Plenty. But something has happened this time. I never thought of bringing tourists to places like this – to the Virgin's shrine, the plain village *vodou*, all the places I think of taking you . . . I wake up with an idea. Just wake up with it. And each place in my idea is a place that brings blessings. So I ask myself, what luck do you bring? What special kind of luck do you bring?'

This made me feel odd. I wasn't used to being an object of mystical speculation. And it was a troubling responsibility. Special luck can be good or bad. Investments in your passenger may go up or down.

3

Tree Gods, Sperm Squirrels
and the Things

One of Isidore's ideas had come to him.

'Quick, quick! We have to go to Ouidah!' He leapt up the steps to the hotel terrace. 'The novices are coming out of the convent!'

I was comfortable on the terrace, nursing a cold drink, looking at families wandering the sea borders in their best clothes – families who came from far inland, maybe from as far as Mali, Niger or Burkina Faso. They wandered a long time because they'd never seen the sea before. Sometimes lone adults would stand staring across the waves for hours, while I stared from my terrace perch a hundred yards behind them. Often the shore roamers were people with robes, hairstyles, faces of a kind I'd never seen before – seas for me.

I was lazily considering that I might shift from monitoring the shore patrols. The jumpy, splashy Sunday-afternoon throng in the hotel pool might be worth braving for a while – just to cool down enough to be at optimum comfort level for sunbathing. Then I might have another cold drink, read a bit, stare at the beach a while longer, by which time it would be five o'clock, when the pool would be closed to non-residents and its chipped-tile blue would be mine, all mine . . . But here was Isidore, jumpy-splashy into my wallowing sloth.

It was supposed to be his day off. We'd agreed that a day off was a good thing. I paid him for it, felt I had to or Isidore might have battled on for weeks before admitting he needed to spend time with his boys, go to Mass with them, feed them, check they were powering ahead with their studies and not crying over hats.

I needed a day off, too. I'd seen too many new things, heard too many of Isidore's stories, and my head was full. Craziness might happen if I couldn't do some reflecting, reordering and emptying into notebooks. Bright and early Monday, we were off for another tour away from home base, best if no one had paternal worries or craziness. So why was he here now, disturbing the Sabbath with wild talk of nuns in Ouidah?

I'd been brought up by nuns; some sort of unleashing of their trainees on the public was not my idea of a night out.

'You better change your clothes. Come on. You can't go in that shorts outfit.'

'Isidore, I thought we were resting today.' I tried not to let my whininess get out loud enough to hurt his feelings.

'What's wrong with you? I heard this was happening and I thought you'd like it. You can write about it. Do you want things to write about, or is resting more important?'

OK, so his feelings were hurt, but now so were mine. I had spent my whole morning off writing notes and trying to read the local paper – my French did not come easy enough for that to count as resting.

'What are they going to be doing, exactly?'

'You'll see. Hurry to get changed so we can have seats at the front.'

So what was this, a nun revue? Sisters of Mercy do songs from the shows?

Isidore was drumming on the tin table – I wasn't moving in any way he'd be satisfied to call hurrying.

'Honestly, Annie, we should get there in time to see the novices come out of the coven; it's a splendid ceremony.'

Coven?

'Coven?'

'The coven for vodou novices. The young initiates are coming back into the community, they dance, they . . .'

I'd completely misheard the French. I was out of the shorts outfit, skirted and in the Peugeot.

Ouidah was about five miles down the coast, a small town with trees and tumbling Portuguese buildings, attractively soft and old after Cotonou.

On a previous visit, we'd arrived in the middle of a road-improvement programme, gone at with great enthusiasm and little logic – every road in the town was dug up at once, ready for resurfacing all at once. Anyone not driving a tank had to park up on the edge of town and walk. Walk carefully, so as not to fall down holes deep enough for a bit of a Metro system to be thrown in under the new roads. I wasn't much bothered; illogical road excavation was such a constant of London life that central Ouidah's open-cast quarrying approach to the job only felt like an extreme of a familiar nuisance. Isidore was outraged. He stopped by the first group of mud-splashed labourers he saw and set them straight.

'What have you done it like this for? Why didn't you do it one road at a time? This is ridiculous. I've got a white person here who has to walk in this heat. Ridiculous!'

A sweat-drenched, exhausted man looked at me, then sneered at Isidore and muttered something in Fon.

The mutter incensed Isidore – 'Idiot!' he shrieked at the man. 'Big stupid idiot! No wonder you have to dig in mud for a living! Come on, Annie, come this way, out of their mud.'

A laugh passed around the road menders as I trailed in Isidore's raging wake.

'You see the mentality of Africans?' He spluttered. 'Stupid idiots. No wonder this country is backward.'

Way too pedantically politically correct for this, I certainly didn't want Isidore saying it on my behalf. 'Roadworks are the same in England; they do it in the middle of the day when people need the roads. I don't mind walking. I get to see more this way.'

'That's not the point. You're paying for a driver – why should you walk? And it's too hot for you, you'll get sick.'

He was so annoyed and I was still not in the least annoyed – but there was a beat of the argument I'd missed: 'What did the man say in your language?'

'He's an imbecile. Never mind what he said.'

'I want to know.'

'You don't.'

'I do.'

'You . . .'

It was hot, we were in the middle of piled-up red mud where the road should be and now we were doing pantomime . . . 'Tell me, Isidore, whatever it was I don't care.'

'OK.' He scowled down at the mud on his shoes. 'He said it's good for white people to walk, it serves them right.'

I laughed.

'You think it's funny?'

'Sort of. Cheer up. Where are we going, down here? You see how much I like walking?'

Isidore laughed and steered me away from my route into someone's back yard.

In Ouidah of all places it probably did serve white people right if discomfort befell them. Ouidah had been where Portuguese, Dutch, French and English traders built forts and conducted their slave trade on this part of the coast. Herded from all over West Africa, the slaves were brought to the marketplace in Ouidah, in front of the house of Dom Francisco Felix da Sousa. He was a Portuguese who came from his father's failing estates in Brazil to find a new fortune in trading people. He organized the trade with ruthless enthusiasm. He was a barking mad, debauched brute, eventually murdered by a barking mad, debauched king of Dahomey, who found da Sousa too much even for his peculiar tastes. Da Sousa was the role model for the slave trader in Bruce Chatwin's novella *The Viceroy of Ouidah*. I would have said that Chatwin immortalized him, but his name and excesses were written repeatedly in any history of the Atlantic slave trade anyway.

The various kings of Dahomey did deals with the Europeans and thought they could control the port and profit from the slave trade on their land. The traders' needs escalated from hundreds to tens of thousands. Once the kings had locked themselves into the brutal trade, those among them who found it distasteful realized it couldn't be stopped. And if they didn't control the European traders, anyone could be taken – including the kings themselves.

From the marketplace the slaves had to walk to the coast – another mile after hundreds. In 1727, Dahomian King Agadja planted a tree, still standing, that was called The Tree of Forgetting. Slaves walked round this – nine times for men, seven for women. When their circuits were completed they would forget their identity, their culture and their real names for the rest of their lives. This slave ritual was modified by the next one they performed: passing round a tree closer to the shore. The slaves walked round this three times, to ensure that their souls would remember their identity and come home after death.

When the slaves saw the boats they'd put up last-minute flailing fights or start screaming and praying. King Agadja once witnessed such a scene and didn't want to see it again.

'Both trees were an idea the King Agadja gave the Portuguese to trick people,' Isidore said. 'It was a trick to keep them calm as they went on the boats.'

'But surely the trees made it clearer to them that they were going for good.'

'It was a spell.' Isidore looked vague. 'I think the King put a spell on them with the trees to make them go calmly.'

It still seemed contradictory, overcomplicated . . . But wasn't there always a lot of ritual involved in brutality? Systems constructed to blur what was really happening, as much for the perpetrators as for the victims. A technique, I'd have called it, not a spell.

Where the slaves had boarded the boats there was now a long, bleak beach. Stranded in the middle of this emptiness was a sculpture called 'The Gate of No Return'. The fifty-foot-high arch was flanked by four gaunt depictions of enslaved people. Densely packed along the surface of the arch itself were thousands of clay bas-relief enchained figures. On the seaward side were two statues of Revenant, the costumed ritual-dancers of vodou who received the spirits of the dead, waiting here for souls to come home.

If you stood in the centre of the arch, all that lay ahead was ocean. A wind blew across the flat beach, so it was never restful; always a feeling of being alone at the sharp edge of the world.

The artist, according to the inscribed marble at the sculpture's base, was actually one co-ordinating several. Local artists – not something Benin lacked.

Isidore was more interested in another inscription.

'You see this? It says Soglo got UNESCO to give money for this.' He sighed. 'Ah, really, when Soglo was president he did a lot of good work.'

Unfortunately, the democratic Nicéphore Soglo was President of Benin only from 1991 to 1996. Kérékou had run the show for nineteen years before him and came back again afterwards.

More Soglo good work – bright-painted clay statues of divinities, kings, and cheery vegetables on plinths lined the road back to Ouidah from The Gate. In the heart of town, Isidore took me to the old Portuguese fort that was now a museum; high white buildings round a courtyard of mango trees.

A somewhat desultory guide with Eric Morecambe glasses showed us round the displays of maps, guns, old photographs and etchings. A second guide joined us with a group of Germans, irritating Eric Morecambe with his loud translations into German. And I don't think it helped the Germans much – I hardly speak German at all, but I could tell this translator was hurling a mixture of German, English and French at his charges in no apparent order.

Eventually, Eric Morecambe left them behind, saying something terrible to the other guide in their language. To me he said in French: 'They're spoiling it for you, madame, and I have so many things to explain.' He walked faster to keep us well ahead.

'He thinks you look richer than the Germans. He doesn't want to share his tip with this other man,' Isidore whispered as we almost raced right past a big, bright wall hanging, covered in cartoon-like appliqué of colonial history – black people growing small crops in the sun; black people being grabbed by luminous-pink people and put on boats; black people growing big crops in the sun whipped by luminous-pink people; black and pink people fighting; pale-brown people getting off boats waving to black people growing small crops in the sun.

'Was this made here?' I asked, stubbornly halting beside it.

'Yes, yes, craftsmen here. The slaves went away and when they came back from Brazil they had all changed colour. They had gone the colour of *café au lait*. You can buy a book on appliqué in our souvenir shop out here. Out here, madame . . .'

I caught up, and did buy the book.

Appliqué was everywhere in Benin. It was originally a decorative tradition favoured by the royal house of Dahomey. The method of sewing bright cut-out fabrics on to plain backgrounds was used for the display of emblems; for making story-pictures of battles; for ceremonial flags and fancy sun parasols. In craft markets appliqué-decorated items were piled high – hats, jackets, tablecloths, wall hangings, shoulder bags . . .

My book showed classical Beninois designs and modern variations. I spotted something that was politely not mentioned in the book. Matisse cut-outs. The similarity was immediately obvious in the bright abstract shapes on ancient hangings and souvenir cushion-covers.

African ethnic was oh-so fashionable in early-twentieth-century France – *objets* from Africa adorned salon tables and Josephine Baker danced on salon tables dressed in bananas. Influence from Africa was unavoidable, if slenderly acknowledged.

I still don't know if it matters that so many celebrated European artists drew inspiration from African art. Even though it often seemed to be the kind of inspiration drawing better described as copying. Picasso's work (and if you have one handy about the house you can try this for yourself) held up beside West African masks, carvings and paintings look like they all came out of the same studio. Same eyes, mouths, noses, materials and slips of perspective . . . I don't know much about art, but I know what I can see.

Eric Morecambe got more of a tip than Isidore felt he deserved, but I'd been moved by his glasses-fiddling charmlessness, and by a remark he made as we passed a large, massively detailed etching on the way out. There was the King of Dahomey greeting a Portuguese emissary. The Portuguese was alone; the King was surrounded by a vast entourage of ministers, relatives, wives, soldiers, slaves, pets and dwarves. A platoon of cavorting humpbacked dwarves.

'You see the malformed children?' Isidore pointed at the dwarf platoon. 'In the times very long ago they used to be killed, but the kings of Dahomey stopped this because they had a genetic trait in their family producing many malformations. We have to be good to them so their spirits don't return angry to earth to do harm. They have their own divinity, Tohossou. The Tohossou spirits live in the water but you should never return them to water against their will.'

'Yes,' Eric Morecambe agreed earnestly, pushing up his glasses. 'In olden times, the mistake was to drown these children. That's what their spirits hate most. Now we know better, now we know to cherish them like little gods.' He had tears in his eyes at the very thought of them; he was ready to hug and cherish the next little malformed child in the door. Money melted out of my pocket.

More money left me in the Temple of Pythons. The pythons were sacred, representing the divinity known as Da, Dan or Dangbe, bringer of life, movement and fertility. The clay-hut temple was painted with snakes and rainbows – rainbows were another symbol of this divinity.

The temple had been destroyed by Kérékou, then restored with

Soglo's UNESCO money. A stronghold of vodou and southern opposition to Kérékou, Ouidah suffered considerably during the time of the People's Republic. Kérékou hounded the vodou priests and forbade public ceremonies. Unfortunately for him, a drought and near famine in the mid-eighties confirmed vodou belief that the gods would send punishment for the desecration of their shrines. Kérékou's unpopularity abroad compounded the work of the gods – very little foreign aid came in to salve the drought.

One of Soglo's first moves was to have an international festival of vodou in Ouidah, as well as building shrines, restoring shrines and generally showing that he was on the side of the gods. Being a friend to the Americans, he also had the back-up faith that he could obtain foreign aid if the gods didn't send rain.

But it did rain. 'These are the things that happen in Benin,' Isidore said. 'So we know why we believe.

In their new temple, the thirty or more very big, sacred pythons were thriving. Small boys attended them and the tourists. Although the snakes were genuinely used for vodou ceremonies, the lure of a python-cuddling photo-session brought in a steady stream of visitors to help pay for upkeep of the temple, and the small boys.

'They're well fed,' the small boys assured me as I stepped very carefully into the round clay lair of the beasts. They slithered along floors and ledges, coiled round beams and each other . . .

'Touch them,' Isidore urged, prodding gingerly at the back of one.

They seemed reassuringly sleepy. I don't have a particular horror of snakes but I don't think it does to rush grabbing at them all 'Yee-hah' and inhibition-free. A small boy did just this, yanked up two gigantic brutes in each hand and slung them round his neck. He picked up a third great-granddaddy of a snake and tossed it at me. I thought I'd die or even scream but it just flopped in my hands, dangerous as a draught excluder, no feelings one way or the other about what became of it.

Snakes are surprising to touch – soft and dry. You always forget 'expensive handbag' when you see them slithering around, and expect a damp and slimy, inside-of-a-binbag texture. While the thing lolled lifeless it felt quite pleasant, and I looked very brave. A second small boy tapped my camera – why didn't I put a snake round my neck, like his friend, have a photo like that? The pleasant-feeling snake in my hands was suddenly rousing itself, darting its forked tongue and seeming far too alert to make a comfortable scarf. I was about to request a more suitable snake for casual wear but the lead boy was already hefting the perky snake up for me to put my head under its potentially neck-snapping middle.

It seemed to like it round my neck and subsided to its previous torpor. The second in command snapped me from all angles while I grinned, feeling more foolish than fearful as the Germans came into the yard pointing at me.

'Good,' said the lead boy. 'Good snake.' He pulled it off me and approached the Germans. Second in command showed us to the python shrine on the other side of the yard; a very small hut with bowls on the ground.

'The big house is where they live. This is where they are worshipped,' Isidore said, as he left an offering of coins in one of the bowls. 'This snake divinity is very important to the Fon. We must never eat snakes.'

'Who eats snakes?'

'Yoruba.' He shuddered. 'Nigerians.'

Oh, the Nigerians . . . I was learning that, in Isidore's opinion, every abomination known to man was carried out on a regular basis by Nigerians before they were halfway out of their cradles.

It is my opinion, still, that Isidore has never visited Nigeria; it's just the place that he knows all the dragons be. If they haven't been cooked for tea.

The real heart of Ouidah's importance to vodou was in its sacred forest. In vodou, kings, like twins, never died – they were said to have gone hunting in the forest. Or, in the case of King Kpassé, fourteenth-century monarch of the Xweda people, they turn themselves into a tree of the forest, while fleeing the King of Dahomey and his army.

Kpassé was a peaceable, fisher-agriculturist king and didn't stand a chance when the Dahomians decided they needed a sea port. The Dahomey Fon moved in on the Xweda, mispronouncing them as 'Houeda'. Then the Europeans came and mispronounced further, creating Ouidah.

The Fon were never really the enemies of the Xweda; they were forced to serve the powerful kings of Dahomey, who although not, as legend had it, the descendants of panthers arriving to take command of the land, were not local lads either. Who they really were and where they originated took me and Isidore quite some investigating. But, for now, they were the ones after a coastline. They had to trade slaves to the Portuguese and French in order to buy guns to protect themselves from the Yoruba next door, who were trading with the British slavers and getting guns that they used to catch slaves to sell for guns to protect themselves from . . . Every kingdom on the coast was caught in a vicious cycle. West African rulers realized that their choice was either to sell slaves or be enslaved. And gentle farmer-fisher kings went to the wall – or rather, the forest.

Before the slave trade the tribes of the southern Benin region had rubbed along together quite amicably. After the Dahomey Kingdom fell and the colonialists became the common enemy, the tribes went back to peaceful co-existence. From a longer history of rubbing along than of fighting, the Xweda and Fon worshipped similar divinities: thunder, fire, water, earth, iron . . . Their religious rites became amalgamated and they worshipped together in Ouidah's sacred forest, with a heavy emphasis on the spirits of trees to remember their old King Kpassé.

All around the quiet forest were representations of divinities ingeniously made from recycled bicycle parts, oil drums, car engines . . . Some were humorous, some elegant, some managed to be both. A beautiful teenage boy with a soft voice introduced himself as the guardian of the forest; he told us which divinity each fantastic abstraction represented, before politely suggesting that it was customary to pay him for this service.

'She knows that.' Isidore frowned at the guardian. 'You've seen me before. Do you think I don't tell my tourists that?'

The guardian looked embarrassed. 'Of course. It's just we had a bad experience with a group of French yesterday. Five of them – my brother showed them everything and they gave nothing.'

'Oh. French.' Isidore made a face. In his world view they came even lower than snake-eating Nigerians. 'She's not French, so don't worry about her.'

The guardian smiled faintly, too worried by Isidore to admit he was still unconvinced I'd pay him properly.

The guardian led on all the same. We came to a large dead tree with several clay bowls around its cement-propped base. This was Kpassé. Some of the bowls held coins; one held cooked rice.

'If you need anything from the spirit, you can leave an offering here,' the guardian said.

Isidore put a coin in a bowl. I said I didn't think I did need anything.

'No. Of course. These things are a matter of faith.' The guardian smiled politely, perhaps a little sorry for faithless me.

As we walked back through the garden of gods, the guardian told me something about his faith that completely confused me. He said vodou was monotheistic. Once he explained himself, it made sense. There was one, unknowable Creator-God, too great for us to approach or imagine. How could we possibly? This great God was worshipped through comprehensible divinities – thunder gods, water gods, gods of iron and trees – umpteen departmental divinities. But there was only one real god in vodou. Just as in Christianity the more approachable and recognizable Jesus Christ and Virgin Mary performed an intermediary function with the Creator, so the vast pantheon of vodou divinities were simply an approach to the truly mysterious.

'God has given us all the gods,' Isidore interrupted. 'You see? This is how we can be Catholics. The great God has given us all of it. It's the same.'

When Isidore bustled me back to see the novices, the guardian of the forest was pleased I'd returned – I had tipped him very well, to show that I wasn't secretly French. I'd also listened to his explanations very intently – it was hard not to be a little mesmerized by him. He had the high-arched, Lauren Bacall eyebrows and butterfly long eyelashes that I was beginning to notice as typically southern Beninois. On more male-faced men, like Isidore, it was a striking set of features; on the fine-boned, soft-skinned forest guardian, it was disconcertingly androgynous. Gender was blurred further by the guardian's voice, not yet broken although he said he was twenty. It wasn't undignified or squeaky; he spoke like a girl with a quiet, husky tone.

'Come, it will be a while before the ceremony begins.' With a confusingly laddish roll in his gait, the guardian led us to the clearing in the middle of the forest, where piles of hard, village-hall-type chairs were set out in a circle. It looked as if a couple of hundred people were expected.

'You should sit here.' The guardian indicated a block of seats under a fat-trunked tree. 'You'll have a clear view but you'll be behind the musicians; it will be safer.'

Safer?

Apart from a few older men who were putting out chairs, who presumably might turn at any moment, there was no immediate sign in the clearing of any danger. If danger was coming, it would be from the focal point of my clear view – it would come roaring out of the twenty-foot red and white doors on the opposite side of the clearing. This was the entrance to the coven, guarded by surly-looking men. They were there to save me from myself – if anyone uninitiated tried to go through the red doors they would disappear, forever.

The musicians – drummers with various-sized tam-tams – arrived and set themselves up in front of us. They began drinking rum and laughing at some great Fon jokes shouted among themselves. There was a young one and four wiry old men, all jovially welcoming me and saying I was best off behind them for a good view of events. But there were unlikely to be any events for an hour yet – it was still too hot for events. They didn't mention possible danger; was this a trick? Or did they not know about whatever it was that the guardian knew was likely to fly out of the coven doors to eat us, once it was cooler?

The red and white of the doors were the colours of Shango, the god of thunder. He was very much a he, represented by a double-headed axe. Shango frequently shared a temple with Hevioso, god of lightning, represented by a ram's head spitting fire. Isidore said for his father and himself Ougon, god of iron, was very important. Ougon was represented by a mound of earth, source of iron, and was sacred to all those who used iron tools for work – from farmers and blacksmiths to hairdressers, butchers and taxi drivers. Isidore didn't know if Ougon was represented at the coven of Ouidah, but there was certainly a cult devoted to Sakpata, the divinity who controlled smallpox. Epidemics had once raged in the Ouidah area, and placating this god was essential.

'What gods are represented depends on the livelihoods and problems of the area,' Isidore told me. 'But thunder and lightning, they are the weather and life; they are always important. You know, our religion is hard to explain. But I will try as things happen to explain them.'

No things to explain were happening in the forest just yet, although a crowd was gathering, adjusting their seats to be sure of shade from the late-afternoon sun. Whole families were settling themselves in a picnicking, noisy, lighthearted spirit – no sense of preparing for something scary to fly out of the red doors. Fruit and biscuits were passed round and musicians began to play in fits and starts.

Isidore and the guardian had a discussion about photography and it was agreed that Isidore could take pictures; people would find it intrusive if I took them, but he could claim to be a relative of someone involved in the ceremony. Later, Isidore got the hang of taking photographs, but I think he didn't want to admit to the guardian that he'd never been in charge of a camera before, let alone a zoom lens. So I have a fine collection of ears, ankles and blurred headbacks to show for my day in the sacred forest.

Or perhaps the divinities themselves prevented their rites being photographed with any kind of accuracy by an employee of a faithless foreigner . . .

More picnickers gathered. The drummers drank more rum and drummed with more purpose.

'It will be soon,' said the guardian. 'I'll be here all the time if you have a question.' He took a swig of rum from the musicians and wandered off with some newly arrived pals.

Seconds later, the gates opened. The crowd cheered and the first set of novices came out, accompanied by some very old, elaborately dressed men and women. The novices were children. Very young children, feathered, beaded, beribboned, draped and painted fantastically, dancing their way across the clearing.

'Children?'

'Yes.' Isidore seemed to think this was an idiotic observation. 'They must be children under ten to enter the coven.'

I'd expected possessions, dropping-dead trances, chicken-head biting and tremors of fear. But I was at a village-school play. Parents waved and applauded their participating offspring. The tiniest children had only a sketchy, meandering notion of their roles and soon wandered off towards the audience on sighting Mum. Mums and aunties hugged the straying toddlers, dabbed faces with spit on hankies, straightened costumes and sniffed back their proud, joyful tears. And the parade of gyrating infants kept coming.

The little girls – little girls being the same the world over – were trying hardest and doing best. One girl of about eight years old, the red feather in her headband indicating a novice of the god of thunder, went up to the drummers and wagged her finger at them – they'd just changed their rhythm and she didn't like it. She waited, they changed again and she resumed her dance. She danced a spectacular full-body shimmy with fancy footwork and got a cheer from the drummers. Applauding adults from the audience came up to her and gave her money; she beamed with delight in herself. An old lady in a similar headdress beamed with pride; this child was clearly her star pupil. Other pupils, particularly the toddler boys, continued to wander off in a daze or stare, wide-eyed stunned, at the crowd. The old lady kept patiently catching the strays by the hand and setting them back on track, keeping them vaguely involved in the circle of dancers as they moved round the clearing.

The kindly old lady was a priestess, one of several doing the joyful circuits with the children. The nice old dancing grandfathers, with a toddler by each hand, were the vodou priests.

'The old ones are proud,' Isidore said. 'They taught the children everything.'

What was everything? And why did they need to know it now? Half of them hadn't even reached an age where they could say 'everything', let alone learn it.

The guardian, looking a little rum-red-eyed, returned at a signal from Isidore.

'Oh yes, they have to be under ten when they enter the coven. This way they can learn the secret language for the religion. They learn dances, the secrets of the divinity and the rituals, but the most important reason they have to be young is for the language. When children learn a new language it is easily imprinted in their memories, not like with adults. The children go into the coven for a year. After a year they spend a week – this is the start of the week – going back into the community.'

He stopped. A tiny boy was being led out of the coven, three if he was a day. He was dressed in a sarong-style garment, a *pagne*, ropes of beads and the red-feather headband of the god of thunder. He was loudly applauded as he blinked at the crowd and clutched tight at the hand of a priestess.

'That is the son of a king,' whispered the guardian. 'A special child.'

'So children from certain families are chosen?'

'Sometimes. It depends on the family tradition. Sometimes the elders see a child and realize it is called. Or the parents see signs at the birth. Sometimes a child knows itself it is called by a particular divinity.'

'How do they know?'

'When children go to a ceremony they hear the music. It's the music that tells them. The priest notices how the small child reacts, wanting to dance because the drum's sound appeals to them. Each divinity has different drum sounds. The child hears the sound that calls them and they know.'

Confused though the smaller ones might have been about which way to face in the Ouidah graduation show, the children did seem to be having a really good time. They were straying to their families in the audience only in a spirit of enthusiastic recognition, not bat-out-of-hell racing to escape the brutal rigours of coven life. Whatever they'd done in there for a year, they'd loved it.

I was finding it harder to understand the guardian of the forest because rum was making his soft, high voice into something only dogs could hear; fortunately Isidore had run out of film and could provide more intelligible explanations.

I asked if the parents could visit the children in the coven. No. And the children couldn't have trips out, unless they were ill or obviously unhappy.

'They go home after this week of ceremonies,' Isidore told me. 'That's when they have their problems, because all the time they are in the coven they speak the vodou language. So they're confused at home; they can't speak the normal language of their parents. If one of their parents isn't an adept, one of the initiated, they have to call someone who is to see what the child wants. Gradually, after about twenty-one days, the child returns to normal. Later, maybe years after, if there is a vodou ceremony, or if they hear a certain rhythm on the drums, it comes back to the child. They start to speak in the language, they go into a trance and then they dance, dance, dance . . . Dance till they collapse. They re-enter the coven; they are born again into the religion – this can happen many times, but they've been prepared since childhood.'

Isidore and the forest guardian exchanged a few remarks. Isidore grinned at me.

'He says you'll soon see.'

'See what?'

'What I'm talking about.'

'The drum is very powerful now,' said the forest guardian. 'When they learn drumming in the coven they play on their chests with their hands, or with little sticks on tree trunks so they don't waste the powerful sound of the tam-tam.'

Something was happening in the crowd: a big man was swaying, muttering . . . He staggered forward . . . The crowd around him went into an excited uproar, some stepped back from him to give him room, some stepped forward – they steadied him and began stripping him of his Western clothes. They took off his shirt, wrapped a *pagne* around his waist, tied a scarf LA-gangster-style round his head; someone placed a white feather in his mouth and handed him a bell in the shape of a double-headed axe. He was in the male costume for an adept of the god of thunder. He was ready. With one final, all-body sway, he launched himself into the centre of the clearing. He danced, danced, danced . . . Swooping, feet-flipping dancing – hard to believe that he was moving the way he was without falling over. The crowd went wild, screeching cheers and clapping. After fifteen minutes he started to slow down, bleary-eyed, reeling. Two god of thunder priests ran at him with a large cloth. They covered his head with it as they half-carried him away through the red doors into the coven.

The cloth over his head was his shroud. He had died again to be reborn at the end of the week of ceremonies.

Another man was muttering, swaying, dancing . . . Then another . . . Four or five men in trances. Each trance set up craziness in the crowd like a goal scored. The kids melted to the sidelines. The older priests and priestesses started dancing furiously, emerging from the coven doors were the star strikers – the representations of the divinities. A man, all in green with an entourage of dancing, semi-naked youths, was Kpassé, the tree god. A scrawny, ancient and toothless man was dancing maniacally in a shoulder yoke with red balls on each end, a representation of the thunder god. In his wake, an old lady with a red-feather headdress danced at the crowd with another double-headed-axe-shaped bell – people bowed and touched it while she muttered a blessing over them. The drummers gulped down swigs of rum and escalated their rhythm.

A crowd of dancing women with white turbans and white dots painted on their faces came out of the coven, initiates of the smallpox divinity, Sakpata. I asked Isidore why there weren't any Sakpata novices?

'Maybe tomorrow is their day. There are so many divinities, they have different days in this week.'

So many divinities . . . Who was it I was depending on for my house in Bloomsbury?

'You know what divinities were there. The twins, Legba and Ougon.'

'Ougon was the mound with the stakes?'

'Yes. You don't remember?'

'So there are always a lot of divinities together?'

'Not always. If there are several the place is more powerful.'

'Yes, yes, it's getting clearer now.'

'Sometimes you say you understand something when you don't. Always ask questions, Annie, or you won't learn.'

If I'd asked Isidore all of the constant bee-buzz of questions in my head he'd have changed his tune and begged for the occasional silence. And I was sure he hadn't said anything about Ougon at the stake mound. Isidore had undoubtedly concluded that I wasn't very bright, fair enough, but withholding information from me then taunting me for ignorance was no way to help me progress.

I didn't have time to argue with him. Another manifestation of the thunder god emerged from the coven. A man in a white robe wearing a red and white striped fez hat. 'Oooh,' said the crowd, awed.

'Ah,' said the forest guardian, nervous. 'This divinity, he's very bad. Everyone's scared of him.'

Sure enough, everyone was backing away, some running far into the trees.

'Are you scared?'

'No,' the guardian said unsurely. 'Not behind the drummers. But if I was out there I'd be scared. This is the bad side of the thunder god.'

The bad side continued circling and chasing.

'Are you scared?' I asked Isidore.

'No,' he said with a manly smirk. 'This is a game. There are manifestations that are frightening, but this is a game.'

It was – plenty of glee in the crowd's *frisson* of half-fright, as if they were watching some horror-film creature.

I didn't feel afraid of Bad Thunder Man but I was afraid that he, or one of the other divinities still strutting their stuff, would pick on me for being a *yovo*, and that that most terrible of frightening fates would befall me: acute embarrassment. Thankfully, apart from the thunder priestess shyly giving me the bell benediction, no one seemed to be paying any attention to me. But when I got up to leave, everyone started to leave. As I said goodbye to the musicians, whose rivers of sweat must have been at least half rum by now, they stopped playing. Dancers drifted back towards the coven doors or into the crowd.

'So it's over?'

'Now you're leaving, it is,' said the guardian of the forest.

I laughed, thinking this was only flattery.

The guardian gestured at the crowd, now streaming round us, headed for the road. 'They wouldn't leave if you were still there.'

I looked at Isidore. 'Is that true?'

'Didn't you notice? The people were looking at you as much as the dancers.'

I hadn't, not at all. It must have been very discreet, because in the three hours of celebration I'd been surprised, and relieved, that my *yovo*-ness had been so unacknowledged.

'No,' Isidore insisted. 'They wanted to see what you were doing all the time. To see how you were reacting.'

'Did I react all right?'

'They were pleased. You stayed a long time. You were smiling and asking questions. They were pleased with you.'

A Somali taxi driver in Soho once told me that Africans go to Europe blind, because they don't know white people, and Africans who return to Africa are always too proud to say what it was really like. What it's 'really like' is what made me feel a bit of a fraud when people were pleased simply by my just-sitting-there presence in the garden.

*

'I'm glad you liked it,' Isidore said as we drove away through the approximately restored red-dirt byways of Ouidah. 'You will see plenty more vodou. We are the cradle of vodou here, as they say. Ah, there are many things like this for you to see . . . And *gri-gri* magic, look. Look at this man. They're always catching things here.'

A man at a crossroads was holding up what looked like a runover fat, tailless squirrel. It was an *agouti* – a sort of fat, tailless squirrel. Also known as tree rat.

'He wants to sell it. I don't like to buy meat from here. They catch it by witchcraft. You'll see, every time we come past there'll be men with animals here.'

Apparently there was good hunting but very few children in this district. There was a sorcerer here who could take a man's sperm and do a spell to make him an endlessly successful hunter but incapable of procreation.

'Usually they have a few children first, then they do the spell to become good hunters. Always they're out here selling *agouti*, deer, rabbits . . .'

I asked a cynical question about the dense woodland on either side of the road, and the possibility of large populations of animals in dense woodlands.

'Woods has nothing to do with it. There are plenty of places with woods. But no one catches the amount these men do. Ah, Annie, there are things in Benin . . . I know so many incidences of witchcraft. There are things in the villages, even in the city there are plenty of things.'

The spermless hunters gave me a chill, and annoyed me some-how. They seemed sinister nonsense after the joyous ceremony in the sacred forest. Of course, what I wasn't getting was that vodou needed dark tales of trade-offs of children for squirrels, needed witchcraft like the Pope needed the Devil.

Sensing I'd developed some kind of bad mood since seeing the sperm squirrels, Isidore suggested a walk on the Cotonou shore.

'We've been sitting a long time. Let's make an appetite for dinner.'

The air off the Atlantic was cool and clean. Vodou was still with us. Lying on the tide line, tangled with seaweed, driftwood and shells, was a little string-tied bundle of cloth; a few yards further was a bundle wrapped in a palm leaf. They were offerings to the sea divinities. Probably from fishermen, for safety and good catches. Fishermen seemed to be everywhere there was water, busy working at their work alongside beach tourists, industrial sea-churnings and aquatic military manoeuvres.

From my idling and staring terrace at the Hôtel de la Plage I saw fishermen all day long. To the left of the hotel, hidden by a curve in the coast, was a dense shanty town where fisherfolk lived. They to-ed and fro-ed across the hotel view, keeping to the sea's edge, skirting the dry, raked sand that marked hotel terrain. To the right, their vanishing point was the hotel's perimeter wall. Behind that were high concrete sheds housing a commercial fish market and boat-repair shops. Beyond these was the old open-air fish market, where small traders plied their wares, right up to the edge of the main national harbour.

Flotillas of hollowed-tree-trunk canoes – *pirogues* – were moored between naval gunships and towering cargo boats. They were brightly painted with eyes, wave patterns and mermaids; they had names like *Believe In God*, *God Helps Me*, or *God Provides*.

There was a scattering of much larger wooden fishing boats, constructed from sealed planks by Ghanaians, the greatest fishermen of West Africa. A rich Beninois might buy a grand Ghanaian boat and bring it home; but he needn't bring Ghanaian fishermen with him – there were plenty living in the coastal shacks of Cotonou. According to Isidore, 'Where there's good fish, there's Ghanaians.'

Cotonou was variable, fish-wise. Often over-fished and troubled by pollution from the industrial port that hemmed the fishing boats into a small dirty cove. Even the heftiest of bravely painted Ghanaian boats looked cowed beside oil tankers and container ships. Sailors in the modern monster-ships might have been praying to the sea divinities to keep them safe, but it was the fishermen who did the serious sea-god cosseting.

Every nine days, the fishermen of Cotonou didn't go out to sea.

Every nine days, their sea divinity, Zombade, had his market day and they didn't want to annoy him while he was doing his shopping. If he was disturbed on his market day, disaster would befall the fishermen.

There was plenty to be done in the port while Zombade was busy with his messages – nets to repair; *pirogues* to reseal or repaint; coloured sails to stitch; outboard motors had to be repaired or just fidgeted around with, like most motors owned by males. The port was a warren of activity on its closed day, but on a fishing day . . . Boats and nets were hauled about, fish hefted by the giant bowlful, women and kids swarmed in and out of everything. The kids sold sweets, cigarettes, drinks, bread . . . The women sold . . . actually, several of them were perched on benches, elegantly coiffed, selling themselves. But mostly the women sold fish. The tradition was that the women bought the fish off the boats and resold them. Resold them with great vigour – they could sprint a hundred yards in gold-medal time to tell a *yovo*: 'Mrs! Buy fish!'

The women also cleaned the fish for their customers, descaling and gutting at blurry speed with scant regard for their fingers as they ripped away with tiny, sharp-sharp knives, all the while talking and yelling like, I suppose, fishwives.

The fishwives yelled at their kids to go and sell bread to the *yovo*; they yelled at Isidore, wanting to know if I was his wife. He translated this repeated question for me, perhaps forgetting he'd taught me that 'yes' in Fon was a sort of agreeing-sounding exhalation – '*ehhh*'. 'No' sounded like the Tellytubbies' '*ehoh*'. Isidore had been exhaling at the women.

He admitted sheepishly that it was more fun for him to say yes and bask in the onlookers' fantasies about how rich and important he must be to have a white wife.

There were white wives, and white husbands. They were usually found on Sunday afternoons on the beach at the other side of town, picnicking lavishly, seldom without some kind of staff in assistance. Some of the whites might be embassy staff or NGO advisers; some of them ran bars or little craft businesses – it didn't take much money to get you into the luxurious-lifestyle bracket. I didn't go about my home life with a permanent driver, guide, translator, bodyguard . . . But in Isidore I had a staff of at least four, on a daily rate that might have got me one taxi ride across London. It wasn't a bargain I was proud of; it was what I could afford and what Isidore said was fair, in our small scheme of things.

Generally, my staff and I found the picnickers' beach too crowded on Sundays. But regardless of French bikinis, American paddlers, Lebanese frisbee throwers, their pets and offspring, the fishermen worked their work. The fishermen were why I'd come back to this beach again and again, on weekdays, when I could have them to myself.

My first day in Benin had ended with a walk on this coconut-grove bordered, seemingly endless swathe of sand against green-blue water. Paradise to me; old hat to Isidore.

We saw men pulling in a fishing net, two lines of men about a hundred yards apart, gradually bringing the ends of their v-shaped net closer and closer. It took around three hours of hauling, tug-of-war-style, to bring the net up to the beach in the last of the afternoon sun. The men sang and they stamped their feet in rhythm to keep their pulling co-ordinated. Occasionally, one would swim out through waves that would make the most kamikaze surfer hang up their board. The swimmers would dive under, trying to get a closer look at the progress of the net. Then they'd chat to whoever was left minding the boat, far out in the water. The boat minders were chosen from those who'd done their hard work earlier in the day, laying the nets wide into the sea. Everyone else had to join the effort to bring back whatever the net had captured after a day of being manoeuvred round the ocean.

As the fishermen began to tire, neighbours and passers-by ran to put a hand to the ropes. Everyone stamped and sang. I asked Isidore what the call-and-answer song meant. He looked embarrassed, said it was Ghanaian, he didn't understand it, but I've a feeling he did and it was something a bit raunchy.

As the net came closer, women and children joined the haulers; the front men were slipping now, drenching themselves in the water, but the v-shape up the beach was gradually closing. Children who larked about were banished; the big men who'd been pulling for three hours had no patience with larking.

More women were coming down from the huts by the coconut palms, carrying bowls and baskets, ready to buy the fish. If there were any. Other women brought fresh water for the men to drink, or cakes and sweets to sell to onlookers. Non-labouring children tumbled about in the surf catching the rising excitement as the net came closer. Ever more children scampered down the sand to see what would come in. Adult onlookers stood on tiptoes for a clear view of the moment.

There was nothing much.

The men dropped to their haunches, disgusted. A pathetic little haul after all that work. The sun was going down and the day was wasted.

Or not. The men perked up to sell what fish there were and to begin the last heavy work of bringing the boat up on to the sand. Tomorrow was another day. The sea glistened blue and the sky tinged pink. Children skipped back to the coconut groves, where a constant chopping sound indicated that someone was bringing in a harvest for them to inspect. If there were no fish, there were always coconuts to drink, eat and make into toys.

I stood looking at the women disperse, bright clothes and empty baskets trailing away. In the distance, there was a haze of spray as Atlantic breakers crashed. Suddenly, I turned to Isidore – 'This is . . .' He was too busy doing commiserating man's talk with a fisherman to notice I'd spoken. It didn't matter. This beach and the fishermen had become the magic wonders of Benin for me. Isidore, with his 'things', his supernatural wonders. Well . . . we'd see. I wanted him to prove it to me. To find a world full of magic is all any of us want, isn't it?

4

Where's the King Put the Car Keys?

According to Isidore, king visiting was as important as understanding vodou, if I was to have any notion of what really went on in his country. But even meeting the kings didn't guarantee me a clear grasp of facts. The kings' own accounts of their lives and histories were so enmeshed with legend, it took a ruthless narrowmindedness to discover what was most likely to be the dull reality – the plain 'This happened, then that happened', with no people turning into trees included.

Believing in iron gods and sperm squirrels as he did, Isidore wasn't always sure what I meant by, 'But what really happened?' He told his story of the Dahomey kings with a bias towards the quality of the story, not the actuality. To complicate things further, half the historical volumes checked back at home had their own bias towards making the old kingdom of Dahomey into a white man's worst nightmare of barbaric savagery.

'This history business will need detective work,' I told Isidore.
He laughed. 'Good, let's do that, then, let's go.'

Isidore yelled long obscenities in Fon and French at a driver behind
us, as we crossed off the main Cotonou road towards the well-
signposted Historical Royal Palace of Allada and Air-Conditioned
Hotel. We narrowly missed a brace of oncoming mopeds. Had they
crashed into our rear, Isidore would have decided it was somehow
their fault for exercising their right of way. He was that kind of driver.

The day was just beginning, so I tried not to have my nerves
jangled by Isidore's tendency to sudden road rages and hair's-
breadth manoeuvrings. I tried not to be cynical about how the
signposting and the well-maintained leafy avenue we were driving
down suggested I might be getting as close to Dahomey royalty as
a Beninois might get to ours on a trip to Trooping the Colour.

There were no king-viewing coach parties nor any crowd barriers
in the centre of Allada village's red-mud buildings – and the road
was eventually potholed enough to suggest that this might not be
a sanitized museum experience, with a king who'd scoot out, wave
at us and hurry back indoors.

A woman approached the car when we parked in an oval-shaped
village square. This being a royal area, the main marketing and
meandering-animals action of Allada was a few hundred yards down
the road ahead of us. The village oval was strictly for special events
– and to me, the woman was just that. She was of a certain age, in
a loud, floral-print 1950s dress, orange lipstick and caked, clown-
white face make-up. She was not white.

'Good morning. Delightful to see you. I am French also. Excuse
me, but I seem to have a problem. I need my fare home. Can you
help me with some coins, my dear compatriot?'

As I fished in my pockets for coins, Isidore was pointing at a
painted clay statue of a sword-wielding warrior.

'This is Adjahouto, also known as Togbegouin. He started the
kingdom in the thirteenth century . . .'

'Have you seen this woman?'

'Yes, she is mad. She'll go now she's got some money, come on, the palace is here. Come on, don't waste time on her.'

The woman had gone. She wouldn't get to Paris on what I'd given her, but it had taken her laughing all the way to the market.

Being a statue, King Adjahouto needed no coins and wasn't going anywhere. In the thirteenth century, had you wanted to go calling on him, you'd have had to go to Tado, a town now in Togo. In the fifteenth century, three of his descendants decided to avoid drought and possibly a smallpox epidemic by crossing into what is now Benin. The first place they established for themselves was Allada.

We walked past a tree, shading a collection of aged, limbless beggars. They leapt, as best they could, towards us – hands or stumps extended, faces eager.

'Later,' Isidore told them. 'She is here to see the King.'

They nodded with sombre understanding, stopped the begging action but continued to cluster round us. They'd seen as much promise in my move towards my pocket as in Isidore's 'later', so, for now, they could relax into purely social involvement with our visit – but they didn't want to lose sight of me.

'Over here, madame.' One beggar pointed a half-hand at a plain cube hut to our right. In front of us was a balconied clay bungalow, roofed with corrugated iron like the rest of the buildings but made distinctive with sky-blue washed walls and murals of scenery and panthers.

'This one with the paintings is the palace,' Isidore said. 'But first we have to see the secretary.'

The beggars escorted us over to the secretary's unembellished cube, babbling excitedly when the half-hand man told them I was from England. Then he added, with proprietorial joy, like he'd made me himself out of old chips: 'This one is not French. You see, people from all over the world come here. I knew this one was not French. Look at the eyes, look at the yellow hair!'

In his windowless room, the secretary gave us typed forms to fill in, detailing who we were, where we were from and the purpose of our visit. Isidore had warned me never to mention book-writing-type purposes, as he feared it would turn people's heads and cost me inordinate amounts of money. I wrote what he told me: that my guide had informed me it was courteous to call on the King when visiting his domain. This was technically the done thing and, unless seriously indisposed, a king should receive a foreign emissary. But the likes of me?

'It doesn't matter if you're nobody big. I told you, I've brought tourists here before. If he didn't want them, he'd take down the sign.'

The secretary, a teenager in a crisp khaki suit, suggested that we might need an envelope if we had a gift for the King – as luck would have it, he did have a pile of envelopes available here on his desk, for a penny each . . . Isidore said that the equivalent of five pounds would be a generous gift. The secretary made a face suggesting that, although he found it embarrassing to do so, he felt obliged, with Jeevesian discretion, to disagree. I held up ten pounds; Isidore winced, the secretary nodded and asked us to please take a seat while he took our completed forms to the King.

We waited. The secretary's hut was hot, with nothing to look at but stationery.

'When we are in the palace, do as I do,' Isidore said.

'Will he see us? It's been ages.'

'He keeps people waiting to show he is a king. It'll go well. Just do what I do and don't give away any more money.'

After nearly an hour the secretary manoeuvred us past the beggars, across the terrace of the blue bungalow and into the throne room.

'It is customary,' the secretary said, nodding back at the beggars who were retreating to their shade tree, 'for his majesty's guests to give donations to these subjects. When you're leaving, just some small coins for food. The King can't afford to feed them all every day by himself.'

Completely ignoring Isidore's injunction, I said I'd see to it. I'd never met a king before. I wasn't going to start quibbling over coins now I'd got as far as a throne room. Whatever was customary for the King's guests, I would have had my small coins tugged right out with my heartstrings anyway – the half-hand man put his good hand in the good hand of a blind old lady beggar with a stump arm and led her, like his cherished young bride, back to a comfortable spot under the tree with him.

The throne room had a couple of fancy rugs on its clean concrete floor, fresh-washed clay walls and the veranda along one side made it pleasantly bright and airy after the secretary's stuffy hut. Bright and airy to show who's king.

The throne itself was the only furniture – an armchair draped in purple cloth with Egyptian hieroglyph motifs. On the wall behind the throne were several framed photographs of the King of Allada. Directly over the throne was a drawing of Toussaint L'Ouverture.

'You know him?' Isidore pointed.

'Yes, he's famous. He freed the slaves in Haiti.'

'Yes, he fought Napoleon and freed the slaves in Haiti. He was very brave. It's good you know him; he is an ancestor of the King.'

The secretary had asked us to leave our shoes outside on the terrace. For the time being we were to make ourselves comfortable sitting on the rugs; he would warn us when the King was coming. He then sprawled on the rugs to one side of the throne room and seemed to doze off. After about ten minutes, as if telepathically alerted, he sprang into action. To the right of the throne was a plain wooden door; as the secretary scurried out of this I saw a thick red curtain behind it, no glimpse of inner-palace activities or a squint at their wallpaper. It was another ten minutes before the secretary reappeared and told us the King was on his way.

'Does madame know what to do?' he asked while glancing nervously back at the wooden door.

'Me?'

'Copy me,' Isidore said. 'I already told you.' Then he asked the secretary, 'Shall we begin?'

'Yes, he's on his way now.' And the secretary threw himself face-down on the floor.

Isidore hurled himself down, hissing at me, 'Come on. No, no, put your head right down so your forehead touches the ground. You can't look at the King until he tells you.'

I didn't look, but I heard the door open, followed by an impressive amount of majestic rustling.

'Welcome to you. You may sit up.'

Visually, the King of Allada was worth the wait and thoroughly deserved to make an entrance. He looked the proper royal silk-and-embroidery show – like a king should look if he's planning to make a go of the job. His majesty, Kpodegbe Toyi Djingla of Allada – we'll call him Allada, for short – was a tall, elegantly haughty man of about forty-five, with the splendid kind of full-horseshoe moustache I haven't seen since Jason King was on telly in the seventies.

Allada was quite handsome, in a gaunt, over-moustached sort of way. His forehead went up to alarming heights before it encountered a gold-threaded black fez, a match for his gold-embroidered slippers. His long silk robes were rich crimson. Gold-chained amulets were strung round his neck and he had hefty gold rings on his fingers.

In one hand he held a gold sceptre decorated with the double-headed axe of Shango the thunder god; in the other hand was a two-foot-long gold sceptre, in the shape of a crook, with a troupe of golden elephants marching along the back of it.

Following Allada, then positioning themselves around the throne, were three middle-aged women in richly coloured *pagne*. One woman held a long-handled, fluffy feather fan; the second held over the King's indoor head a golfing-sized umbrella decorated with leopard emblems. A third woman held a lidded silver bowl. This last ceremonial item was a spittoon. Great ones for chewing tobacco, the Dahomey kings of old always had a woman to follow them round catching spit, to prevent their regal fluids being taken by ill-wishers and used in subversive spells.

These three women were palace servants, not wives, the King explained. Some visitors thought they were wives. Some visitors, he added, were repulsed by the notion of the spittoon, but it was a purely ceremonial object – 'We Dahomians ceased to use spittoons at the same time Westerners ceased, if not before.'

I felt he'd marked my card. Some visitors might not expect politics, but there'd be plenty.

After explaining his entourage and accompanying objects, Allada asked me where I'd come from and what I thought of Benin so far. I made a lamely flattering response to the latter question – understandably this seemed to bore Allada. He gave me a dead smile with too many teeth and, with suspicion, asked Isidore his name, birthplace and occupation. Isidore had visited him four times but Allada gave no glint of recognizing him, although he smiled a more lively smile at the answers and called him 'my son'. He praised his 'son' for respecting tradition and bringing his visitor to the palace . . . Suddenly Allada broke off his praise and looked at me sharply.

'This is a genuine traditional kingdom. It is not children's game. We have been here hundreds of years looking after the people at grassroots level. We're the ones they come to, not the governments. Governments change; we are always here. We know the families by name, we know the history of land ownership and the good and bad in individuals. All over Africa, you'll find that the traditional kings remain. Even when colonialists expelled and killed traditional rulers, or when misguided governments tried to destroy us, we were always in the people's hearts. When the situations change, you'll always see the traditional kings return. It is better that we work in association with political governments – better for them, I mean. Then a land has continuity and the full co-operation of ordinary people. Otherwise they are lost.'

I wondered if he'd have talked such big talk to Mathieu Kérékou at the most communist and short-tempered phase of his presidencies. No time to watch and wonder – Allada had sailed on, leaving me gasping in a wake of long words. He was talking circuitously about various forms of monarchy around the world . . . Once in Dahomey, they had been absolute monarchs; now they were very like the British royal family. A fine royal family. The death of Princess Diana had been a terrible event – how saddened he'd been by the loss of such a lovely young person. I started to think perhaps he'd known her, tear-welling as he was in his eulogy, but he said: 'Yes, I watched a very moving tribute to her on CNN.'

I must have looked surprised; he added, 'My English is excellent, would you prefer me to speak English?'

I admitted this would be easier for me.

Allada's voluminous way of talking had been hard to follow in French but somehow, though initially his speaking in English had seemed easier, understanding all he was saying only clarified how confusing and boring much of it was. For close on an hour we listened to selective histories of Africa, then present-day African politics, country by country . . . It was getting hotter in the throne room; the light breeze of fresh air from the terrace had died away. I wondered what happened if visitors kneeling at the King's feet fell over while he was talking.

I rallied myself to take proper notice when he came to Toussaint L'Ouverture. He said people were mistaken about this leader of the Haitian slave revolt – Toussaint L'Ouverture was not a slave, as people said, but was of the royal house of Dahomey. He was a prince of Allada who went to save the Haitians from slavery.

I wanted to have found a little-known truth in the palace of Allada; but I have since checked and am sure I was right to have my doubts about Allada's story at the time. I don't know why he told it. Possibly to glamorize his connection, or to lift the Dahomey kings out of their muddy history.

It was well documented that Toussaint L'Ouverture was born in Haiti, in 1743, the son of an educated slave who was possibly a member of the Allada royal household. The kings of Dahomey frequently fell out with each other and sold each other into slavery, and the Allada branch of the family often seemed to come off worst in these clan fights.

At the time of the slave revolt, the Dahomey kings were still trading slaves. They weren't, as Allada insisted, sending their princes across the Atlantic, at their own expense, to save Haiti as part of their war against the French.

The slave revolt in Haiti was not started by Toussaint L'Ouverture, who was a slave until the age of thirty-four; it began from several sources. Interestingly, one uprising began after a vodou ceremony to Ougon, god of war as well as of iron. Ougon spoke through a priestess and told the Haitian slaves to rise up and they would succeed. Toussaint L'Ouverture wouldn't have been involved in this uprising; he was a Catholic and didn't approve of vodou. However, by 1791 Toussaint, who'd joined the slave revolt as a medical officer, had become one of its leaders. He inspired and co-ordinated the successful revolt, becoming Governor-General of Haiti in 1796. In 1802, Napoleon Bonaparte decided to retake Haiti. He didn't succeed but he captured Toussaint. In 1804 Haiti achieved full and final independence; Toussaint L'Ouverture had died the year before in a prison in the French Alps.

Even if I'd had the facts at my fingertips in Allada, I doubt I'd have had the nerve to contradict an unfamiliar monarch in his own throne room. If I'd had a chance to get a word in anyway . . . Allada talked long against colonialism and the theft of his people's rights by foreigners. What he skipped right over was the Dahomian kings' involvement in the slave trade.

Present-day racists love to cite the Africans selling Africans as justification of the slave trade, colonialism and their own dishonest beliefs – conveniently forgetting the frenzied 'sell or be sold' atmosphere that the Europeans created. Forgetting also that the small battles fought between African peoples – the Yoruba and the Fon, for instance – turned into bloodbath wars as the Europeans armed and encouraged disputes to ensure the constant supply of prisoners of war to be sold on to the slave ships. The Yoruba kings and the kings of Dahomey had to feel that it was their enemies they were selling, because they knew they were selling human beings; the Europeans, however, didn't feel that this was what they were buying.

The kings of Dahomey had slaves of their own; they didn't understand that in the Americas a slave was not a servant, a soldier, a mistress or someone who could work hard, become a court official and trusted friend. The slaves of African kings were sometimes free to go home after a few years' useful servitude, and their children were not automatically made slaves. Theirs was nothing like the life of slaves in the New World, where so much effort was made to maintain the perception that slaves were not the same as human beings.

Perhaps Allada was loath to give me too much information in case I was one of those whites eager to have the blame for slavery shifted away from Europe.

Or maybe he just forgot to mention slavery because Allada had a very idiosyncratic way of telling history – one minute we were up to French colonialism, then suddenly we'd swooped back to the thirteenth century. In Tado, where the kings lived at the time, a very odd thing happened with a local princess and a panther: they had a child. This child, Togbegouin, was so naturally ferocious that he grew up to murder the established Tado King and take control of the area, all while still a mere slip of a boy/panther cub. Togbegouin extended and consolidated his kingdom at Tado. Under his sons, the powerful kingdom flourished but eventually there was a dispute over the succession. Three royal brothers set off from the over-crowded Tado royal household, deciding to make new kingdoms for themselves. First they arrived at Allada and took charge of the area. Then a brother went north to Abomey and another went south to Porto Novo. Eventually the Abomey branch became most powerful, calling itself the Kingdom of Dahomey, with Allada and Porto Novo remaining nominal kingdoms under Abomey's rule. Porto Novo broke away, with French assistance, in the late nineteenth century and the end of Dahomey was nigh.

Having told me these edited highlights of his origins, Allada's eyes narrowed.

'You foreigners always ask about the panther. It is, of course, a metaphor.' He looked at me contemptuously. 'The panther is an explanation for our royal household being so powerful. We're not children. We don't believe these stories. These stories are myths only, you understand?'

I don't know what he was having a go at me for – he started it, with the panthers. If it worried him that much, he could have skipped straight to the feisty nature of his family. Maybe it was the heat, but Allada's temperament was getting increasingly opening-night prima donna. Isidore, understanding little English, was nevertheless

listening with rapt respectful attention; the fan, spittoon and
umbrella ladies were beginning to look very wilted but kept nodding as if listening – and I'm sure I was giving the impression of
attentiveness – yet somehow his majesty wasn't getting enough
attention. It seemed he needed to up the drama of the situation by
developing a wild staring look and a tone of voice so close to
hysterical it made me suspect he might be a little high-pitched,
psychologically. Strung far too tight not to snap. It was a scary
demeanour that definitely suggested the pantherish family trait, or
indeed what I later discovered to be a cousins-marrying-cousins
family trait.

Having pounced about the panthers, he flung himself back in his
throne as if magnanimously deciding not to slap me in the face for
my stupidity. He did another time-loop in his story and went to
the period when the kings of Dahomey were in decline.

'The kingdom was strong, but then the kingdom became like the
ancient Rome of West Africa, decadence fuelled by the corrupting
influence of Western opportunists. Our dignity was restored in the
1890s when our King, Gbehanzin, fought the French and the
English . . .'

He went into a lengthy account of Gbehanzin's many military
manoeuvres, footfall by footfall, but suddenly it seemed he'd even
bored himself and he leapt out of the past and slap into modern talk
about World Bank interest rates and continued exploitation of
Africa by the West . . . I started to whimper internally, thinking he
was starting a whole new opera of tedium – but he was preparing
the ground for his grand finale. A tirade about relative economics
quickly got to the specifics: how the upkeep of the palace and roads
around it was as expensive in Benin as it would be in Europe. I
needn't think he was some bush dweller, grateful for a few pounds
– he had an historical residence to restore and international corre-
spondence and contacts to maintain; he had innumerable poor,
uneducated subjects who looked to his kindness for survival . . .
And he obviously needed to buy a lot of jewellery, I thought to
myself, just as an unholy female shrieking started from behind the
wooden door.

The King flounced his robes and stormed out, furious, slamming the door behind him. Spit, fan and brolly lady merely shifted their feet and made small, embarrassed smiles.

The woman's shrieks intensified, Allada barked something ferocious, the woman shrieked, there was silence. Allada came back in looking irritated but making no excuses, no comment at all on the startling interruption.

'So,' he said, giving me an almost impish smile as he settled himself in his throne again, 'I know my secretary has given you a donation envelope . . .'

What had he done to the woman?

'I hope you won't insult me with what's inside your envelope.'

Holding my envelope in both hands, as Isidore instructed, I bowed low and gave it to the King. He immediately counted the contents and I waited for the tone of voice I'd heard behind the door, instant crazy rage, envelope flung back at me . . .

'This is acceptable,' he muttered, stuffing the envelope into the folds of his robe. 'Now, have you any questions, Miss from England?' He smiled with his too many teeth and widened his eyes. I wasn't asking a question, no way I'd risk anything that might start him talking again . . . Before I could clap a hand over his mouth Isidore asked: 'May she take a photograph of you?'

Surely this wasn't done? Surely this would provoke crazy shouting?

Allada pouted and sighed wearily. 'Oh really . . . I do hate to be photographed. I really don't like it.'

I was happy to accept this and flee – but Isidore was gushing a lot of 'it would mean so much to her she's never met a king before'-type gush. It worked. Allada became all gracious condescension.

'Ah, indeed. She's come so far. Of course she must have her photograph.'

He summoned me to sit at his feet and fussed at the umbrella, spit and fan ladies to straighten their hair and stand nicely. They fidgeted with their heads obligingly; only an all-body genteel glow of perspiration gave an indication of how long they'd been standing guard. Allada re-titivated his own robes and jewellery, and fixed his face in a flashing grin for the camera.

They say it's good for the health to drink a litre and a half of water every morning when in a hot country. Better for the health of the kidneys to enquire in advance of filling up with liquid if you're likely to be meeting a local sovereign who can keep talking for two hours.

Shoving money at the hobbling and limbless, I rushed for the car, gasping at Isidore to get me to a café or hotel.

'You're thirsty?'

'The opposite. What about this tree?'

'There's a man sitting there with a goat. OK, calm down. The hotel's just here.'

'He does talk a lot,' Isidore agreed once my kidneys were saved and we were comfortably settled at a table in the Allada Royal Hotel, owned – unsurprisingly – by his gold-trimmed majesty. 'But it was interesting for you to hear the history, wasn't it?'

I'd sounded too impatient with the experience and Isidore was looking hurt. 'Oh yes, it was fantastic. I loved it.'

Isidore had decided there was enough genuine enthusiasm in my reassurance; he drank his drink and looked content. I couldn't quite leave it at that, though – I had to see if it was just me or wasn't Allada, and his household . . . wasn't there something a bit . . . ?

'A bit mad?' Isidore pondered with mild surprise. 'I don't think so.' He shrugged. 'He does that bizarre staring with his eyes when he's excited, but I don't think that's madness.'

OK, if there was no such thing as madness in the house, what was all the Mrs Rochester carry-on in the back room?

'Isidore, he was yelling, there was a woman screaming . . .'

'Oh, outside?'

'Yes, yes.'

He laughed. 'That? That was his wife. She was angry that she couldn't find the car keys. She wanted to know where he had put them; he is always putting them somewhere silly. So he went out and told her to stop shouting, he had them in his pocket. She shouted he should leave them on the hook like she'd told him, his pocket was no use to her. Then she went out.'

The original inhabitants of Allada, the Tofinu, had been quelled by the arrival of the panther-sprung family from Tado. But it took the Dahomey kings several centuries to make them get out and stay out.

The Tofinu then did an extraordinary thing: they fled a few miles down the road and built a new civilization entirely on water. They'd learnt something about Dahomian kings – that they had a religious taboo forbidding them to cross water to do battle. Centuries later the Tofinu still lived in their stilt dwellings in the middle of gigantic lakes and considered themselves never really defeated by the marauding panther family.

Our journey to the lakes was short but there was still time for Isidore to boss me around.

'We'll thoroughly deal with the lakes this afternoon, then visit the other two palaces – Abomey tomorrow, then Porto Novo. So you will have seen the three royal sites of Dahomey. But it's also important to see the King's origins at Tado. Maybe you'll need a visa for Tado, as it is in Togo, but it's only just over the border so we can try.'

'There isn't going to be a panther there, is there?'

The middle of itinerary planning was no time for childish jokes.

'No. You know there won't be a panther, it's just a story. Now, we'll be at the jetty for Ganvié village in a moment, a very interesting place but don't give the people any money unless I say so. They are very greedy for money in Ganvié.'

In the small car park alongside an immense stretch of dark-grey water, Lac Nokoué, the money greed of Ganvié villagers manifested itself. There were scores of pushy boys selling souvenirs, noisy youths offering themselves as guides, car minders, car cleaners . . . There were tough women selling bananas, tomatoes, bread, onions, peppers . . . But they were nothing like as tough as the women buying and selling fish on the plank jetties. Maybe there's something for scientists to discover in fish oil, something that provokes aggression and loudness in females? There were the ubiquitous swarms of children asking for sweets or *cadeaux*. And not a single person there was dressed in the same colour or pattern of cloth. Noisy people, noisy outfits – this was no stretch of water you'd want to come to for a restful commune with nature.

The most persistent hustlers of the Ganvié jetties, the boatmen, were already making a group of young English tourists get tetchy. Isidore suggested we share a boat with the English to economize, but I declined their gesticulating company on the grounds that if I was going to get into an argument with boatmen, I'd rather it was my own argument.

Visitors bought their official admission ticket and a boat ticket from an office run by very slow-moving old men. The boat ticket gave a choice – a place on a large, collective-tour boat with an authorized guide, or the hire of the next small fishing *pirogue* in line. The moonlighting fishermen's *pirogues* were much more exciting but less safe and had no guide. The office would take a split of the boat-ticket price, leaving the moonlighters only two pounds for several hours' work – hence the need to firmly establish with visitors the need for a good tip before setting out. Hence tetchy arguments.

Once the office had pointed out our boatman, Roger, a bulky, middle-aged man with cauliflower ears, Isidore told Roger I was very fair so he needn't worry, tip-wise. So that I wouldn't be worrying what 'fair' meant, Isidore suggested I give Roger the equivalent of five pounds at the end. Then Roger explained he was just the boatman; if I wanted a guide who spoke good French I'd need to take his friend Luc and pay him separately. Another three pounds, Isidore whispered. Why not? I didn't want to be like the English group, now separating into *pirogues* and bickering hard to avoid the encumbrance of guides and being evasive about the possibility of boatmen's tips.

Roger donned a straw hat the size of a bin lid and paddled us out of the log jam of *pirogues* around the jetty, on to the vast, choppy lake. Once the jetty vanished from our stern we could have been at sea, the watery wastes around us surged so far on out of view. We had the wind behind us; Roger hoisted a patchwork sail and we sped towards the largest lake village in Africa, home to more than fifteen thousand people.

The Tofinu used to hunt and cultivate the fertile land around Allada; when they were finally driven out, they took to cultivating the water. They didn't just fish the lakes – they also farmed under-water. Maybe I've made that sound a bit too exciting. What they did was simply to keep up their stocks by breeding and fattening fish. All across the lakes they used tree branches to make enclosures, between fifty and several hundred yards across; here they trapped the fish with rich tempting foliage gathered from the shores. The fish were shut in and fed more foliage while they grew in size and number ready to be caught. The fishermen encircled the inside of a trap with a length of net, then closed it in on their fish. The encircling method took a lot of men and time, so during the process there was a diversionary game played of diving in to catch a fish by hand. This succeeded surprisingly often, as the fish had grown slow and lazy in the trap. And probably, when it came to strength and speed in the water, there weren't many fish in the world who could compete with your average Tofinu.

There was so much activity to watch – fish traps being built, repaired or plundered; men standing precariously on the prow of *pirogues*, throwing graceful swirls of white net into the water hoping for chance catches outside the traps; boatloads of women returning from the shore with purchases of bright, primary-coloured vege-tables. I watched, figured out what people were doing and com-pletely forgot we'd taken on the expense of a guide.

Luc, more of an age to be Roger's son than friend, was a dreamy-looking youth who seemed to suffer from a paralysing shyness, possibly not ideal in a tour guide. After our session at Allada his reticence didn't bother me, but Isidore liked people to do the job they were paid for. He coaxed Luc into a faltering explanation of fish-trap construction.

Without Isidore, I don't know what poor Luc would have managed to do for his money, because Isidore asked questions I wouldn't have known to ask.

'Luc, tell her about the start of Ganvié.'

'Oh yes.' Luc looked flustered. 'It is very interesting.' There was a long pause. I don't know if Luc was downloading the information into French or finding his courage, but the wait was too long for Isidore.

'So? What's this? Suddenly it's a secret?'

Luc and Roger laughed. Something broke free in Luc and he talked-talked-talked, in fast, heavily accented French.

Then Luc seemed to realize he was talking aloud and took fright – stopping abruptly, mouth half-open. Roger smiled at him, avuncular, encouraging. But Luc's eyes were wild with panic. He'd nothing left.

'Did you understand?' Isidore asked me.

'Yes, yes.' I nodded, smiling at Luc as close to avuncular and encouraging as a girl could be.

Luc seemed to relax slightly and nodded at me. 'We'll soon see the village. I will explain more.' He concentrated on the paddle he was using as the boat's rudder as if there were some important problem he had to stare at to fix.

I realized how disturbingly well Isidore had got to know my face. Some blankness in my eyes must have told him I'd barely managed to grasp a word of poor Luc's explanation – two very different forms of bad French had just not met in the middle. So, despite my assurance that I'd understood, Isidore repeated Luc's information at a careful pace, in clear French, until he was satisfied that my 'Yes, yes, I understand' was matched by a convincing look of comprehension in my eyes. Luc's pride was saved by Isidore telling him his explanation was great, but my French was not.

'The best thing,' he told Luc, 'is remember to talk slowly, as if to a child.'

Having me defined as severely retarded did wonders for Luc's confidence. He grinned at me. 'You're not French?'

'English.'

Luc and Roger seemed to think this was just great.

'Later,' Luc said, 'I will sing you a Tofinu song, if you sing an English one.'

I promised there would be songs.

Enhancing Luc's account with his superior narrative skills, Isidore presented me with more magical history. Ganvié, in the Tofinu language, means 'The people are saved'. In 1717, after many years of fighting, King Abodohoue of the Tofinu feared the Dahomey kings would finally defeat and enslave all his people. Abodohoue had considerable magic skills, so he turned himself into a white bird to fly across the lakes, searching to find an island where his people could live – knowing that the Dahomians would never cross water to do battle, an island home seemed the perfect solution. He found an archipelago of small mud islands; now all he needed was a quick way to move all his people to the islands. He turned himself into a crocodile and persuaded all the crocodiles in the lake to help him. The crocodiles carried the people to the tiny islands on their backs. The people took wood with them with which to begin construction of the houses on stilts we see today. The stilt houses allowed what little land there was to be reserved for the keeping of livestock and growing of vegetables.

In return for their help, King Abodohoue made the crocodile sacred; the Tofinu people constructed crocodile totems and were never to eat the creatures. Unfortunately, Abodohoue's brother, Sô-Tchanhoué, was jealous of his success in rescuing the people and he spitefully ate a great feast of crocodiles. Abodohoue banished him further into the lake. The brother took some followers and established a community, still in existence, named after crocodile-guzzler Sô-Tchanhoué.

Rising on pillars out of the lakes were carvings of a crocodile and a white bird, marking the entrance to Ganvié. Ganvié spread far, but in the fifty-kilometre stretch of lake it was invisible from the shore. Wooden stilt houses jumbled together around patches of earth where animals meandered and small crops straggled. The people had added to the scraps of terra firma first discovered, mixing sand and sea shells with lake-bed mud to extend the islands. But mostly they lived on the water, swimming from house to house, or grabbing anything from a car tyre to a tin bath as boatage – when there wasn't one of their many canoes available. If they felt like keeping dry, there were dense networks of wooden walkways to cross – to walk the plank in Ganvié just meant to go next door.

In an Ancient Mariner fashion, these people had to either collect rainwater for drinking or go with buckets to one of the points where it was pumped clean from below the lake bed.

The lake's crocodiles were preying on my mind as I watched small boys leap from the veranda of a wooden house and swim towards us.

'There are no crocodiles now,' Isidore said. 'The water has become salty so there are no crocodiles. Just fish.'

I told him there were saltwater crocodiles in Australia. He wasn't having it. 'Crocodiles can't live in saltwater. There are no crocodiles here now.'

If there ever were any. 'But this crocodile thing . . . it's a legend anyway.'

'Yes.'

'So what really happened?'

Isidore frowned. 'That king, he was a very powerful magic man, powerful enough to turn himself into a crocodile.'

But, but . . . ?

'But he didn't really.'

'Maybe. You must remember, there was a lot of magic in those days. Does it matter? It's what the people believe. I believe it.'

That was me told, then. I'm guessing the King told everyone to grab a log and make a canoe. The facts were that the people did flee to live on water and remained there to this day. They became a closeknit community who loved their breezy independent life.

'We hate to leave here,' Luc told us. 'If we go to the city it's too expensive, we miss our families and the air makes us suffocate.'

'It's a good life here,' Isidore agreed. 'They always find fish and tourists. They can build a stilt house in the village just as they please. They don't have to buy land like land people.'

Luc was pleased. 'That's right. If you come from here you can make a stilt house any time you can buy the wood. Even if you don't come from here, the chief will probably give you permission. The water around the village is for all the people. Out there, the water is private.' He gestured towards the open lake and explained that areas of the water were owned by families, like fields would be. Families marked their ownership by always building their big, corral-style fish traps in the same place. Some of these vast traps had been in the same place for hundreds of years.

Poorer people could work for a trap-owning family, catching the fat, lazy, cultivated fish – although there were still enough fish roaming the undesignated lake areas to make it worth a poor man's while to head out there with his nets or a line.

As the land round the lake had long been cleared of anything useful, the wood and palm branches used to wall the traps and hay for fattening the fish had to be bought inland. If you inherited a trap, you needed to make the money to maintain it. If your trap was neglected, your fish might be poached by the poor; some of your fenceposts and palm fronds might be pinched; the people with an adjoining trap might begin to encroach on your territory as the trap walls started to collapse and the demarcation was no longer clear. Quarrels over this kind of thing blew up occasionally and the village chief had to step in and say: 'Yes, yes, I remember this family's trap extends from here to here – you neighbours need to get back.'

'How can he tell? Does he have maps?' I asked, looking out at trap after indistinguishable trap.

'No. He just remembers.' Luc looked out over the traps, as if trying to memorize them himself. Although his terror had receded, he did prefer any activity to talking.

I'd been too busy listening to Luc to pay much attention to the small boys who'd been dog-paddling round us, showing off a rowdy form of synchro swimming and yelling for '*Cadeaux!*' They now changed the display to backward somersaults off the prow of a

parked *pirogue*, yelping '*Yovo, yovo! Cadeaux!*' I found some sweets
and took their photograph. A few *pirogues* along a new circus display
of wet naked children began: handstands over into the water,
cartwheels into the water, dive-bomb splashing . . .

We passed through stilt forests and down tiny waterways. More
children were clinging to crossbeams under their houses or dancing
on verandas, holding out hands for *cadeaux*. A laughing little girl
poled past us on an old door, two tiny sheep behind her on her
vessel. 'Give my sheep money, they're hungry!'

Just as I was wondering about the safety of very young children
handstanding at the edge of their verandas, ten feet above the water
a toddler fell with a wail backwards out of a window. No one
batted an eyelid. He splashed upright in the water, spitting and
laughing, an older brother yanked him by the scruff of the shorts
into a *pirogue* and paddled away with him.

Luc smiled at my panic. 'All children swim here. All! The water
is the ground to them.'

We made one of the compulsory stops on the Ganvié tour, The
Francophone Salle de Réunion, an elegant stilt café constructed for
a conference of francophone African leaders in the early nineties.
There were grand wide steps to draw up to and it was one of the
few stilt constructions that was whitewashed and not battered,
moss-grown or half-sunk-looking.

As all hands on our deck helped me clamber ashore, a little girl
with a spiky dinosaur-type hairdo came across the water, paddling
frantically with her hands, sitting in a brown plastic washing-up
bowl just big enough to hold her. She was a very funny sight and
she knew it. 'My photo, my photo, *yovo!*' she demanded. I took
one, then she paddled in a frenzy to get to the steps in time. I
waited for her and handed her down some sweets. This pleased
her: 'Good *yovo*, good.' She grinned a tooth-short grin.

A child's voice from a stilt house behind her called out, to see
what was going on and if it was worth bothering with.

'*Bonbons!!*' she yelled back, and paddled away in her basin.

When I left the café she was at the foot of the steps with a baby brother in her arms and a clutch of small companions eager for shares. One male, one female French tourist – the international budget-traveller type with ponytails and weather-worn rucksacks who'd shriek with rage to be called tourists – came out of a *pirogue* and said something disapproving to me about '*encourager*'. Encourage her to what? Use her initiative? Have a laugh?

The French couple also complained heavily about being brought to the café, suspecting high-priced drinks; they talked down their mildly protesting boatman and left. Possibly they'd have been shamefaced to discover that their admission tickets entitled them to a free soft drink in the establishment.

The café proprietor made his money, though, because it would be a hard tourist who wouldn't buy a drink for the boat people who'd just sweatily paddled them to the door.

Over the very sweet local drink, *fizzi*, we relaxed in the breeze and talked about water life.

I was still worried. What if a baby fell in?

'How would a baby fall in?' Isidore frowned impatiently. 'Babies are on their mothers' backs.'

'No one drowns here.' Luc smiled to mollify my near sulk at Isidore. 'I've seen even a small baby fall in and float. But you see how we are here, all on top of each other. No one would miss seeing a baby fall in.' He consulted Roger in their own language. Roger shook his head. 'No, we both never heard of a baby drowning. Sometimes men drown, out on the lake. There was one in a storm, got thrown out of his boat and his leg was caught in a fish trap. Storms are the enemy here. They bring floods – you see how the houses are all falling? The water pulls at the underneath of them in floods. There are such big floods in the rainy season, everyone has to go and sit on the roof for a few days. But there are advantages. Fire, crime and famine, we don't have those.'

'No crime?'

'Tiny things. Like I told you, moving posts from a neglected trap. Otherwise, no. Everyone knows everyone too well. It's not like Cotonou, where strangers arrive every day unnoticed. It's hard for us in Cotonou. We're used to this nice life here.'

It did seem like a nice life. Ganvié smelt vaguely fishy and muddy but there was none of that sewagey rottingness that wafts at you in Venice – the water here was full of life and a clean wind came off the lake . . .

'Do the children go to school?' Isidore always liked to know.

'Yes. We have two schools. On stilts. It's unusual for people to have further education, though. Because that means leaving. Some do. There's a man from here became a doctor. Another woman went to university, married a politician and has lots of shops in Abomey.'

Isidore made a face at the mention of Abomey. 'My wife was from Abomey. Those people are no good.'

Luc and Roger agreed vehemently. *Abomey . . . Oh là là!*

Not for the first time, I wondered about the wife – but we were on the move to the next compulsory stop.

We wound round more stilt legs, waved at endless handstanding, *yovo* yelling, corkscrew-diving infants, and dispensed every *bonbon* on my person. The mention of Abomey seemed to have tempted Isidore to consider the simple life in Ganvié. 'They need very little here,' he sighed, trailing his hand in the water like a frilly lady at Henley. 'The most expensive thing is wood and clothes.'

'And boats,' Luc said. 'We buy the boats inland. But a good boat can last twenty years. Oh, and we have to buy fuel for cooking fires,' he added, perhaps in case his tip disappeared in the notion that he'd no need for money.

The second compulsory halt was at a stilted, barn-sized souvenir shop. Luc and Roger stayed outside. Isidore was immediately accosted by a stunningly beautiful young salesgirl, in traditional wraps of new, blue floral cotton. She urged me to go and make my choice, as if she couldn't get me out of the way fast enough. Setting a chair for Isidore beside her own, she went all flittery and fluffy round him, and didn't seem to care if I bought anything or fell out the window and drowned.

There were appliqué banners, cushions, tablecloths . . . All with stilt houses on them. There were wood carvings of stilt houses. Paintings and raffia mats with stilt houses on them. The crafts on sale at Ganvié were mostly bought from inland markets and resold at inflated prices. Isidore had warned me not to buy much, but said there were little comedy carvings I might like. These were coarsely cut wood models of doctors performing operations, dentists pulling out teeth, children in school, a lady at a computer, people on a bus . . . They were very knowingly cute, faux-naïf, but I had to have them.

I brought my armfuls of wood people back to Isidore and Miss Fluffy. Now she was twittering as well as fluffing her display feathers, touching him on the arm, looking into his eyes . . . She was beautiful enough to be a supermodel and nearly young enough to be Isidore's daughter. Very irritated to have to deal with my purchases and hear Isidore say that we were in a hurry, Fluffy showed him out, talking sweetly to him all the while, pouting coyly with her eyes full of 'Take me, take me!' warm promises, while I got only one of those looks up and down that beautiful women can give ordinary women, full of mockery and disdain for our minor charms.

I scored a point because the next thing she saw was me laughing and whispering to Isidore. 'She liked you,' I teased him. 'And she's very beautiful.'

He grimaced. 'What do I want with a young girl like that and all the babies she'll want? These girls . . . She sees me with you and thinks I'm rich.'

'She doesn't think I'm your wife?'

'If you were my wife it wouldn't matter. She thinks she'll get to be another wife for me, living off you. That's what they're like.'

I felt very old and frumpy and wished I had fallen out the window and drowned.

On the boat jetty in front of us was something else to upset me. The ponytailed French couple were sitting with an old woman. She had an array of carvings and drums set out at the top of the steps, shading herself with a parasol. The French boy was arguing with her in slow, elaborate style as if he had all the time in the world, although their boatman was looking very fidgety behind them. While he bargained, as the budget-traveller guide in his rucksack had undoubtedly told him to, he kept making strange melodramatic faces. I don't imagine his guide book told him that when dealing with Africans it's best to be ludicrously over-emphatic.

He exuded self-importance and seemed convinced that he knew how to bargain like a native. The self-possessed old woman smirked slightly as she interrupted him: 'Listen, take the drum. Learn to play music for your wife, your mother – all your family will be happy when you play music.' Probably what she meant was: 'If you're playing music, at least you won't be talking and we'll all be happy.' She started tying carrying string round a large, ugly, loosely made tam-tam.

'Oh, madame.' The French boy smiled excessively. 'And your mother will eat well tonight if I buy at your price.'

The old woman laughed. 'My mother? She's been dead for ten years.'

The French boy was undaunted: 'Madame, your price isn't possible. If I pay that I'll have to eat sand. I'll have to crawl on my belly and eat sand.'

The old woman stared at him. Isidore and every boatman on the jetty stared at him.

'You'll have to what?' the woman said eventually.

'Eat sand,' the French girl interjected, making eating motions.

'This girl . . .' Roger began incredulously. I don't think he ran out of French; the words in any language escaped him.

'What's wrong with that man?' Luc asked me.

'He thinks that's how Africans talk,' I said.

'He's an idiot,' Isidore said.

'Does he think Africans eat sand?' Luc was so bemused he looked like he might reel away off the end of the jetty.

'I don't know,' I said. 'He thinks this is a good way to bargain.'

'By talking like a lunatic?' Isidore made an exaggerated face in imitation of the Frenchman.

Our noisy laughter provoked a glare from the still bargaining Frenchman. I wanted to shout something at them about not encour-aging Ganvians to buy craft works inland and sell them at inflated prices. But it was enough to see them, later, struggling out of their *pirogue* with the ugly great drum, and to know that for all his smug knowingness the Frenchman had bought what Isidore called 'a type of monstrosity you can get cheaper anywhere'.

We'd almost done with Ganvié, but Isidore had one of his ideas: 'There's something you'll like even better then Ganvié. I asked Roger and Luc if they will break the rules especially for you and go on to the next village. They say they will, if you remember the extra distance in your tip and you don't mention it to the boat controller back at the car park.'

If Isidore thought the next village, Sô-Tchanhoué, home of the crocodile eaters, was worth it, then so did I. Gleefully, Roger and Luc paddled out the other side of Ganvié into more wide lakescape. Fishermen fished their traps out here, but there were fewer boats.

Luc called out an answer to a question from some half-naked fishermen mending a trap, then said to me: 'I have told them you are from a charity project. This will be our story.'

Our story seemed to satisfy the half-naked fishermen. Luc and Roger had now taken their shirts off in the late-afternoon heat. There was definitely a fisherman's physique – big upper bodies from hauling things and paddling; lean legs from swimming more than walking. Not mentioned in the guide books as an attraction at Ganvié, but quite memorable.

After another half-hour of mixed paddling and sailing, we reached the dowdy crocodile eaters' village. Being less accessible than Ganvié, it was poorer, less populated and less trained up in the tourist game. Children did no tricks for sweets; they simply stared at me, astonished. Just as well, really – my pockets were cleaned out of encouragement.

Quite a few adults froze on their terraces, seemingly horrified at the sight of me.

'The villagers are nervous you might be from the government,' Luc said, as one woman on a walkway shrieked with alarm and ran inside her stilt house. 'But if you were from the government you'd have a motorboat.'

Isidore pointed at the reason for village nervousness of official-
dom – huge boats, the size and style of garbage barges, secreted in
channels behind houses, half-covered in branches. These were
smugglers' boats. In the dead of night they chugged out from their
coves behind the stilt houses and crossed miles of inland water
networks into Nigeria, coming back laden with fake Nike trainers,
televisions, fridges, mopeds, stereos . . . but mostly petrol. Petrol
was officially twice the price in Benin. Illicit trade was so rife it was
virtually uncontrollable.

Sometimes police boats would swoop along the waterways but
the smugglers knew the byways better – and the police weren't
going to start shooting at a sixty-foot hull full of petrol.

It would be some interfering government insistence – egged on
by official petrol suppliers – rather than an unusual burst of police
enthusiasm, that would send them out this way at all. Scouring the
waterways too enthusiastically could lead to encounters with far
worse villains than the petrol scallies. Boats full of armed drug
smugglers might be out there, plying another frequent trade from
Nigeria. And the worst thing about drug smugglers was they didn't
bother trying to negotiate a bribe; they'd just kill you. No Beninois
policeman was paid enough to make dying worthwhile. So, generally, the police didn't busy themselves too frequently in the remote
lake-backs. It was easier to catch the petrol sellers on dry land.

All along the roadsides of Cotonou were rickety wooden stalls
selling wine bottles full of smugglers' petrol, glinting in the hot sun.
Often, pieces of rag were stuffed in the necks to seal the bottles,
so the roadsides looked like extensive markets for firebombers –
Molotov cocktails off the peg.

A wine bottle held enough to top up one of Cotonou's swarm
of mopeds. The larger amounts needed for cars were in big bottle-
garden jars underneath the stalls. Some funnels, a piece of plastic
tubing and you had a petrol station.

The petrol stalls were a terrifying sight, always being just skimmed
by speeding mopeds, missed by inches by thundering jugger-
nauts. People with cigarettes in their mouths funnelled petrol,
attendants lit their food fires close enough to cook while minding

the stall . . . I kept thinking about that childhood summer amusement of setting fire to dry undergrowth with a piece of broken glass. One good refraction and half of Cotonou would barbecue.

There were official petrol stations but hardly anyone used them, except for foreigners and people driving company vehicles who weren't paying for the petrol themselves. If there was no unofficial petrol the country would have ground to a standstill in a matter of weeks.

If there was a police bad-hair day, usually caused by it being a long time until next pay day, they'd do a tour of the petrol stalls looking for backhanders. If you refused they'd smash up all your wine bottles and confiscate the gallon jars – so a backhander was easier.

'It's not a good living, petrol selling,' Isidore mused to Luc and Roger. 'Very dangerous, there's a lot of hassle and accidents.'

'I'd never have a petrol stall,' Luc agreed. 'Smuggling is better.' He smiled at me; all shyness had left him now. 'You'll find there are two categories of smuggler, madame.'

'Two categories?'

'Yes, those who get rich and those who get caught.'

His joke brought him right out of himself and he sang us Tofinu songs all the way back. It was a hard paddle against a brisk wind, so on the final stretches Roger joined in the singing to keep himself buoyed up and set the rhythm.

Back at the jetty, one of the old boat controllers from the office appeared and wanted to know where we'd been for so long.

'My husband knows someone in Ganvié,' I said. 'We had lunch with them.'

The controller wandered off, irritated to have caught no one out. Luc and Roger shook my hand, grinning and whispering, 'Good lie, very good.'

'Very good lie, very good,' Isidore said as we drove off. 'Who is the husband – me?'

'No, it was some other man. But he fell out of the boat and drowned.'

'Oh dear, that's a shame.' He laughed. 'You should have said something; we'd have saved him.'

We realized we were starving but braced ourselves to survive on a bunch of bad bananas a woman in the car park had intimidated me into buying. We'd never make it to Abomey before nightfall otherwise. Personally, I didn't want to be arriving after dark in a town with walls built from human blood.

5

The Goodfellahs and Their Bellies

'This is my favourite. You see, he is pushing balls of mud up the man's bottom. Pushing, pushing until he's full and actually chokes to death.'

I wasn't witnessing some strenuous local sport. This unusual use for mud, and bottoms, unless I've led a very sheltered life, was depicted on a bas-relief decorating the palace of Abomey.

It was disturbing that our guide, Edgar, delighted in the image quite so much, but if you had to pick a favourite, what were the choices? Jolly, bright-painted reliefs of people having their hands chopped off, necks bitten, stomachs stabbed, backs flayed, heads sliced or whole bodies shot to bits by the rifles of the busy warriors of Dahomey. My favourite was what looked like a crowd of little men with hatchets stalking an alien spacecraft. Edgar said this was just a depiction of an attack on an enemy's hut, which was disappointing.

If you didn't find a favourite artwork among the bas-reliefs, there were the palace's wooden doors, made festive with carvings of horses strung round the neck with human heads. Or there was a throne inside, resting on feet of human skulls.

'Are you Fon?' Edgar asked Isidore. 'OK, then I can say this: sometimes if African visitors ask whose skulls these are, we say we don't know. But they are the skulls of Yoruba kings.'

Edgar, a precise young man with glasses, was studying the history of the palace and had written a guide book in English. He didn't believe the much-broadcast old chestnut that the walls of the city were made with human blood.

'As you go around, you'll see these protecting walls stretched a long way. Kilometres. And they are high, in fact eight metres high. And they were built by slaves with bricks. Clay and straw bricks. It was hard work for them, killing many by falls and crushings. So in my view what is meant in fact is the English expression 'blood, sweat and tears'. Not blood used like water in cement.'

I thought this sounded very wise. Nice to have a common-sense rebuttal to histrionic colonial chronicles of the kings of Dahomey as 'savage and brutal beyond human imagining' (Richard Burton), at a time when nineteenth-century France, Belgium and England had policies abroad that involved a surprising amount of massacre, rape, thievery and flogging, for people who claimed to define humanity.

Admittedly, I had an image of the Dahomey kings as a sort of Mafia gang, the Sopranos of West Africa, tough men doing a tough job and who still had wives, families and private troubles they'd love to have taken to a therapist had they not got to watch their backs, never show weakness, and do things to challengers they'd have preferred not to. I'd fancied that another architectural feature we were supposed to shudder at in Abomey, the bodies-in-the-walls rumour, was some kind of cement overcoat, burying them under the flyover-type punishment.

'I don't think there are people in the walls,' Edgar sighed at my question. 'In fact it may be some fell in the foundations by accident and died. But why would the kings want their angry spirits in there forever?'

Isidore spoke to Edgar in Fon. Edgar replied in English.

'No, no bodies in the walls have been found, just bones nearby. Like from a battle.'

I was distracted from the corpse debate by noticing that Isidore must have been following the conversation. 'You speak English?'

'I don't,' Isidore said in French, smiling coyly. 'I understand but don't speak it well.' Then he grinned at me, speaking English. 'I am not speak good.'

His English was probably about the same standard as my wildly approximate French. But Isidore, I suspected, didn't like doing things he couldn't do well. Our tour moved on, in English for me, with Isidore swinging from Fon to French as the whim took him, and understanding all.

The Palace Museum compound covered fifty acres, but was only a fraction of what had been contained in the original city walls. Each of the twelve kings of Dahomey constructed his own residence; there was a taboo against inhabiting a previous king's home. Of the twelve Abomey palaces, constructed between 1600 and 1900, only three were in reasonable order. Work to restore the rest went on in fits and starts, largely dependent on foreign project-aid.

Although not yet butting in to disagree with Edgar's debunking approach to Dahomey history, I think Isidore hated to see good stories wasted by Edgar's prosaic 'in fact's.

'They say, if you walk near the ancient walls at midnight you will disappear forever,' he whispered to me as we crossed the vast central courtyard of the Palace Museum. I didn't believe it, but once told that the deep, dark red of Abomey was blood, it was hard to feel you'd want to go roaming the town alone in your nightdress.

Isidore then held up our progress, involving himself with some of the artisans who plied their trade in the courtyard – weavers, carvers, metalworkers, embroiderers – all doing something fascinating to watch. But for Isidore it was the weavers with their wood-frame looms that were the fascination.

'I would love to learn this. I would love to have a loom at home to relax with in the evenings. I've seen little ones, you know, small enough to put on a tabletop. That would be perfect. I could do it in the evening and watch telly.'

Did I tell you Isidore had muscles like a full-grown Ganvié fisherman? He was no slip of a wilting, weaving milksop. But I didn't doubt that he would love to weave of an evening. It would be a clean hobby, absolutely suited to his fastidious attention to detail and the gentleness under all his bossing and scowling. I also felt sad about the weaving; it was a lonely man's plan for his evenings.

Edgar wanted us to move on from staring hypnotized at whirring shuttles and taut thread.

'There is a lot to see,' he reminded me. 'In fact, here in the courtyard is an important place itself.'

He explained how supplicants would wait in the courtyard, hoping that their bribe to an official would get them in to see the King. Local officials were obliged to wait every day in case an announcement was made that had to be relayed to the common people. The waiting could be excruciatingly long in the reign of King Guézo (1818–1858). He was very superstitious and consulted oracles before deciding whether to appear before the people at all. If the oracles were against it, the supplicants and officials could be hanging around in the heat for days.

Guézo, sitting on his skull-footed throne, had a spectacularly bizarre temperament but he was a tough, clever king, admired in retrospect by his people for insisting that Dahomey was the centre of the universe. His son Glélé struggled to maintain Dahomey against Yoruba wars and growing European trickery and belligerence; he wasn't tough enough or bright enough. The final ruler, Gbehanzin, was handed a kingdom that was already lost.

Guézo was the most written-about Dahomey king, the epitome of decadent barbarism for European chroniclers; he was fictionalized by Chatwin and committed to celluloid by Herzog in *Cobra Verde*. But for a swashbuckling, big-budget action hero, Gbehanzin would be my man.

Ruler from 1889 to 1894, Gbehanzin was fortunate to inherit an immense arsenal of firearms, accumulated during Dahomey's slave-trading years. He was going to need them.

The Europeans had gone off the slave trade; it was no longer the money spinner it had been. The palm-oil plantations established and controlled by the Dahomey and Yoruba royal households were much more valuable. Palm oil was a principal ingredient in soap, the new big thing in Europe, both domestically and industrially. It was essential in the production of wool and cotton cloth. As the Dahomey and Yoruba kings kept putting up their prices, the palm-oil shippers called for consular and military backup.

In the Yoruba kingdoms, the kings also controlled tin and gold monopolies – it was believed there must be gold in northern Dahomey. Using the excuse that they were cleaning up the last of the slave trade and trying to civilize West Africa with commerce and Christianity, the French, British and Germans fought their way into occupation of the land in order to control the new valuable trades. As the French troops arrived in Dahomey, Gbehanzin fought to save his people from being made slaves in their own land. Several times he came close to defeating the French, but the English arrived to assist their co-colonialists with gunboats and more ruthless military tactics. Gbehanzin was forced to retreat, burning his palace at Abomey rather than leave it for his enemies. He battled on from the bush, living among the ordinary people as they fought together, but was eventually captured and exiled to Martinique. Possibly he had too much influence here with former slaves, because the French moved him to Algeria, where he died in 1906. His son brought his body back to Dahomey for burial in 1928.

If I were directing *Gbehanzin: The Movie*, there's an event shortly before his capture that I might overlook in the interests of making a film for all the family. When he knew capture was inevitable, Gbehanzin dashed south to his mother's home. He cut her throat, cut the throats of forty-one of his mother's female servants and forty-one of her male servants. They were all buried together with full ceremony. Gbehanzin performed these alarming rites so that mother wouldn't be taken prisoner by the Europeans and humiliated. Or worse, she might be killed by the Europeans, who would disrespect her corpse.

Locally, Gbehanzin was the most frequently depicted Dahomey king, in painting and statuary, a tall, handsome man smoking his trademark long-stemmed pipe, wearing a dark-blue robe, usually pulled back to reveal a broad chest . . .

Ever on the hunt for gore, Isidore stopped by a low oval hut, surrounded by animal skulls.

'Edgar, are you going to show her Guézo's tomb?'

Edgar looked mildly frustrated. 'Yes, of course, but first I wanted to explain the . . .' He smiled acceptingly. 'But if you like we can go straight on with the tomb. It is Guézo's tomb now but in fact when he was alive it was his temple where he did sacrifices to his gods. The outside wall here is normal, but if you look through the door you can see there is an inner wall. This is made with earth, alcohol, seawater, palm oil and sacrifice blood. Things important to the divinities. There are still sacrifices of animals done here. But in the previous times there were human sacrifices. Some. Prisoners of war or people who had betrayed the Kingdom or offended the gods. Their blood was smeared on the walls for the gods. This is my other theory where the idea of blood walls in Abomey comes from. Don't worry, in fact it is only animal sacrifices now.'

Much was made of Dahomian human sacrifice by European chroniclers. Human sacrifice was not a regular practice. It was a religious tradition that the kings' priests demanded in times of crisis. Those sacrificed were traitors, significant enemies or spies. It was a form of public execution, given more substance than merely exacting society's revenge, because it had a religious dimension. There are modern states with a death penalty showing little evidence of a need for higher motive than revenge.

On the charts and lists of Dahomian succession displayed around the palace, I noticed there was something wrong with dates. Had there been some outbreak of republicanism between 1797 and 1818?

Edgar smiled broadly when I spotted the omission. Adandozan, the bad-fairy thirteenth king, had been removed from the records, despite a twenty-one-year reign of much sound and fury.

'In fact,' Edgar beamed, 'my studies tell me this may be an

injustice. Many believe we shouldn't even speak his name. They say in life and now in death he was an evil spirit and we shouldn't summon him. I'm not afraid of this, are you?'

Unspeakable acts on the résumé of Adandozan the Unmentionable included: usurping the throne from his brother Guézo in the first place; ripping open the wombs of pregnant women to obtain foetuses for doing spells; feeding prisoners to hyenas and leopards kept in cages at the palace; castrating men suspected of plotting against him. And he suspected many, being alcoholic and paranoiac. So it was brave of Guézo to start listening to princes and ministers who were plotting against Adandozan. The plotters were particularly bothered by things Adandozan did that nowadays might actually take the edge off his demonic reputation. For instance, he opposed the international slave trade. He found the continual waging of war rather tiresome – this was a serious treason, because the kings of Dahomey were obliged by a sacred traditional oath to create a kingdom greater than the one they inherited; that is, to invade some neighbours. If there was no war there was no loot, no captives, and profits fell. He also upset the royal retainers and palace priests by not making sacrifices and offerings to his ancestors. Ceremonies and sacrifices meant profits for attending priests. Adandozan deprived many royals and hangers-on of their inherited privileges, even sold some into slavery. As palace retainers kept the history of the household, it is debatable how much of Adandozan's reported cruelty was true.

When Guézo accepted his friends' offer to make him King, there was a bloodless coup and Adandozan the Unpopular was imprisoned in his palace. Guézo kept him there under house arrest, refusing to execute him. He said he would not execute anyone who had once occupied the Dahomey throne. This was generous of Guézo. He and Adandozan had the same father but different mothers; Adandozan had sold Guézo's mother into slavery. Yet Guézo left Adandozan unmolested in a palace back room. Adandozan can't have drunk too copiously or done anything too annoying back there, because he actually outlived Guézo.

Edgar concluded his attempt to rehabilitate Adandozan with a final gesture at the tomb of Guézo. 'Guézo did nothing against his brother but he knew that you can kill someone by giving them a bad name.'

Unsurprisingly, Guézo developed a system of loyalty that didn't depend on family ties, known as the 'Blood Oath'. Absolute mutual fidelity was sworn in a ritual of religious seriousness. If either party betrayed the sworn friendship, the betrayed could kill them or have them killed. In fact – not just with names.

Moving on from tombs, Edgar showed us large collections of weaponry, mainly Portuguese cannons, exchanged at a rate of fifteen men or twenty-one women per cannon. In the yard outside here was a French-made heavy machine-gun. Edgar had a story to tell us about this: 'Ah, this is a favourite story of mine. In 1870 the Germans and French were at war in this part of Africa. The French army retreated; the Germans captured this gun from the French and took it back to where they were settled in Togo. Then King Gbehanzin, through a Togolese arms trader, bought this gun from the Germans. But then Gbehanzin needed some Germans to come and train his men how to use it. Four Germans came. They painted their faces and bodies black so the French wouldn't know they were helping Gbehanzin. But the French were amazed when the Dahomians attacked them so well with the machine-gun and they sent spies to Gbehanzin's camp. They found out that the men in charge of the machine-gun did not have African hair. The French captured the four Germans and executed three of them.'

'What about the fourth?'

'He was Belgian.'

'So what happened to him?'

'I don't know, he was Belgian. Now, here is where some American experts have been working to help us to restore the bas-reliefs. The ones on the walls now are replicas, but in here the originals are being restored. The palace is a World Heritage project.'

There was a lively amount of work going on and a photographic display showing the progress of the restoration.

'They will keep the replicas outside. The real ones will stay here to protect them from the weather. This building is more modern as you see. It was in fact the headquarters of the French colonial administration. They deliberately built it right in the heart of the palace.'

Isidore nodded. 'Like Dahomey itself.'

Edgar smiled, bewildered. 'Like Dahomey?'

'You explain things very well, Edgar. Will you please explain to her, in English, where does the name Dahomey come from?'

Edgar understood. 'Oh yes. I see what you mean when you say Dahomey itself. Oh yes, very important. Would you like a mango?'

He pointed to an over-burdened tree, surrounded by ripe wind-fall fruit.

'She will get sick if she eats fruit from the ground. She will have her lunch later,' Isidore snapped.

Sometimes Isidore . . . Edgar was looking foolish and told off. Remembering I was quite a big girl really, I made a suggestion.

'I would like something. I saw a café in the entrance. Shall we have a drink there?'

Edgar smiled and walked alongside me. Isidore followed, glowering over my wilful impudence. A small beer seemed to make him glower more. Edgar drank pineapple-flavoured *fizzi* – he'd need to keep himself steady; he had an important explanation to give and Isidore was making him nervous.

'In fact, the proper name in Fon is Danhome. This means, in the stomach of Dan. Abomey also is wrong. It is Agbome, which means in the middle, or stomach, of the moat. Because there was once a moat around the city. Danhome is more complicated. When the brothers came from Tado to Allada, the youngest, Do-Aklin, went to Kana and settled. The local chief, Dan, said he could settle if he liked and gave him some land to farm and another piece of land to build a house. Then Do-Aklin died and his son, Dako-Donhou, asked for some more land so he could build his own house, not live in his father's. Dan said yes but that was an end to the land the strangers could have from him. But when Dako-Donhou died, his son Houegbadja asked Dan for even more land. In fact it was a different Dan by this time, or he would be very old . . . Dan said,

"No. You strangers are too greedy, you won't be happy until you've built your house in my stomach." Houegbadja said, "In this case, I will do that." He killed Dan and buried him in the foundations of his palace. So then, as you see it is Danhome. In the stomach of Dan. Houegbadja was in fact the one who started the rule of always having to expand the kingdom by war. He was the real first King of Danhome but his father is given place in the list for respect.'

Edgar glanced at Isidore, hoping for approval. But Isidore only grunted and half-nodded. What was wrong with him now?

'This is a good explanation. But you forgot the dog.'

Edgar clearly hadn't forgotten the dog, just didn't want to talk about it. 'Ah but that story . . . I'm trying not to tell her things I don't believe myself.'

Isidore looked close to building houses in Edgar's stomach, knocked back the dregs of his beer and launched himself into his story.

'Here's what happened. Dan summoned his friends, saying, "This man Houegbadja is out of control, we'll have to kill him. We'll dig a deep, deep hole in front of my house. We'll cover it with palms. I'll invite him to come and see me, pretending I'll agree to give him more land. Then he'll fall in the hole, we'll throw in spears and kill him." But Houegbadja had a magic dog, who told him that Dan planned to kill him. So Houegbadja went to Dan's house well armed, taking his dog with him. Approaching Dan's house, the brave dog ran ahead, fell in the hole and died. Upset and furious, Houegbadja leapt across the hole, ran inside, strangled Dan and slit open his stomach. Houegbadja turned to Dan's household and told them to get red sand and construction materials. He threw sand in the stomach, threw in stones – he had begun his house.'

There was something about the way Isidore told a story, doing the voices, actions, adding gore and animal magic . . . Edgar looked crestfallen. All he could offer in competition was dry reality.

'We must remember that it wasn't Houegbadja who established a secure, centralized kingdom. This was left to his son Agadja who in 17 . . .'

Isidore scowled. Edgar gave up. But he showed me a short pamphlet he'd written about Agadja; I bought this while Isidore sat stony-faced.

As we crossed back out of the courtyard I gave Edgar a tip, without consulting Isidore.

From out of a deep scowl, Isidore suddenly asked Edgar something in what sounded like affable Fon. It was. Edgar looked pleased and switched to French.

'You want to see the King of Abomey, madame? Oh, he is very nice. You should see the First Minister to make an appointment – let me write his address.'

More talk in Fon with the address scribbling; Isidore and Edgar parted as if they were best friends.

Despite Isidore's attempts in the car to win me round with talk of some other Dahomey King gore and magic, I remained monosyllabic, deciding that the bossiness and interference in my life had to be firmly tackled over lunch.

With the mango as an example, I told Isidore he didn't always have to answer for me.

'But you can't eat mangoes from the ground.'

'I'm not talking specifically about mangoes, I'm saying I can say yes or no for myself.'

'What if you don't understand the question? Remember I can see from your face if you don't understand.'

'Edgar asked me about the mangoes in English.'

'If you want mangoes they can bring them here in the restaurant washed for you.'

I paid the bill before he made me insane. I'd think of something, he'd soon see how well I could fend for myself . . .

Without Isidore's supervision I'd have had no clue how to ask passers-by the way to the first minister's obscure address down the back warrens of Abomey town. This wouldn't be the day, then, that I showed him.

★

Cosy in an armchair, the First Minister was quite happy to arrange for us to see the King of Abomey. He asked me where I was from and wanted to know if I had a purpose to my visit.

'No, she has no purpose. She's a tourist,' my answering service said.

'That's good,' the First Minister smiled. 'It will be a relaxing visit. Nothing official. The King likes that.'

He consulted a large red appointment book. 'Ah. I'm afraid it will have to be tomorrow afternoon. If you can call here first at two o'clock I'll take you over there.'

Tomorrow was fine. Isidore always had a Plan B for my days. Did I make plans for the day? About as much as a mango made plans. So I had no right to still feel vaguely sulky with him, but I did.

En route to Plan B, I had to visit the bank in Bohicon, a thriving commercial town outside Abomey. Bohicon had begun as a ribbon development of traders on the main road to Abomey and eventually became significant in its own right. It was easier to build modern facilities, like banks and railway stations, here, where half the land wasn't the semi-sacred site of the ancient palaces and where there weren't a lot of backhanders to be paid to living minor royals.

I had to wait for ages in the bank. So did an elderly man next to me. He scowled, sweated, a vein in his temple throbbed. After fifteen minutes, he jumped to his feet, bellowing: 'I'm an old man, I can't waste the time I've got left in here!'

The outburst helped him queue jump. Non-bellowing clients like me left the bank after an hour in the frustrated mood Beninois banks always provoked.

Isidore, perhaps suspecting the slow bank-bureaucracy would mean I'd come back and take it all out on him, was waiting to placate me with a bag of peanuts he'd bought from a child near the car.

'Sure they won't make me sick?' I snapped.

I felt bad instantly when I saw his wounded face. Some of the money I'd changed in the bank was for his wages. When I handed them over, he was so pleased I resolved to slap myself with windfall mangoes and several other rotting fruits if I was ever horrible to him again.

'This is a good job for me. Regular money every day. You don't know what a rest that is from my usual life. Sometimes days go by and no customers need taxis. I'm there, ready to work, work very hard, but nothing comes. I'll always pray for you and your family. I know my life will change now, because of you.'

He folded the money into a tatty leather shoulder bag he kept under the driver's seat. I felt sad. All this hope pinned on me.

Plan B was an attraction Isidore had only heard tell of, so we roamed the bush outside town, Isidore consulting every passer-by for directions. He began to fret that he'd been misled by mere rumour, but eventually a woman nodded and waved vaguely at the bush beside us. Isidore parked and excitedly scouted ahead into the undergrowth, me following, beginning a slight whimper as we headed into a pride of huge, humpbacked, horned cattle with a nasty look on their faces. A teenager was pulling water up from below ground in a bucket – neither he nor Isidore seemed to notice we were surrounded by bus-high beasts with ten-foot pointy horns.

'Yes, it's here,' the teenager told Isidore. 'It's full of water from the rains, that's what I'm getting for the cattle.'

He was encouraging these creatures, giving them water? Any minute now they'd be goring me, trampling me, flapping me to death with their humps . . . Isidore didn't seem to care, just kept raving delightedly about finding 'it'.

There was a small excavation and an abandoned bulldozer nearby, half-sunk in red mud. This wasn't 'it'. 'It' was a rectangular hole at the back of the excavation, door-shaped, not natural. 'It' was a house underground.

The teenager put his bucket aside and led us into the excavation.

'Last month they find it. They were dig to build a house for a minister and suddenly the machine falls in a hole. They continue dig with spades and realize it had fallen through the roof for one room. They climb down and find more rooms, bowls and pipes inside where the people lived. They say some scientists are coming. They will pump out this rain and look in the house. For now the water is useful for me. Come, look inside.'

The door opened into a vast chamber below ground. Isidore flashed a torch. Halfway down there was water, but the dry portion was square cut – definitely a made room, not a cave.

'They go down by ladders then hide the doors with mud and bushes. No one finds them.'

Isidore smiled wryly at the teenager. 'Ah, those Fon of Abomey.'

'Yes, yes.' The teenager nodded.

'They made this, the Abomey Fon?' I was trying to concentrate despite cow fears.

'No, no.' Isidore made a patient-schoolmaster face. 'People made them to hide from the Dahomians of Abomey. Hide from being slaves. A few houses like this have been found. Perhaps this family succeeded. If the underground houses were discovered, the soldiers would make fires at the entrance with peppers and dry leaves so the people begged to come out.'

There was some more talk with the teenager about the Fon of Abomey and the terrible things they'd done. The teenager was a Fulani, a cattle-herding nomad. Isidore, ever alert to find information for me, asked the teenager why he was so far south, explaining to me, 'The Fulani usually don't like these populated areas.'

'There have been poor rains in the north,' the teenager said. 'We go north again soon. The cattle need more space. I like it here. There are unusual things to see. Of course we knew about the Fon of Abomey but now I have seen their palaces for myself.' He waved a hand at the door to the underground house. 'They say the minister won't build here now. It will be bad luck for him.'

The wickedness of the Fon of Abomey was Isidore's topic for the drive back to my hotel.

'But you're a Fon.'

'Not like them. You forget, they came here from Togo, the kings. They were Adja people. They took our language, made us work for them. The Fon around Abomey became mixed with the kings from Togo. But a poor Fon from the countryside like me, I'd have been a slave.'

The bad Fon, the Adja, the good Fon . . . And then I read in Edgar's pamphlet that the whole region was essentially Yoruba. It suddenly dawned on me it wasn't that complicated. We had French, Belgian, Dutch, Danish . . . but were all essentially Northern Europeans. Isidore wasn't displaying some self-flagellating oddness talking about the Fon and their badness; he was Irish, if you like, talking about the English.

The bad Abomey Fon he railed against included, I recalled, his former wife. Being of a gossipy low mentality I did want to know more about this, but had decided I couldn't ask; he'd have to tell. Meanwhile, I'm sure she was at the bull'seye of his attack on Abomey Fon.

'And you know, Annie, the Abomeyans haven't changed. They're full of tricks, all swelled up with themselves, always making big backs.'

Faire gros dos was a French expression I'd never heard before; it made me choke laughing. I kept watching out the car windows for big-backed behaviour as we drove through Abomey.

'No,' Isidore concluded, 'they can still never be trusted.'

'And they make big backs.'

'They do.' He laughed at how much I had to keep saying this now I'd learnt it. 'And the King of Abomey, he has a big back, big front, you'll be very pleased. He's the fattest man in the world!'

I'd seen his photograph and couldn't quite believe Abomey was standing upright in the middle of his courtyard, addressing a large group of children when we arrived with the First Minister.

'Ah, the school visit is running late. Can you wait here? I'll call you as soon as we are organized.'

The First Minister bustled through the arched entrance to the courtyard and disappeared. Too hot to wait in the car, we hung around on one of two thoughtfully placed stone verandas by the entrance to the palace, a palace right across town from the homes

of the ancient kings. This palace was painted breeze-blocks and
corrugated iron in an ordinary, chickens–and–kids–darting area of
town.

The school party in the courtyard cheered, sang a song, and poured
out into coaches parked behind our car. They shouted '*Vive le roi!*'
as they waved out the windows, and seemed to have had a good
day out. The First Minister asked us to be patient a while longer –
the King needed to rest a moment. There was then talk in Fon
about a gift for the King. We were ahead of him; we had our
envelope ready.

It was very hot now, stifling. How could a man built like three
sumo wrestlers in one skin not be lying packed in ice somewhere,
gasping at an oxygen cylinder? But Abomey, apart from a lady wafting a fluffy fan over him, looked wide awake and ready to party.

Although his palace was much larger than that of his thin relative
at Allada, the King of Abomey's throne room was scruffier and felt
more like a domestic sitting room. He was on a plain sofa, not a
throne. No fancy robes, simply a *pagne* round his lower half,
enabling me to register the full amount of stomachs he had. He was
waiting for me, not the other way round, and he didn't have a
cavalcade of beggars outside on his porch. Through the door beside
Abomey's throne there was no curtain, no secret screamers – it was
the kitchen.

Here Isidore and I could sit on comfy chairs, rather than constantly kneeling on the floor as we'd had to when Allada allowed
us to get up from prostrating ourselves. We'd taken off our shoes
and prostrated ourselves when we came before Abomey; he told us
we were very polite but it was a hot day for that kind of thing, we
should please relax and take a seat.

One of several women sitting kittenishly on the floor around
him went to the kitchen and brought us Coca-Cola while the King
told the fanning lady to take a seat and switch on the electric fan.
She did this, smiling at him fondly. The Coca-Cola lady asked if
I'd prefer whiskey. I didn't. But the First Minister impishly asked
for a tot in his glass.

'Coca-Cola and whiskey.' The King laughed. 'He's seen this on the television, now he has it all the time. What are we to do with him?'

His considerate warmth took the edge off Abomey's unusual appearance. He seemed classically fat and jolly. And so what if he wore a carved silver muzzle over his nose making him look part Hannibal Lecter? I decided the poor man must have some kind of nose affliction and was making the most attractive job of covering it up that he could. It certainly wouldn't be kind, or remotely well mannered, to say anything, but Isidore had pleaded with me while we were waiting.

'When you see him, ask about his nose.'

'I can't do that. Anyway, maybe he's like Allada and I won't get a word in.'

'You can still ask him some questions. Ask about the nose. I've always wanted to find out.'

'No, think of some other good questions.'

'You can ask about the enthronement ceremony for the kings of Abomey; I think that's interesting,' he suggested, not interested. 'You know, it will be OK coming from you about the nose.'

'No.'

'Please.'

'What else can I ask him?'

'I don't know. Ask how many wives he has.'

'That's not very interesting.'

'Isn't it? I like to know. Anyway, this king doesn't have many official wives but they say he has a lot of women and children around the district. They say women like him a lot.'

I could see it. Abomey had a naughty glint in his eye that belied his avuncular way of talking. He had a laugh in his voice, a constant real smile and he exuded a contentment with his considerable self, unabashed to be half-naked in only his sarong skirt, a bracelet and a neck chain. It wasn't just me – I could see the women around him wouldn't have swapped him for lean and handsome in a million years. Maybe he was doing some Fon of Abomey trick on us, rippling his flesh in a subtle to and fro to hypnotize the girls . . . Anyway, I was not upsetting him with talk of his nose.

The King asked me where I was from. Ireland, inexplicably, stirred an alert interest from the women. Then there was some confusion, as I thought he asked me what I'd been doing – I talked about the underground house. Everyone looked politely confused. Hastily, Isidore explained that the King had asked what my job was, a look in his eyes asking me how dumb was I, to barge in, shedding all tact, talking carelessly of the unpleasant past? Then I think he was ready to drag me out of the room and bury me alive, when I announced that I was a writer. The First Minister flinched, some of Abomey's smile wilted.

'A journalist?' the King asked coldly.

'A novelist,' I flustered. 'I write stories about the Irish people. Romantic stories,' I said, quickly disguising myself as Maeve Binchy.

'Love stories?' asked one of the women.

'Yes. Love stories.'

The women whispered among themselves, very interested.

'She is a romantic girl,' said the King. 'That is very nice.' And he twinkled at me, all mention of underground houses forgiven.

The force of the twinkle made me brave. Now I was looking at the silver face-thing and I had to know. I could do it, I just had to be tactful.

'May I ask if the decoration on the King's face is traditional in Abomey?'

Nobody seemed bothered. Nobody said, 'You wicked girl, don't you know that the King's nose was eaten away by a terrible leprous infection in his childhood? How could you be so cruel!'

'It is traditional,' the First Minister said, as if I'd asked how he thought the weather would turn out. 'When the King goes out he is surrounded by people. This protects the kings from germs and bad smells. Also it serves to distinguish the kings of Abomey from all other kings. It used to be made of wood. Now it is silver or gold.'

The question I thought was the innocuous one produced a 'tut' from the First Minister, a weary laugh from the King and flinching among his women. The enthronement ceremony?

'It is very complicated, too much to talk about,' the First Minister answered quickly. He muttered something to the King, the King shook his head and smiled tolerantly.

'Tell us about this Queen you have in England,' he asked. The women made enthusiastic sounds. 'What is she like as a ruler?'

I explained that she didn't rule at all, she had only a ceremonial role. The women looked disappointed but the King seemed delighted to hear this, perhaps pleased to find he wasn't the only monarch reduced to entertaining school trips.

The King asked if I had a camera. He'd like Isidore to take a photograph, with me in it, but I had to promise to send a copy. The women shifted around so I could be cosy with them at the King's feet.

With a seemingly stern remark, the King pointed at the luminous-pink nail varnish on my toes. The women giggled.

'He says he likes this,' the First Minister laughed. 'He's telling the women to do it too.'

The First Minister said that if I had no more questions, the King had to rest before his next appointment, it had been a busy day so far. Isidore nudged me; time to hand over the cash. While the King feigned disinterest, chatting to Isidore about life in Cotonou, the First Minister checked my enveloped gift, pronounced it satisfactory and told me to hand it to the King with two hands.

'The two hands are respectful,' he said. 'Also, in the old times, it was to show you didn't have a knife or a gun in the free hand.'

Regardless of knives or guns, or even germs, in my free hand, the King hefted himself to his feet and gave me an only slightly sweaty handshake goodbye. He came right to the door, wishing me well, and entered into an excited discussion with his womenfolk about my slip-on shoes.

'Look, what are they, elastic? See, she just pulls them easily. Ah, not all elastic, that part is cotton. First Minister, you see the shoes we need here? Part cotton for coolness, elastic to be quick. Ah, the foreigners have all the shoes, all the best things.'

Isidore didn't know if there was a living king still lurking in the original palace of the Dahomians at Tado, but he did know a small border-crossing near Abomey. He thought it might be worth a try at getting through there without a visa. After all, Tado was only just over the border – we'd hardly be in Togo at all. Perhaps he could persuade the border guards to let me slip in and out quietly. For a small tip, a tenth the cost of a visa.

On the Benin side of the border, two policemen were playing backgammon under a tree. They didn't disturb themselves when our car drew up, just carried on playing after a cursory glance established that we weren't heavily armed drug runners in a tank. Isidore sauntered over, made some helpful suggestions to the senior officer about his game, then began a long, easy-going discussion. The smiling senior officer won the game and came over to the car to explain himself to me.

'Madame, as far as we are concerned, you can go past, no problem. But them, down there,' he pointed to the khaki uniforms on the Togolese side, 'they are not like us. If you don't have a visa they will want you to give them money. Lots of money. Or they might beat you. They are not like us. So I am sorry but I cannot recommend going over there.'

I agreed, best not to get beaten. Isidore gave the policeman a small tip for his trouble.

'Nice man,' I commented as we made a disappointed U-turn.

'He's not a nice man. He's blaming the others but he wouldn't let you through. He's just blaming the others to get a tip. I know Africans. I know the mentality. And we have to see Tado. How can you be a detective of the kings of Dahomey without seeing the origins?'

I told him there was always next time. I would get myself properly equipped with a beating-proof visa.

I started to remember something I'd read about Togo expelling the representatives of Amnesty International. A ferocious sort of administration. Not the kind of country to treat illegal entry lightly. I could have been arrested, sent to live on food vouchers in the Togolese equivalent of Milton Keynes and had to wash car windscreens for cigarette money. How could I be a detective then?

No, no need to be downhearted about Tado. In our trawl for Dahomey kings, we'd also Porto Novo to cover to collect the set. Although because of a long-running lineage spat there was currently no one on the throne at Porto Novo; there was a palace, and Isidore said Porto Novo was the prettiest town in southern Benin. He did know best, some of the time.

6

Don't Tell Me It's Raining, I'm an Actress

'Other places you get Yoruba who are normal, but these Yoruba of Porto Novo, talk, talk, talk for the sake of talking. You think their teeth will fall out from so much of it. And *gri-gri*, ah, they are mad with *gri-gri* here. And you'll never see them work as hard as a Fon. Ask anywhere in West Africa, "Who works hard?" they'll say the Beninois Fon. Gabon, Ivory Coast, they need us there to work. Now we should rest. At five o'clock we'll start our attack on Porto Novo. There is a lot to do.'

Isidore didn't think the Yoruba of Porto Novo were all-round bad and making big backs of themselves in an Abomeyan fashion. He did like them. But you could hear what he meant by the talking if you got wedged in a clutch of them at the market. Yoruba had a sort of clanging sound in it, whereas Fon was tinkly; so noisy Yoruba on all sides, on a hot day, you could start to feel as if you were trapped in a belfry as war broke out.

Looking at them was loud on the senses but in a more pleasant way. They moved around in dressed-to-kill bird-of-paradise robes and wound cloth headdresses – bright-coloured caps for the men. Fancy-looking people weren't the only pretty things in Porto Novo; Isidore had been quite right about how attractive the town looked.

In between ornate nineteenth-century Portuguese architecture, all tiles and curly ends, there were flower shrubs and luxuriant greenery. Porto Novo was a small, sleepy town compared to the traffic-fumed race of Cotonou. Elaborate, tumbledown and taking a leisurely pace to incorporate long-chat time, it was always a shock to remember that Porto Novo, not striving Cotonou, was Benin's capital city.

Our attack on Porto Novo started with the museums. The Ethnographic Museum was housed in such an appealing old Portuguese mansion, with magnolia trees in the garden, I was more inclined to lie down on the steps and dream I lived there than to be marched round on a tour, then whisked away to a new item on Isidore's itinerary.

Isidore was talking to the lady guide in Gun, the language of the coastal people of Porto Novo; he probably wanted to know something important about the museum but it was clearly the day when he was destined to be surrounded by trivial-minded women. She didn't answer his question – she had one of her own.

'She wanted to know your age. She is surprised. She says a woman of thirty-eight here isn't thin like that. She says she is thirty-two and you're younger than her. I told her Westerners take vitamin pills to stay young.'

'It's not that easy.' Lotions, potions, gyms . . . I laughed. 'You should tell her I have to . . .'

'Are we here to talk about you? I want her to get on with explaining.'

Getting on with it for the sake of Mr Exasperated, we looked at Fon and Yoruba ceremonial masks, tableaux of traditional Fon life, old rifles, spears, copies of treaties signed by local rulers with the French and finally some huge carved doors captured from the

Yoruba kingdom of Ketu by the Dahomians. It was a small museum, clearly presented and soon done with. Now we could talk.

'I want to know what kind of vitamins you take,' the lady guide said, the instant she'd finished dutifully naming the masks, tableaux and so on. 'So thin, isn't she? I expect she will look like that at fifty.'

Isidore shrugged. He wanted me on the move to my next educational visit. I was about to say I didn't take vitamins, just lived a vain and self-absorbed existence, but she seemed to prefer talking about me than to me.

'Is she your wife? How many children does she have?'

'None, she has none.'

The woman looked at me with a mixture of pity and acute embarrassment. Quickly she wished us a good journey and rushed away.

'She thinks there's something wrong with you,' Isidore said. 'She's very sorry for you. Sorry for asking, so she ran away.'

He said there was no way I could have explained it to her; even if I said it was my choice, she'd have thought I was making excuses for my tragic barrenness.

'A woman like that, from a simple background, how could she understand? You can see she was simple, just wanting to talk about silly things instead of the artefacts.'

Isidore loved a good artefact. I tended to think they were just there, whereas a nice little chat could be a universe.

There was less chit-chat at the extensive Da Silva Museum; a male guide in a hurry to get it all shown and close up for the day. The building was also known as The Brazilian House, constructed at the turn of the century by a family of returned slaves from Brazil, the Da Silvas. They came back to make a lucrative new life in the palm-oil industry, diversifying into cloth manufacture and printing presses. Their home was now laid out with artefacts aplenty, including samples of the cloth the Da Silvas manufactured and Portuguese crockery, cutlery, weaponry, costumes . . . There were portraits of eminent Beninois and Brazilians of the nineteenth and twentieth centuries and a genuinely interesting collection of documents chronicling the history of the slave trade – bills of sale, treaties, maps, early abolitionist tracts and an anti-abolitionist statement signed by Napoleon's Josephine. Unusually, I impressed Isidore by having a halfway intelligent question.

'I thought Josephine was part black, from Martinique?'

The guide looked almost as impressed as Isidore – 'I heard that, too.'

'So why . . . ?'

The guide looked at the framed tract, then gave a shrug. 'What else would she do?'

There were women behaving in complicated ways at the café we'd chosen for dinner. An afternoon drink there had been a gaping at the setting, can't-believe-I'm-here moment for me; Isidore thought there were too many mosquitoes.

Porto Novo was built across gentle sloping hills surrounding a lagoon. Our café was perfectly located for a clear, high view of the sparkling water, little fishing canoes busy near the shore, larger ones heading away over the horizon. The tables were under spreading trees, there was music, friendly staff and, just to the back of the café, the railway tracks, bringing the excitement of the twice-daily train from Cotonou wheezing past at barely a mile an hour. The carriages were brightly painted wood, like a Victorian toy, and the diesel engine made a noise and smell I haven't come across since I was toy age. I ran to the five-bar crossing gate behind the café and waved hyperactively at laughing, waving passengers.

'The train is cheap,' Isidore said when the hullabaloo was over and I was sitting back at the table like an adult. 'There's this one and another that runs north to south. But there are a lot of accidents. And the seats are wood. You're better off in the car.'

'But it would be fun to see what it was like, for a short journey at least.'

'You don't have trains in England?'

'Not like that.'

'Hmmm.' Isidore began a conversation with our friendly waitress, Natasha, about last month's train accident. Four dead. Twelve maimed. One woman had her leg torn right off at the hip . . .

I got the message.

In the evening, the trees were strung with fairy-lights and Natasha told us it was chicken or chicken for dinner.

Natasha was a hefty girl in a T-shirt and the same baggy, three-quarter-length cotton khaki trousers as I was wearing, so we'd bonded over this. Natasha's trousers were very important in the events of the evening. As was her very small, sweet face. This face, along with her chirpy smile, didn't quite disguise a girl you could tell had initiated a lot of brawls in the school playground, and won. In contrast, Estelle, older and the boss, was a slim, gentle Togolese who looked like her life had been one sadness after another, borne with fortitude but increasing weariness. She seemed to be the sort of woman who made Isidore go all melty round the edges and he was soon softly teasing her about chickens and extricating her life story.

The chickens teasing was because of the pickiness of his passenger, who found it hard to search out any meat on the average Beninois chicken. Beninois chickens led a hard life, running around underfoot and living on scraps. A well-rested chicken, artificially reared to meaty tenderness, was a rare thing and known as '*poulet cher*', expensive chicken. The scrawny average chicken was '*poulet bicyclette*', bicycle chicken, having the sinews of a Tour de France champion. You might as well suck on some chicken-tasting elastic and sticks – but it was cheap.

Estelle said she could have found us *poulet cher* if we'd warned her, but the menu only offered one that had endured a hard-pedalling life. She did have some eggs that hadn't suffered too much – would I be happier with an omelette and chips? Unadventurously, I would.

Perhaps Estelle had been waiting for someone like Isidore to come by that day, someone who'd ask her about herself, so she didn't have to drag her life around with her, putting a brave face on it. She quietly passed it on to him, needing someone to say, 'Ah Estelle, you must be in pain. Take a seat, have a drink with us.'

Estelle didn't own the café, she worked for a rich Porto Novian. Once, she had owned a small café in Togo, with her husband.

Togo's gun-toting government troops had taken against someone in her street, pushing him around, provoking a riot, followed by the shooting of every male over ten, dead in the road. Her husband had been on his own doorstep. How could she stay in her house? She took her children and came to relatives in Benin.

Forgetting that he'd spent the morning trying to get me to gyp Togolese border controls, Isidore showed his solidarity with Estelle by telling me how bad Togo was. How their insane dictator murdered any opposition, filled every byway with secret police and had these soldiers who'd gun down citizens for nothing. Togolese refugees came to Benin, particularly in the south where the Fon, Gun and Mina peoples had similar languages and a shared vodou culture. Benin was a haven in the region now, somewhere people could have peace. Estelle smiled sadly; a haven wasn't home.

Natasha was also from Togo originally, but had lived in Benin as long as she could remember. She had no major tragedy to report, just that there was no work in Togo except farming and fishing. Togo was full of misery and Benin was on the up, full of small opportunities to get a little way ahead, so her family had moved.

Having told Isidore all she wanted him to know, Estelle disappeared to cook dinner. Natasha attended to a newly arrived Beninois army captain and his wife. Just as she put the drinks on the table, a high-pitched shrieking started from the railway tracks. Natasha charged out, bellowing in French, 'Get lost! Go away or I'll sort you out! Go away, I told you, go!' Schoolyard Natasha emerged. She stormed back in and started crossly roaring something kitchenwards. Estelle made a soothing response.

The captain asked Natasha what was going on. She straddled a chair at our table to let us all in on the drama. Early in the evening, an old woman had come in, walked across the restaurant and dropped her purse – coins rolled everywhere. The old woman burst into tears. Feeling sorry for her, Natasha and Estelle had crawled round the floor – *crawled* – for ten minutes, collecting the coins for her until they were sure there were no more to find. The old woman then started a hue and cry, calling Natasha a thief, Estelle a whore, claiming she was 850 francs (75 pence) short and that the girls had taken it. She'd gone on and on until they'd had to shout at her and chase her out — now she was back with the same story. Wailing outside, saying the women had robbed her.

'Last time I help anyone,' Natasha concluded, swung off her chair and went to yell abuse at the voice from the railway tracks.

Before Natasha could catch her, the voice from the tracks materialized in our midst, sobbing and holding out a handful of coins to the captain.

'My dear general,' she sobbed. 'I can see you have a kind face; please help me. These Togolese whores have stolen my money. This is all I have. I had eight hundred and fifty francs and they took it.' Then, in a very different tone of voice, she shrieked at Estelle who was coming from the kitchen to see the show. 'There's the other whore! A fat whore and a thin whore from Togo!'

To finish his drink in peace, the captain said, 'That's enough, now', handed her 1,000 francs (£1) and told her to go home.

Natasha exploded. 'Don't give her anything, she's a liar!' She snatched the 1,000 francs and gave it back to the soldier.

A siren scream came out of the old woman. 'My money! You thieving prostitutes. You see how they are with an old woman? My family have lived in Porto Novo since the time of Dahomey and my father was a customs officer and my mother was a doctor. I'm not used to this, I'm a proper person from this kingdom and now I'm being set upon by savage foreign whores.'

The captain tried to give her the money again, signalling Natasha to back off.

'You're a liar!' Natasha yelled in the woman's ear. 'Take what this man's giving you and get lost!'

The old woman flinched tight and sobbed harder. Real tears down a wrinkled, refined little face. 'Oh, what happened to my life? Oh, my dear white lady . . .' She came over to me. 'Look how these savage whores are treating me. My dear white lady, I am from a good family, my family knew many whites, they came to our house when I was a child. And now look at me, please help me and protect me, white lady, please.'

Her tears and her little scrumpled doll-face nipped at my feelings as much as they had the captain's. There was a polish about her that did support her story of social fall; her clothes were smart, her hair carefully plaited, she had gold earrings and the little leather clip-purse she brandished as Exhibit A was shiny new. Her fall had clearly not taken her to sleeping in the gutter or neglecting to wash. Whatever madness had overtaken her seemed too sad to merit the jeering imitation Natasha had just started – 'Oh, my dear white lady . . .'

I reached for my purse. Natasha shouted, '*Yovo*, don't!' Isidore frowned at me disapprovingly, the old woman screamed at Natasha, 'Who are you, you whore with your big head, your eyes like a sheep and your mouth like a bat!'

Natasha was too bewildered by the insult to fire back more than a quiet echo. 'Mouth like a bat?'

'You whore with your banana-planter's trousers, you don't even dress respectably, fat girl in banana-planter's trousers of a whore!'

My banana-planter's trousers obviously didn't make me a whore, because the old lady came tugging at my arm. 'Help me, dear white lady, help me please. They stole my money.'

I gave her 1,000 francs; I couldn't help it. Natasha decided that was the end – she grabbed the old woman by the shoulders and frogmarched her out to the railway tracks. 'You've got her money, it's over, now get lost, you old bitch!'

It wasn't over.

From outside the old lady kept wailing, 'My dear white, she's hurt me.'

Isidore told me off about the money. Natasha started throwing stones in the direction of the railway tracks. Estelle stopped her. 'Leave her, Natasha, she'll go.'

There were more plaintive cries of 'My dear white lady' from outside, while Isidore and the captain concluded that the old woman probably did this all over town, counting on the softhearted and her ability for relentless-nuisance value to keep herself fed.

Isidore turned to me, genuinely puzzled. 'Why did you give her money? You saw the captain here tried to do the same. It's what she wanted.'

I shrugged. 'She made me sad.'

'Me too,' said the soldier.

Natasha flopped into a chair by a vacant table. 'It's me that's sad. Imagine being told you've got a bat's mouth. What's a bat's mouth like, anyway?'

'And we've got banana-planter's trousers,' I reminded her.

She kissed her teeth. 'Yeah. Old fool. These are high fashion, aren't they?' The thought of high-fashion garments being so mocked propelled her to a final roar into the night against the receding complaints of the perhaps not so mad old woman, with 2,000 francs' profit clipped in her purse.

Isidore was late, tired and grumpy in the morning. He sat down with a steadying tonic water and told me the trouble. After his good dinner at Chez Batmouth he'd slept well, until banging and screaming in his corridor woke him. He put on his shoes and shorts and ran out. A neighbouring guest was also in the corridor, along with an aged night-watchman and a male receptionist. They all gathered at the door of a room where two women were beating and pulling hell out of each other.

The neighbour said he'd heard knocking, the receptionist knocking on the door that was now open on the catfight. He'd come out of his room and seen the receptionist there with the big woman, who'd then barged in the door and pulled the small woman out of the bed.

'So remember,' Isidore looked up from his drink, 'the receptionist had brought the big woman to the room. Now the big woman was slapping the small one, pulling her hair, tipping out her handbag, ripping her clothes, even tearing up some pretty new shoes the little one had, screaming she was a filthy whore, a dirty whore . . .'

Was there some kind of whore-calling festival going on in town that week? Would I look at someone sideways and get forced to join in?

'The small one was crying and trying to defend herself and protect her clothes but she was no match for the other. The man, the husband of the big woman, was just sitting on the bed with his head in his hands.'

'The little one was with her husband?'

'Exactly. The big one, she had an advantage, she was dressed in shorts, a T-shirt and trainers. She'd arrived there ready, dressed for a fight. Whereas the small girl had been asleep. Then the husband started to get dressed. The big wife screamed at him – "Don't you feel ashamed? How could you? You were lying with me in bed and then you got up like you were going to the toilet and you go out and find a prostitute!" The little one wept, she said she wasn't a prostitute, she was only trying to find a little money to feed her two children. The big one just laughed at her and turned to her husband: "See what you've gone after, this thing on the streets who's already had two children." The little one cried more, said her husband had gone off with another woman and abandoned her. "Well, my husband won't abandon me!" the big one said, and she walked off with the husband following. He muttered "sorry" to the little girl but just left her there with strangers.'

Isidore had helped the little one pick up her things. In her bag she had some make-up, a plastic bottle and a folded carrier bag. He'd asked her what the bottle and carrier were for. To get palm oil and food for the children once she'd found money. Her children were with her mother, who was very poor.

'Oh, Annie, I felt for her. She was a young girl, very pretty, with all her hair pulled and clothes torn. She said the man had brought her to the hotel several times, but she expected that was over now. She tied her clothes round her and walked out crying. It was awful. My heart went out to her because she had to walk into the street with her clothes torn and her new shoes in her hand all destroyed. I'd given her some money to get the food but I should have given her a lift in my car, but I was too tired and confused to think of it. It was awful looking at her walk away, because I could see how ashamed she was. Oh, if you'd seen her, just a young girl of just nineteen, nice pretty girl and her life was ruined already.'

I didn't need to see. He had me close to crying.

'Poor Isidore,' I said, hoping to stop him sinking too far. 'All in all you've heard a lot of shouting women in the last twenty-four hours and you've had no sleep.'

'Exactly.' He laughed. 'Please don't start shouting with another woman this morning or I will lose my mind and run mad in the marketplace.' He took a sip of his tonic water. 'Luckily, it's not far to the palace so I won't fall asleep driving.' He took one more moment with his memory. 'Really, that poor girl, her shamed face . . . that will haunt me.'

Despite exhaustion and haunting, Isidore gave me a thorough tour of the town on the way to the palace. There was photograph taking at the fancy-painted and curlicued mosque, once a Portuguese cathedral, then a hurried escape from fast-talking Yoruba marketwomen insisting I needed bananas, presumably to go with my banana-planter's trousers, non-whore cut.

Constructed in a retro French-colonial style were the fancy new buildings of the administrative district. Porto Novo was still the official seat of the government, although the President, most businesses, and the majority of the urban population lived in Cotonou. It was the port part of Porto Novo that had gone wrong – silted up and not deep enough for modern commercial shipping. Cotonou was deeper. And flatter, better for the international airport, so the foreign embassies were there, and the flashy foreign hotels like the Sheraton and Novotel. Yet sleepy dowager Porto Novo, crusted with faded finery, still managed to keep its name in official gazetteers as the capital.

And Porto Novo had its kingless palace, extensively restored but without any displays of artefacts in its considerable number of baked-mud rooms. I liked the lack of exhibits, it felt like the King had just moved out.

The last major monarch in residence had been King Toffa. A tricky fellow, he'd allied himself with the French against Dahomey, benefited for a while, then learnt that the Europeans had little respect for him once they'd had the use of him. He didn't get the independent kingdom he'd been promised; the French kept Porto Novo, along with the rest of Dahomey, for themselves.

It was said King Toffa was poisoned by the French – an ironic end, because he'd worked very hard all his life not to be poisoned. He never ate anything that hadn't been prepared in his own household and never ate or drank in public; this was partly out of fear of poison but also a tradition among Dahomian kings, to prevent the public seeing that a king was an ordinary human in need of sustenance.

The woman who prepared the King's food had to eat first from each dish at a place of the King's choosing. It couldn't just be any woman. Toffa had 200 wives, rotating their residency in the palace because a woman menstruating was not allowed anywhere near the building. Traditionally, the only permanent female resident in a Dahomian palace was the Queen Mother, or a post-menopausal aunt. Toffa's mother was dead and he couldn't abide his aunts, but he had among his 200 a wife of sufficient age for the permanent resident-female job – only she could prepare the King's food.

More paranoia showed itself in the King's main reception hall. There were two doors – a very tall door and a tiny door. The tall door was for the King, the tiny door for everyone else, forcing them to arrive in an obsequious posture and making it inconvenient for attackers to rush in brandishing weapons. Frenchmen with guns surrounded Toffa all the same and by the end of the nineteenth century he'd somehow been slipped the killer morsel that saved the French the further expense of his house arrest.

Our female guide showed us along a terraced gallery that led to an open-air auditorium. Here the King would address the people, drill troops, or be entertained. The auditorium, still used for public entertainment, had covered terraces on three sides, a raised stage and stacks of plastic seats in the stalls area. Apparently there was to be a theatre show that evening. A touring group called Echoes of the City were coming. This company had a male troupe and a female troupe; tonight it was the female troupe appearing, with stories of women's lives. The guide said I could certainly attend if I wanted, but did I realize the performance would all be in the Gun language? I said I didn't mind; it would still be interesting for me to see what the show was like. The woman understood this and showed me where to buy tickets. Isidore was sceptical but said he'd collect me at eight if I really wanted to go.

'But the show starts at eight.'

'It won't start at eight, or even half-past. I know African time. OK, don't look like that, I'll collect you at a quarter to eight.'

'I'd just hate to miss it.'

'Five pounds a ticket?' Isidore said scornfully. 'Of course we're not going to miss it.'

Isidore had no further drama at his hotel and arrived at seven-thirty looking keen and rested.

'I realized that getting there early was a good idea. I want to park near the palace, where there's supervision, so some Porto Novian won't steal my car radio.'

I wished they would. Isidore's choice of music, especially for early mornings, was atonal, jangling, Fon folk songs that required wordy explanation hard to take in before I was fully awake. Normally I liked African music, but there was something about the songs Isidore delighted in for top-volume reveille that was like nails down a blackboard through a loud hailer.

Ensuring the continuation of this torment, we found a place to park right outside the palace and were given a numbered wooden disc by a man who billed himself the official car-minder for the evening. He wanted some money from Isidore.

'Don't be ridiculous,' Isidore told him. 'I'll give you something if I come out and find you haven't stolen my car.'

The man was too indignant to speak.

More indignation as Isidore marched me to the head of the queue at the palace gate, shouting something that sounded like '*Yovo* coming through!' A girl in a Nike outfit stood at the door, telling Isidore I couldn't come in. He had a sharp discussion with her, saying *yovo* quite often and angrily. Intimidated, she relented and indicated a chair behind her on the porch where I could sit. There was a lot of very uncomplimentary talk from the queue about *yovos* as I went in. It was starting to rain, which added to the resentment of pusher-in *yovos* who were going to be sitting in the dry.

I was mortified. Particularly when the Nike girl closed the door on the dampening locals, telling them she had no idea when the doors would be opened for them.

'I wish you hadn't done that,' I said to Isidore. 'Why should I be the only one in here?'

'You want to stand in the rain? And it's not just you, look.'

A well-dressed Beninois couple were sitting opposite me on the wide porch. By the cut of their clothes and weight of their jewellery, I guessed they were local dignitaries but they didn't seem to know any more than we did about what was going on.

Beyond us there was a courtyard full of statues of divinities looking very beautiful and mysterious in dim floodlights. The palace behind them was in darkness. Then the rain fell heavier and the floodlights went out.

Hurricane lamps were lit for we swells on the porch. We could hear the sound of a gathering, agitated crowd outside.

At around eight-thirty, the Nike woman was joined by a burly man who hurried from the direction of the palace. He took the Nike woman outside with him, perhaps for moral support as he began loudly asking people to calm down. He shut the door behind him. I could hear further cries for calm from him against a rage from the crowd. The man and Nike quickly flustered back in, rain-drenched and pushing the door closed on angry wet faces barking questions.

Presumably the same question Isidore asked: 'So when are they starting?'

'We just work at the palace,' the burly man shrugged. 'They have a problem but we don't know when they'll start. They're very difficult people.'

There were now hammerings on the door, and singing started, presumably the Gun equivalent of 'Why Are We Waiting?'

At ten past nine there was a flurry of activity. A neat, nervous young man fiddling with a trendy pair of spectacles arrived from inside the palace. As he rubbed rain spots off his lenses, he introduced himself as the theatre director and told us it was the rain that was the trouble. He sat next to the local dignitaries, ready to give a fuller explanation . . . Suddenly four paratroopers burst through the doors, slammed them shut behind them and demanded to know who was in charge.

I'd spent my nap time reading about Benin's nine coups in twelve years. There was now a considerable uproar outside – had the crowd decided to pass the waiting time by staging another coup? I noticed the paratroopers weren't armed – was this good or bad?

Good. They wouldn't be shooting anybody. Or bad. Now they were inside the paratroopers seemed vague and not particularly ready to act. They wouldn't be much use if the crowd had phoned Bob Denard to come over with some of his pals.

Their laconic sergeant found out who was with him on the porch, then told the theatre director to go outside and explain himself. The director played for time, telling the sergeant how the rain was making it dangerous to use their electrical equipment on the outdoor stage, if the wires . . .

'Don't tell me,' said the sergeant. 'Tell them.' And he opened the door on the baying crowd outside.

The director adjusted his glasses and bravely stepped into the doorway. A howl of fury went up from the mob. I figured the first person to be torn to pieces after the director would be a dry, sitting-down *yovo*.

Not exactly springing to the rescue, the sergeant was looking at his hands like he wished he had a nail file. But then a bizarre horseless cavalry came swooping out of the palace. Two towering women in enormous robes and headwraps bore down on us. Everything about their walks, fluttering hands and battle-cry eyeliner said these were actresses. They stood themselves either side of the director and one of them began to address the crowd with formidable projection.

'Gentlemen, ladies and children of Porto Novo, we apologize for the wait . . .'

She was astounded to be interrupted by a great bear of a man who came roaring up to the gate. 'Never mind that. Why have you taken my money for nothing? It's disgusting behaviour. I've got my children here, my wives . . . All my wives are wet now, what am I supposed to do with them?'

The actress heaved her breast at him and looked down her nose like Cleopatra smelling gone-off asp. 'There is absolutely no need to shout.'

This made the shouting bear-man shout and push forward more. 'No! There's no need to shout! I'll just come and box your ears for you if you don't let us in. Taking our money, stupid woman . . . Can't you see it's raining?'

The actress gave us her Boadicea. 'Are you threatening me? Don't tell me it's raining, I'm an actress! I know it's raining!'

She quivered with rage, eyes closing in the face of the unspeakable horror of a common shouting man.

But shouting man shouted more, the wet wives shouted, the director tried saying something that verged on shouting, both actresses gave us their shrieking Medeas . . . The paratrooper sergeant turned to me and gave his weary Sergeant Wilson from *Dad's Army*. 'Oh really, do we need all this shouting?'

One of the younger paratroopers told the screaming actresses to get out of it; they ignored him. He pushed them back firmly but respectfully and closed the door. The actresses strode off, adjusting their headwraps, complaining vociferously that he should have left them alone, they were dealing with the situation and now how could they possibly perform after such an ordeal . . . The director whimpered away after them.

Sergeant Wilson sighed deeply as he listened to the hammering on the door.

'I expect I'll have to do something,' he said, doing nothing.

Isidore then became the hero of the late hour. He suggested that Sergeant Wilson let the people come in, sit down in the auditorium and see for themselves that the stage was awash. At least that way they'd get more comfortable, not be left in the street feeling neglected and cheated. They'd continue their wait in a much calmer frame of mind.

Sergeant Wilson nodded sagely. 'This is a solution,' he said. 'And one is needed.'

Isidore motioned me to my feet so we could get ahead of the crowd. Too late – the doors were opened and a people-dam burst.

But the instant the charge inside began, rage turned to euphoria. Being let in was all it took. Sergeant Wilson beamed at me and Isidore as we were swept past him into the sodden auditorium.

Everyone scrambled for the benches under the covered galleries, spurning the muddy ranks of wet plastic seats. Music played, small girls were selling iced juice, yoghurt and little fishy pastries. We were happy. We were in, we were chatting, relieved and ready for action. The stage was wet, dark and empty.

I wanted to try a fish pastry but had no small change, nor did Isidore. A stranger on the next bench bought us a portion and laughingly offered to buy pastries for everyone in the place she was so glad to be finally sitting down. The rain continued to pour but we all seemed to feel that getting in to the auditorium had become the event itself.

A small boy in his Sunday best ran away from his parents, danced in the rain, slipped over in a perfect non-hazardous pratfall and everyone, except the mother who'd be washing out the mud, went wild with the fun of it.

Other children were wiser about rain danger – a line of five small girls marched down to the stage to see what they could see, holding a length of clingfilm over their plaited heads. As women came in, all dressed to glitter in public, they'd devised fantastic means to protect their elaborate hairdos – *chapeaux* of carrier bags, shower caps, road maps . . . One woman had a car-seat cover wedged on top of her high *coiffure*.

While we tried to judge the Strange Headgear Contest, Isidore told me that two years previously the Benin government had attempted to introduce a compulsory motorbike-helmet law – a sensible move, considering the millions of rickety Vespas teeming round the potholed roads. But women's outrage at having their expensive hairdos ruined and their headwraps crushed thwarted all attempts to enforce the law.

'They'd rather break their necks,' an eavesdropping man behind us laughed. 'We've got some rum, would you like some?'

Just then, there was a whoop of excitement as the actresses all came out on the stage in a dim light. They made speeches in Gun that were so long and impassioned I thought the play had started. I shushed Isidore as he said: 'There we are. Time to go.'

They'd told the audience to hold on to their tickets and come back the following Saturday, or get a refund at the palace gate in the morning.

Isidore put our tickets back in his wallet, saying grimly, 'Oh, I'll be there, girls. Five pounds a ticket!'

We were full of fish pastries, feeling like we'd had a good night out and seen plenty. We decided to forget dinner and just call at Chez Batmouth for a nightcap and an update. Smiling sad Estelle told us the old madwoman hadn't been back to bother them, but they'd been very busy so it was as well we didn't want food as all she had left was a potato.

I couldn't quite relax; the drawback of Chez Batmouth, its mosquitoes, were out in force. What was that pricky feeling on my left ankle, the back of my neck? I cross-examined myself about how diligent I'd been with the repellent lotion – it was all right, I'd been neurotically diligent as usual. I hadn't heard the question Isidore asked me, so he repeated it. No, to be honest I had heard it, just hoped I hadn't. He asked me if I could find a girlfriend for him in England, someone who'd want to live in Benin, someone educated like me who could help him set up a small business. This was the real jab into my skin that would spoil things. Every time he sensed I was in a good mood, he would put in a request. When I went home could I send him some trainers like mine, nice sunglasses, shirts . . . ? Now a girlfriend.

I'm not an ungenerous person – and God knows, he deserved some handouts in his struggled life – it just made me feel that I was only a rich customer to him, to be played carefully for maximum gain. Fair enough, maybe my fault, maybe I kept doing things to make him feel like just the driver . . . Except that just at that moment I'd remembered it was my birthday, and I was with someone who didn't even see me as a person.

A descending melancholy was swept aside as I noticed an eerily beautiful sight across the lagoon – tiny lights, all in a straight line, flickering against the water.

'Those are the shrimp fishermen,' Isidore said. 'They go out in their boats with lanterns to draw the shrimps to the surface. Then they all move forward together, skimming up the catch as they go.'

I hadn't answered the question about the girlfriend.

'I can't send someone just like that.'

'I know,' Isidore sighed. 'But think about it sometimes.' Then he laughed, as if he was with a real person. 'Anyway, after all the screaming of women and girls we've had in Porto Novo, I ask myself if I really need a woman.'

To help him make his decision, Natasha started some mouthy tirade about the mosquitoes, slapping herself and yelling at the air.

7

Butch Up, Ladies, It's Party Time

'I have to tell you honestly, all my brothers are bastards.'

Nice talk when we were on our way to visit them. And Isidore didn't mean their legal status; some buried rage about them had been jolted out of him by a bump in the red–dirt road to his home village.

'They work in the fields, fish sometimes, but they take two, three wives, keep having children then cry to me for money. They say, "Only you can read and write, only you can meet *yovos* in the city and have money . . ." Where were they when I needed encouragement to stay in school? Really, they are my brothers but if you ever see them treat me fairly, be extremely surprised. Anyway, don't be annoyed, but I have given them the impression you are like a girlfriend to me. This is in case there are ceremonies that are interesting but cost money. If they hear you are a customer they'll think you're too rich. But I'd like you to see the ceremonies. You'll see real village life.'

*

There were nine brothers and four sisters – the sort of situation that arose when a man had three wives. Having indulged himself in the three wives, Isidore's father was now suffering the long-term effects – his compound was leaping, crawling and skipping with grandchildren, who all had some kind of noise to make.

'My father's an old man, he wants to sleep, he wants to talk calmly with his friends but all the time, yow-yow-yow from the kids.'

On the way into the village, Isidore pointed out a plot of cleared land and some breeze-blocks. This was where he hoped to construct a retirement home for his father away from the undersized madding crowd.

The house would be built facing the sacred forest of Oro, a cult very important to Fon and Yoruba men – and very secret. Decisions were made about the organization of the community, transgressions of social codes debated and there was rum drunk, fun had. In the time of Oro ceremonies, women had to check before they went out into the road in case Oro was there. If a woman saw Oro she would die or go mad.

'What does he look like?'

Isidore gave me a very old-fashioned look. 'If I told you, *I* would die or go mad. Try any trick you like, I won't accidentally tell you.'

Isidore's father was an elder of the Oro cult. In addition to being the local blacksmith, healer, spell caster, witch catcher and midwife, delivering most of the babies in the village and for miles beyond.

There was a medical centre with visits from hospital-trained midwives in the village. There were also midwifery services at a Belgian convent seven miles away, but most people trusted only the traditional methods of Isidore's father.

The bastardy of the brothers wasn't any worry for me as we arrived at Isidore's home compound, in a small Fon village, a long way from the last town in south-central Benin. It was the too-clever-by-half-sounding father I didn't want killing me, sending me mad or simply giving me a disapproving look.

I expected an unsettling presence housed in a big, startling, metal thwacker of a man.

'Le Vieux', the Old Man, as Isidore called him, a more respectful title than our usage, was only around five foot five and slight as a bird. A dignified bird, moving gently and delicately, not skittering with any kind of troubled busyness. His skin was completely unweathered, soft and clear. Had I not been forewarned I would have been very perturbed by his voice. 'My father talks like a woman,' Isidore had said. 'It is tiny, his voice, it never changed from a boy.'

The blacksmith sounded like a child with a mild head-cold.

Some months later, an English sculptor told me that working with metal wasn't a question of muscle – it required sensitivity and patience. It required acute powers of observation, to know when the metal was at the right heat to be moulded – a hair's-breadth decision. Blacksmithing wouldn't sit peculiarly with Le Vieux's more obviously subtle arts.

In addition to looking nothing like the man I expected, Le Vieux also looked slightly Chinese in a high-buttoned, long-sleeved shirt, a sarong-style *pagne* and wide-brimmed hat. The voice, far from being undignified, caused you listen to him carefully. He had a presence that shimmered with steady confidence. He smiled constantly, drawing you to him, although his eyes seemed to look right past you to something more important.

Le Vieux was fit as a fiddle; Isidore said this was because he never smoked, never drank alcohol and never worked in the fields. It was the fields that destroyed people. The alcohol-drinking, field-working brothers looked a lot less well preserved than sixty-six-year-old father. Not older exactly, just more battered.

The family grew maize, peanuts, manioc and vegetables; in the red-clay compound there was plenty to eat but barely enough cash to clothe the extensive throng, let alone school them. There were children up walls and down wells; grinning horny-handed brothers showed me at least three babies that had been born that week and one born yesterday. Probably a few more emerged from the weary-looking wives while I was there; it would have been hard to know if someone was giving birth above the constant yelling, laughing, maize-pounding, goat-bleating, chicken-squeaking, toddler-bawling noise.

Having greeted me in his soft voice, Le Vieux sat with me for a few minutes, although we could only communicate via Isidore. There wasn't much to translate: Le Vieux had no questions; perhaps that was a form of politeness. Perhaps he didn't need to ask questions . . . but I didn't have the feeling he was witchily reading my mind. He just sat at his ease, smiling, making rare quiet remarks.

'My father apologizes he can't speak to you in French.'

'I'm sorry I don't speak Fon.'

'He says perhaps one day you will. He is too old to learn new things. He depends on me for new things.'

I could see Le Vieux was pleased with me, not going to denounce me as a liar available for marriage, or generally perceive my inner-most faults and expose them. But the person whose presence he really doted on was Isidore. He watched with pride as Isidore spoke to me in French, glowed when Isidore showed me where we were on the French road map. Isidore had told me, 'If anything happened to kill me, my father would die soon after.'

Le Vieux had wanted to pass on his secrets to Isidore. 'But I live in the city, I can't take over from him. He's a little bit sad about this. But also proud I have education, so we've put the matter to one side.'

Some men from the village arrived. Leaving me in the shade of a palm-thatched lean-to, Isidore and his father excused themselves and went into the father's one-room house in the compound with the men and some of the brothers.

'I have to leave you a while. If I don't sit and tell them my news they will think I've got swelled up with myself and have come here to make big backs in front of them.'

He knew this would leave me highly amused.

I was sitting in a light breeze, I had a view of trees and a downhill path that seemed to have an increasing amount of traffic, mostly children; whatever errands they were on required many return trips along the path with the view of a *yovo*.

Although the rains were only beginning, my memory of the village, Dovi Dove, was of greenery, trees and swathes of wild grass. Apart from people's houses, Dovi Dove had nothing in particular. There was a primary school, a two-room medical dispensary and one flaunty mansion of a house that Isidore said belonged to a customs man, as if this were enough explanation. Apparently if you wanted to get rich in Benin, a backhander-filled career in customs was an easy route – once you'd bribed your way into the job.

Gradually I was no longer alone in the lean-to. The compound's women and children crept over to look at me and touch my funny hair. Two old women with five teeth between them were the wives of Le Vieux. Not Isidore's mother. She lived elsewhere, a long story I'd yet to be told.

The young woman with the day-old baby had washed, powdered and dressed up the baby for me to hold. It was gorgeous – and terrifying – in its best frock with matching pants and little bundles of fresh rag for a nappy. What if I dropped it? Held it in some wrong way and its head fell off? I didn't know if this was a welcoming friendliness or if I was supposed to give her some money, or even take the baby away with me. It wouldn't have been the first time I'd been made such an offer.

Isidore talked frequently of poor children being taken by childless French people to unimaginably fabulous foreign lives. I had snapped at him about the humanitarian and political obscenity of this use of Africa as a cute-baby farm, and alarmed him so much with my sudden, loud, soapbox leaping that he probably wasn't going to utter the word 'baby' again in his life. Let alone continue what I suspected was a veiled strategy of hinting about the poor babies in his family. So with a gurgling, powdery newborn in my hands that I wanted to run, run, run away with, I'd have to practise what I'd preached and hand it back when it was time to leave.

Trying to be a shrewd traveller can dip into harsh cynicism; not everyone had an ulterior motive for communicating with me. It soon became clear that the mother of the newborn wanted only to show her off. We made cooing noises about its little hands, feet and dimples . . . But just as I dropped my defences and simply enjoyed the baby fussing, a strapping young man with ulterior motives came by. He acted surprised to see me but I felt his stroll by wasn't an accident; he'd heard there was a *yovo* on the manor and out he'd sped.

After introducing himself as Paul, a neighbour, he sat himself beside me and asked if I was with the nuns.

No, I wasn't a nun, I was a visitor to the family.

'You're visiting Benin. Do you need a chauffeur?'

I said I had one, thank you, and busied myself straightening the baby's straight dress; there was a shoving vibe of being after something coming off him, so strong I had no need to examine my conscience for undue cynicism.

Paul was dressed in new jeans, new T-shirt and newish trainers. He spoke impeccable French and was, as I said, a big, healthy young man. What irritated me, apart from his determined intrusion, was the baleful, imploring look he seemed to switch on in his eyes as he sat down.

Isidore had warned me not to give any gifts of money, except to his father if I wanted to. His father was discreet and wouldn't provoke jealousy. Particularly, I was to play dumb if any of the bastard brothers summoned up enough French from their ignorance to ask me for money. While Paul, looking healthier and wealthier than any of the maligned brothers, launched straight into a sob story, the brothers had smiled at me, introduced me to their wives and left me in peace.

Paul's story, dropped in my lap right away, was not a thing with feet and hands to coo over. He said he worked in the fields but this only provided a few months' work and he needed other work. He would do any work, driving, farming, cleaning . . . I tried explaining again that I did have a driver and was just in transit, in no need of further employees, but he insisted – I must help him by giving him work. Probably understanding his tone more than the French, the women drifted away, leaving only a toddler to mind me and baby. Paul had embarrassed them.

It did occur to me that Isidore had commandeered me as an employer with this kind of instant, full-on approach, but the same instincts that told me to give Isidore a chance, told me that Paul was not to be trusted. Fairly soon, I knew I was right. He asked me if I was alone. I said no, I had a husband in London and Isidore was my driver, guide and friend here. No pause to reflect. Paul asked: 'Are you happy with your husband?'

I said yes, adamantly.

Switching to his other theme, Paul said he would give me his address so I could recommend him to people for work. He wanted my address so he could write to me. I said no, that was pointless, I was never at home, always travelling, usually with my husband with whom I was so very happy . . . Paul still insisted on having my address. I was just about to be rude to him when Isidore poked his head out of Le Vieux's house. I think one of the bastards must have alerted him to the possibility I was being hassled. He asked if I was all right; I made a crosseyed face to contradict my assurance that I was. Isidore said something sharp to Paul in Fon. Paul seemed flustered; he followed Isidore into Le Vieux's house and greeted the company.

I heard him say: 'Who's the white woman? She's just asked me for my address.'

So when the sneaky snake came out, I glared at him and he slithered off up the path.

Isidore re-emerged at the same time, telling me it wouldn't be much longer, but there were arrangements to be made for me. Soon, we'd go and find me a hotel. There was one in Cove, he thought. Of course I was welcome to stay in the compound but he doubted I could survive the noise, heat, lack of a mattress and running water. I didn't argue.

The women and children clustered round again. The children stroked my hair, I stroked the baby. There was loud talk and laughter from the men's meeting *chez* Le Vieux. Soon, it broke up and the brothers came grinning at me and shaking hands. Only two were younger than Isidore but they all looked older. A still fresh-looking grandson of about seventeen spoke enough French to say: 'You will enjoy tomorrow, madame; you are very welcome.'

Le Vieux came to his door, smiled and gave me a little wave.

'Le Vieux is going to make arrangements so things are perfect for you tomorrow at the village ceremony. He likes you.'

'He doesn't know me.'

'You're good to me, that's what matters. Now he would destroy anyone who hurt you.'

I hoped the people hurting me wouldn't be coming thick and fast out of the evening – I was feeling quite tired now.

There was a long search for a hotel along roads that looked like someone had gone ahead of us in a bulldozer with extra tree-felling attachment. The road then became unworthy of any stretch of the word and was more a gap between the houses of Cove town, full of boulders, ha-has and interesting rain-eaten terraced effects. Isidore told me he'd learnt to drive in Cove so the stunt manoeuvres required held no fear for him. Nevertheless, it took strained concentration on top of a long day's driving and conferencing. Probably, although he didn't complain of it, he'd also undergone some emotional wear and tear from encountering the bastards.

In a side street, the hotel Isidore had been looking for had sort of collapsed in on itself. It was just a roadside bar and overgrown rubble.

'You used to have eight rooms – where are they?' he berated the lady behind the bar. She shrugged and carried on talking to her friends. Incensed, Isidore drove off into the night, towards the empty bush.

'Are we going to another town?'

'There is no other town. Abomey is seventy kilometres. If we do that at night on these roads I'll die at the wheel. This is terrible. I'll have to take you to the nuns.'

I was very grubby, weary and felt babyishly tearful about having nowhere to go in the dark night, but turning up destitute on a convent doorstep seemed a very bad end to come to.

'Will the nuns give me a room?'

'They're supposed to help people. They'll have to.'

The mood Isidore was getting into, he'd have decked a Reverend Mother if she crossed him. He stopped to ask a group of young men on mopeds the best way to the convent. There was some agitated debate; I thought there'd be a row, but then Isidore almost smiled, setting off in pursuit of one of the moped men.

'There is a new hotel at Zagnanado village I thought was just a bar. He says there's fans and meals and everything.'

We hadn't eaten since breakfast, which wasn't helping matters.

There was nearly another hour of precarious night-driving. The hotel was outside the village, on a route used by truck drivers from Nigeria. The rooms were chalets round a vast central dancefloor. There were no ravers, just one drunk asleep at a side table. The young boss, Gerard, seemed to suffer from some kind of insanity.

Gerard would narrow his eyes, grind his teeth and scowl when listening; grin with his eyes glazing over when speaking. Isidore thought he might be on cocaine, a strong possibility on the Nigeria road – truck drivers spread it around them like dust.

We were hungry but almost too tired to eat; Gerard, in between doing a new thing of scratching a lot and shuddering, said he could make us omelettes quickly, so that we weren't hanging around too long before sleep.

In the bar there was a teenage girl washing glasses – Gerard sent her to the village to buy bread. Funnily enough, I had thought of saying we didn't need bread, thinking this might save time, but . . . The girl was gone for ages. After twenty minutes, Gerard was fuming round the dancefloor giving out about her as he stacked chairs on to tables and chased the drunk off the premises with a lot of unnecessary pushing and shouting – the poor man had been leaving without objection when bidden.

Isidore said Gerard shouldn't have sent a young girl out alone at this hour. Gerard looked like he was considering pushing and shouting at Isidore but realized he'd be dealing with someone his own size. They went out to look for the girl in Isidore's car; with me not being a young girl, obviously it was fine to leave me alone in a roadhouse at this hour.

Fifteen minutes later no cocaine dealers with machetes had arrived to disturb me, but I was very relieved to see Isidore and Gerard back with two baguettes.

Apparently the danger wouldn't have been coming from the road. While Gerard cooked the omelettes Isidore whispered.

'I've taken that room there, five, on the other side of the compound.'

'Of course,' I said. 'You can't drive all the way back to the village again.'

'Partly I was dreading that,' Isidore admitted. 'But also, I can't leave you alone with Gerard. He is not just strange. He is a real mad person. Do you see the young girl didn't come back?'

I had wondered.

'When we found her in the village he leant out of the car and screamed at her, screamed at her till she cried. She'd only taken so long because she'd had to walk the whole village to find bread at this hour. I made her get in the car and took her home. He screamed at her all the way in the car, accusing her of going with men while we were waiting for bread. He's extremely peculiar.'

When the food came I was so exhausted I could barely swallow a mouthful, but also worried that Gerard might break a bar stool over my head if I didn't get most of the baguette down me. Isidore ate his share like a wolf; I tried to get him to take mine.

'No, I can't, I really can't, just leave it.'

'He'll shout or something.'

'I'll shout back.'

I couldn't bear the thought of it. I slipped the bread in my bag, saying I'd save it for breakfast. Isidore thought this was very funny.

'Scared of that lunatic, aren't you? OK, let's sleep before we fall down.'

As we went to our chalets, Gerard flew out of his kitchen in a panic. I thought he'd seen my manoeuvres and was going to accuse me of bread stealing. 'Do you want breakfast?'

Isidore shook his head.

'I just want coffee,' I said, giving Gerard what I hoped was a calming smile.

'OK, just coffee, of course,' Gerard said pleasantly – not looking mad, just for a moment there.

★

Although my last sight of Gerard wasn't too worrying and Isidore was only a dancefloor away, I felt my room was very exposed. I was right by the cocaine sprinklers' road, only a corrugated-iron door with a flimsy bolt between me and marauders. They could burst through there into the compound, burst through my room's flimsy wooden door with its flimsy lock . . . There was further easy access through the metal window slats, if they'd just wanted to poke a gun barrel through and shoot me. I was very tired. The electric fan was making the heat agitated and hotter. So that was plenty of heat. But I wasn't overheatedly imagining that the room was alive with insects and that the one sheet on the lopsided bed seemed to have led a full life, free from dull spells in soap and water. I decided to sleep in my clothes, inside a cotton sleeping-bag-liner I intrepidly kept for such situations. The stand pipe over a hole in the corner, my bathroom, could wait till morning.

I couldn't sleep. I couldn't believe I couldn't sleep and intense irritation turned to galloping palpitations when there was a loud bang on that compound-side door. There was more banging, followed by what sounded like a shuffled, grunted fight outside on the road. Gerard was probably doing all this by himself to sort out some of his inner demons, but I wondered if I should get Isidore. I could just make a dash for it . . . I couldn't. Better to crouch in my cotton bag, quaking and wishing I'd never heard of Benin.

The sound continued, stopped.

The minute it seemed I'd finally got to sleep, there was a knocking on my door and it was first light. Washed, brushed and immaculate, Isidore looked a little disconcerted, if not repulsed, by his unkempt, sour-breathed companion, her eyes glued together with yesterday's mascara, hopping about in some sort of blue sack.

'It's early. I'm going to Dovi Dove to meet with my father and make some arrangements. I should be back by nine o'clock.' He fled the sight and smell of me.

It was six o'clock. I fell back on my squalid bed, too weary to feel ashamed of myself. Isidore had probably got up and washed the car before he washed himself, and found petrol, and said his prayers.

After a couple of hours' groaning and dozing in my pit, shame did drive me to the stand pipe and clean clothes. If I could just get some coffee I'd be almost acceptable by the time Isidore returned.

It was a clean-smelling morning, birds were singing, Gerard was in the middle of the dancefloor counting his cooking pots. Perhaps he wasn't counting them, perhaps he was arranging them for a formation finale to the cooking-pot *Come Dancing* he'd been compèring out here. Whatever it was, it was a mistake to interrupt him with a cheery 'Good morning' and polite request for coffee.

He swung to his feet and glared at me, yelling: 'Coffee? I asked you if you wanted coffee last night and you said nothing! I'll do it, but you said nothing!'

Oh.

I thought of pointing out that the conversation hadn't exactly run like that, but he might have taken the head off my body with a soup tureen. I meekly crept to a chair with a view of the road, willing Isidore to come back early.

Putting on one of his other personalities, Gerard made an attentive fuss with cups, saucers and paper serviettes as he served the coffee, smiling obsequiously and hoping I'd slept well. He went back to the kitchen and started screaming like Beelzebub. I watched for green bile coming out but the young girl ran out – she skidded on the dancefloor in her haste, panicked herself upright just in time and started gathering the cooking-pot display. I decided that if I pretended to read the guide book at least it was a big thing to hit Gerard with if he flew out the kitchen door in Linda Blair's nightie trying to snap my head round 180 degrees . . . If Isidore would hurry back he'd got some holy water in the car. Five past nine. Come on, Isidore.

At a quarter to twelve Isidore hurried in, as well he might. I'd been through fear of a road accident to suspicion he'd gone on an all-is-forgiven drinking binge with the bastard brothers, and was coming close to the conclusion that he'd never even got to Dovi Dove because Gerard had snapped his neck and was figuring out how best to divide his dismembered body between his small cooking pots. Mostly, I'd sunk into self-pity.

Gerard was sane and matey with Isidore – yes, I'd had my coffee, he'd looked after me . . . I was so relieved to see Isidore, I barely heard his explanation for lateness as we fled the bipolar disorder of hospitality Chez Gerard.

There'd been a considerable amount of negotiating, entirely for my benefit. The matter was now settled and it would all begin at five when the day began to cool. 'It all' was a *gelede*, a fiesta-type experience Isidore had described but I couldn't visualize. He said there would be music, dancing, puppets, and masks. I wouldn't believe such a small village could produce such a show.

The *gelede* was, like so much here, a complex business. A Yoruba tradition, it served a religious and social function. Witches and the troublesome side of divinities like Shango, Ougon and Legba were kept away by the ceremonies. It cleared the air for the new agricultural season, summoning good fortune and chasing out bad. In the preparations and execution of the *gelede* the community was bonded and entertained. Producing a fine *gelede* was a matter of pride. There were forms of the mask dancing in villages for deaths and honouring ancestors; there were forms used in preparation for war. But the *gelede* I'd see was for ensuring harmony in the day-to-day life of a community.

There was also – and why not – money in it. Fortunately, there would not be an exorbitant amount of my money in it. Isidore said he and his father had worked a sort of pincer movement on the relevant villagers: 'I told them you are my girlfriend – sorry, but it does change things. Then my father told them that if you took photographs you would go home and show them, then more whites would want to come and see what our village can do. My father spoke to them very seriously, he said you had come from thousands of miles away and they had to represent the village in a good light – not go acting the fool and playing any old thing. They had to make sure you went back with an impression of them as talented, nice proper people. They listened to what he said. They wanted fifty thousand, now the price is twenty thousand. This is good for them, very good and not too much for you.'

Less than £20. No, not too much.

'A local person with money would pay more than that. But I must admit less money than this would be collected around the village when the *gelede* is done in the normal way, simply for communal celebration.'

'It's fine. I'm happy, really.'

'Good. Also my father has sent you some wise advice. Don't give them all the money in the beginning or they'll feel they don't have to try too hard. Give them ten now to buy drinks and feel encouraged, put the rest in an envelope and give it to the chief drummer at the end. The envelope is important – this way the villagers don't see what the players are getting and get jealous. And you must hand over the envelope yourself; if I hand it over the people might say I lifted a portion of the money from the envelope.' Isidore smiled triumph-antly. 'It will all make you very happy. Now, do you know where we're going? You'll be pleased. We're going to a forest where some of the Rolli people live. Remember I told you about Rolli people?'

I did. I was an attentive passenger, in case of this kind of spot test. The Rolli were a sparse tribe who seldom appeared outside their own villages, notorious for their skills in magic arts and their withdrawal from the modern world. They were supposed to be a subgroup of the Fon but Isidore said their language sounded incom-prehensible to him, and they used Yoruba to communicate with outsiders. There were Rolli, deep in the forests, who would still take fright at the sight of a car. Let alone a yellow-headed *yovo*. We'd be going to their market, so we'd be meeting the less timorous Rolli.

It was the Rolli magic that intrigued Isidore. Le Vieux had lived among them a while to learn their secrets, and Le Vieux was not one to be easily impressed with other people's magic. Apparently the Rolli magic could particularly do wonders in the gynaecological field: 'They can make women have two babies in one year. You'll see Rolli children and think they are twins but they've been born nine months apart. The magic means the Rolli women can breastfeed while pregnant.'

Robust would be my word for it rather than magic. This also seemed to apply to Isidore's claim that Rolli babies, even in times of drought or fever, seldom died like babies in the villages around them.

Homoeopathic medical knowledge was my other theory.

'If you are wounded, even very seriously, if you find the Rolli they can put potions on your wounds to cure you. They're incredible. You see all these little lakes and rivers. In the rainy season they flood. When there are floods, the Rolli people put their children in a large basket, six to a basket maybe, and give them a mixture of flour, mustard, salt and pepper to eat, so they won't drown. The adults wade through the waters, pulling the children in the basket behind them without worrying a child might fall out because the mixture keeps them safe.'

But if the children were used to floods and . . . I said nothing. My constant search for the logical explanation was beginning to bore me anyway. The explanation was too easy to find. And made no strange bright pictures out of the world's muddy, tangible stuff.

We came to the edge of a tiny village. 'What time is it, Annie? Oh. Where has the day gone? I wanted you to see how the Rolli do their courtship. They take a very long time and it all happens in the market. Now, imagine, the young man has seen a girl he likes. He goes to her stall in the market. As he comes close, he turns his back, he stands in front of her with his back to her. He says nothing. He waits, he goes away. He does this several market days. Each time he says nothing – back turned, he waits, he goes away. But all this is the signal for the girl, if she likes him, to alert her parents. They find out who the man is and start investigating him. Does he have a respectable reputation and good maize fields? The Rolli are known for their excellent maize fields. If the family tell the girl he is acceptable, she can start talking to him the next time he comes to her stall. He can reply, they can talk. But still he must not turn to face her. They will not meet face to face until the marriage day.'

Arriving mid-afternoon we were too late to see any backwards wooing, but Isidore pointed out some young women sitting in the shade behind their stalls, all dressed up in their best *pagne*. 'In the evening some more young men might come.'

Even without the wooing, the Rolli were a sight to behold. Small in stature, they made sure to be noticeable by covering themselves in dark-blue tattoos. The men had scars, small squares cut into the cheeks, as well as a second skin of tattoos. These could cover the whole body – tiny flowers, geometric symbols, symbols of divinities – dense, delicate decorations that needed staring at. I tried not to, but then there was a lot of shy but persistent staring at my *yovo*-ness so it was only fair . . . Children under five didn't stare – they fled or burst into tears.

We made our way out of the market, in search of the Rolli at home, heading into a forest of long-trunked trees with all their leaves at the top, like trees a child would draw. The forest path, in leaf-dappled green light, was the proper kind of path to go along to find something magic in a fairy-tale. For Isidore the magic was discovering that the Rolli were having a small Catholic church constructed at the edge of their village; it was very unusual for them to convert from traditional religion. The priest, a Fon from Cove, was inspecting the construction and joyfully shared the news that fourteen Rolli were now baptized Catholics – and, with their own church, surely there would be more.

The priest spoke the language and volunteered himself as a guide to the Rolli forest. He particularly wanted to introduce me to what he called 'The Women's Pot Team'.

In the hut of The Women's Pot Team, one very small tattooed woman balked with fright at the sight of me, then extended her hand apologetically.

She was making clay water-jars, big enough to hold several gallons. I'd seen these jars in the market and assumed their exact finish must come from a factory. Or at least a workshop with potter's wheels and all kinds of professional pot-smoothing tools. She was making them completely by hand, starting with a lump of clay, pulling and pushing with no equipment except for a small plastic comb she used to decorate the edges. How she made the pots so perfectly round and smooth was bewildering.

She said she could make three of these large pots in a day and sold them in the market for £1.50 each. She showed us smaller pots; she could make ten of these a day. They were more elaborately decorated, something she'd just done to amuse herself. She picked one with four handles shaped like little hands, and gave it to me. I wanted to pay her for it but she refused.

The priest interpreted: 'She says it has given her great pleasure that you've turned up here from your foreign country and praised her work so much. She says there are eight women who make pots, but the others are at the market. They'll be very happy when they hear about your visit.'

The thing was, she was out here in the middle of nowhere, making these perfect objects just for people to put maize or water into them, selling them for the price of plastic washing-up bowls, but as I asked questions and talked about the pots, I could see she knew how good she was. Perhaps no one would ever call her an artist, but she knew that's what she was.

The excursion to magic land brought us back to Dovi Dove sweaty, dirty and running late. I had thought it would be the form to dress up for the *gelede* but there was no time to do more than splash our faces from a water bottle. Isidore agreed that ideally we should be in party wear – 'They'll think it's strange we've turned up looking like we've been working in the bush, but let them worry about that.'

'They won't be insulted?'

'No, they'll just be surprised at me in particular, that I didn't want to make big backs in good clothes.'

We picked up Le Vieux, who giggled with delight when I greeted him in Fon. 'Hello', 'goodbye', 'yes', 'no' were still as much as I'd managed to acquire. Le Vieux was a bit of a giggler all round, which was very endearing and yet another trait I hadn't expected to find in the top local shaman. He also got car sick and seldom went any distance he couldn't walk or cycle. As this was a special occasion, and we were only going down the hill, he did sit, warily, in the passenger seat.

Under trees at the edge of a well-worn clearing, straight-backed

wooden chairs and a table covered by decorative cloth were set
out for me, Isidore and Le Vieux, the guests of honour. A dozen
men had already started playing high tam-tam drums in the centre
of the clearing, another dozen were dancing round them in a
shuffling circle. Children were beginning to gather at the edge of
the clearing.

By the time we'd settled ourselves, more children and more
dancers arrived – the drummers upped their pace. Within minutes
there was a crowd of dancers circling the drums. Realizing how
many people were involving themselves and looking at me, I smiled
broadly to show how much I was appreciating it so far.

Smiling may have been a mistake. Once I'd started I felt it
was churlish to stop. Unaccustomed as I was, I'd never read the
handbook on how to be a guest of honour. I'm sure handy hint
number one must be *Don't start smiling at the beginning of a ceremony
of indefinite length*. By the end of the *gelede* my whole face hurt like
I'd bruised myself with my own smile muscles.

Far more eyes were on me than on the proceedings. Hundreds
of these eyes belonged to children – I'd never seen so many
under-tens, yards deep, left, right and behind me, utterly agog and
half-scared, whispering about me and following my every gesture.
Most of the under-fives were naked. Pants and occasional T-shirts
were added for modesty until the age of about ten for boys, then
they dressed like cut-down adults. Girls put on wraparound skirts
and T-shirts after passing the slightly earlier pant age of about seven.
I wished I was at pant age, or even pre-pant age, as my modestly
covered arms and legs simmered in the heat. But most of the time
I was so astonished by the sights, I forgot my discomfort.

Isidore said that the gathering multitude was nothing like the
mob that would have turned up had there been more notice.
Outlying villagers and families working in the fields wouldn't have
heard since this morning. If there'd been a few days for word to
get round, then I'd have seen a crowd . . .

The circling dancers began a song to accompany the drums. A
Yoruba folk song. Several of the dancing men looked far older than
Le Vieux. One had a trailing limp, one had a goitre on his neck

almost the size of his own head, some had digits missing from their hands or infected sores on their legs, or infected eyes – village life was hard; it was rare to survive as unblemished as Le Vieux.

The dancers turned and turned, making a dip-and-rise motion as they went, with a lot of upper-body action, seeing as footwork was restricted to the circle. A village elder with a long horsehair whip shouted encouragement to the dancers while flicking the whip at the children to keep them back from constant near entanglement in the show. As the children pressed further forward, other elders took up palm switches to smack them back into line. Despite tears, shrieks and crumpled faces, the children would soon forget the pain of a switch hit and edge forward again.

Some squabbling and pushing among the adults started as the mouth-removing local rum, *sodadi*, took hold. Men swayed and rolled into each other, annoying the more sober. In bursts of exuberance drunks came up to shake my hand, each time as if it was for the first time. Things became really chaotic when the drunks joined in the children chasing, causing more shrieking and tangled disorder than any child would know how to create.

The dancers still turned and turned. Every time I leant back there were little cheeps of anguish as I inadvertently crushed the tiny fingers of children clutching the back of my chair. There was some nipping and biting to have the precarious privilege of clinging to my chair, getting that chance to surreptitiously touch my yellow head.

I noticed something odd about some of the men dancing and clapping round the drums – they were women. Burly women in men's clothes and hats, dancing with male vigour and grinning at me. They danced in synch with each other, like teenage girls do once they've practised for hours at home. They were not at all like the baby-holding or dressed-up man-catching girls around the perimeter. I tried to get a photograph of a particularly self-possessed woman in male attire. When she realized what I was doing, she grabbed her friend and they came right up to the table to dance for me.

According to Isidore, in the *gelede* women had licence to act the fool, blow whistles, wave flags, sing loudly and wear men's clothes for fun. One of the functions of *gelede* was to keep the balance of male and female energy in the community, to harmonize this, preventing conflict between the sexes. Sometimes men, particularly the younger ones, put on items of women's clothing to satirize women, to remind women of what proper behaviour should be. Women dressing as men was more unusual but served the same purpose. It was the spirit of misrule let loose so order and balance could return.

There was another thought I had. The men-dressed women were definitely quite winky and flirty with me; was this part of their role play? Or was it their secret? I did extensive research, showing the photos and discussing it with one gay woman-friend in London. She said: 'Well, don't quote me but in my expert opinion I'd say you were right. Why wouldn't there be lesbians? They just let the men think it was a way some women liked to have a lark.'

The *gelede* was an old, old system of keeping harmony in the community, so why wouldn't there be ways to harmonize the less conventional citizens, allowing a space for them?

The who-knows-but-maybe lead lesbian of Dovi Dove appeared beside me, energetically cooling me down with a plaited straw fan, just at the moment I thought I'd expire. After she'd kept going for ten minutes I tried to get her to rest, but she just smiled and carried on.

Shouts went up as tall figures draped in cloth were brought into the dancers' arena.

'Now you'll see,' Isidore squealed.

The tall figures had helpers to steer them. One was positioned in front of our table, his covering cloth was removed and the show proper began, with accompanying uproar from the audience.

Under the drapes was a tricky thing to describe. Starting from the simplest part, the feet, bare with rings of jangly bells round the ankles – Isidore called these castanets . . . Then, as part of the cross-dressing tradition of *gelede*, the leg ends of trousers were sticking out from under a long, bright-coloured skirt. The hands had woollen knee-socks over them instead of gloves. The upper body and head were entirely covered by a circular cloth, like the night cover of a parrot cage. On the covered top of the dancer's head, perched like a hat, was a brightly painted mask, with a pink face staring serenely ahead. On top of that was a wooden toy. The first toy was a block of blue wood with a shark's fin protruding from it. As the dancer stamped his castanets and shook his body rhythmically, the shark's fin moved across the blue wood as if through water.

The next dancer was uncovered and came forward; his toy was a wooden acrobat that, after considerable stamping from the dancer, turned a somersault. Then there was a toy man holding a machete, who eventually chopped off a snake's head. A man standing by a motorbike lifted his leg, got on the bike and, after more hard dancing, he got off again. The adults in the crowd took particular delight in a figure of a woman, a prostitute, standing outside a little hut, looking at a man with 500 francs (50 pence) attached to him. She went towards him, went away, towards him, away again, obviously refusing his cheapskate offer. Then the door of the hut opened, the woman went in and the man quickly followed. Huge cheers, as the puppet prostitute had apparently accepted his price.

There was a panther that jumped on a lamb; a child spinning a hoop; a woman who picked up a baby – creation after creation paraded out. Old men steering the puppet dancers kept coming up to the table, telling me that this was nothing compared to what they could really do, if they'd had some notice . . .

The whole village was glowing proud with the devices, made by their local artisans.

'These things show you African inventiveness,' Isidore shouted over the cheers, pointing at a horse that bucked. 'Sometimes there are acrobats at a *gelede* but Le Vieux said this is what you'd want to see – the dances, music and toys special to Dovi Dove's life.'

I must have seen at least thirty complicated toys. Sometimes the toy bearers began with variations on the dances, waving horsehair switches and woven palm fronds, taunting us before beginning the real dance – the stamping and head waggling that set the toy in motion. Some string pulling was disguised by the sock gloves but the toys' actions always looked like some wonder of balance controlled by the dance alone.

Although my grin was hurting me, it was coming from real joy. Le Vieux chuckled contentedly when a spontaneous rush of screaming and clapping overtook me on seeing the last toy, a top-of-the-bill crowd pleaser – a man by a telephone table, who picked up the telephone, put it to his ear and put it down again. We went wild.

'This is new!' Isidore shrieked. 'Always something new!'

The toys were finished but the drumming and dancing continued and when it should end was now up to me. Le Vieux advised me to give my envelope to the crowd controller with the horsehair whip. He held the envelope aloft and the crowd cheered. The woman fanning me finally let her arm rest and went back for a last frolic round the drums with her friends. What a day out.

We began to move towards the car, me gripped all round by small children – wading through small children. I made the mistake of shaking a child's hand goodbye. Immediately an ocean of clam-ouring little hands thrust up at me. Then the children were firmly pushed aside by my butch fanning friend, holding out a firm handshake. I gave her grateful thanks for fanning me for so long; I don't know if she understood me – she seemed to come over shy and confused. Then, just before she turned to go, she gave me a big smile and winked at me, I'm sure of it, suggestively.

Anyway, then it was all back up the hill to Chez Le Vieux for an exhausted-but-happy post-mortem. The older brothers, being very involved in puppet making, were still busy with dismantling the ceremony. Isidore excused himself to go in for a private conference with Le Vieux, but the compound women, children and young men crowded round me proprietorially, showing off to passersby on the path; everyone had seen me but they'd got to take me home.

Paul had made sure to attach himself to the family group. I was starting to find him a bit sinister. At one point in the *gelede* I'd looked across the crowd and there he was, staring at me – he'd been waiting to catch my eye. Every so often he'd rear up in a different spot, so there was no point avoiding looking where I thought he'd be. Nothing wrong with staring – anyone else I'd barely have noticed – but there was something about him.

'He lost his father just five days ago,' Isidore said the night before when I'd complained of Paul. 'Things are bad for him.'

Now Paul had worked his way through to me.

'You remember me?'

I smiled politely and kept myself busy with the hair-plaiting lesson three little girls were giving me. 'Yes, yes, I remember.'

I had a quarter of a child's head to work on and wasn't progressing very fast. This was only basic plaiting. A wife who worked as a hair-dresser told me that a full adult plaited head, with added nylon arti-ficial hair, could take two days to finish. Half a day if the head was shared. For all that fiddly work she made about 25 pence an hour.

Quizzically eyeing my efforts, the woman added that doing children's natural hair plaits was easy. Usually a matter of fifteen minutes. The current fashion for the spiky, startled-stegosaurus look on little girls was done with tight winding of plastic thread round the hair, and needed plenty of time or a gang of apprentices working on shares of the head. She said she didn't honestly think she'd rush to take me on as an apprentice; I seemed to have 'the fingers of a farmer'. This made us all laugh a lot but Paul was still trying to weave himself into my attention.

'I think you've forgotten me. And I need help.'

I looked at him, souring the atmosphere with his tragic expression. I knew what it was then that upset me. Not the begging – begging was either a yes or no matter to me – it was that underneath his mournful grovelling he despised me.

'Think of me,' he said, leaning in at me to look into my eyes.

'Yes,' I said.

Yes, I'm white, just hate me, can't you? Don't do this to yourself. I was angry for him; he'd make himself go mental because he'd never be brave enough to tell me how much he despised me. I was angry he'd put me at the hub of this, put all the power over his self-respect into my hands. I was also annoyed for the rest of the village – no one had asked me for anything; simply been hospitable, and dignified.

My plait section was getting very tangled. I thought there'd be a reprieve from Paul when Isidore emerged announcing that Le Vieux would like his photo taken with me, but first he had to talk with Le Vieux in private for a while longer, he hoped I wouldn't mind. I made myself smile and nod obligingly.

So I wouldn't feel neglected, Le Vieux sent out two large bottles of grapefruit *fizzi*. One of the old wives gave me a clean metal bowl and poured the entire contents of one bottle into it for me. She eked out the second bottle among the children. I could feel Paul watching this, wanting to point out the unfair distribution-of-pop situation to me as if I was too heartless to notice. I offered my bowl to the second old wife nearby but she insisted vociferously it was for me. The first old wife stayed my hand as I went towards a child who'd had the last dregs.

'It's for you, she says. The children have enough,' a teenage grandchild told me. So I lived with my embarrassment, that was my own and not provided by Paul.

Paul then started a long whinge about how normally the money given to the *gelede* performers was held up for all the people to see, but in this case, because the money was hidden in an envelope, the people couldn't see how much was given.

I was very grateful to notice that the French-speaking grandson was listening and relaying Paul's plaint to the returning brothers. They looked disapprovingly at Paul.

'Do you understand me?' Paul went on. 'The people shouldn't be kept in the dark like this; you should tell me how much you gave.'

I said: 'It's not for me to say.'

Paul started to get petulant: 'This shouldn't be a secret. It makes the villagers unhappy if they don't know what you've given the players.'

Le Vieux had advised me and I would stick to his advice – who better to know what the form was than him? I said crossly, 'Well, then ask the players what they got.'

The grandson laughed delightedly, passed on the joke to the

brothers who smiled and nodded. The hairdressers showed me that both the plaits I'd finished were now unravelling.

Paul wasn't done. Suddenly, in very good English, he asked if I spoke English. Being so taken aback made me stupid – yes I did, of course I did, I was English. I glanced at the grandson – he raised an eyebrow to tell me he was alert to Paul's new trick, speaking English to isolate me.

In his new language, Paul said: 'I lost my father five days ago. He is dead.'

I said, with as much compassion as I could muster out of material that was predominantly anger: 'That's very sad. Very sad. I'm sorry to hear that.'

'So you must help me, even if you can only give me a little money. You must.'

Compassion was gone. 'I'm sorry, but I can't help everyone.'

I turned away to resume my hair-plaiting studies, but Paul was pleading: 'Help me go to London, let me stay with you in London. You have to give me your address. I want to leave this village and find work in London.' He held out a pen and paper. In the nick of time, Isidore came out saying it was time for photographs.

Le Vieux selected a nice floral shrub to stand beside and fussed at Isidore about whether he should do up the top button of his shirt or not. We decided on done up. Le Vieux noticed the grandson was wearing smart leather sandals; he borrowed them for the photos, giggling and urging me to get the sandals in the picture. This was tricky – he was at least a head shorter than Isidore.

All the giggling and titivating, the high voice . . . I thought about the androgynous forest guardian at Ouidah. Harmony between the sexes contained in one person must have been a useful trait in a vodou celebrant.

Paul was shaken off in the photo session, although I could sense him still around, staring resentfully. Then there was too much to do, with saying goodbye to Le Vieux, old wives, young wives, brothers, children, a little girl with a quarter of her hair gone very wrong indeed . . . Isidore was loud and laughing with them all, the golden boy. Paul was at the back of the throng as we settled in the car, but suddenly he was by the passenger door looking plaintive. 'Don't forget about me.'

As we waved off, scampering kids in our wake, Paul stared at me reproachfully till the last instant. I hoped he wasn't putting some kind of *gri-gri* on me. Well, let him try. As we left Dovi Dove behind, Isidore pulled over to the side of the road.

'I just have to do something for my father,' he said.

He had two small, brown-paper packets in his hand with sort of cubist-hieroglyphic writing on them – Fon. 'My father wants me to have protection from anyone envious in the village. Especially with such a long journey ahead of us.'

From one of the packets he took what looked like a piece of charcoal. He traced it from the nape of his neck, across his head to just above his eyebrows, leaving a clear line down his forehead. The other packet was a soap he was instructed to wash with every night.

'Do you think we're in danger?'

He gave a slight smile. 'I couldn't ignore this if my father advises it. So no, now there is no danger. You can think it's strange but my father has seen too much. I don't ignore him in these matters.'

He tucked the magic products in his shirt pocket and drove on.

I was sceptical about *gri-gri* but I wished I'd been able to talk to Le Vieux. Not to cross-examine him about the existence of magic but to hear of the things he'd seen that made him devote his life to it. Then there were his more visible skills – the babies he'd delivered, the physical illnesses he'd cured homoeopathically. I wanted to hear how he described his skills for himself. I only had Isidore's respectful awe to go on. And the gentle presence of Le Vieux, that I did feel he'd sent with us on the long journey north.

8

The Good, the Mad and the Bewitched

There was a marked lack of accidents on our journey north.

We were driving so slowly it would have been quite an accomplishment to have an accident anyway. Isidore was in a quiet mood, meandering the road to Savé, a quarterway mark of the country. Our plan was to reach the very end mark in a couple of days, so I did wonder if we needed to take it quite so easy.

It's a rare person who finds adult encounters with their family an unmitigated joy, so I think Isidore was a bit emotionally spaced-out. Relief that the bastard brothers hadn't done anything bastardly, indeed that the whole family and community had done him proud, let him relax into an ambling form of post-traumatic stress syndrome.

When he did speak, his voice was flat, vague: 'This place is called Glazoué. I have to buy some presents for family here.' We'd taken twenty loaves of bread to Dovi Dove but apparently we were now visiting an aunt who had no time for bread. 'She makes bread herself. What we need is cheese, but the cheese is north of here. We'll bring cheese on the way back. For now I think I'll get tomatoes. What do you think?'

I said I thought tomatoes would be fine. You see how the usual fast-snapping, decisive Isidore brain had gone? All powers of command replaced by vagueness and dependency over mere grocery decisions. I didn't mind, I could take the helm for groceries, but I hoped I wouldn't still be in charge if we had a scramble alert, with incoming serious troubles off the starboard, or indeed any, bow.

'You'll like my aunt. She's always happy. She laughs and loves God. I'll stop in this market, OK? We'll get some tomatoes. And I will get some bread for my mother, if they have soft bread.' He smiled sadly. 'Now she has no teeth she has to suck her food like a child.'

Mother? He'd sprung that on me. He said nothing more about her. Made a lackadaisical attempt to bargain over the tomatoes and bread, gave in to the price in the first round of argument, got back in the car and carried on talking about his aunt.

'My uncle and aunt are the kind of people who are always cheerful. It's their philosophy. If you've got riches, you're going to die; if you've got nothing, you're going to die – so why not just laugh and live in the joy of Christ every day, and you will attract good things towards you.'

As we pulled up at the aunt's roadside home, there was one member of the family who didn't laugh too much in the joy of Christ at the sight of me. A plump toddler boy was horrified the instant my yellow head appeared – he let out a siren wail of alarm and ran behind a tree. From this safe position he kept staring at me and screaming objections to my presence. Aunt thought it was just a question of getting him used to me, and tried putting the boy in my arms – he fought like his life depended on it, kicking and biting at aunt, punching me, yelling. Embarrassed, aunt put him down and the child fled back to his tree, sobbing with rage. As apologizing aunt and uncle made me take a seat on a log bench, the child re-emerged brandishing a long stick, then ran at me and whacked me across the face with it. There was mortified pandemonium. The struggling child was separated from his weapon and chased into the house, where he stood in the doorway, glaring at me and letting fly occasional screams of fury. Angry with everyone – couldn't they see there was a wrong-looking thing in the compound and he'd only been trying to save them?

He'd left me with a stinging red welt across my face that lasted a good couple of days. I told distressed aunt it really didn't hurt at all. Isidore wasn't quite so solicitous about my wellbeing.

'Ah, he's never seen a *yovo*,' he laughed. 'He doesn't know what you are. You're like a monster. Like a bad dream.'

'Thanks. My face does hurt, you know.'

'Yes.' Isidore, the proud uncle, smiled as he looked at my injury. 'He's a very fine boy, a strong boy to have done all that damage at his age.'

I told him that if he'd like to test the health and strength of any other nephews on my face I'd be more than happy to oblige.

Aunt wanted me to try some of her maize beer to restore me to health. She served it in gourds, and promised it had a wealth of nutrients. Apparently she made a tidy profit from her beer business, probably contributing to her chubby-cheeked joyousness as much as joy in Christ. She was a completely round woman. It would have been physically impossible for her to have a miserable streak – the streak would simply have been forced to curve up into a smile.

I was trying to just have a sip of the beer but she urged me to finish my gourd. It was frothy and tasted weak but it was stronger than it seemed. I missed the car-door handle on the way out, sat down too heavily and took a disordinate amount of time to remember how to light a cigarette.

'I lived here for a year. It's a very happy house,' Isidore told me as he supped his beer, gossiping with girl cousins and tousling the hair of their many offspring. 'There was a sugar factory in Savé. I went to work there at fourteen and lived here. My uncle taught me the beginning of driving sitting here on this log. He had no car but showed me the feet actions, the gears and so on, with a stick and some flat stones.'

Uncle came out from the house with a plate of fresh-roasted peanuts for us. There was a limb-flailing, peanut-spilling re-enactment of the driving lessons, while aunt busied herself hanging out large red and white washing and somehow hugging a child or several at the same time. She always seemed to find a free arm for hugging. Two arms for Isidore when he left; I suppose she knew him well, knew he was feeling fragile. She saw the bread in the car and asked him who it was for. She squeezed him harder when he said his mother.

'Good boy,' she said in French. I asked what she'd added in Fon.
'She said she keeps an eye on my mother every day.'

I found it hard to register that the bent, near-blind lady, apparently in her nineties, was younger than my mountain-hiking, glowing-complexioned sixty-eight-year-old mother. That's vitamins, a health service and not working in the fields for you. Isidore's mother was all worn out and moving cautiously, as if everything ached. At a couple of yards, I was too far away for her fading sight to register me.

Isidore was getting the soft bread and a share of the tomatoes from the rear seat, telling me he'd introduce me in a moment. Mother peered right into the car to see who he was talking to and was only inches from my face before she withdrew sharply, exclaiming, '*Yovo!*'

I don't think it was only near blindness – it was also the confusion of the very old. Once she'd seen me she dithered by the car, needing someone to tell her what to do. Isidore handed the gifts into the two-room clay house; his niece was there, a bored-looking teenager. He apologized to me, he needed to talk privately with the niece . . . He said something to his mother as he went into the house. She remained by the car in a daze. Suddenly she leant in again, shook my hand and started talking rapidly in Fon. Isidore hurried out and led her into the darkness of the house.

After about five minutes, Isidore re-emerged, talking with his niece. His mother followed and began moving some cooking bowls from beside the door to a fire at the side of the house. She seemed to have forgotten there were visitors. I got out of the car, thinking I should be helping mother with the bowls.

'We're leaving, where are you going?' Isidore asked.

'Oh. Well, I'll just say goodbye to your mother.'

He didn't seem to think this was necessary. '*Maman!*' he called. She looked up, startled.

I went over to her to shake her hand again. She seemed flustered by me and my extended hand. Isidore merely said goodbye from beside the car; she looked at him, or in his direction, and I thought I saw tears. She stayed in exactly the same position until we'd driven away, maybe longer.

His mother was sixty-four. She had worked in the fields, walked miles to sell things at market and now, Isidore said, 'It's close to the end for her.'

Understandably, he didn't want to dwell on this and quickly told me about his sister – he was very worried about her and had urged the niece to make the sister come to Cotonou to see him.

'Her husband is driving a local bus. It is not a good job. So now my sister is working in a cotton field to make money. Women can't do this work, it's terrible work, it kills women to do this. In our village some of the men wanted to change the crops for cotton to make money, but cotton goes wrong very easily. And often the buyers are cheats. My father persuaded the village against cotton – at least with the old crops, if they don't sell, you have food. And working on cotton fields for someone else, it's too hard. I've given my niece some money but my sister has to stop this work right away. In Cotonou I can get her some things to sell in the market, cosmetics, plastic bowls, something like that. That's women's work.' He sighed. Didn't even flicker with anger when a moped cut dangerously across our path. 'This is the trouble, Annie. There's no one but me to look after everyone.'

He played music for a while to soothe himself. I always had plenty to be getting on with, looking at the overloaded bush taxis, the villages at the roadside that were endlessly full of new detail.

He'd acted like his mother was someone he barely knew, been almost curt with her compared to his affectionate chatting with his aunt and father. Sometimes, curt was caring too much – it was hard to linger round someone who used to be vibrant, looking after you, reduced to decrepitude and confusion.

Isidore had always talked about his childhood in terms of him and his mother, Le Vieux not getting a mention until tales of his adult life. Why didn't mother live in the village? Had father simply been a busy man in Isidore's childhood, always out doing *gri-gri*, delivering babies . . . ? What did Isidore know about me, except for the bare facts of how many brothers and sisters and a made-up boyfriend I had to keep remembering to lie about? So I always stopped myself asking anything, waited to be told.

After listening to his music for about ten minutes, a Nana Mouskouri tape – the singer was inexplicably popular in Benin – he said: 'This is where the sugar factory was, down that road. Then it closed. They say the town of Savé had a curse put on it. When things are started round here they always go wrong. The sugar factory was excellent for the whole town and it's been disastrous here since it closed.'

'You worked in the sugar factory at fourteen?'

'Not the hardest work. My mother was worried about me so she sent me away from the village. The atmosphere was better at my aunt's, everybody had money from the sugar factory. I could write, so I had a job writing the deliveries and bills and that kind of thing. My mother knew if I had to go on in the fields I would commit suicide. At least this way I could use my education.'

'Your mother lived in Dovi Dove, then?'

'She prefers to be near her own people now she is old. Then she was in the village with us children and my father's relatives. He was not there very much because of the problems with Kérékou. He went north, into the bush. Also, he wanted to go north. There is a different *gri-gri* there, he wanted to learn it. The children were not a problem for my mother, except me. I had started at school and wanted to continue. But the money for books, pens . . . she tried. I tried. I would finish at school and go to the market to help her or other people there, any jobs to find some little money. In the end my uncle said I was only thinking of myself, I had to work in the fields. My mother saved me with the sugar factory. Then my father came back and arranged for me to go to his friend in Cove and be an apprentice taxi driver, live in his house and do the paperwork. This way I could use my writing and numbers. So the taxi driving began. My mother still thanks God I don't work in the fields.'

He paused, as if he was offering up a short prayer himself.

'I was lucky. I drove the local taxis in Cove, then Dassa. The boss in Dassa sold me this car in bit-by-bit payments. He was a good man. He died last year.'

There was a sad, reflective pause, I thought we were going to have more Nana Mouskouri, but we were going somewhere else entirely. Somewhere awful.

'You doubt *gri-gri*, I know you foreigners do. But I have seen with my own eyes. If it wasn't for *gri-gri*, you'd see a different Isidore today. Perhaps I'd be . . . I don't know, a teacher or in a government office. Feel like a respected man. When I started at school in Dovi Dove my parents saw I was good in school, but that little school was not advanced – there would be no point, those villagers don't send their children to school. My parents decided to send me to my mother's brother in Cotonou. He had a good house, down by the beach where you like to watch the fishermen. He was a builder, a top builder who often worked for whites. He had four children and a wife from Ouidah. I stayed there and went to a private school in Cotonou. At the weekends I swam in the sea and learnt to help the fishermen. Sometimes, if my mother came to the market in Cotonou, she visited me. She was happy to see how this life suited me. I lived this way for many years. Then my uncle decided he wanted to take a second wife from Dovi Dove. He told the Ouidah wife he'd be bringing the second in a few months' time. The Ouidah wife was completely against this. In a few days, she said her father was ill and she had to go home. This wasn't true. She'd gone to Ouidah to get her parents to give her *gri-gri* to kill her husband. She got the poison in a string, put in the strands of the string. She would cook it in a dish with strong flavour. A few days after her return, my uncle wanted beef for dinner and gave her money to buy beef. This would have a strong flavour. The wife didn't eat with her husband; she always ate with her small children in the other room. As I was older I ate with my uncle, so I was with him when the wife served the beef.'

I was already troubled by that string. Beef joints came tied with string, and not just in Sainsbury's – I'd seen them tied in Porto Novo market.

Isidore said his uncle was always afraid of being poisoned anyway, which is a rational expectation, I suppose. Can any of us start to eat our dinner and honestly say we know it couldn't be poisoned? Unlike the rest of us Devil-may-care diners, uncle had done *gri-gri* to warn him if he was going to be poisoned. He would always take a small piece of food to test it before eating. He'd look at it in the spoon, and if he felt a shock through his body, he'd know the food was poisoned. On the night in question, uncle stared at the food in his spoon for a long time. Then he stirred the food in the dish and found the string. He screamed out for his wife to come in.

'What's this?' He showed her the string.

'I don't know,' she said.

'Get down on your knees and tell me the truth.' He started slapping his wife round her head. Apparently uncle was always a bit handy with his fists around his wife and children anyway.

'Not you?' I asked.

'No. I was careful to keep quiet around him, and I think he was afraid of my father. Anyway, he beat the wife and shouted, "Tell me what you've done or I'll break your neck!" She was weeping, she said she had put some *gri-gri* in to make him not want the second wife. "Liar!" my uncle said. "You've tried to poison me. Eat this beef, eat this beef dish yourself." She refused. He went to the other room and found out she'd cooked vegetables for herself and her children. He came back and beat her until he broke her arm and put out her eye.'

Maybe she had tried to kill him. Who wouldn't? The second wife wasn't what drove her. That was only the final straw for a broken-down, desperate woman. The final straw that broke her arm and put out her eye.

I didn't tell Isidore what I thought. It was only an opinion and he had his version of the story seared into his heart. 'A few weeks later, when she came out of hospital, my uncle drove his wife to her parents in Ouidah – he threw her out of the car in front of them. "Look what you've done. I know you Ouidah parents, it's you who encourage your daughters to poison their husbands so you can have his money. You can have her back with nothing. I never want to hear from any of you again."'

That done with, the uncle moved in the Dovi Dove wife. Everything was peaceful for a time but the Ouidah wife and her parents weren't done with him – they did more *gri-gri*, this time to send uncle mad. Now he started beating the second wife, the children and Isidore – madness overwhelming his fear of Isidore's father. The violence escalated, until one day he came home, went to his room and came out with a machete, screaming at them all. He chased them out of the house, trying to hack them to bits with the machete. No one was hurt. They fled to the house of friends from Dovi Dove. When they'd recovered a little from the shock they were all taken back to the village.

'For a few days my uncle was heard screaming in his house, break-ing things with the machete. Nobody dared go in. When he did come out he started drinking in bars. He'd drink one or two drinks, then throw down an enormous note, so the people would chase after him, saying, "Your change, sir, your change." And he'd scream at them and hit them in the face – "Who are you to tell me I forgot my change? Who the hell are you to tell me anything?" He did this all over Cotonou. Eventually relatives from Dovi Dove came to his house, tied him up and took him to the village. It took five years for him to be cured. My father cured him. He's quiet now. He has a small masonry business but he's not the man he was.' Isidore glanced at me. 'So you see, actually it was *gri-gri* that ruined my life.'

Our slow drive had finally brought us to the town of Savé, nestling beneath its bosom-shaped hills. Finding a new person to talk to in the Bosoms of Savé Hotel was a useful distraction from our sad visit to the past. The beautiful receptionist knew Isidore from previous visits with his *yovos*. She told him business had been slack since the closure of the sugar factory but she remained optimistic – they were on the main road, they had air conditioning and tourists travelling north needed to break their journey around this point. Isidore agreed and praised the hotel's fine facilities.

When our meal was served the receptionist excused herself. Isidore whispered, 'Look at this dining room. It's fallen apart.'

He tapped his chipped dinner plate, then gestured round the room. The light fittings were broken, the murals of countryside scenes were peeling and faded. Isidore's chipped plate was probably the least damaged piece of crockery on our table.

'Even a year ago it was better. She's putting on a brave face. She is the owner's daughter. She runs this for her father, her husband was killed in a car accident. You see what I mean about Savé? Things go wrong for people here.'

'When was her husband killed?'

'I don't know, I've known her for years and he's always been dead. I forget what she told me.'

I noticed he wasn't eating much, still speaking in a vague and depressed way. Trying to cheer him up seemed very crass, considering what he'd just told me. I wondered if I should suggest we call it a day so he could rest up and find himself again. But he was enough himself to have a plan.

'There's a King of Savé; I think you'll like him.' He pushed his picked-at meal away apologetically. He needed to escape from me. 'I'll go to the hostel for drivers – it's very nice. I'll meet lots of drivers I used to know. I'll call for you in an hour.'

No instructions for me to nap, wash . . . nothing.

I'd become so infantilized by his bossing me about, I felt bereft and insecure without it. I didn't think there was anything to be done for him except tread softly till he pulled round.

The King of Savé was a Nago king. The Nago were a Yoruba people who had broken away from the main Yoruba empire some time around the twelfth century. Their language and culture had become more like that of the Fon, who had battled them into submission in the eighteenth century and chased them off the best of their land.

The Nago remained a very scattered people, little groups of them the length and breadth of Benin. Although they managed to keep some kind of hold on Savé, the Nago had a tough, Fon-bothered history and consequently the population of the French Caribbean has a high percentage of people of Nago descent.

At the present-day palace of Savé, you'd only know you were visiting a king because it said so on the gate. REMOVE YOUR SHOES, it also said. Children were streaming in the gate, coming home from school with their satchels and khaki uniforms. The King's nephews, nieces, grandchildren, grandnephews . . .

A teenage grandson introduced himself as Bertin, told us the King was out back and of course we could visit. He led us through a side gate into a farmyard.

'There's the King by the steps – no, no need to take off your shoes, you'll be outside. The King likes to sit outside in the evening, to see the animals and take the air.'

There were bicycle chickens and midget goats clambering all round the scruffy yard. In the shade of the palace wall the cuddly, grandfatherly-looking King sat on a deckchair, surrounded by very old elders – on upturned buckets and crates or lounging on the steps. One had a book in his hand, reading aloud. He stopped as we approached and Bertin explained us. Used to kings now, I thought I'd better drop to the ground face-first.

'No, no,' Bertin said. 'Please sit. My grandfather doesn't need that.'

The King said something as Bertin found us crates to sit on.

'My grandfather says he thanks you for your respect but he is only the hereditary leader of the community, called a king, but there is no true king but God Almighty.'

A young woman came with a bowl of water for us, handing it to Isidore first. He tipped a splash of water on to the ground before drinking.

'It's a courtesy,' he told me. 'To give something to drink to the dead of the house, the ancestors.'

I asked if I should do the same. The elders shook their heads.

'This is a Christian house,' said Bertin. 'My grandfather doesn't believe in these old ways.'

The old King smiled benignly and asked if we were Catholics. I figured it would be best to say yes; Isidore said the same. The King looked at Isidore with surprise and spoke in Nago. Isidore, bottomless well of abilities, also spoke Nago.

'His majesty is telling me to concentrate on my Catholicism, there is more wisdom in it than in the old ways of our ancestors. We are all only men before God. He is here to guide his people but he is only one of them.'

The King was dressed in plain, many-times-washed robes and old leather sandals; no jewellery or fancy royal equipment. Isidore seemed as taken with the small, serene King as I was, accepting the kindly toned telling-off sheepishly but without resentment.

The elder with the book in his hands spoke to me; I realized he was also the elder with one eye: 'The King is quite tired now. As you arrived we were reading from the Bible. The King likes to hear some words from the Bible every evening. Then, as he goes to rest, he contemplates what he has heard and lets it guide him the next day, so he can help us all the best way he can find.'

The one-eyed elder put on glasses and opened his Bible. Everyone shuffled a little to get comfortable, like a big treat was coming. The elder was about to begin, then looked at Isidore. 'Our Bible is in Yoruba – can you tell her about the reading afterwards?'

'Of course,' Isidore said.

Bertin had a better idea. 'One moment, please.' He ran into the palace and came back with a Gideon Bible in French. 'This way she can follow.'

Everyone murmured contentedly.

The elder announced the chapter and verse, Bertin flicked the pages for me. 'Isaiah one. One to nineteen.'

I looked but didn't read. We had the last of the sun now, a breeze rustling a plump ancient tree in the corner of the yard. Chickens scratched, goats murmured – over the wall children laughed and made slap-footed runs in flip-flops; carefully spoken words of Yoruba closed the King's eyes in meditation.

'Hosea four, verse five,' Bertin whispered. Thin pages slipped gently on. An arc of tiny birds sailed out of the palace eaves and vanished across the red-touched sky.

'Acts of the Apostles. Three, nine.'

Isidore's hurt seemed to be fading as the elder's voice stroked over him in the rhythmic rise and fall of Yoruba. There was a drum in the sound of Yoruba, some times hard-struck, this time soft passes over the skin.

The reading ended. The King opened his sleepy eyes and spoke. With the elders, Isidore listened attentively, nodded occasionally.

Bertin whispered: 'The King gives his interpretation. What God has promised us, comes to us.'

The quiet, gentle group were still sitting in the dwindling light as we left the yard. I'd given a small gift of money to the King; he'd blessed me and handed it to an elder. The elder, Bertin explained, who kept charge of money that belonged to the community. The King didn't keep such gifts for himself.

'I like the Nago people very much,' Isidore reflected. 'The simplicity of them.'

He drove away for the night with a contented smile on his face. I felt as calm and at one with the world as a little Buddha.

I didn't contemplate the Acts of the Apostles so much as the behaviour of Isidore, in light of all the new information.

I decided I had to be as straight with him as I possibly could – not let him down by dashing his hopes that I'd turned up as some kind of good luck at last. I'd be very clear about what I could promise him. I couldn't be the embodiment of good fortune but I could make it my job to be such a nice customer; he'd always look back and see he occasionally found some fairness in his life. Then perhaps he'd start to expect some fairness from the future, not be waiting around for the piece of string that would turn up to wreck everything.

Big-backed thoughts of an overtired brain. I had some kind of string-related nightmare and was woken very early by an unnecessary amount of roosters in the back yard of the Bosoms of Savé Hotel. Isidore turned up full of beans, banging on about old mates up at the drivers' hostel who thought he was the bees' pyjamas and kept him chatting all night. Ten minutes after breakfast he was playing his most jangly no-tune music, driving Formula One pace and talking incessantly about the Peugeot's need for new tyres, new seat covers and a man he knew in Cotonou who could get them cheap and if he earned good money working for me he could get a new rear bumper and buy a television but did I remember I said I would try to find him a white wife but I hadn't said any more about that why hadn't I said any more about that?

Restore his faith in the fairness of life? If I'd had a piece of string I'd have thrown it at him.

9

The Yam-Stuffed Dogs of War

When Isidore said game park, I thought giraffes. I was going to say how much I'd love to see a giraffe but the game-park lecture wasn't finished: 'This way is to Pendjari Parc, the other way is Parc W. Each park has a section for hunting and a section for looking. Pendjari is much more developed by the French. They like the scenery and they make a big fuss about the people there, the Somba. Which is idiotic because most of the Somba don't even speak French. And there are Somba, especially the women, who never saw a white person to this day.'

'Isn't the President a Somba?'

'Kérékou is not typical. He's a very well-educated man. Anyway, we'll go in the Pendjari Parc direction and you'll see. The region is called the Atakora. There are very interesting . . .'

'Will we see giraffes?'

'Giraffes? What do you want with them? They're animals, will that be very interesting for the book? All the tourists rush to see the animals and see nothing else. I'm surprised you're talking about giraffes. And if we have to go into the game park it will be expensive, very expensive.'

I tried to think of an intellectual reason for a jaunt in the safari park. But it was just for myself. A childish yen to see a wild giraffe.

Isidore relented. 'We can see the prices if you like but the French have it all sewn up. Also, it is May. The end of the dry season. They close the parks when the rain comes. But you know who your driver is, he can arrange things. I suppose if they're not used to them people would like to read about giraffes.'

So, book editor was a new job Isidore had given himself.

With his next breath he was doing his main job – being Lord High Chief of Bossing Everyone Around: 'See this village? It's called Peanut. All these women, all they sell is peanuts.' He parked the car. 'Get out, have a look.'

There were wooden stalls of peanuts, upturned basins used as peanut stalls, right-way-up basins full of peanuts . . . peanuts in plastic bags, shelled and unshelled peanuts, roasted peanuts, salted roasted peanuts . . . We bought a couple of small bags to show willing, then took a walk into the village of Peanut. Isidore seemed to be looking for something. He heard a noise coming from a hut and put his head in the door.

'Come, this is what I wanted to show you.'

A machine for shelling peanuts. A rectangular metal frame on legs. A hand-turned grinder on top. Broken shells trapped by a grille, peanuts falling through. It seemed very hot work. The women demonstrated for a while then stood around looking embarrassed. So did I. Isidore picked a handful of broken shells out of the machine.

'These can be used, too, for making house bricks or for the fire. The peanut is a very useful plant. Do you know how it grows?'

Among many callings he'd missed, he'd have made an excellent *Blue Peter* presenter.

Somewhere north of Peanut, we passed the *yovo* line. '*Batture!* *Batture!*' Ending like 'hooray', the word for whites in the north was the new yell from the roadside. Except if we passed the lanky, cattle-herding Fulani. They'd just lean on their long herding sticks and stare.

'You see how many more Fulani there are here? The other tribes here are Bariba and Dende and some other tribes. The north is full of small tribes. The Somba are called that altogether but really they are many tribes, the Detamari, Natemba, Okoma . . . many. They all joined forces in war and slaving times but they are slightly different and . . . Oh, look at these imbeciles!'

He thumped on the horn. A small round Peugeot, grandfather to ours, swung off the road. Three men were waiting, with the fattest, woolliest sheep I've ever seen. The tiny car oozed passengers and luggage already, but somehow, with everyone sitting on the front seat and trailing luggage out of the windows, they managed to shove and heave, and heave, the monster sheep into the back seat, and the three men followed.

'I don't believe they did that.'

'Oh, these bush taxis load up too much. I hope they pay double for that sheep. Bush taxis is a terrible job. If you don't overload, you don't make enough money to survive. If the police set up a road block and catch you overloaded they'll fine you, or want a bribe. There's more road blocks now because they're also fining the drivers for drinking. Good, really – they have an inestimable number of accidents, inestimable! The drivers often keep themselves going with rum and kola nuts. Some of them drive all day, totally out of their minds. You are very lucky to have me.'

Probably. The rum was always over-proof and kola nuts had the bracing effect of being caffeine packed but were also inconveniently hallucinogenic. I could see only one advantage a bush-taxi driver might have over Isidore.

'I expect you're more expensive.'

He laughed. 'Much more. But *yovos* don't like to be in big accidents to save money, am I right?'

Depended on the *yovo*. There were *yovos* who travelled in Africa as if saving money was the object of the journey. A peculiar thing to do, really, in poor countries, where people had the notion that tourism might be an industry for them to make a little money out of. Budget tourism made certain guide-book companies rich, made 'adventure' tour operators rich – but not the locals of the countries being adventured into on a shoestring. It was a weird kind of neo-colonialism, the way the youth of wealthier countries were allowed to forge their characters in other people's poverty. But who was I, log in my eye, to think this thought?

When we reached the northern capital, Natitingou, I needed cigarettes and Isidore needed to find a phone box, to check his children were still alive. Giving me a quick cross-examination to confirm I was halfway competent with Beninois money, Isidore left me to shop alone.

The shop was a great barn of a place, habitual stocking-up point for safari tourists. It was also, apparently, the fun place to be in Natitingou. At a small bar in the corner, a whoop of teenagers were fixing up coloured lights and playing James Brown very loud. One boy, who'd probably seen James Brown on the endless stream of music videos shown on Benin TV, demonstrated the way you might behave on stage if you were James Brown. And, indeed, a sex machine.

It would take Isidore a while to get through on the none-too-funky phone lines, so I could take my time, enjoy myself listening to music that wasn't Nana Mouskouri, watching the James Brown boys and trying to remember what I'd come in to buy in the first place, getting bedazzled by the piled shelves of catering-pack French food.

When Isidore peered in the window to see what had become of me, I hurried to join the checkout queue behind a very grouchy, grey-bearded Australian tour guide. I'd seen his protégés among their camping equipment in two big orange trucks in the car park. What I couldn't believe about them was that they were *inside* the trucks and two of them were playing cards. They weren't lured out to see where the James Brown was coming from, weren't even watching the streams of people on their way to the evening market with all manner of baggage on their heads and clothes on their backs . . .

The grey beard was berating his two African assistants, who might have been Ghanaians. The Australian was in sweaty old shorts and a filthy T-shirt; the Ghanaians wore neat jeans and spotless white cotton shirts. They were smiling as they brought baskets of shopping to put with the Australians'.

'What have you bought these for?' he yapped, taking tins of tuna fish out of their baskets.

'It's fish, very nice,' said one of the Ghanaians.

'That's useless. We haven't got a bloody tin opener!'

The Ghanaians looked politely quizzical. With all the equipment strapped to the trucks, all the little Swiss Army Knife kits adventure tourists always had, all the equipment on sale in this store, including several types of tin opener, what was he talking about?

'Well, all right, but you work out how to open them,' Grey Beard said, piling the tuna-fish tins into his basket. The checkout girl had already begun ringing up his purchases. 'No, no, hold on, start again – haven't you rung that bread twice?'

'No,' she said.

'Well, start again so I can see what you're doing.'

She wasn't having this. 'I didn't ring it twice. Did you see me?'

'Yes,' I said, although I hadn't.

The Ghanaians smiled at me. The Australian ignored me. 'Well, start again anyway. How can anyone think straight with this bloody music?'

To save herself the trouble of splitting his head with a can of tuna fish, the girl started again.

'Sorry about this,' the Australian said to me. I ignored him. Then he looked at the Ghanaians who'd sensibly decided to forget about him and watch the James Brown show. 'Are you guys helping me or not?'

They went to put the purchases in cardboard boxes while the Australian watched the checkout girl like a snake waiting to pounce. Although they'd maintained a smiling surface, the Ghanaians knew what century it was. As one packed the cans of tuna, he held a can up and said to me: 'In Ghana we open these with knives.'

So I was right about Ghana. 'We do the same in London,' I said, letting my eye drift to the display of can openers. 'It's not very difficult.'

The trucks were starting up as I came out; the Ghanaians were driving.

'What took you so long?' Isidore grumbled.

'An Australian. Not very nice,' I said.

Isidore looked surprised. 'These?' he nodded towards the noisily departing trucks. 'I've seen them before. They come all the way from Ghana in those trucks, up to Pendjari and back again.'

'I think Australians are nice,' Isidore continued. 'I admire them. They're poor but they're still determined to travel.'

'What makes you think they're poor?'

'Look how they travel, crushed in there like cattle. Sometimes they sleep in those trucks. Or in tents. I never saw them in a hotel. Once I saw them go to the market, buy meat and vegetables and cook them on fires at the roadside like we do. It's always puzzled me how people that poor can afford to travel at all.'

'Isidore, they're not poor. They're mean.'

'Really?'

'Do you know what would happen to a truckload of Africans in scruffy clothes cooking food at the roadside in Australia? Same in England. But that type of Australian . . . Even him being here is just weird.'

Then, despite confinement in a small Peugeot, I found I'd leapt on a soapbox. Fifteen minutes of Isidore's life passed slowly while I ranted about the mistreatment of Australian Aboriginals.

'That's very sad,' Isidore said when I'd done. 'I never knew there were black people there. Well, I don't know about you but I think we should get our dinner.'

It had been the same when he'd asked me if it was true there were people in Europe who didn't like black people and I'd told him at length about the Stephen Lawrence case. It was like he hadn't heard me. Maybe it was too much information of a kind he hadn't expected. Information that made him reel too much to comment. Or maybe it was boredom.

★

We took a side road full of deep holes; unconcerned, Isidore drove and talked.

'I think you'll like this hotel. There is a French place, very fancy, but the prices are French. This place is like your hotel in Cotonou, a bit strange. It was built as a hotel but then in the revolution it was taken over as police headquarters. A few years ago they made it a hotel again, some local people have the lease. The police still have their station at the back and visiting police chiefs stay here, so it's very safe.'

The Hôtel Belle Vue had a circular, 1950s colonial-style high-terraced mansion as its central building and small, square, terraced buildings dotted around it housing the accommodation. It did have a *belle vue* from the bougainvillaea-draped terrace, out across the town to the mountains beyond, catching a clean breeze and scents from the plants lovingly tended in pots and beds around the main building.

The dining room was laid with white linen and crystal fit for the highest police chiefs in copdom. We were the only diners. I ordered something called American Chicken from the menu of mixed local and French dishes – I was hungry, I didn't want an adventure. For some reason, perhaps because it came with chips and the waiter described it as chicken with herbs, I imagined a Natitingou version of Kentucky Fried Chicken that would be tasty and plump . . . But it arrived the usual old cycle-weary collection of bones and sinew.

'Oh dear,' Isidore scowled at my plate. 'Bicycle chicken.'

'I know,' I said. 'I thought because it was American it would be car chicken.'

Isidore laughed like a drain and kept laughing over 'car chicken' for days afterwards. At least I didn't bore him all the time.

I know I was weedy about the food, living mostly on rice, vegetable sauces and omelettes, but the food here could go very wrong for me. The inland fish from rivers tasted of mud and had teeth; the sea fish were invariably the type with an armoury of small bones. The chicken we know about, pork would have been foolish, beef was like shoes and any other meat available was overwhelming, or frightening, and made ancient Celtic taboos rise up and warn me I'd run mad after a mouthful.

I had tried a popular Yoruba dish of stewed oxtail and greens, tasting too wintry strong to be eating in a hot country. Bravely I'd supped on tree-rat cutlets – tree rat has a very powerful, gamey flavour. (I say gamey, but I always think people say gamey as a polite way of saying 'gone off'.) I'd declined a pot of calf cheeks and a plate of sheep's God-knows-what. Goat I didn't mind but nobody seemed to eat it. I did mind snails as big as your head that Isidore had picked up to show me in the market, their sucky faces and antennae waving in my face: 'Ah, these, the Fon love to eat these. We slice them with a little lemon and some garlic ... delicious. High protein.'

I don't know about the Fon, but it sounded to me like the French had got among the cuisine with their peculiar ways and dreamt up the dishes of Satan for the dinner table.

It could have been worse. I could have been in Burkina Faso and opened a pot of baked bats. Isidore said that when you cut open a bat's stomach you'd find a baby bat inside. If you cut open the baby bat's stomach, it had a baby inside ... I don't know how long the Russian-doll-with-bats business went on before you managed to get to the core of your dinner, but it wouldn't be one I'd be trying. Even if Isidore did recommend it as an excellent dish for preventing witchcraft.

There was a scruffy old man shuffling about watering plants on the Belle Vue terrace. Isidore whispered, 'You'll think he's the gardener. But actually he's the boss. His wife must be away or we'd have heard her by now. I think she's called Françoise, a very frightening woman. Come, let's buy him a drink.'

Isidore wasn't buying the boss a drink to console him for having a frightening wife – after a brief preamble about the progress of the gardens, he shifted to his real purpose, a conversation about four-wheel drives to take me to the safari park.

'Ah, a shame,' said the boss. 'The one we usually have here, my wife has taken it to Cotonou on business. She wants to buy some special furniture for her computer.' He smiled, not frightened, clearly delighted with his Françoise. 'She has a computer here now, she understands it completely. Isn't that amazing? But you know what she's like.'

Isidore nodded and said the old man's wife was 'formidable'.

'So, she will be gone a few days. She has some relatives to visit, too, so I can't help you I'm afraid. Besides, you know the safari park has just closed, officially.'

'Officially?' Isidore didn't need two bites at a hint.

'You know how it is.' The boss shrugged. 'It only closed two days ago. You could plead with them, say your journey was delayed or something. Ask when you get near there, at Tanguiéta. I'm from Tanguiéta myself; we are very helpful people.'

'Still a chance of a giraffe, then.' Isidore beamed at me as we set out early next morning.

I was getting just as excited about finding the people who lived beyond Natitingou, the Somba, Kérékou's people. Isidore wasn't too fussed about them: 'They are very wild. Very tough and none of them go to school. Kérékou only went to school because a priest found him tending cows as a small child. He talked to him and thought, "This child is very intelligent, he should be educated." He argued with the parents until they allowed him to take Kérékou to the Jesuit school. He was exceptional in school. At fourteen he went to the military academy. He was exceptional there and then exceptional in the army. Then he was President. Very clever. Very tough.'

'So he's a Catholic?'

'He's a communist. He was. Who knows what he is today, mostly I think he's just interested in staying President.'

Kérékou's nickname was 'The Chameleon'. Chameleons were supposed to be able to walk across branches without breaking them – that is, Kérékou could be boss and no one would even notice his light touch of command. Chameleon was more apt for his political and religious shifts. When he defeated Western-favoured Soglo in 1996, he declared himself a born-again Christian; a useful way to get a lot of American aid money. He went so far as to say that Soglo, who had declared vodou the national religion, had been removed from office by Jesus's intervention.

Who knows, maybe Jesus did run about in the 1996 election campaign making death threats to election and court officials to ensure Kérékou's return, regardless of what the voters wanted.

I'd thought Kérékou's re-election had been puzzling. But apparently no one had been more puzzled than the majority who hadn't voted for him. Ninety-six had been one of those Florida-style elections, many a ballot box slipping into a swamp, and a defeated politician helpless amid accusations of 'sour grapes'.

Kérékou had bailed out of power and allowed democratic elections just as the economy was collapsing and revolution looked certain. During the short tenure that Soglo did have, Kérékou orchestrated at least two attempts at a military coup. So he'd never really been away.

The country's majority, the Fon, were traditionally wealthier and better educated than the northern population. Their natural allegiance was to Sorbonne-educated liberal Soglo, but as the Fon were more likely to have status and property to lose, they were not the type to start a violent revolt. This didn't mean they were happy with the situation.

'You know most of the police and the army are Somba,' Isidore said. 'Because they're thick. Easy to order them around. And they're tough. Big and wild people. You've seen their faces, even the women, barbaric.'

The Somba's side to the story was, of course, that when the Fon had been in charge they'd sold everybody. Under the French administration it was the Fon who had posts in civil administration, business opportunities . . . Now it was the northerners' turn. Although Soglo had poured resources into the north to show there was no favouritism, the northerners preferred their man Chameleon in the presidential palace. And Kérékou, for all his faults, created a balance in this country that colonialism had cobbled together from unmatched peoples.

★

What Isidore meant by the faces was the Somba scarification. He pointed out a couple of tall, wiry Somba women as we stopped for petrol. He called them over; they wouldn't come until he held out two tempting empty mineral-water bottles – very useful for storing oil, or carrying water in the fields. They stared a moment, made a dash and grab for the bottles and strolled off waving them triumphantly to some friends over the road. I'd had enough time for a good look. The women's cheeks were crisscrossed with lines, like someone had prepared them for life as herringbone-check swatches. Kérékou had the same checky-cheek scarification.

The scarification was no longer universal. The younger generation of Somba might be excused the chopped-up face; but other adult initiation rites were commonly practised, a source of horrified fascination to Isidore.

'When a man is going to be married he dances in a circle of men in front of the bride's family. He has to smile and dance, smile and dance while the men whip him with whips. Whip him with whips till he bleeds, but still he has to smile and dance. One hour, two hours. If he shows tiredness and pain, then he is not strong enough to be a husband.'

I never saw the whipping but I did see young Somba men dancing at the village of Boukoumbé. They held small sticks in their hands, representing weapons, and to the accompanying high-speed drum they went round and round in a circle, knees bent, up straight, knees bent, up straight, knees bent . . . They did this from eleven in the morning, with a skull-bleaching sun beating down on them, until six in the evening. Only occasional ten-minute breaks to chat to the crowd.

Apparently they'd done the same thing from seven to midnight the previous evening before a hearty drinking spree.

The Somba dance was part of their equivalent of a *gelede*. An animist people, they needed to summon strong spirits from the earth for the new agricultural season. They also believed in re-balancing the male and female energy of the earth and the community. These strapping fellows did their military-looking, testosterone-laden dance dressed in their sisters' clothes.

I'd arrived before they were ready; a local elder said the dancers were getting changed. I imagined the traditional Somba costume I'd seen in photographs – leather loincloths, strings of beads and Viking-style helmets with horns. But the dancers stomped out of their houses in skirts, bras, women's wigs and· pointy-rimmed ladies' glasses . . . Then danced like they were out to show Arnold Schwarzenegger and several big male lions what macho really meant.

The Somba of certain regions were accepting enough of tourism to let their dances be photographed, for a fee. I didn't think this made what they were doing any way artificial, but the search for authentic Somba life and suspicion of fee paying seemed to obsess French tourists.

One couple outside the Belle Vue were badgering their tour guide about seeing 'the real Somba' as they loaded their four-wheel drive.

'It will be the real Somba you're taking us to see, the real ones?'

He said wearily, 'Oh, they're all real.'

'Not just doing it for tourists?'

'Doing what?'

'Living their old-fashioned lives.'

'They live how they live. They don't know it's old fashioned.'

One of the educated, modern-living Somba, who'd gone on to be the President, had been appalled to see a French documentary about his people living their old-fashioned, real-African lives, wearing hardly a stitch of clothing. He'd rushed around making them put on trousers, go to school and stop being quite so authentic. It made the place look untidy, and backward.

Despite Kérékou's trouser fussing and the frequently passing tourists, even the Somba close to town and the main safari-park road seemed reserved and detached, seeing no reason to make more than cosmetic changes to what was a successful and enjoyable way of life. But Isidore knew where to find Somba who weren't used to the French and truckloads of Australians passing the back gate.

He'd planned a route into the most inaccessible territory for a small Peugeot, not telling his customer until very late in the adventure that he had never actually done the journey before.

The red dust from the road north covered us and the car in minutes. A glance in the wing mirror told me the sad truth – I'd be spending the rest of the day with clown-orange hair and a tomato complexion.

There wasn't much unfolding of the Atakora's red and green hills before I saw the *tata somba*, the famous high castles the Somba people lived in. The *tata somba* had been built the same way for at least five hundred years, turreted fortresses that looked oddly like northern-French châteaux. Odder still, the greener swathes of the tree-littered countryside were reminiscent of parts of Normandy.

The *tata somba* had only one small entrance on the ground floor, for livestock. There was a middle level for storage and the people lived on the top, getting home via wooden ladders that could be pulled up quickly in case of trouble. They slept in the round turrets, cooked and communed on the central flat roof.

They'd built the houses this way because their fertile hunting grounds were frequently invaded. When they retreated to the top of their castles they could repel invaders with arrows, spears or boiling water. In slave-raiding times the high castles came into their own. The robust Somba made excellent slaves, but catching them was hardly worth the hassle. Because another smart thing the Somba did was not to live in communities. There was only one family per castle. Another family's castle would never be closer than 500 yards away – reputedly the distance an arrow could be shot. It would be a world of trouble, even with guns, to capture a Somba castle – and then you'd get only one family. You'd have to do the whole thing over again to get another single family out of their fortress. All this and you were travelling through mountains then, not the weather- and time-crushed sandstone hills of today.

Living under a big sky, the Somba believed the stars were our souls. Our unborn souls came from the stars and when we died we returned there. The night sky was full of people yet to be and people who had gone from earth. The sun, the moon, the wind and the earth were their divinities. Their animism had broader strokes, less cluttered with detail than vodou; the beliefs were similar in the conviction that each human's spirit is part of the overall lifeforce. When alive, you are responsible for your lifeforce – you should ensure it honoured the world around you, so that when you died, it returned to the universe, strong and positive. Being a hunting, wide-ranging people, the Somba didn't have particular sites for honouring their divinities and ancestors – the gods and ancestors were all out there with them, in the wind, the earth and the stars.

Adding to the impression of French scenery, the road was very straight and shaded with neat avenues of trees at any stretch crossing a stream.

'Yes, this road was the French,' Isidore said. 'They always put trees like this. We'll turn off at Boukoumbé and you'll see how bad the road gets. The French usually turn back at Boukoumbé so they can sleep in Natitingou, or they go on the better straight road, through Tanguiéta to the French encampment and hotel at Porga. Not us. We'll take the back way to Tanguiéta. You'll be able to see Somba till you're sick.'

Sure enough, past the campsite at Boukoumbé, the road narrowed, bloomed with holes and the tree avenues disappeared. There were more people, though, friendly and curious.

'I thought they'd be more nervous here.'

'No, they think my old car is a bush taxi. On the big road they think all cars are tourists who might annoy them. Or take their photo to sell for money. To them that's like stealing, because the Somba are very strict to charge money for photos. Out here they don't know that – they're just interested to see who's in the bush taxi today. Look at these men – they're going to eat that.'

Three men were examining a dead dog at the roadside, prodding it with long sticks and discussing it.

'They're deciding how much time it's been there, if it's still good to eat.'

'They eat dog?'

'They love to eat dog. Haven't you seen them with their dogs all the time?'

I had. Lean, low dogs following Somba men across the landscape or fleeting somewhere on their own.

'I thought they were pets, not livestock.'

'They hunt with the dogs. They train them very well to hunt, and they put magic potions on their eyes so the dogs can see in the dark – that way, the dogs can follow an animal underground into its hole. Then the dogs start to get older, slower and less useful for hunting. So they keep them near the house. They feed them on rum and yams until they get very fat, then they eat them. It's very good.'

'You've eaten it?'

'Once, to see what it was like. It's good. Like old tree rat. You wouldn't know it was a dog. But still, I'd prefer not to do it again.' He laughed. 'But you! You would never eat it, even taste it.'

'Maybe I would, to see.'

'You wouldn't, you're a complete coward in food.'

To avoid conceding this point, I shared one of my favourite snippets of trivia with Isidore: that apparently dog meat was used by the Chinese as an aphrodisiac because its indigestible nature made you stay awake all night. Maybe that was why the Somba had so many children?

'They don't need indigestion to encourage them. They just have lots. But what else is there to do out here except make children?'

Up in their breezy high castles, running across green slopes hunting and making babies of an evening . . . I told Isidore I might run away to be a Somba, it seemed a good life.

'Not for a woman working in fields and having all the babies out here; hardly any medical care or cleanliness.'

Ah, not running and hunting, then.

'And in winter it's terrible here. Terrible. You now what a Harmattan is?'

'A hot wind from the desert.'

'Who told you it was hot? It's cold and full of dust and makes a terrible noise. That's why they make their castles round. In Harmattan times they sleep in the round rooms so the wind goes round and they hardly go outside for the wind and the cold and the dust. We get it a little in the south, but up here it's terrible.'

'I read somewhere it sends people mad.'

'Of course it does. But they are all mad together up here, so they don't know it.'

We passed a collection of dusty children and their dogs by the roadside. The dogs were at the alert, racing-fit phase of their dogs' lives. The children were pulling bits of cardboard on strings for toys. Or as a preferred choice of pet. Pets they wouldn't have upset themselves eating.

'Oh, their life is bizarre,' Isidore continued. 'Look at those children, filthy. The Somba never wash from the time they're a child until their dying day.'

Having just passed some Somba girls washing in a stream, I pointed out that this wasn't true.

'I don't mean women. Women always wash all over the world. I mean the men. After childhood they only wash for circumcision and marriage. How would you like that?'

'When I do run away to be a Somba, I'll make my husband wash.'

'Make a Somba? Have you seen their muscles? How will you make him? Nothing will make him wash. They're not interested in pleasing you. They grow vegetables, they hunt, grow vegetables, hunt, out in the sun without hats, never washing, getting blacker and blacker until they die.'

I still thought there was something about it. This top-of-the-world, red and green landscape . . . Obviously it would be the life of a Somba man I'd want. And once you'd got used to it, why wash? There'd only be more dust the next day so why not wait till the rains came to get clean? Dance about half-naked in a field in the rain being at one with the stars. Fantastic.

I watched two rangy Somba men follow their dogs over the horizon – striding, striding and gone.

Of course, the apparently free Somba men did have that pre-marriage whipping ceremony to worry about. And the malecircumcision ceremony. They'd be isolated from their family in a small, round, windowless hut. Sealed in. Going to the toilet in there, fed only on water and millet gruel passed in through a slit in the straw roof. Seven days, they'd be in there, without a moment's peace because at night the other men of the family would bang on the roof and walls of the hut, thump on drums and make a constant racket to keep them awake. When they emerged, blinking from the rowdy darkness, they'd be washed, taken away amid dancing and drumming, to be cut and chanted at. All this would happen when they were about seventeen years old. Somba men didn't have to drink lager and fight on football terraces; the route to make them feel like men was clear and memorable.

It was inferno hot. I was throwing mineral water down my neck and sweating it out like a very efficient water-using machine, so by now I'd two empty water bottles at my feet – useful containers for someone.

I told Isidore to slow down as we approached a tree clump indicating a stream under the road. A woman and a girl were sitting on a low wall, with bowls on their knees, taking time to chat before collecting water. Suddenly the girl noticed the car slowing down; she screamed, threw her bowl in the air and ran into the stream below. The older woman turned to say something to her, then glanced back at the car. She saw me, flung her bowl in the air and ran into the stream, and on, grabbing the girl by the elbow, urging her to run. They ran way, way across the bush until they were far behind us.

Finally they took a pause to look back. Isidore was laughing like a crazy rum-fed hound. 'Watch,' he said.

He started to reverse the car rapidly, roaring backwards towards the poor women, who fled again – and this time they kept going.

'Stop, stop, that's mean!' I shouted at him. Isidore had stopped. No longer able to drive, he was laughing so much. It was sort of funny, but I felt too sorry for the women to allow that. 'Stop it. It wasn't funny.'

He paid no attention. 'Oh, these people.' Tears were rolling down his cheeks. 'First the little one's scared of the car, then they're scared of you!'

'It's mean. They've left their bowls behind.' At least they didn't have maize or something precious in them.

'We can't take them their bowls. If you get out of the car to look for them, they'll kill themselves.'

He assembled enough sense to change gear and drive forward again. A hundred yards down the road we came by a group of young men. They seemed uneasy but didn't shriek and flee. One of them spoke French. Once he'd laughed with Isidore over the story, then shared it with his mates, he asked me to give him the water bottles.

'I'll go and find the girls. Explain what you wanted.'

'What did they think I wanted?'

'Oh, these girls, they must be from way out in the bush. They still think people in cars will come and take them.'

'Take them?'

'Take them away and cut off their heads.' Him, his mates and Isidore thought this was hilarious.

As I turned to wave goodbye to the men, I thought I saw two female figures stand up from the bush grass, far, far away.

The world is not small.

Just before his head fell off, no need to take him and chop it off, Isidore finally stopped laughing. Until the diversion with the girls, a question had been tiptoeing around in the back of my mind. I decided I'd found a way to phrase it.

'Isidore, I have a question that's a bit delicate.'

'You want to piss?'

'No, no, not that.' I'd got over any delicacy about that a long while ago. 'No, this is a delicate question and if you don't want to answer, just say you can't answer.'

There was a pause. He seemed to be bracing himself for the worst. 'OK. Ask your question.'

'Is there circumcision for the women in Benin?'

He seemed relieved this was all it was. He answered readily, with anthropological detachment.

'Not with the Fon. Generally not in the south, I think. Up here, I know the Somba do it; so do other northern tribes, like the Bariba, maybe the Fulani – they're Moslems. It's usual with Moslems. When I was young I was friends with a Somba policeman. I asked him why they did this, you know, they cut off the clitoris.'

I'd been trying not to say clitoris, or any female-undercarriage words, but Isidore seemed blithely content to keep saying clitoris and to drive round potholes at the same time.

'My friend said there were two reasons. The first reason was because in the olden days the Somba women used to extend their clitorises. They'd pull it and pull it, even put little weights on it so it was big, like with a horse, protruding. They thought this was attractive, and so did the men. But then one woman who'd made hers very big suffocated a baby with it while giving birth. When this happened, the elders met and decided from then on the clitoris should be cut off.'

What kind of a legend was that?

I said nothing, wondering about the time when men saw the clitoris as a fine thing, the bigger the better. Did it really happen? Maybe way back, when the world over, from Mesopotamia to the forests of Europe, there was supposed to have been a dominant goddess-culture. Was there a cultural shift, the coming of male religions, Islam, Christianity, some external influence that made the elders change the culture? Or did cultural traditions change because of one suffocated baby? Was the exaggerated tale of what women might do, if left to do what they wanted with their bodies, invented later, to back up a cultural convention?

Isidore still had to explain the second reason. It was more predictable.

'The man's second explanation was that the clitoris itched the women. So they'd start to rub it and this made them want men too much. They'd get crazy for men and end up as prostitutes.'

'Oh,' I said.

★

Female circumcision, practised in regions of Africa, the Middle East and some of Indonesia, was referred to by campaigning organizations and Western feminists as Female Genital Mutilation. African women's organizations felt this encouraged a perception of them as the world's eternal victims and that, in its anger, the term Female Genital Mutilation had a subtext of accusations of savagery: because this was something that Third World people did, it could be dismissed without comprehension as barbaric.

I would never defend it. Women who refused circumcision could be forced into it or excluded from society, often in societies where survival depended on inclusion. But one of the contributing factors to the continuation of the practice has been the criticism and attempts to discourage it. Particularly from Western missionaries, charities, journalists and medical practitioners.

Female circumcision was not a religious requirement – it was a cultural convention. Opposition to the practice that was Western led or influenced often entrenched the men of the community against what they saw as a post-colonial criticism of their society. And their argument – that the individualism and sexual freedom of Western women was not all it seemed – was, of course, accurate. We weren't doing so well. In order to look young, we paid dearly for surgical mutilation of our faces, had fat sucked out of our thighs, put silicone in our breasts and threw up our dinners (or simply didn't eat at all) – in order to distort our appearance to suit our social conventions.

Burkina Faso, Ghana, Togo and the Central African Republic had outlawed female circumcision, but it was not illegal in Benin. Studies showed that female circumcision was still practised by about twenty per cent of the Fon people. Fifty per cent of the Yoruba and sixty per cent of the northern tribes, the Bariba and Somba tribes, practised the removal of the clitoris in puberty.

Isidore always tried to be honest with me; I think he just didn't know all the facts. The diminution of the practice had probably come from decisions made by the Fon women themselves. The banning of the practice in Ghana came from a grassroots movement among women. In Senegal, many communities abandoned the practice overnight when a consensus among women simply decided this 6,000-year-old practice would no longer happen. A key factor in the sudden change seemed to be the spread of education for women. What the key factor would be in stopping us deciding that not eating until we disappeared was the best way to gain social approval – well, who knows?

I didn't have an extensive debate about female circumcision and the meaning of female life with Isidore at the time. I needed to do some research, and thinking. And he'd ended the conversation quite soon after it had begun, not because he wanted to change the subject, but because he saw a gang of Somba children by the road and stopped to ask them about something that was preying on his mind more than clitorises. Where on earth were we?

He didn't like the children's answer. He started down the road of gravel scree and sudden water-worn gullies with a scowl.

'I thought we would be nearer Kobli by now. It's still ten miles. On this road that could be another hour. And then that's another two hours to Tanguiéta. This road is much worse than I thought.'

I could see he was getting tired. It was close to four o'clock and we'd had nothing to eat since breakfast. We should have set out earlier but on leaving the petrol station some electrical wire in the car had come loose, looking like disaster but just being a time waster. So, cleverly, we'd left Natitingou late, with half a packet of biscuits and mineral water for provisions.

'Maybe we should eat something at Kobli.'

'There'll be nothing for you to eat there. I know some people there, they'll give me something, but you better eat the biscuits.'

I started to ponder what might happen if we broke down out here. There were fewer and fewer people around and the road deteriorated by the mile. We probably should have had a four-wheel drive, tents, a satellite phone and full SAS rations. Still, someone might come past on a bicycle, eventually.

Out of the hot-red nowhere, a lorryload of sweaty men rounded a corner and pulled up beside us, waving their arms as if warning of some calamity on the road ahead. Isidore greeted them affably but quickly plunged into a ferocious disagreement. He shouted, they all shouted, and he spun the car off fast round the gravelly corner.

'*C'est impossible. C'est pas possible*!' he muttered furiously. 'I'm so sick of Africans.'

I liked them, myself, so I said nothing. It took a while before he was collected enough to give an ordered recap of the argument.

'Those men wanted me to give a lift to a man who had to go to Kobli for a tyre for his truck that had broken down. There, that must be it by the road here.' We passed a small, mournfully lopsided lorry. 'I said I couldn't take him as the car was hired privately to the *yovo*. They asked me to ask you. I said you were my employer, I couldn't ask you things.'

'Of course you could have asked me.'

'I decided not to, because after getting the tyre the man would then have to be taken back from Kobli to his truck, wasting your time and petrol. And we're very short of time here. And what if the man attacked you? You're my responsibility and it would be my fault if you were attacked and strangled.'

I wasn't too happy about being made to look like the worst kind of *yovo*, but with time and tiredness against us it was probably the best evasion.

'Then the man who needed our help said I was an African with no concern for his brothers, his brothers who had been suffering in the sun to repair the road surface for me to drive my *yovo* on. I was bad.'

'Repaired the road where, exactly?'

'Further on. Anyway, this is what made me fed up. Africans. Always, if you won't help, because you can't, they start saying you don't care for your brothers. But how can I risk it? He grabs you, I fight him but he stabs me, then strangles you, strangles you until you're dead, takes your money, your suitcases and throws your body in the bush.'

'Maybe you'd win the fight.'

'No. Better for me to be stabbed dead. Otherwise he'll tell the police I was part of it. Or, if he took out his knife like this – cut my throat while I was driving – how would I have a chance to fight? No, really, you're lucky you've got me; some drivers would easily attack you out here alone, take your money and leave you strangled in the bush.'

When our travels started, I had been wary of Isidore – unreliability, unwanted snogging, and small-con tricky stuff were the worries I'd crossed off my list. The bush-throwing scenario wasn't one that occurred to me. Good job, really, or I'd never have left home.

The road did seem to be wider and pothole free on the approach to Kobli – more of a crossroads with houses than a village. In a breeze-block compound Isidore's friend, the local doctor, was not at home, busy at the small clinic that served the people for miles around. His wife made us welcome with soft drinks and bowls of cassava dumpling. A harmless food that tasted of nothing.

Revived by cassava, *fizzi* and company other than mine, Isidore was confident about the next leg of the journey.

'We won't make it before dark, but they say the road is quite good most of the way. There's a local election coming up so some repairs have been started.'

He also seemed relieved to learn from our hostess that there was a hotel at Tanguiéta, where white people had been known to stay and not die in the night for lack of amenities. He admitted he hadn't been entirely sure there was a hotel.

'The hotel is called APP. À Petit Pas. This means a little place but it also means there's no reason to look for a big place. Little by little – like the saying, "Little by little the bird makes its nest".'

I've no idea what he was talking about.

Big by big, Isidore made the most of the fairly smooth section of dirt road to try and get us to Little by Little Bird's Nest Whatever Hotel before darkness. But just as the good road ran out, so did the light.

'Maybe another half-hour,' he said, putting on his headlights. He hated to do this, said it wasted petrol, but we were nowhere and the road had some frighteningly deep gullies on one side, and then they'd be on the other side . . . We crawled along and I could sense Isidore's burst of energy leaving him.

Our lights picked out shadows of people at the roadside; I tried not to think about vengeful road-mender bush throwers doubling back on us. But people did seem to be lurking by roadside clumps of trees with unnerving lack of obvious purpose.

'What are those people doing?'

'Looking to see what car this is. There's not much to do here at night.'

I tried to keep awake so that Isidore wouldn't be suffering alone. I played children's games in my head to spur us on through the night – *By the time I've named every seventies pop star I can think of we'll be in Tanguiéta . . . By the time I've named every type of biscuit . . .* No, not biscuits – they were long gone. Not food . . . *Every name for a type of . . .* Isidore slammed on the brakes. There was real trouble: we'd nearly been skull-cracked, totalled. A herd of donkeys charged across the road in front of us and off into the nothingness.

'Beasts!' Isidore yelled at them. 'You're called beasts and you are!'

It was more apt in French, beast and stupid being the same word. At first the donkey ambush relieved Isidore's tension, he'd had a good shout. But then it gave him a new worry: 'If we hit a big cow we're finished. There's lots out here. Even on good roads people hit big cows and they're finished.'

Big cows, oh no . . .

Shadows of people no longer emerged – we were heading further from anywhere and I had a chilling thought about a fork in the road we'd taken a while back.

Just when it seemed as though Isidore was about to start sobbing at the wheel, doomed to drive on a dangerous road at night until he was dead, we turned a corner and saw the flickering lamps of Tanguiéta. Then, as if it had been waiting for us, the town blazed in jubilant electric light.

'Must have been a power cut.' Isidore had a catch in his voice, close to tears of relief. He crashed the gears, he was so overcome.

Down a side road was Little Bird Little Hotel. Surrounded by a high corrugated-iron wall topped with razor wire. Isidore hammered on the gate, disappeared inside, leaving me and the Peugeot in an ill-lit market, hung around with malevolent-looking youths, staring, undernourished children, big women posed as if they fancied a street fight and wandering goats trying to look as much like they'd the Devil's eyes as they could.

The metal gates opened. Isidore drove into the courtyard and a man called Emmanuel locked us safely into his little nest. Small cottages surrounded tables, shrubs and trees; each cottage had a terrace with potted plants and gingham curtains at the windows; the trees were strung with fairy lights.

Emmanuel, our five-foot-one messiah, face scarred like a golfer's trousers, told us he could bring us chicken and rice in half an hour. He had a problem with water – there'd been no running water for two days – but he would go immediately and bring us buckets for our rooms.

Isidore fussed with my window, shutting it and telling me this would keep insects out. With just the feebly turning fan and a corrugated-iron roof to the tiny cabin, I could see a hot night ahead.

Yawning strenuously, Isidore said, 'He's given me the cabin next door. Is that all right?'

'It's three pounds a night; the only place cheaper is sleeping in the car. And if you have to get in that car to drive again tonight you'll die.'

'I am exhausted,' he confessed as he went next door. 'Exhausted, hungry and covered in dirt.'

I thought he was likely to lie on his bed and pass right out.

I showered from a bucket in a stone stall in the corner of my sweat-box room, then crossed the courtyard with my torch to where Emmanuel had indicated the toilet. The torch was a bad idea; if there'd been no light I'd only have gagged on the stench and would not have seen the swarming cockroaches, four-headed millipedes and slithering, small some-kind-of-death-worms. I fled and decided the plug hole in my shower stall made a safer convenience. I'd noticed some little pipes coming from the cabins into the flower beds – if recycled shower water was going out to water the garden, I'd just have to live with wee-wilted geraniums on my conscience.

Having poisoned the plants, I made my getaway to the courtyard. I sat under a sparkly lit tree at a wooden table, refreshed by cooler air and a drink. A wave of tired happiness came over me. A warming wave of joy welling right up from inside. Probably some kind of physiological response to receding fear of death by donkey or strangulation.

An all-body joy to behold, Isidore emerged from his cabin in nothing but flip-flops and a sarong. Water from his shower still glinting on his biceps. Biceps, triceps, all the ceps . . . A welter-weight boxer's body that I hadn't fully taken into consideration before. Obviously he hadn't reckoned that I'd already be washed, brushed and out in the courtyard to see him gad out half-naked. But after an initial bridling embarrassment, he decided we were all too tired for formal dining attire.

'I started my wash then realized I should do it after the car.'

He did notice me noticing what a fine figure he cut with just a cloth wrapped round his middle. As he took his car-cleaning rags out of the boot he had a secret naughty smile on his face. I quickly forgot what I suppose was a moment of temptation in the Garden of Little by Little when I realized the punishing madness of what he was doing.

'You can't clean the car now.'

'There may not be time in the morning. I can't leave it covered in dust like this – it's bad for the car and makes me ashamed.'

Much as I wanted to wallow in exhausted-joy stupor, I couldn't have this. I got to my feet.

'Give me a cloth. I'll help.'

'You? No, sit and rest, the car is my problem.'

'I can't sit and rest, watching you work when you're the most tired.'

'I'm stronger than you. Please, sit down. You'll make me ashamed. What will the people here think? That I'm so bad at my job my *yovo* has to help clean the car? Really, it wouldn't be right.'

'This isn't right.'

He ignored me. I hung around the car, shifting from foot to foot, contemplating taking a rebellious run at a cleaning rag, when Emmanuel came out of the bar and dancing area at the back of the yard.

'Did you want something, madame?'

'No, nothing.'

'The food will be ten minutes. Another drink?'

I ordered a drink for Isidore.

'I'll bring it, madame. Please sit down.'

'You see,' Isidore grinned triumphantly as Emmanuel left. 'He thinks white people should be sitting down.'

Isidore finished the work just as dinner arrived. He dashed to his cabin and reappeared washed once more, and back in his shirt and trousers.

'Ah, bicycle chicken!' he said gleefully, and fell on it so hungrily it wouldn't have mattered if it had been made of old spokes and handlebars. He had the marrow sucked right out of bones and not a rubbery sliver of skin left on his plate. Then he finished the mound of sinew and bone left on mine.

'Now,' he began, when finally full, 'the programme for tomorrow . . .'

Emmanuel was opening the gates to a four-wheel drive full of young Africans. They seemed as bewildered to be in Tanguiéta as I was, and disappeared into cabins begging for buckets of water.

'They are from Cotonou,' Emmanuel explained. 'They have been here to make a film about the Somba villages.'

That would account for the cameras they'd been carrying, then. And their confused demeanour. City folks. Never mind London, Cotonou seemed to me like a far-off dream of very swish tall glass and tarmac now. If I saw a traffic light I'd probably throw my bowl and run for the long grass.

The camera crew had left a scruffy, chain-smoking Somba with the vehicle.

Isidore whispered to me: 'You see, they're leaving him to sort himself out and sleep in his vehicle. That's how drivers are usually treated.'

Having made me feel like the holy saint of employers, he resumed the posting of orders for tomorrow. We would get up at six, go to the rangers' station at the animal park and persuade them to let me have an off-season peek at giraffes.

Then we'd go back, looking at Sombas again, if I liked, spend the night in Parakou, a town roughly halfway down the country, then another early start to get me back to Cotonou in time for my evening flight home.

'I think this best avoids a wasted moment,' he concluded. 'You go to sleep now. I'll quickly talk to Emmanuel. See if he has some local knowledge to help us with the animal-park question.'

I pottered in a moronic, too-tired-to-remember-how-to-use-a-toothbrush daze. It was now nearly midnight. Maybe a lie-in would be a nicer thing than a giraffe.

To get any oxygen at all I had to position the fan to blow right in my face, and I was just sinking into a windswept doze when there was a furtive tapping at the door. Malevolent youths? Devil goats?

'Annie? It's me. Isidore,' he called softly.

The clock said one-thirty. I hauled a sheet round me and opened the door with probably a cross goatish-Devil-type face myself.

'Isidore, we have to get up at six.'

'I know. But I went to a bar in the market and I found a man with a four-wheel drive. Emmanuel says we must have one for the park.'

'Must we? OK.' Anything, just go.

'But the four-wheel drive is rented to someone tomorrow afternoon, so in the morning the driver will call his boss in Natitingou and get another four-wheel drive up here — it could be here by the fast road by eight-thirty . . .' My mind was glazing over. All I really seized on was eight-thirty – that could mean two extra hours' sleep.

'Great,' I said. 'That's fine.'

'But he says it will cost twenty pounds and tips. Is that too much?'

Twenty million pounds wasn't too much to get Isidore off my doorstep.

He was still talking . . . 'Apparently there's a back way in to the park so it doesn't even matter if it's closed.'

'Fantastic. See you in the morning.'

'You see, how much I work hard for you?' Isidore grinned, hovering.

'I do. Thank you.' I shut the door, it was the only way.

Maybe my goggling at his torso had provoked this needy nocturnal hyperactivity, but I was long past any flicker of temptation. I lusted only for my lumpy, itchy-sheeted bed.

Five-fifteen, again with the tapping at the door . . . Isidore had lost his mind in some way and it was a great shame but I'd have to kill him.

'What? What now?'

He looked upset and awkward. 'I'm sorry, but Emmanuel says the water is running now. It will stop again at six. I didn't know what to do. I thought you'd want a shower and might be cross to miss the water. I decided I had to tell you.'

Cross? A charmer like me? I grunted something and shut the door, yanked on the water, had a rage at my towel for being so bone idle as to still be damp, and my half-witted shoes had put themselves exactly where they'd get covered in water . . .

This mild fretfulness was showered out of me. I went into the daybreak cool of the courtyard – flower scents, birds in the trees and Emmanuel presenting me with a cup of coffee. I felt that peculiar wave of joy again.

All was not going well. Isidore was up and around and roaring at a man by the gate. He seemed to win. The man stomped off with a defeated slouch.

'Ah, these people,' Isidore growled his report. 'Really, that man,

he . . . Did you get coffee? I told Emmanuel it was essential; he
went to the market specially. But that other idiot, he's wasted our
time. Now he says the office in Natitingou is closed, but if I give
him some money for petrol he could get to Natitingou and back
to find the second driver. What if he just disappears? He says I've
insulted him. I told him I was the one insulted, because he thinks
I'm stupid.'

The film crew came out and involved themselves in our problem.
They said if they didn't have an appointment in Natitingou with a
Somba expert they'd have happily taken me to the animal park
themselves.

'But it's closed,' an older, late-rising crew member came over to
put a stop to our nonsense.

'I know,' I said. 'But apparently there's a back way in.'

'Are you crazy?'

A question I frequently asked myself. But not at this moment.

The older film-man looked round at his young colleagues, plung-
ing them from helpful enthusiasm to head hanging. 'Is no one here
thinking this through? How dangerous that would be? And you're
encouraging her?'

I thought it through. 'You mean I could get hurt by a leopard
or something?'

'Leopard? No. You'd get shot as poachers.'

Ah.

Everyone looked shamefaced and foolish. Except Isidore, who
looked horrified. All his fears for me and he hadn't thought of that
one.

'Oh my God, I didn't think . . .' he stammered.

It didn't matter. It was almost funny, what we nearly did to
ourselves. 'Isidore, it's really not important. I can see a giraffe the
next time.'

The senior crew-man had more news for us. 'Giraffes? Where
will you see them? There's no giraffes in Pendjari.'

Isidore said of course there were, he'd seen them in a guide
book.

'It must've been a very old book, then. I promise you. I made an information film on the park last year. There used to be giraffes, decades ago, but they migrated. Right across to Niger and Cameroon. The climate changed. They've gone.'

Isidore looked like he'd pass out or throw up.

IO

The Price of Everything

The film crew left and I had to put Isidore back together again.

He sat in the car with his head in his hands, muttering. 'I've wasted your time.'

I'd said 'It doesn't matter' quite enough; it was time to be firm and remind him that he was the one who said giraffes were a frivolity. And how could I have had my time wasted? I'd seen Sombas, I'd seen all kinds of dog dinners, night donkeys and Emmanuel's fairy-lights . . .

He took down his hands with a slight sniff. 'It's all an experience for you.'

'That's the point – that's why I'm here. It's all things I never saw.'

He nodded thoughtfully. I held my breath. He seemed to be rallying.

'They have a big market here. Would you like to see it?'

'Of course.'

He pulled himself up to his full self. 'Come on, then, pay Emmanuel. If we take the good road we could be back in Cotonou by tonight. You can relax in your hotel there and not be rushing on the plane straight from the bush.'

'Excellent idea.'

In daylight, Tanguiéta was cheerful, bustling, the main market for miles around rather than the last-chance saloon at the end of the earth it had seemed the previous night. There were people from Niger, Burkina Faso, Nigeria, selling all manner of things, wearing all manner of different clothes. The malevolent youths must have been kept in a box while the sun shone.

Giraffe shame forgotten, Isidore became very agitated about some old men sitting under a tarpaulin selling fish. Terrible, tormented-looking fish; flyblown dried fish with their eyes still in – fish from the inside of Mervyn Peake's head.

'Look at those men with the fish. How bizarre.'

I examined them more closely . . . Nothing. The men looked fine; it was the fish that were peculiar.

'Well, I've never seen that in my life before.'

'What?'

'Men selling fish. Women sell fish. Men catch them. It's too bizarre.'

He strode over and tried to strike up a conversation with the men but couldn't find a common language. He was in a complete lather of excitement to find out where they were from, doing this extraordinary thing. I was in a hurry to get away from the look and smell of the horror fish themselves, never mind if high-heeled drag queens were selling them.

'They're from Niger, from the border,' a small eavesdropping boy selling bread from a basket on his head told us. 'They fish the rivers on the border and come here to sell. They like their women to stay in the house. My mother told me. Come on, *batture*, buy my bread.'

I bought some to have food for the journey. Isidore smirked at the boy and the half-dozen pre-pant brothers trailing behind him.

'Look at you Somba children with your no soap and small eyes. I hope you won't kill us with your bread.'

The bread boy looked indignant; the small brothers stared at me from their very small eyes fringed with huge furry lashes. Somba children did look odd. Isidore thought the small eyes and paintbrush lashes had evolved because they'd lived for centuries in the windy dusty highlands. But the children often had sticky-out, slightly pointy ears, and shaved heads, making them look like standard photofits of aliens from space, with their dots for eyes. And the staring, naked children were usually covered in a thin film of grey dust, which gave them an extra unearthly hue. All in all, a funny thing, for people who came from the stars.

We moved on through the food section to the chainsaw massacre of the meat stalls. Hacking, splitting and ripping of flesh going on, with far too much insouciant gore splashing for a hypocritical omnivore like me to be confronting, with its matching accessories of sour butchery smells and sliminess underfoot. This was even worse than the horror fish – but then I saw a woman with something in a bucket that looked like nothing anyone should be handling without asbestos gloves, let alone selling at a food market. Fly-dense, smelly slabs of hairy grey blubber. It couldn't be food, it couldn't be food, it couldn't be food . . .

'If people can't buy meat they boil this with the vegetables. They can use it several times to give flavour.'

It was a sheep's skin, what you got when the wool and flesh were removed. My liberal conscience reeled . . . Such things couldn't happen. I would do something. I would . . . I would get to the vegetable section as fast as I could push through the crowd.

A group of women selling shiny red peppers nudged each other and giggled about me.

'Madame Pantalon! Buy some peppers!' one of them shouted.

They all screamed with laughter, all shouting, 'Mrs Trousers, Mrs Trousers, buy peppers!'

'A woman in trousers is funny to them,' Isidore said, frowning at the rib-clutching, hysterical women.

'Mrs Trousers, come back here and show us your trousers!' they yelled as I retreated into used clothing and stationery.

I thought that if for some reason I ever decided to open a brothel, Madame Pantalon would be an ideal name. Saucy but with a hint of well-travelled sophistication, exactly how I would want my brothel to be.

'Posters!' Isidore waved me over to my favourite type of market stall. This was a particularly fine collection of posters. You had to know what to look for. In between blurry prints of African pop stars and garish reproductions of Michael Jackson, the connoisseur could find treasures like *Warning Story of Goat Abomination.* This was a cartoon story of a woman who doted on her goat too much when pregnant. Her baby was born half-goat and had to be taken away by the elders to be destroyed. The goat remained smug in its stall, having caused so much trouble; so, ladies, don't trust them.

This time I bought *Jet-Set Man Hair Fashion.* This was a type of poster usually put up outside barber shops, with drawings of the styles a Jet-Set Man could have, including 'Trendy Man', 'Boss of Business', and 'Very Jamaican Man'.

I was about to cast my expert eye over another poster stall but we had to get back to the car fast. A big man, totally stark naked, was bearing down on us. He was unremarked by the traders as he strode along aimlessly, talking to himself and letting it all hang out – but when he saw me, he changed direction with determination.

'The lunatic wants you,' Isidore panicked. 'Let's go!'

We escaped along the better road to Natitingou and seemed to be back on tarmac in good time. The heat was rising. I dozed a while and woke to see another large naked man in a sunhat striding the side of the road.

'Look! Is he mad?'

'Of course he's mad. They walk around a lot, mad people, I don't know why.'

'Are they always naked?'

'Very often naked, yes.'

'Maybe he's going somewhere. I mean, how do they live – does anyone look after them?'

'Who? The family can't look after a mad person naked like that. They have to send them away. People give them food sometimes. Or they eat from rubbish piles. It's a terrible thing. People go mad just like that and they're finished. In Cotonou there's a big building that's a house for the mad. Otherwise they're just outside in the markets.'

'Is it the serious cases in the house?'

'I don't know who's in there. Different kinds of mad people, I think. People go mad in different ways, you know.'

'I know.'

'Usually it's *gri-gri*. Sometimes it's drugs. And then –' he said this as if it was the most astounding thing – 'some people go completely mad just of their own accord.'

But usually it was *gri-gri*. People exploded, flung themselves from cars and dropped dead, but *gri-gri* most often destroyed people by sending them mad. They didn't go blind, deaf, develop a limp or become prone to painful indigestion. They lost their minds at the drop of a calabash, or a string in the meat dinner.

Not everyone was a nerve edge away from blindness, deafness, limping or indigestion. But madness? Not such a long leap away for any of us. Especially if we lived in a hot country, with the grinding stress of constant poverty; the grief of children dying at birth; friends and relatives dying young with cholera, malaria, Aids – even minor road accidents meaning death. A poor African's life could be a high-wire act above immediate and irreversible disaster. Not an aromatherapy oil or prescription for Prozac in the house to nip trouble in the bud before it got out trouserless in the market-place. All very handy for the ill-intended *gri-gri* man.

I had a sleep-deprived, too-hot, vaguely carsick irritation gathering in my nerve ends as the high-speed journey progressed. I could have done with some heavy drugging to help keep me stable. But I only had my willpower to stop me showing my irritation with

Isidore as he ate bread noisily and wouldn't stop tapping the steering wheel.

Suddenly he said with unrestrained irritation: 'Why don't you speak? If you don't speak, how can I know what your character is like?'

I was in no mood to be told off, nor to entertain him with my character.

'Don't you know my character by now?'

'You leave it to me to guess; you never speak.'

Didn't speak as much as him, that was for sure.

'I do speak. I'm just tired now.'

'Oh well, even when you're not tired you keep quiet.'

He shoved a cassette in the tape player and turned up the volume. I was outraged. Here he was taking his tiredness out on me while I'd been digging my nails into my palms not to get annoyed with him . . . Well, now he was for it – I was going to shut my eyes and pretend to sleep all the way to Cotonou.

Having my eyes closed made me feel more carsick, and there was always something to see at the roadside – markets, nomad children thwacking sticks at their giant cattle, cotton factories, palm-oil factories, strings of women and girls carrying water containers on their heads away from the splashy fun at roadside pumps. Along one stretch of road, women were breaking stones for a living. Young girls chiselling boulders into centimetre fragments that they sold to road menders. Ashamed? I should have been. But Isidore was turning up the cassette volume – if I asked him to turn it down there could be another irrational fracas . . . Stone breaking at midday? They didn't know they were born.

After half an hour, Isidore seemed to think better of berating and tormenting me and turned the cassette down.

'This is a good song. It says don't complain if you have no money, no clothes, no children, no bicycle, because God has written that you should be poor. Just as He's written that someone else should be rich.'

'That's not true,' I snapped.

'Of course it is.' Isidore clearly regretted his attempt to communicate and turned the volume back up.

I didn't think it was true, in my terms or his. How could you think people could control the world with magic and at the same time accept that everything was preordained and way beyond your control? Oh, it was too hot for this. I suggested we stop for lunch. He didn't want to stop until we reached Parakou.

'Parakou will only be twenty minutes. And what could you eat in these villages that you wouldn't be complaining about anyway?'

We still had most of the length of Benin to go. Three hundred and fifty miles that was really double that with the bad roads. I wanted to slap him in the face with a village dinner and scream until we were both dead. But I never thought about firing him and switching transport. Inconceivable. He was a fact of my life now, a given that had to be coped with.

Still, it was a shame that it had come to this on the last day.

Isidore coped with me by playing a new tape, the dingiest yet.

'This is my favourite cassette,' he announced. 'Because it's about Jesus.'

He tapped the steering wheel and sang along in enraptured delight.

The singer was a mawkish, off-key ungifted creature – accompanied by a Yamaha organ and a drum machine. All the great music in Africa and I was trapped with this, unfortunately a lot of it in French so I understood too much of the caterwauling about the lovely helpfulness of Jesus.

It did seem helpful to Isidore; he was almost pleasant over our fish lunch, telling me why even Benin's primary roads were so bad, the tarmac peeling off leaving lagoons of red dirt to dip into and wreck the suspension.

'It's the government's fault. They give the road making to a French company, because they always give a lot of bribes to the ministers here. And they make rubbish roads. Do you and I know how to build roads? No, but we know you need drainage in this climate and don't just put a thin layer of tarmac on the mud. As soon as it rains, the roads are gone and the French company has to to come back over and over to repair the roads, getting rich – and Africans can't drive anywhere. People think it's us, they think Africans don't know how to make roads. Really, how will we progress?'

I agreed. Benin heaved with Peace Corps workers, foreign charity projects, all doing fine things – but there should have been no need. If Africa wasn't continually interfered with, manipulated, hamstrung, abused . . .

'You see, exactly,' Isidore said. 'Most Africans are like me, men who want to earn their way. I don't want a charity project to give me medicine for my own children, but I have to accept it. If someone says to me, "Here's an opportunity", I take it. You see these people in the villages, sitting in bars, lying under trees – you think they wouldn't start running if there was a chance of earning money? *Oh là là* . . .'

We nodded over the bad ways of the world, pals again.

Parakou heaved with people, especially round the central petrol station. While Isidore went in to pay for our petrol, I scrabbled through the pile of cassettes to find something nice. There was a Cotonou band called Panteres Noire, sort of funky African reggae – Isidore didn't have it. There was internationally famous Angélique Kidjo – Isidore wouldn't have it. For one thing, she came from Ouidah, where all the women were witches. Secondly, her music that we loved so much in the West sounded thin and foreign to listeners at home. 'What's the point of Angélique Kidjo's music?' he'd said to me. 'You can't dance to it and it has no story. If music doesn't have either of those, what's the point? Listen, she was lucky some Frenchman took her away because she used to sing in bars in Cotonou and people would put on cassettes to drown her out. We're not like you Europeans, we're not impressed by singers just because they're slim and pretty. If a woman's the size of a house but her songs are good, that's what we want.' On the television shows, the most repeated songs were jubilant dance music from the Ivory

Coast, a style called zouk, or there were big women singing songs with a story. I found a tape of danceable, tuneful local man, Stan Tohon. Stan would keep us cheerful with his songs of lively warning of what became of you when you didn't use a condom. I was about to swap it with the Jesus cassette but had to give money to a family of beggars pawing in the window at me – a small boy with a harelip, an old blind man, a little girl making deaf-mute noises.

'You gave them money?' Isidore asked, shooing them away.

'Well, look at them. The disaster family.'

He laughed scornfully. 'Here comes their cousin.' He threw a coin to a disfigured boy hurrying towards the car. 'You know, next time you're in Parakou you'll see the blind man with different children. There's a boy with a stump and a girl who drags her leg.' He chuckled. 'Really, how can that be a family? When will you learn not to do things without checking with me first?'

I started to plot revenge on him but sometime into the next drone of the Jesus tape I fell asleep.

I woke up to find women beside the car calling me a *yovo*. I'd slept my way south. Isidore had pulled up to buy vegetables to take home for his children. He looked very hot and tired, and was arguing with the vegetable women as if he was at the very end of his tether.

A line of women in long white robes and white hats, like sous-chef caps, were crossing the road ahead. Celestine Christians. Benin was full of churches, chapels, tabernacles . . . As well as the Catholics there were Jehovah's Witnesses, Seventh Day Adventists, Methodists, Baptists, Presbyterians, Pentecostalists . . . There were plenty of Moslems, even some Buddhists, but the majority embraced imported faith alongside the practice of traditional African religion. The Celestine Christians, however, were a cult who combined many of the practices of vodou with the language of Christianity. They danced and drummed to summon angels. They fell into trances and received clairvoyant messages for the congregation from messenger angels, or from Jesus himself.

The church was founded 1940 by a local man who wanted to rid the villages of the greedy power of the *vodounon* and to provide a form of Christian worship that wasn't contolled by foreigners. The sect had become very popular. They used prayer to heal and to protect themselves from witchcraft. They always faced seaward when they prayed. They were devoted to the sea, the source of life, and would frequently process the beaches with incense burners and shaded candles, singing melodiously as they went. There was something very beautiful about their wafting progress along the shores. Isidore respected their simplicity, the lack of greed among their priests – but he didn't like to get too near them. 'They're against all *gri-gri*. One touch from their white robes and all my protection would be destroyed.'

The women were gathering under a tree with benches round it – a Celestine Christian church needed to be no more than that.

'They're starting a ceremony,' I remarked as Isidore came back with his purchases.

He scowled at me. 'We haven't got time for that.'

I was very sorry I'd woken up.

Ten miles outside Cotonou, darkness fell and we started to hit the first heavy traffic we'd seen in days. It took two and a half hours to get through a creeping logjam of trucks, taxis, bicycles, handcarts, pedestrians, flashy cars, cars that were mere smoke-belching engines with scraps of bodywork clinging to them – all in the thin two-lane highway into town.

Any gaps in the traffic were filled by mopeds and scooters. There were more people in Benin with a moped than could write the word moped in any language of the world.

Mopeds and scooters needed no licence, no MOT, no road tax or insurance. They could be bought cheap in Nigeria or secondhand for £30. These unregulated and often ancient conveyances were designed to carry two people; in Benin they frequently carried families of five, with shopping. They were the main source of Cotonou's heavy pollution problem and involved in an estimated minimum of seven gut-spilling accidents a day, three fatalities a week. The most dangerous were the fast-weaving *zemi-jan* drivers. These were moped taxis, driven by wild young men in numbered, coloured shirts – different colours in different towns, yellow and green for Cotonou. Driving dangerously was a matter of necessity – they had to work fast to get enough of their low fares to make a living.

Zemi-jan was Fon for 'take me quick' – which they did, if they didn't kill you. Dicing with peril was a matter of pride; it was a laddish job with much wearing of baseball caps and sunglasses, especially at night. They were not always sober and needed to work such long hours their judgement could doze right off on them.

Policemen kept striding into the road, pulling up overloaded taxis for spot fines, picking on *zemi-jan* drivers who'd driven too near them and blowing piercing whistles that added one too many sounds to the cacophony of engines, screamed abuse and endlessly blown horns. The police gave drivers the added difficulty of seeing where a gesticulating mid-road policeman might be in all the dust and petrol fumes thick as lead-flavour candyfloss.

As we'd reached the outskirts of Cotonou, Isidore had loudly thanked God for a safe deliverance. When I saw the state of the traffic he had to drive through I vowed to be in a good mood. It didn't last. He put on the tape of the Jesus singer and manoeuvred at terrifying speed through traffic that would look wedged tight to a normal person. I was tired, hot, carsick – and I was sure the Jesus tape was giving me a disease.

In case the frequent occurrence of the words 'Jesus', 'Thank God' and 'alleluia' had misled me into thinking that the songs were about smacking up bitches in the hood, Isidore explained the lyrics to me.

'He's saying, "I thank Jesus for saving me, for my life, I don't need anyone but Jesus, Jesus will always help me . . ."' He interrupted his devotions with yelled obscenities at a *zemi-jan*, then screams at a lorry driver. The whole thing was a cheese grater on the nerves. After an hour of this, just at the peak of my anguish about the heat, the traffic, the holy tape and Isidore's incessant road raging, he pulled into a vacant lot. Oh, what now? I just wanted to be in the hotel, be washed, be lying down . . .

He'd stopped so he could clean the dust off my suitcases in the boot. So they'd be nice for me to take into the hotel.

'You'll be depressed if you open them for clean clothes tonight and the red dirt gets in.'

He could barely lift his cleaning rag, he was so shattered, but he didn't stop till he'd scrubbed at every lock, zip and buckle.

'When your plane leaves, I will go directly to pray you come back,' Isidore said in the airport. 'You've been very good luck for me. And become like a friend. I'll be shocked if you forget me.'

Something had happened. Nothing romantic, like notions of hurling my life away to run a beach bar in Cotonou, but I felt a good deal more emotion than I usually felt when I paid off a taxi driver.

I tried to be honest with him; it could be a matter of six months, but I would write, send sunglasses and come back.

Isidore checked I had all my papers, handed me my suitcase and said that even if it was going to be longer before I came back, I should tell him frankly, so I'd see how he understood my problems. He didn't want me to think he'd be just impatiently waiting to take more wages from me. We had travelled together, eaten together, laughed, shouted and told each other a lot of things. He hoped this meant we had trust between us.

I made assurances of trust in response to his big speech. He gave a delighted smile but his eyes were very sad. In his experience of *yovos*, Isidore hadn't found us to be creatures that did real friendship. We got on planes home, leaving a trail of promises we'd forget about on landing. He'd be left with a withering hope, not so much as a promised letter appearing.

As well as risking his hopes on my promised return, Isidore, cornered, risked imposing on our friendship. He sent me a simple, dignified letter explaining that his mother had died. The family were looking to him to foot the bill for the funeral expenses. He had already paid for the hospital expenses incurred in the last months of her life. So now he was desperate. Could I advance him some of his wages from the next trip? He knew it was a lot to ask but £200 would be so much more important to him now than later.

He finished the letter saying he would completely understand if it wasn't possible, but asking me was all that was left to him.

I wrapped French francs in a bundle of old T-shirts and sent them off.

He was a resourceful man. He could have coped without me, in some car-selling way. Gone back to driving bush taxis, maybe had to take the kids out of school, all retreated to the village . . .

I had a few moments of cynical thought about being wrong about him. Then I thought, so what?

When I did go back to Benin, he told me how he'd opened the parcel in the post office and publicly wept when he saw the money. He'd been so desperate, the family would be shamed, his mother would be disrespected – but he opened a parcel and it was all lifted from his shoulders.

Worth it, then, for myself.

11

The Men with Horses' Feet

'As you will be here for many weeks, we will see everything. We will rummage through Benin like a sack of rice,' Isidore said in his next letter. First, we'd rummage up the other side of northern Benin, the Borgou region. Less well trodden by the French, full of peoples and places even he hadn't seen and, most exciting of all, the Borgou was full of witches . . . If I didn't believe in witchcraft after the Borgou, Isidore didn't know what he was going to do with me.

When he greeted me at the airport I could see he wanted to hug me but held back. How could he be in charge of me if he got too soppy and emotional?

'Are you going to wash? Are you hungry?'

I wasn't that hungry, airline food having swelled me up like a great swollen brute of a thing; but I was so excited to be back in Benin, I wanted to get out and on the town.

'I'll just quickly wash, change some money at reception and off we go.'

'You don't understand,' Isidore said. 'You don't need money. I want to invite you to dinner. I'm driving you to a very nice restaurant. Don't argue.'

He chose Chez Fatou, a medium-smart African restaurant, so I already felt bad that the meal wouldn't be low budget. He knew the staff and encouraged much fuss-making of me, telling the waitress I was like an extra big sister sent by Jesus.

Jesus's gift ate only a salad because she really wasn't hungry. The television in the corner was showing a programme that appeared every evening, a prime-time show of memorials for the dead. Mr Whatever, eighty-two, sorely missed . . . You didn't have to be just-dead to be on the dead-people show – photos and announcements came up for people who'd been dead for fifty years. All this was accompanied by a Yamaha-organ version of 'Nearer My God to Thee', and went on for half an hour. I didn't think this was suitable viewing for someone recently bereaved, and so I distracted Isidore, asking if it was just my imagination but had the staff back at the Hôtel de la Plage been replaced by android clones who worked with speed and efficiency?

Some diversion to explain android clones . . .

'No, they are not, as you say, machines in the people's skin. But it's all changed. New management.'

It wasn't only the new efficiency. In my rapid run in to drop luggage and change for dinner, I'd had enough time to see that the hotel had been transformed. The staff's former haphazard apparel had been replaced by neat African-print uniforms, there were living flowers in the plant pots, all the public areas had been given a lick of paint and the rooms were £5 dearer because there were now minuscule televisions perched on top of the wardrobes.

'The manager has changed everything. Put a bomb under the people. You know how they used to be, asleep.'

I liked how they used to be – friendly although bewildered about what their job might entail, lolling, giggling, gossiping and watching the vast hotel crumble around them. Now the government wanted to sell the hotel and everyone had to look sharp or they'd be out of a job.

★

The hotel had been built by a French entrepreneur in the 1950s. He loved Benin and made great friends in the post-independence governments. He was nearly deaf, so he tended to talk very loud. When Kérékou seized power, the Frenchman sat on the terrace giving out to his cronies about Kérékou, very loudly: 'Who's this oaf from the bush in charge now?' he'd shout. 'Some ignorant thug, he won't last.'

A few days later, nearly deaf though he might have been, the Frenchman heard that Kérékou's men were coming to arrest him. He packed a bag of money, got in his car and was over the border to Nigeria, never to return.

Kérékou made the hotel the property of the people – that is, the property of Kérékou and his associates. It was used for ministerial conferences, military get-togethers and entertaining a diminishing number of foreign visitors. No one bothered to maintain it; the staff were on the civil-service payroll – unless they were cleaners, paid too little to care.

The new manager had been unable to clear out the excessive number of staff, mostly distant relatives and dependants of ministers – but he made sure they all had plenty to do. There was constant titivation of public rooms, ashtrays emptied mid-cigarette, chairs polished while you were sitting in them . . .

Kérékou's first notion had been to offer the hotel at the knock-down price of £1 million to the now deceased deaf Frenchman's son. Surprisingly, he told Kérékou what he could do with his offer. Now the hotel was on the market for £2 million.

I missed the old Eastern European seaside-resort ambience, the long hours roaming the corridors in search of a waiter, the Monty Python everything-off menu – if it continued improving it would be a fine hotel, with nothing to laugh about at all.

In the fine surroundings of Chez Fatou, Isidore fussed at me for eating so little. 'I think it's because I said I'd pay.'

I assured him I'd eaten as much as I wanted.

'Well, it's a very small dinner to thank you for your kindness. Ah, look, this is a good song.'

The dead-relatives show had ended and TV Benin was back to its dominant broadcast fodder, locally made music videos. A man dressed for LA gang warfare began his song outside the Sheraton Hotel for millionaires but sang the chorus to poor children in a rural village; Isidore translated: 'He's telling the children, if someone does something good to you, remember it the rest of your life. If someone does something bad, forget it, give it to God to deal with.'

Isidore paid our bill. And, like the song said, I remembered how much £5 meant to his coffers.

Outside, the fairyland of the night markets was alight. Wooden-box stalls of groceries, lit by tin-can oil lamps, stretching way back into the darkness. Even the stalls with bottles of petrol and paraffin had naked-flame lamps. It was nine o'clock and the streets were teeming with children who looked like they planned to be out playing for hours yet – those who weren't over five and in charge of a stall. We passed my favourite local hairdressers, Dingo Coiffure and Thank God Lady Hairs, just along from Padre Pio Householdry – this wasn't an advice centre on how to live with a male relative bleeding from feet and hands; it was a place to buy plastic buckets and bowls.

Seeing as it was my first night back, Isidore was allowing me to stay up late and suggested a drink on the hotel terrace. At one newly painted terrace table was a family of smartly dressed Africans, at another were two middle-aged, unshaven, dodgy-looking Frenchmen. This was the usual clientele, middle-class Africans and dodgy French. The Africans behaved in normal ways to indicate people on holiday or business trips; the French sat around drinking and muttering things to each other and seldom went out. They always seemed to be waiting for something.

'Oh, you know, import-export,' Isidore said when I asked what they did. 'Cars mainly. They sell secondhand cars that come into the port. Often the ships are late, or more often the cars are delayed in customs.'

'Secondhand' was a generous description of the cars flogged off in Benin, with every cassette player, seatbelt, windscreen wiper and possible extra removed. And how many cars did the country need?

Some of the Frenchmen were so low down the profit pole, they made a living driving the cars to sell in inland states like Mali and Niger. The sort of job a young person might do for fun – but these middle-aged men? You just knew they'd done something terrible back home. These were the men the Foreign Legion wouldn't have.

According to the CIA – I looked up their report on Benin on the Internet, nothing fancy – Cotonou was a major drug-trafficking and currency-fraud route out of Nigeria.

In many ways, drug and currency deals were innocent compared to what some of the French were doing. Things that the CIA didn't bother to monitor because they weren't part of organized international crime. They were worse, small evils, not even actual crimes.

Isidore pointed out an ugly Frenchman of about sixty, arriving in reception with a very young, slightly dazed-looking African girl. She wore new but cheap Western clothes. She had hard-walked, wide feet crushed into gold girly sandals, and held her gold handbag like she wasn't used to having one.

'This bastard,' Isidore growled. 'He gets girls from the bush, right out in the poor bush. He takes them around with him, buys them some clothes and promises he'll take them back to France and marry them. How could they know better? Look how ugly he is, but always these pretty young girls from remote places. Just educated enough to speak French like an infant. Then after a few weeks he pays his hotel and leaves them. Maybe he found her near Natitingou and he'll leave her here. They're ruined, how can they go home? They find their way down to the red-light district to survive – he makes a prostitute of them. Or he gives the girl to a friend of his, makes a prostitute of her that way.'

'You should tell her.'

'She won't believe me. She'll think I want her for myself or something. She wants to believe him, not me.' He sighed, then brightened. 'There was one girl he brought here, she was from the west somewhere, near Togo. But she wasn't so innocent as he thought. She didn't believe his stories. When he went out on business she took everything from the room, even his shoes, and she disappeared. Look at him, his hands are all wrinkled like a toad. Now he doesn't leave the girls in the room when he goes out. The girl has to sit around the hotel public areas feeling ashamed.'

I hoped the toad would get ten kinds of clap and die; but he wouldn't, would he? The little girls would be the ones to get his diseases.

'Really it makes me sick to see him.' Isidore stirred a straw in his Coca-Cola like he wanted it to be the toad's entrails. 'I'll never drive him, even if my children are starving. I stand by my car and say "I'm busy", like that, so he can see I'm not.'

I observed that I'd seen quite a few elderly foreign men with beautiful young African girls on the beach, girls way beyond the man's wildest dreams of possibility.

'If an old foreign man is nice to a girl and improves her life, why not? If he marries her and takes her to Paris, both have gained. But actually, those girls on the beach, usually they are prostitutes.'

'Oh well, at least they earn more than a few new clothes.'

'Exactly, those girls know their game. But these bush girls he tricks . . . Look at that one, she looks fifteen at most.'

'Maybe we should tell the police about him?'

'As if they'll do something. It's very bad, but if we worried about all the bad people in Cotonou we'd have no time to enjoy a Coca-Cola. Or make plans. Let's make a plan.'

We were eagerly unfolding the road map when two troubadour musicians shuffled on to the terrace. I'd seen them last time – a tall, thin man with a short, limping acolyte. They roamed the terrace, the tall one vaguely strumming a guitar, the short one singing Elton John songs off-key. Then they'd hover by tables, usually mine, muttering incomprehensible mutterings, interspersed with 'Please, madame' until I had to pay them to go away. This time, Isidore saw them coming.

'Quick, let's get out of here. I can't stand those idiots.'

He folded the map and was moving to the troubadour-free inside bar when he had a better idea. 'Shall we hear some good music?

Why not, this is a celebration. These idiots make me ashamed; let's hear some good music.'

I realized we were heading for what I'd primly christened The Rough Bar. Every time we'd passed it on the way back to the hotel it seemed to have a loud-music, ladies-of-the-night, sailor-flinging ambience. It was always packed.

It was always packed, Isidore said, because it had good cheap food, live music and, admittedly, a lot of prostitutes.

We took a seat in The Rough Bar's small side-garden and Isidore complained to the waitress that they were playing tapes – where were the musicians?

'He's having his dinner, he'll be here in ten minutes.'

'He? Usually there's a group.'

'The others are playing at a wedding.'

The Rough Bar turned out to be run by a woman called Rita, Isidore's heroine. Rough Bar Rita had started out selling beer from a box and, now she had this, drove a nearly new Mercedes and owned a minibus that she rented out for a good profit.

'Ah, that minibus, that's such a good idea. Rita will never starve, even if her whole restaurant burnt down.'

'She would if the restaurant burnt down with the minibus parked outside.'

'The minibus is never parked. It's always hired out. If it breaks down, she has the restaurant. In this life you need two businesses; just one taxi is not enough.'

I ignored Isidore giving me precise details of the cost of second-hand minibuses. I watched the girls frying fish on charcoal griddles at the back of the restaurant and the small market across the disused railway tracks, mostly late-night fish sellers from the port. Some ragged boys ran along the tracks with strange bundles and glances over their shoulders.

'They've been stealing from the commercial port,' Isidore said. 'The port here, it's full of little thieves. They get on the boats in the dark and take everything. Last week even the pillows off a sea captain's bed, even his sheets.'

Then we witnessed a glorious ragged-boy coup. Half a dozen of them rolling a full oil drum that they'd stolen from a Shell delivery. They scampered and rolled triumphantly, little Robin Hoods off into the night.

The ragged boys would likely be running down the railway line to where it once crossed the beach in front of the Hôtel de la Plage. They'd go skittering on to the old port, now a collection of tumbledown nineteenth-century buildings, shanty dwellings and a half-collapsed iron wharf.

The wharf was a spectacular wreck of rusting metal, surrounded by half-sunk boat hulls. Apparently someone had offered to buy the wharf for scrap metal. Kérékou refused, saying it was part of Benin's history and he'd be having it repaired. Repairs didn't seem to be going apace; and it was strange that Kérékou had voiced an attachment to the old wharf, because the mercenary-led coup that attempted his overthrow in the late seventies had started with the mercenaries landing at this very wharf. But then, that time, Kérékou did win.

The time when Kérékou didn't win, the late 1980s, one of his troubles was the drop in world oil prices – just as Benin discovered it had offshore oil. Benin couldn't afford to exploit the resource. They had to sell it at the low price of the time to the likes of Shell, to then have it refined abroad and imported back into Benin, at a very good price for Shell. So hooray for the raggedy boys, rolling their barrel across the beach, past the old wharf and somewhere into the hell's kitchen of the fishermen's mouldering shanty town, where the police seldom ventured and people lived among the sewage that swept out of the city and back in, just at the spot where the poorest of the poor had their homes.

Isidore had once walked me up to look at the old wharf. The pretty scrubbed beach outside the Hôtel de la Plage disappeared round the corner behind us – ahead was a beach thick with slime, used Durex, plastic bottles, jagged tin lids and kids to-ing and fro-ing through this, their garden. Isidore warned me never to walk this close to the shanty town alone.

'These people will steal the nails from your fingers and strangle you.'

What he held against them even more was that they didn't wash. They were filthy. Presumably they'd been living there, close to the old port, before Cotonou expanded. Now they stayed because it was the closest they could get to the new port; even though Cotonou's town planners had decided it was fine for the city to literally dump on them. It wasn't their choice – life had made them filthy.

The musician in Rita's Rough Bar played the guitar well and began with a few tuneful Bob Marley covers. At Isidore's request, he switched to singing in Fon. All these songs had a similar-sounding, nursery-rhyme tune. In his gentle voice and the intimate setting, they sounded a touching, comforting type of music, not the same as the mournful yowling Isidore had on tape. Interestingly, Isidore didn't think the musician sang the songs properly because he'd watered them down to sound like *yovo* music.

As with most Fon songs, they were fables. Some of them were a mini-opera. Isidore would translate one inconclusive-sounding story, but then the next song would continue the tale. He translated in whispers; flames crackled as the fish-fry girls worked; little thief boys skipped back along the railway tracks striking their blow against multinationals; a moon came out from behind the clouds as market women settled to plait each other's hair in the warm night, sharp with charcoal smoke and salty sea.

'The song of the mouse and snake . . . The song of the true friend . . . The song of the clever wife . . . Ah, now he sings this one. It touches the heart very much. A man has two wives. The women both have children but one woman dies. The dead woman has one baby. The second wife starts hitting the child of the dead woman, hitting it with a stick. The singer sings against this and says if a child has no mother it is to be pitied. The singer says if you are a mother and you die, your child will suffer. He sings now to the child – "Take courage, this is nothing, God the good will send help and rescue".'

I panicked about this inopportune ballad of poor orphans but Isidore seemed perfectly happy. He gave the musician a tip and drained his glass. 'Ah, what a nice night. It feels like a reward.'

Reward-like and musically fine though it might be, Rough Bar Rita's garden had a seething insect population. We walked back to the car, flapping buzzy clouds away, watching our footing because people were lying asleep in the sandy vacant lot between restaurant and road. They'd camped for the night beside or underneath parked-up fish lorries. One sleeping man narrowly missed being run over as Isidore reversed the car.

'Move!' Isidore shouted. The man just turned on his mat and curled himself tighter. 'These are all thieves that sleep along here. Never walk this port road alone at night, or even in daytime. They jump out from behind the fish lorries, grab people by the throat, strangling and strangling until you give them your money.'

Officially, the port road was the most likely spot for night robbery in Cotonou. Gangs of mugging youths, very occasionally, cruised the area. Somebody had to do the job – why should Cotonou be excluded from the reputation of harbour districts across the globe? Sailors coming out of Rough Bars the world over got ripped off inside and rolled outside. But statistics made no mention of strangling. Maybe Isidore had an irrational fear of strangulation – or maybe he just liked doing vigorous air-strangling actions to scare me into obedience.

'OK. Sleep well. Welcome back. Be ready at nine, to leave for the Borgou.'

'How soon before we see a witch?'

'You can joke. You just hope you don't see one.'

The skies of the Borgou were not thick with shrieking hags on brooms. The land was densely populated, small-scale agricultural, in contrast to the rangy emptiness of the Atakora hunting lands.

The Borgou probably had reasons to divest itself of elderly ladies, gorging themselves at the larder with no further strength to dig a field for themselves. There were male witches of assorted ages, but predominantly, as in the heyday of European and American witch fears, it was old women who were the main trouble. Older men were the repositories of wisdom, but non-working, nonreproducing women – what useful role was there for them? Perhaps some childminding and midwifery – but this was exactly the work that could lead them into trouble. Children often died in this harsh environment. Disease, malnutrition, minor infections . . . Somebody had to be scapegoated.

Isidore blamed the proximity of Nigeria for the witchiness of the Borgou districts. And as for the Nigerians themselves . . . Isidore and his Cotonou taxi-driver friends could sit outside the hotel telling tales of Nigerian sorcery till the owls came home. For instance: once, a very well-dressed young Nigerian in the back of Isidore's cab had told him how he'd acquired his three-storey house in Cotonou. He'd cut the first baby hairs off the first of newborn twins. He mixed these hairs with soap and washed his own hair with it over a basin. He rubbed and rubbed until there was plenty of lather, then he carefully scraped the lather into a basin. As the lather fell it turned into large-denomination notes. Isidore said nothing to the young Nigerian man but he knew there was a detail to this alchemy the Nigerian had left out – the baby whose hair you cut would get sick and die within seven days.

'So what was he really? A drug dealer?'

Isidore tutted at me. 'I just told you what he was. A sorcerer of extreme wickedness who didn't know I knew the results of his methods. That's why people here with twins cherish them carefully as babies. You'll see it in the papers, Nigerians coming here stealing twins.'

I did check the local papers most days – must have just not spotted those stories.

The beautiful lady boss of the Bosoms of Savé Hotel was the latest victim of the mysterious curse blighting her region. Even at midday the interior of the hotel looked gloomy. She came into reception rubbing her hands on a teatowel, looking exhausted and unembellished.

'Did you want a room, madame?' she asked anxiously. 'I'm so sorry, but the rooms are closed at the moment.'

Persistent lack of custom had left her unable to pay the electricity bill. So no air conditioning, fans or light. The telephone had met the same fate. To add disaster to humiliation, the water supply was cut off until evening because of repairs to the mains. She smiled at me sadly. 'I apologize to you for the inconvenience.'

'There are some,' Isidore said as we drove out of bad-luck valley, 'who say the King is to blame. Because he doesn't attend to the spirits of his ancestors.'

'The nice little praying king?'

'He is entirely Christian. Some people think that's a mistake.'

'What do you think?'

'He worships God. If he didn't, that would make him to blame. All gods are the same in the end. But the people, what they see is what matters to them, not what God sees.'

Such profundity made me sleepy. Next thing I knew, we were driving through Parakou's busy market, Isidore tapping my head to wake me, suggesting a browse round.

He enjoyed himself, because he had a sister living there and, though she was away in Dovi Dove, lots of the market women seemed to be her friends, pulling and teasing at Isidore as if he was a naughty schoolboy.

A little girl attached herself to us, repeatedly urging us to 'buy something' which seemed rather vague. She had some plastic carrier bags in her hand. She followed us and followed us, with her tireless refrain of 'buy something'.

'What does she want? Will she get herself a commission from a stallholder if we buy something?'

'No. She's selling the plastic bags. She wants you to buy something so you can buy a bag to put it in.'

I bought a carrier bag. An empty carrier bag is always a useful possession.

'Thank you, sister,' she said.

I was pleased that such a small child saw me as still of an age to be her sister, not her mother. But that's not what she meant.

'Excuse me, sister, but when I'm older I would like to join you. Can I come with my mother to the convent to talk to you about it?'

Unfortunately for her, she was talking to someone a long way from holy orders and nice habits.

'*Ah, cherie* . . .' I tried to disappoint her gently. 'I'm not one of the sisters; I'm only travelling here.'

'You're just a lady?'

I couldn't promise her that either.

'Ever see a nun with earrings?' Isidore mocked the girl.

Embarrassed angry tears sparked in her eyes. 'I didn't notice.'

I glared at Isidore. 'I do have very short hair like a nun.'

'And you have a nice face like a nun.' The little girl smiled at me, not looking at Isidore ever again. 'I will be a nun, too, one day.'

'I'm sure they'd be pleased to have you.'

She smiled and skipped off, having spotted another group of foreign market-browsers to attach herself to in hopes of carrier-bag sales and a possible noviciate.

We were planning to spend our evening in Parakou visiting the King, but his elderly male secretary seemed to think we weren't fit to be let in. He exchanged agitated words with Isidore. Suddenly it was almost all right.

'But please, madame,' the secretary begged me. 'You must at no point touch the King. And don't attempt to hand him anything directly.'

I said I wouldn't dream of it. But why not?

'This king is very strong in *gri-gri*,' Isidore told me. 'If a woman touches him it drains his power. If you were having your period you couldn't see him at all – your presence would drain his power. That's what the secretary was asking me about. I said you were OK at the moment.'

'How do you know?'

'I just know.' Isidore was only a little embarrassed but I was mortified. How did he know? Had he noticed altered *modus operandi* during toilet stops on the road? Or, worse, perhaps in a hot car . . . I was mortified and a bit annoyed.

'So what, the King thinks I might be unclean or something?'

'Nobody said unclean. Men who have a lot of protective *gri-gri* are afraid of women at that time. Women are extremely powerful at that time. One touch and the *gri-gri* is destroyed. Even if they are in the same room. My father won't let women in that condition even prepare his food, they're so dangerous.'

The round throne room was decorated with wall hangings of Mecca, pictures of horses, some fancy chairs and an elegant writing desk. The King was pleased with the chamber; he'd had it constructed himself, based on traditional Bariba architecture. Although Parakou was at the edge of the Bariba region, the kings were of the much scattered Nago people. Centuries ago, a Nago prince had been sent up to form a buffer state between the Nago heartland in Savé and the Bariba kingdom of Nikki, who were forever raiding and pillaging. The buffer prince did well and many Bariba joined him. He negotiated with Nikki and a truce was called, cemented by shared *gri-gri* ceremonies, and there'd been no trouble since.

I asked why the King of Parakou was a Moslem and the King of Savé was a Christian.

'Ah, to be honest I don't know. I expect we were all Moslems and they converted in Savé at some point when the Europeans ruled. They had much more European influence down there. I'll remember to find out because I'm writing a history of the kingdom. Until now our history has been passed down orally – I'm the first King of Parakou who can read and write. I'd like to give a written history to my sons.'

Even though he was abandoning the power of talk in his kingdom's history, the King liked a chat. He called for tea to be served and became very relaxed in his brocade armchair.

'Now, this is a very informal conversation. You can ask me what you like, but I'd like to ask you some questions too. I don't travel as much as I'd like. Tell me about yourselves. Where are you from?'

Isidore explained himself. The King nodded when I said London but then looked very impressed when I said I was born in Ireland.

'Ah, Ireland. I hear they're our brothers, not one of these colonial powers. Are you married?'

Sticking to my made-up story, I said I would be married soon.

'And you have no children yet? You're how old? Aren't you worried you've left it too late?'

'Maybe. But people where I live have children very late.'

'I know, I know – but you shouldn't wait much longer. Leaving it so late has many disadvantages. Of course, here we're children crazy. My grandfather had sixty wives. Sixty. I think this made my father reflect, so he had just the one wife, but eleven children. I have five wives, halfway between tradition and modern thinking.'

The King, a rotund, healthy-looking forty-five, seemed to me like he enjoyed life too much to reflect overlong on modernity before co-opting a young lady of the kingdom he'd taken a fancy to.

'You know, one time I met a white woman, a Belgian. I took her all around, bought her presents – and I was young then, you know, strong, not too bad to look at. But she said, as I had a wife already, she wouldn't marry me.'

'We're like that, we don't like to share.'

The King laughed. 'More than one wife doesn't please African women either. There's always trouble. Even here, where it's the custom, they don't like it. And there is always trouble between children of different beds.' He grinned cheekily. 'But if we can, we do like to have plenty of wives and children.'

Isidore smiled. 'Your majesty, I understand you have very strong *gri-gri* for women here. I have a question about that.'

The King told him he could ask anything he wanted.

'I wonder,' Isidore said, man-to-man frank, 'if you know how to help a woman with very heavy periods.'

The King didn't bat an eyelid.

'Yes we have *gri-gri* for that. Is this a problem for your wife?'

'No, no, my neighbour's second wife. She's young but she's not managing to have a baby. And her periods are heavy, with very thick dark blood.'

'Ah, yes, I know the problem. There are many things to be done to help with that. Send them to me. Let me give you my card. And here's one for my Irish friend.'

The King handed both royal calling-cards to Isidore. Because he couldn't touch me.

I wondered why Isidore hadn't asked his father to help his friend.

'Two reasons. One, it looks bad to immediately recommend someone from my own family. Two, although my father is strong in these things, if there are further problems the neighbour will always blame me. So I'm suggesting he comes to the north, where they are good at this type of *gri-gri*, particularly the kings and people at the court. Or he could go to the Rolli people. Ah, the Rolli, they are formidable.'

More tales of Rolli gynaecological *gri-gri* as we headed along the road to the Kingdom of Nikki – a bad dirt road with too many trucks driving wildly to Nigeria.

Rolli baby magic involved the treatments I'd heard Isidore mention in his father's repertoire, giving infertile women teas to drink, wash with . . . and the Rolli had other spells that seemed to boil down to buying fruit from pregnant women without haggling over the price and – Hey presto! The next thing Isidore told me about Rolli magic pulled me up sharp.

He said the Rolli could do magic even against guns. Immediately I knew where we were going: the Congo, the Simba boy-soldiers shot to hell because they thought bullets couldn't touch them; the West Side Boys of Sierra Leone in their backwards baseball caps, supplied with cocaine to enhance the delusion of invincibility they thought they had acquired from the magic men.

Isidore began and I was waiting for the dismissal, the evidently existing sensible part of him to butt in saying, 'It's all rubbish, of course – spells don't stop bullets – just thought you'd find the story interesting . . .'

No.

The Rolli gave you a powder. You took a razor blade and cut yourself on the back of your hands, the crook of your elbow, on your shoulders and your chest. You rubbed the powder into these cuts. Then you had to stand in a basket, so your feet were not touching the earth. The magic man was also standing in a basket as he handed you the necessary: a second razor blade dunked in the powder. You chewed this and swallowed it. The magic man muttered incantations. Then he gave you a needle wrapped in the leaves of special herbs; you mustn't chew this, you swallowed it whole. Then it was done. Bullets couldn't touch you, even automatic fire.

I forgot tact: 'You don't believe that. You don't believe that works.'

'I do. It's very powerful. I've done it.'

Despite his insistence, I didn't think Isidore really believed it. The sensibleness in him would make him duck. He fretted too much about strangling and mugging for someone who'd stood in the basket of invincibility.

My dismissal of the basket had been very loud and rude so he sulked a while, concentrating on seeing through dust from overtaking lorries. Unthinkingly intrepid as always, we'd set out on the rocky road to Nikki with extensive supplies of nothing to eat. Not a town called Peanut along the way to save us.

Nikki, when we finally reached it, had the snippy unsettled atmosphere of a border town. The roads were ground up by scores of lorries and bush taxis. It was a passing-through town, a traders' town, hung about with twenty-four-hour malevolent youths and busy, aggressive women who mowed you down before asking you to move.

Nikki was the oldest settlement of the Bariba people in Benin – Bariba stretched across the region through to Kano in northern Nigeria. They were predominately Moslem and dressed, when dressed traditionally, like desert horsemen – heads covered in loose white turbans, bodies in long white robes. They were on average taller and more haughty-looking than the pretty-eyed Fon. But I think the haughtiness was to do with how you had to hold your head in a long swathe of white cloth.

Hot, tired and hungry, the usual well-balanced frame of mind we were in to arrive at places, we were also in territory Isidore didn't know well. He followed a *zemi-jan* driver to the only hotel in town the driver reckoned a *batture* could survive. Isidore didn't trust the driver's judgement, and left me in the car while he inspected the establishment.

I had to get out of the suffocating car. I found myself standing by a stinking, bubbling open drain. I'd run out of insect repellent that morning, so my usual thick coating wouldn't be there to protect me from the insects delighting themselves around the drain. I was past caring.

After a very long inspection-absence, Isidore came out enraged, cursing '*jeunes filles*'. The rooms weren't clean because they didn't expect any guests. The *jeunes filles* were sitting reading magazines and all the rooms were dirty; it was outrageous.

'I told them they should be ashamed. They should have a clean room to show you. I've told them you won't set foot inside until everything's clean. Really, these girls, bush dwellers!'

He had a word for people he deemed, ignorant, unkempt or both – '*broussiard*'. It roughly translated as 'bush dweller'. Usually it made me laugh. But not when standing over drains, listening to his ranting and wanting some sort of wash, even in the world's filthiest room.

'I'll just go in and wash.'

'Where? It's disgusting! And there's nowhere else in this bush village except truck-driver hostels where you'll be robbed. We have to find the King; we need to make arrangements. We might as well go now as waste time here.'

Oh, for God's sake.

He bellowed something ferocious in to the bush dwellers and we roared off.

The small, thatched-roofed palace was to one side of a vast open ground that looked as though it was used for marshalling troops. The other sides of the ground were shaded with flame trees. *Flamboyants*, they were called in French, and they were.

On a deckchair in the shade of a *flamboyant*, the white-robed King was resting and minding the grandchildren. He was very old, wizened in on himself. A baby was asleep on a mat at his feet. Beside us, up on the concrete terrace of the palace, were two girls aged around five, sitting by another toddler girl asleep on a pile of cushions. The calm domestic scene took away all the tension overspill I'd been gathering from Isidore.

The old King was taking snuff and watching me. He smiled, snorted and spat heftily into a decorated calabash beside his deck-chair. He spoke to Isidore in a tired, quiet voice. The problem was Isidore understood very little Bariba. A translation was cobbled together once a ten-year-old boy was summoned to stammer through in broken French.

'My grandfather King says we look Minister of Finance. Him French is good.'

The Minister of Finance was a plump old boy dozing in the cluttered front room of his house surrounded by small cats. There were small cats on his chair, under it, on the coffee table, behind the door, up on the shelves . . . The Minister of Finance was not happy to be disturbed, and talked grouchily to Isidore while taking great thumbfuls of snuff. It seemed to perk him up so much I wondered if it was something else, but Isidore assured me it was tobacco. With much cat shooing and a shout to, I presume, Mrs Minister of Finance, we all trekked back to the palace.

The King said what we wanted was fine by him. But the Minister of Finance had to take us somewhere else to make the arrangements. Off we trekked again.

What we wanted was to see the King's horsemen. Once they were warriors, but now they were featured in tourist brochures extolling their skills in dashing equestrian displays. Our new mission was to see the Chief of Horses, the First Minister.

The First Minister's clay-brick house had an entrance chamber laid out for the reception of visitors. We joined a group of men sitting on mats at ground level. The Minister was up on a platform, lying on a long, cruise-lounger-style chair – why everyone sat on beach furniture this far inland I couldn't tell you.

The First Minister and Chief of Horses had retired from actual riding six months previously, being nearly seventy years old. He was extremely handsome. For the first time, I understood what romantic novelists meant by a fine-chiselled face. The chiselling was warmed to life by his soft calm eyes. His skin was unlined, an ageless face. In some moments a glance at him would guess thirty-five, then some kindliness, some time-won wisdom would cross his features and he'd look decades older. I couldn't take my eyes off him. And he couldn't take his eyes off me. If you'd filmed it, it would be the love-at-first-sight scene. The shocked recognition, another-time-another-place scene. Of all the First Ministers' huts in all the world, you walk into mine . . . And he told the horsemen sitting below his platform, 'If you can ride for me, you can ride for her . . .'

Well, not exactly.

Isidore and I sat on the mat with the nervous, horse-smelling men while the Minister of Finance and the First Minister talked in Bariba.

I do have a thing about the smell of horses, evocative of exciting lives – cowboys, highwaymen, warrior men . . . The scent wafted round the room, a sharp lift on an occasional light breeze. I could hear the stamp and jingle of horses behind the back door. The First Minister listened to the Minister of Finance and watched me.

I noticed, hanging from the roof of his platform, up above where his food bowls were set out, were little bags of *gri-gri* to protect him while he was eating. He noticed me looking at them – of course he did, he had half an eye on me all the time.

What would I have in common with a seventy-year-old retired Chief of Bariba Horsemen? Hard to say. I'd never seen a face like his before. High-cheekboned perfection. Maybe I had seen it on a statue of a long-dead pharaoh. Maybe it was something about men who rode horses.

Apparently some of the horsemen were away in the villages at a celebration but the Chief could arrange for a small display the next morning, after Friday mosque and the traditional Friday salutation of the King. Isidore said he was surprised organizing a special horse display had been so easy. I wasn't, having met the Chief of Horses in a previous life.

Via the Minister of Finance, the Chief of Horses had asked the usual questions – where we were from, where we were going, where we were staying in Nikki. At the mention of my hotel there was a general eye-rolling and muttering, as if there were something to know about the place.

I didn't know much, not having been allowed in it yet. Isidore went in, roaring for the *broussiards*. Yes, yes, the rooms were ready. Lucky for them.

The hotel, with its French-restaurant-in-a-British-sitcom name, Chez John, was only £2 a night. It was huge, with a brag of neon signs inside and out saying Chez John – none of which were lit.

Chez John looked as though construction had barely finished, yet it was dilapidated, dirty and neglected. There were two-storey blocks of rooms and chalets round a courtyard. There was a disco, an outdoor cinema, an unfilled pool . . . John seemed like a man who'd expected something to happen and been disappointed.

The *broussiards* were two girls, one about seventeen – cool, distant and what my grandmother would have called slatternly. The girl who did all the work couldn't have been more than fifteen. She was a sad little girl, with uncoiffed hair, a plain little face, scruffy, oversize Western clothes; every inch of her physicality said 'terrible life and terrified'.

Isidore told her to get us dinner in an hour. I tried to escape to my room. He insisted he follow me to inspect it.

Crossing the courtyard, past the empty two-storey buildings and empty chalets, I didn't understand the place at all. Why had John built this place at most only a year ago and left it to go to ruin? Run by one sulky, slatternly girl and a depressed girl-child, who looked more like they were squatting in the place than running it.

My room was fine, just about clean. Everything looked recently installed, but broken, stained, mould-edged.

Isidore, almost swaying with tiredness, stood in the doorway, pointing out at the courtyard. 'Look at this wonderful place. Someone's spent a fortune and these girls are letting it rot. Really, if I had a place like this, I'd never need to worry about money or food again.'

'Maybe the owner died or something.' It felt like something had gone that dramatically wrong.

'No. He'll be abroad or in Cotonou and he's built this in his hometown, not thinking you can't leave bush dwellers in charge.'

I chivvied him away to get some rest. I wanted to nose round the premises without him.

Maybe John had just built himself a great white elephant, expecting the horse shows would be attracting tourists in droves . . . That would have been a sad story, though, and wouldn't have produced the knowing tone of eye-rolling from the horsemen.

I wondered about the cinema, the discothèque . . . Perhaps people roared into the place at night and it came loudly to life. The metal seats in the cinema yard were stacked and rusting, the whitewash screen was covered in red dust. There was a padlock on the discotheque door. No. Nobody came.

A wash and a lie down had not improved Isidore's mood. And he'd now taken against Chez John even more, and concluded that the owner was someone who'd made easy money so didn't bother looking after what he owned – probably a drug dealer or a customs man. Interchangeable professions, obviously.

We had a drink in the dark, fly-brown bar/restaurant. It had been built fancy, too, with wooden booths and ranchhouse cartwheels on the ceiling to hold lightbulbs. No lightbulbs alive in them. The harsh striplights down the sides of the cavernous room buzzed and showed up the dust. The drainy smell from outside was drifting in.

Isidore bellowed at the depressed child to hurry up and bring dinner. She was hurrying, but as she reached the kitchen door he called her back.

'Is the food going to be hot?'

'Yes,' she said. Petrified of him, she hurried off again.

I tried to make conversation about the horsemen but Isidore wasn't listening, kept making impatient sounds and watching the kitchen door.

She brought two tin plates of congealed rice with meat and tomato sauce. Isidore took one mouthful and roared at the retreating child.

'I asked you if the food was hot. You said yes. It's completely cold. Idiot!' He pushed his plate away.

I smiled at her. She seemed to have turned into a scared little stone. 'Mine's fine,' I said. She nodded and fled.

Isidore didn't eat; he stared at the table. To spite him, I ate every scrap, including the rancid-tasting meat – even if every drain-sucking fly in the place had laid larva eggs in the meat and they grew inside me and ate my intestines and then my lungs, I couldn't forgive him for bullying that child.

He put his head in his hands like he had the world's worst migraine. He sighed. He sighed again. He jumped to his feet.

'I'm going to tell her to pulverize the rooms.'

This was less alarming than it sounded. *Pulvériser les chambres* – spraying them with insecticide. Again, usually, the violence of the French expression would have made me laugh. Pulverizing at Chez John would undoubtedly be essential; but I felt Isidore had been simply racking his brains for an excuse to go on another bullying spree.

He shouted the depressed child back to our table.

'Give her your room key,' he said in a tone that told me bush dwellers weren't the only ones he thought he could bully. He barked orders at the child, cross-examining her to make sure she'd understood.

I knew that what he was interpreting as a defiant look was her trying to hold back tears. Poor skinny, ugly-haired girl who didn't need to be shouted at one more minute in her wretched life.

The other girl came to clear our plates. Isidore started railing about the cold food. The girl seemed to glaze over and seal up. She'd found a way not to feel that the little one hadn't yet discovered. Isidore stood up again.

'Where is she?' The child had barely been gone a minute. 'Tell her to hurry up, we want our keys back.'

Very weepy, the child came back with the keys and a huge can of insecticide. I remembered my room had a tricky lock. Probably more tricky for a scared, sobbing kid with shaking hands. I was starting to point this out when Isidore grabbed the keys and insecticide. 'I'll do it myself.'

★

I paid for the meal and drinks, smiling apologetically at the older girl. She registered no emotion. The child had already run away, slamming a door behind her.

I went out on to the terrace, to watch the street and think what to do about Isidore. I was distracted by red lightning behind clouds in the dusk sky. Beautiful. Then thunder. Was this rain? It wasn't a good time for a tropical storm to wash away the dirt road out of Nikki. Stranding us at Chez John for days.

Maybe I should pack up, find a taxi and leave immediately.

Nothing this bad had come up before. It wasn't just a row; I felt as though I had no idea who he was.

I was certain it wasn't about what it seemed to be about. Was it some overdue, warped expression of grief? Was it to do with me? Some offending stupidity of mine? He couldn't get directly angry with me, so he'd taken it out on the little girl?

Isidore walked over to me. Not angry, not shamefaced. He was cold, matter of fact. 'Can we go for a walk around?'

I agreed. I didn't want his company, but I might as well look at the town.

On the way out, Isidore banged the insecticide can down on the bar and rattled its protective metal cage. The cage didn't speak well of the sort of clientele John had managed to attract. The girls didn't appear.

As we walked around the night market, Isidore began a lot of sighing and muttering of 'Oh really . . .' Like he was desperate for my attention. I ignored him, flashed my torch along the ground to check I didn't fall into a sewage drain to crown the evening.

Finally he completed a sentence: 'Really, that girl. Such a stupid, rude idiot.' I tensed, ready for further arguments, but his mood shifted. He said wearily: 'Anyway, I thought if we had a walk around you might find something interesting to write about.'

It was interesting – lantern-lit stalls, staring people not used to a sulky *batture* strolling the streets after dark. White-turbaned youths lurking on corners; goats, sheep, lorries; people selling mounds of fake Nike, Reebok and Adidas from Nigeria; canisters of smuggled petrol. It was interesting, but I was miserable. I was in the middle of Africa, at night, at the start of a very long journey with someone I didn't even want to look at any more.

I thought terrible things: no wonder Isidore's wife left him – he probably bullied her relentlessly, probably beat her. How could he take his anger about the world, or me, out on that luckless child? We passed a stall selling biscuits and cans of Nescafé. I decided I'd buy these, otherwise getting breakfast would result in scenes and a filthy cup in the drain restaurant. I broke what had been a very long silence:

'I'm going to buy a little tin of coffee. I can make some cold with mineral water myself, that'll do fine. It's caffeine. Otherwise tomorrow there'll be another fuss about nothing and I'll end up with a bad cup of coffee anyway. It's not worth it.'

Isidore sounded sad. 'If I get annoyed with her, you'll get annoyed with me.'

'Exactly.'

'Oh really . . .' He wasn't sad, he was still angry and not at all ashamed. 'OK, go in the shop, it'll be cheaper.'

In the big Nigerian-run shop I'd been served Nescafé and biscuits and told the price. Isidore had hung around outside, probably looking for some cripples to push over, then he appeared at my elbow, roughly demanding to know the price I'd been asked. I ignored him and asked the pleasant shop assistant if he had any insect repellent. He showed me several jumbo cans of pulverizer, so I said, trying English, 'Against insects for the skin?'

'Ah, American.' The Nigerian smiled. 'One moment.'

He rifled shelves under the counter and came back with a bottle of Dettol, which was a good guess at what I wanted.

'No, no, that's not it,' Isidore barked.

I smiled at the assistant and tried brand names on him.

'Sorry, lady, we don't have. How's New York?'

'Fine.' I paid the price he'd asked and, seeing Isidore about to question it, I walked out of the shop. I looked at the now silver-blue lightning in the clouds above. It was going to rain on my horse parade.

I so didn't need Isidore; I could figure the way back to the hotel for myself. He caught up with me, going into a panic, floundering to remind me of his usefulness.

'After the horses tomorrow, I think we should go to Kandi, there's a lovely place to stay up there. We can use it for a base to see everything in that area. I have it all planned. I haven't been to school – I have no one to teach me how to do it – but I can make good plans. I think about plans for you all the time.'

This was awful, abject. Now I hated the situation more – hated that he'd realized he had actually very little margin of freedom to make me angry.

'You'll like Kandi, and at Malanville you'll be right by the Niger river. You see my plan?'

I said nothing. I couldn't bear this grovelling, but it was hard to forget the poor bush-dwelling child's tears.

Outside my door he asked anxiously: 'Nine tomorrow, then. Is that OK?'

'Yes,' I said curtly and went to my room. I knew he hovered but I didn't look back at him.

Once in my room, I wished I had looked back. He'd made me feel sad for him with his last-minute panic.

Isidore's position was less precarious than he thought. He'd shocked me, confused me and upset me, but I realized that I'd have had firing him on my conscience a lot longer than I'd be upset for the child.

The rain that had crashed on my tin roof all night and kept me awake had made all the plants in the courtyard fresh and clean. The air was washed sharp, the sun was shining. Isidore was up, scrubbing the rain dirt off the car. He noticed me, waited mid-scrub to see . . . I called a cheery '*Bonjour*' and at fifty yards saw stress drop off him like rain dirt from a Peugeot. He smiled with unabashed relief. Waited again as I came over, to see if the cheeriness would expand. It did. I cheerily asked how he thought the road would be after the rain.

'It'll be fine. One night's rain wouldn't destroy it. And anyway, it didn't rain all night.' He smiled sheepishly. 'As you can guess, I know because I didn't sleep very much.'

He wasn't getting sympathy, if that's what he was after.

'Anyway, I have paid the hotel bill because I wanted to be finished with them and not have to see them again. Especially not if you were there and there was further disagreement.'

He didn't get it at all, no notion what he'd really done wrong. 'Isidore, there's no point getting angry at people like that, it just makes them scared and makes them worse. That girl needs someone to be kind to her.'

'Well,' he squeezed out his cleaning cloth, 'you think that, I think the opposite.'

I told him he wasn't seeing the girl, imagining her life.

'I don't want to think about her. It's finished now anyway – we don't have to see them again.'

'She did nothing to deserve it.'

He looked at me like now he was going to cry. 'You don't understand. When I first walked in here her speech to me was very rude.'

I didn't understand. There was no point bothering with this any more. We didn't have to see them again.

Hey-ho. You think all you're doing is hailing a cab . . .

Under the flame trees small clumps of people sat in the shade. We had to call in to find the Minister of Finance at the palace and let the King know we'd arrived. In a white skullcap and shiny best Friday robes, the Minister emerged all smiles.

'Good timing. Mosque has just finished.' He interrupted himself as a line of old coves walking with sticks approached the palace from the mosque. One of them in lurid cheap sunglasses looked vaguely familiar . . . it was him, my heroic Head of Horsemen, looking like just one of the old coves. It had been hot yesterday, not enough food, stress . . . Then he came on to the palace porch beside us and took off the sunglasses. I saw his amazing face again. He didn't smile, simply took a long time staring into my eyes. The

Minister of Finance seemed to feel we should all be moving along.

'The ministers have to pay their respects to the King. Follow me.'

We crossed the open ground; the Minister installed us on a mat in the shade.

'Look, the musicians have arrived.'

Under another shade tree, men with drums and a man with an instrument like a very thin alpine horn were settling themselves. The horn, a traditional temple horn, began making long, low notes.

'This tells people mosque has ended and the King will come soon.'

Children were gathering behind me. The King's girl grand-children showing me their best frocks; little boys showing me gymnastics and wanting their photo taken. I indulged them until the Minister started talking again.

'The King asked me to explain the history of Nikki to you.' He shooed away some upside-down boys.

'They say the people of Nikki originally came from Mecca,' Isidore began.

'Who says? Excuse me, my son, I've heard that too but it's not accurate. The people of Nikki are not Arabs. We're from this region of Africa. We've always been in this area. We are Bariba, an African people. A man called Sinoncero was inspired by the teach-ings of Mohammed. He converted the people of this region and led them. He formed us into a fighting race, based on Arab models.'

Perfectly on cue, in white turbans and flowing white robes, two men galloped up on small strong Arab horses. They halted a few flame trees away. Three more arrived, in coloured robes and tur-bans. One had his horse covered in decorative padded cloth as if ready for a medieval joust.

'This one with the padded horse is their leader,' the Minister said.

While I'd been watching the horsemen, the old coves had all crossed from the palace to sit in the shade near us. Including the Chief of Horses, who, sitting with one knee up, seemed to be tall again. Perhaps like most people who looked good on a horse, he had a long body rather than long legs. Suddenly two of the horsemen were off – galloping up and down the open ground, robes flying. They raced; they went up and down perfectly in unison; they went up and down at a frantic pace with their arms held up . . . So much for my suspicion that it would all have gone to seaside donkeys now.

The horsemen came to rest under the trees again, their mounts sweating, stamping, switching flies. The riders began whispering among themselves, looking at me. Then the leader walked his animal a few steps towards us – he spoke to me in slow, heavily accented French.

'Is it you who summoned us?'

I thought I was in some kind of trouble. I decided I'd just look pleasant till I saw what kind.

The leader smiled, puzzled. 'We were asked to come. We're not sure what you want from us. Do you want to see us race some more? Or did you want to take photos?'

Not in trouble, then. I said I'd like to take photos.

'Of course.' He smiled and went to tell the others.

I started to photograph them. The leader said, 'Wait, wait, it can be better.'

He reared his horse up almost vertical and held it there long enough for me to take several pictures. As he came down, the riders in the white robes reared up for me. They all took turns at this pose, perfectly controlled, competing with each other for length of time in the air. Then all of them charged together in an exact line across the open ground, turned together and came back at a high-speed gallop, right towards me. I kept snapping until I was sure I'd be trampled to death but they stopped just short of me in a perfect line.

'Careful, come back,' Isidore kept urging. But now the horsemen were having fun. In turns, each of them would charge into the open ground, turn and rush back, scattering small children and Isidore, as it looked certain that this time it had all gone wrong and they couldn't possibly stop the horse. They always did.

As a fearful Isidore scattered yet again before a galloping horseman, the leader approached him at a non-hazardous walking pace.

'Listen, there is no need for that. This horse is part of me; it's like I was coming up to you on my own feet. All of us, these horses' feet are our feet.'

More like the Isidore I knew, he laughed at himself. 'I didn't realize I'd be nervous. I'm glad I wasn't born here, I'd look a fool.'

The horsemen stopped larking about as the King emerged from the palace. The horn resumed sounding its long, low notes. The Minister of Finance creaked to his feet.

'We greet the King formally now.'

One by one, the ministers crossed the ground to prostrate themselves before the King. Including my hero. He lay flat on his belly, grovelling, hands above him on the ground. He began rolling from side to side like a snake in agony. This was so all of the front of his body would be sure to touch the ground. He made a strange, low 'Uhh, Uhh' sound – a sign of respect used all over northern Benin. Then he was speaking, still prostrate and writhing, showering blessings on the King.

Isidore said that, as he was the First Minister, he made the most elaborate and traditional salutations. I felt it was all a bit beneath his dignity.

The Minister of Finance had remained with us. He suggested we dismiss the horsemen and say our goodbyes to the King.

As we crossed the horse-churned ground he said, 'Mind the mud here. We were lucky with the rain. Usually they make too much dust. You enjoyed it?'

I realized I'd let the horsemen go and knew nothing about them except how good they were. I hurried to find intelligent questions . . .

These days the horsemen were simply farmers who indulged a hobby, if they could afford it. What with weddings, royal ceremonies and curious tourists, if they could afford the horse in the first place the hobby covered its own costs.

Once, horseriding had been a way of life. The King had given horses to his favourite soldiers; horses were like a second currency. But now the wars were over it was just a bit of traditional fun. No particular status was involved, nor were there particular families who involved themselves with horses.

Finally, for no reason at all, I asked how one got to be Chief Horseman.

'They choose the Chief themselves now. Once, the King chose; now, they choose the best and wisest among themselves.'

Best and wisest, retired, was sitting beside the King in the official reception chamber, looking none the worse for his dirt writhing. The King sat in the corner, where he couldn't be seen from the door, an anti-assassination ploy. After the best and wisest, all the other ministers were rowed along the wall to the King's left. Court was in session to receive people, mostly people with problems. The beproblemed were gathering outside, very curious about me, starting to tell me their troubles, show me their stumps and rags.

I didn't know a Bariba word for what was about to happen, but Isidore had taught me a good Yoruba word: '*walhala*'. Meaning mayhem, hassle, brouhaha . . .

Once I was inside the palace the beggars could only wave stumps and call to me. The King's granddaughters held hands with me while I waited in the antechamber. We were joined by a boy-toddler grandchild, adorable in a blue shirt and baby jeans.

I had to take my shoes off to go into the reception room proper. I knelt before the King, thanked him and, of course, glanced sideways to meet the gaze of the First Minister. He'd been waiting for me to do that. He nodded at me with a beautiful smile warming his eyes. 'Thank you,' I said soundlessly and held his gaze as long as possible.

In the antechamber, where the First Minister could still see me, I was filled with some overwhelming urge to pick up, cosset, cuddle and kiss the King's grandson. I knew I was showing off for the First Minister in the most biologically basic way, but I couldn't help myself. Out of the corner of my eye I could see him watching me. I was going to say 'fondly' but it was with a lusty stare, which I guess was what I was angling for. But he was a seventy-year-old Bariba horseman who spoke no French and ate under spells against witches, and I was on my way out the door forever . . .

I was being hustled out the door by a rather exasperated Isidore trying to fend off the gathering stump wavers, ragged youths and women with deformed children creating a rising *walhala* on the doorstep, pushing and shouting for money from me.

'What are you doing? Put the baby down, put on your shoes!'

He hurried me half-shod into the car as the *walhala* of pushing, baying entreaters nearly cut off my escape.

12

Why We're on Earth,
and Other Lessons

Released from whatever bitter helplessness had made him go wrong for those horrible hours in Nikki, Isidore told funny stories all the way north. Once we'd spluttered and giggled for a solid hour, there was nothing to do but look forward.

'We'll go right up to Karimama and Malanville. There's a huge market in Malanville. Huge. I'm going to buy plenty of things for the children there. I'll like to see their faces when they see what I've bought. Maize, onions . . . The Borgou is full of cheap onions. We'll take back so many, it will be fantastic . . .'

As well as witches and onions, the Borgou had more kings than you could shake a sceptre at. Most of them supplemented the small income of small kings with farming. Most of them were Bariba and Moslem animist. Very few had styled themselves as tourist attractions.

The King of N'Dali was too old and sick for visitors. The very old King of some other place told me a story about the first king of the region arriving on the back of a boar but he had to cut the conversation short because he needed to go shopping. The King of Bembereke was very old and asleep on a deckchair amid the gnarled roots of a baobab tree in a courtyard of grandchildren and goats. He was extremely startled to wake up and find a *batture* in front of him.

'What does she want?' he asked Isidore.

'Nothing,' Isidore said. 'She's just interested to know the history of the kingdom.'

'I'm sorry, I don't know anything about that,' the King said, and fell asleep again.

Further down the road, half a dozen houses and a tree graced themselves with a roadsign reading 'Petit Paris'.

The King of Gogounou explained the name to us. It was a recent thing, and it was a joke. The men from the city had come to make maps and roadsigns and couldn't find anyone who knew the name for where they lived. Not happy with this for an answer, they decided the locals were just being deliberately unco-operative and named the place Petit Paris to mock them.

The King of Gogounou was half-blind, very short of breath and had badly swollen legs; nevertheless, he'd come wheezing across his farmyard to welcome us. This cruel dragging of old men from their daybeds for questioning was Isidore's idea, not mine. He said the kings and their elders would know the history of the region, or anything current that might be important, so they had to be interrogated.

I have a kaleidoscope of photographs of Bariba kings. Some of them imparted obscure local facts and recounted long histories, but in my memory odd quirks about them loom more than dry facts. The King of Gogounou, for instance, complained of the preponderance of girls among his twenty-seven grandchildren. And as we were leaving, many small girls trailed out of the palace to look at us. They stood around the car, all gnawing on large, gristly meat bones.

'Ah. Small children with meat,' Isidore remarked, in case I didn't understand what I was seeing.

Opening the car door, he said to one toddler girl with a lump of cow leg held to her face, 'Come on, you, we're taking you to England with your meat.'

She jumped away, the others waved their meat and squealed delightedly.

'I have meat! Take me!'

'Take me! I have meat! I'm not scared!'

I wondered why the King of Gougounou, palace doorways draped with *gri-gri*, found himself helpless in the face of ever oncoming girl grandchildren.

'Can't people do *gri-gri* to make sure they get boys?' I asked Isidore as we continued north towards his final Bariba king of the day.

He looked disapproving. 'They can, but not up here, these people don't know that *gri-gri*. There are Fon who know it, but it's not good. That God gives you a healthy child who lives . . . that's the thing to work for. To make boys, well, my father, he would say it was a bad way to use *gri-gri*. That is the area of witchcraft. You need to be careful what you involve yourself in. Like my father would never do the *gri-gri* to make money – that's witchcraft.'

'I find it difficult to know the difference.'

'It's not difficult. The things that work with the world as the good Lord has given it to us, that's no sin. But wanting more than God has given us, that's witchcraft.'

But it wasn't witchcraft to make babies for infertile women, babies God hadn't given them? The dividing line seemed blurry. Isidore said doing someone harm to get you your wishes was witchcraft. But . . . how come it wasn't witchcraft to carry a small knife tipped with undetectable poison made from rare leaves gathered with a Bariba magic man in the mountains at dawn? This was an accessory Isidore sought to purchase at the court of our final king of the day, the King of Kandi.

King Sakasalle the Third lived in a small, orderly compound, and received us in a carpeted throne room. The throne was a plain wooden chair with a spittoon and a radio beside it. All the time we were with him, he left the radio playing faint music in the background. Maybe he thought we'd be boring.

Sakasalle chewed tobacco and snorted snuff, but these habits didn't seem to have destroyed his health. He looked very young, with clear soft skin and no time at all showing round his eyes. At first I thought he was a boy king – until I spotted the neat grey goatee. The beard was so incongruous that at first I suspected he'd stuck it on to look older. Astonishingly, he told me he was fifty-six.

He had one wife, four children and that was enough. He said he was driven demented by people trying to throw wives at him but he really didn't want any more, and he certainly wanted no more children. He wanted to provide well for the four he had.

His younger brother and a man he introduced as his best friend joined us in the throne room. It turned out that Sakasalle could speak English, having been raised in Ghana. But we needed the brother to do the Bariba to French for Isidore's more peculiar questions.

The people of Kandi were a branch of the Kingdom of Nikki, although now completely autonomous. Kandi, properly Kande, meant 'thanks to me' – me being the King. Sakasalle smiled. 'Not me personally – an ancestor of mine who had trouble with an invading neighbour as he tried to establish his kingdom. My ancestor fought and won and made the place secure. So he said the kingdom existed "thanks to me".'

I was still distracted by how shiny and young-looking Sakasalle was. Even his voice was young. With all the ensuing talk of spells I did wonder about cosmetic *gri-gri*. Perhaps I could pick up a little pot of something for my dressing table. Maybe he was doing something weird with the radio – it always had to be on because he'd *gri-gri*-ed some way to make sound waves beat back the ageing process.

As well as being good mounted fighters, adept in the use of poisoned arrows, Sakasalle's ancestors had been able to successfully consolidate their kingdom through use of their magic powers.

Sakasalle's grandfather was a very strong man. Born in 1901, he fought in the war in Europe alongside Americans, continued in the army for a while after that, then trained in forestry. For a change of scene, he went to work as a forester in Ghana. He was working in the forest one day when a bird came and told him to go home. He went quickly; his father was dead and already an interloping cousin was trying to be king.

Many Kandi people didn't know the stranger from Ghana. He had to fight hard for his right to the throne. Even after he was enthroned, several elders were on the cousin's side and sent all manner of *gri-gri* to annoy grandfather. They'd send goats to run into his house with poison on their horns. They'd send poisoned food. Grandfather would taste the poisoned food and send the rest back to whoever had sent it – by tasting it, he could tell who'd sent the poisoned food. It frightened his enemies to see his cleverness, and that he could eat a spoonful of poison and not die. After a while they stopped messing with him.

Sakasalle's father had remained in Ghana, but was brought to Kandi in time for the people to get to know him before his father died. Sakasalle came with him. Because grandfather lived so long, until 1986, his father was only king for twelve years before Sakasalle succeeded.

There was a pause as the recap of Kandi history ended. Isidore shifted on the floor carpet, taking some rum from the brother's proffered bottle – he'd decided it was time to get down to business. He praised the notorious power of Bariba *gri-gri* and asked if they could help him. One of the things he wanted was *gri-gri* against envy. I thought he had some but presumably you could never have too much.

Sakasalle smiled and nodded. 'With your *batture* here I can see they'd envy you. Now, our *gri-gri* isn't some nonsense like those powders to swallow sold in the markets. We cut it into you or make proper leather amulets that you have with you all the time. Everything in them will be specially prepared. If we do give you things to eat it will also be specially prepared, things to be consumed over a long period of time, with proper supervision. As you must know, if someone takes *gri-gri* they're not used to, in the wrong way, they could drop dead.'

Isidore nodded, he knew.

'Unfortunately,' Sakasalle continued, 'this is not a good time of year for it, with the rains. The rains wash the power out of things. The best time is during Harmattan, the wind cleanses and all things are at their strongest. If you are serious, you should come back then, in . . . when is Harmattan? November. I have an elder who can help you. In November, he'll take you to find the leaves that grow from a certain tree after it has fallen. It's hard to find these fallen trees, and the leaves are best gathered at dawn, so you would need to be all night in the bush. Then you make a soap from these leaves, wash yourself in this every day for seven days, then you'll have great strength.'

They were completely matter of fact, as if Isidore had called in to see if they knew a good car mechanic.

There was some actual car talk because the brother worked as a taxi driver. He came out to cast an admiring eye over the mere Peugeot that was to take us through the Borgou – he'd assumed a four-wheel drive. There was much patting of the Peugeot, hand-shaking and promises of *gri-gri* reunions in Harmattan time. No one shook my hand, obviously, in case I drained them.

Isidore was a happy man. 'Ah, really, the Bariba are strong. I hope I have a customer who wants to come this way in November. You heard them talk of poison? They're excellent in this. In case of bandits on the road I want to get a little knife. When bandits attack, I'll pretend to scratch my leg, and pull it out. If your knife is poisoned you don't need to be accurate. Just cut them and they're instantly paralysed with this poison. Then, later, they die but even a hospital doctor can't find poison. You see, a special little knife I'd attach to my calf in a holder.'

He tapped his leg, stared at the road ahead as if imagining fine triumphs over bandits.

'What kind of bandits are you expecting?'

He laughed. 'No, no, don't worry. There won't be any bandits while you're here.'

'Why not?'

'I'm just thinking of the future.'

'And where will you be going then, exactly, to need a knife?'

'I don't know.' He looked slightly crestfallen. 'It would be nice, though, to have the knife, just in case.'

Just in case, I wanted to put him off the idea. 'You'd probably slip in the mud one day and stab your own leg.'

He thought this was very funny. 'What am I? An idiot?' He could hardly drive in to the hostel for laughing. 'Yes, you're right, with my luck, I'd stab my own leg.'

The Kandi *auberge* was so lovely you'd enjoy a stay there even if you'd just stabbed your own leg and needed to hole up somewhere for your last night on earth. Elegantly homey, the hostel was one of a chain owned by a Frenchman called Guy. The *auberges* were all small, cheap places, twenty cabins at most; only eight at Kandi. Local craftsmanship was used for furnishings, local cloths for curtains and bedding; the grounds were nursery rich with flowers and fruit trees. The menus were simple French or non-tree-rat Beninois, and you could get an excellent cup of coffee.

Kandi was used mainly by small groups going to the animal park on the Niger border. Had the park been open I might have come face to face with an elephant, but yet again I'd arrived when the parks were closed. Some locals came to drink on the bar terrace in the evenings but I was the only guest in the *auberge* for five nights.

As in all the *auberges*, the staff and management here were Beninois. There was Christophe, the chef, a Fon, immediately pally with Isidore – he cooked fat chicken, beef kebabs and a range of fish dishes that never had too many bones or tasted of mud. There was another Fon, Amiée, a woman in her late thirties who cleaned, washed up and seemed sad. Marie, a young Nago woman from Savé with beautiful long plaits and many curves, was the waitress. Hassan the teenage Bariba was in charge of gardening and heavy cleaning and Jacob from Ouémé did the bar, administration and shopping. Actually everyone did all the jobs if they needed doing. 'We're a team, that's the idea,' Jacob explained.

The place was fairly new and the staff had been told it was down to

them to make a go of it. They only had me to make a go of, and they
certainly did. Hassan carried in the cases; Amiée flapped around the
room checking everything was just right; Christophe wanted to get
my dinner on; Marie wanted to fetch me a drink; and Jacob needed
to write down all kinds of things about me in his visitors' book.

Isidore told Amiée he thought he knew her face. He did – she
was from just outside Dovi Dove. She helped Marie set up for
dinner and, after initial enquiries about her status, Amiée started to
tell us her life story.

Amiée had three children with her husband who then took
another wife. The other wife did *gri-gri* and the husband started
beating Amiée. She took her children and went home to her
parents. Luckily Amiée's parents had enough to support the children, because the husband refused to see her, or them, again.

'Through a friend I found this nice job up here. I have even met
another man.'

'Hmm,' Marie said with kindly disapproval. 'Tell them about
that.' She looked at me. 'I know I am younger, it's not my place to
advise, but I don't think what she's doing with this man will be
good for her.'

The man already had a wife and three children. He wanted to
make Amiée a second wife.

'I think it will be all right, if I have some children with him too,
so my position is as strong as the first wife's.'

I could tell by her face she knew this was desperate.

'Do you like him?' I asked.

She nodded.

'Like him? That's not the question.' Isidore looked at me scornfully, then spoke to Amiée. 'This man, does he have money?'

'No.'

'Then why have children with him? You have your children.
You'll gain nothing and lose your freedom.'

'But I'm thirty-five, not new, what other offer can I expect?'

'You have your children, a nice job, your parents sound nice
people. Till now you have everything just nice. You go with that
man and have children, you lose all your advantages. What you

should do is work hard, make a little money, get yourself nice *pagne*, go to the cinema or restaurants with friends. Buy gifts for your children and your parents. Forget a man who brings zero to your life. You need to enjoy life.'

She seemed completely thrown by all this.

'Yes, enjoy your life,' Christophe said, bringing through the dinner.

'Enjoy my life?' She might as well have been advised to run to the moon. 'A woman alone?'

'You won't always be alone,' Isidore said firmly. 'You'll have a better offer than this one, if you keep yourself free and look like a woman who enjoys life.'

'There are no men available for a woman my age.'

'There are lots – look at you,' Marie said, glancing at me for back-up. 'You see how smartly dressed she is, hair nicely done, she's always like this.'

Amiée was spick and span, and pretty. But true enough, what made you draw away from her was the air of a woman not enjoying life.

'I think he's giving you good advice,' I said.

'Are you going to eat your dinners?' Christophe fretted.

'There are men,' Isidore said. 'You could find a divorced man, a widower. Really, Amiée, go to restaurants and cinemas and forget this man here.'

Amiée looked unconvinced; now saving her was down to a last push from me and Marie.

'My sister was married twice,' Marie said. 'The first one abandoned her, the second one beat her. So she took her two children and went home to our mother who has a small restaurant in Dassa. My sister is exactly your age. She has helped my mother build the restaurant into a good business, she has a little car for doing marketing and always looks like a film star. She realized what the *monsieur* has said: enjoy life but forget husbands.'

'Where I come from, you hear the same thing,' I said. 'If a woman is over thirty it's very hard to find a good man – we complain of it all the time – so we get our own money and enjoy life, because a bad man is worse than nothing.'

Marie and Amiée both looked startled. 'But a European man? Those men are good to their women. They only have one wife.'

'Men abandon their wives, beat them and cheat on them all over the world,' I said.

'Really?' Amiée was dumbfounded. 'It's the same?'

'It's the same.'

'A lot of you live happily without husbands?'

'Not always. But we are happier than women who have no money of their own and are trapped with a bad husband.'

'Exactly,' Isidore said. 'Freedom is better than slavery. Hope is better than putting yourself in prison.'

Having incited female riot, Isidore ate his fish dinner.

Amiée looked like the earth had cracked open in front of her. Not in a bad way. It had just never occurred to her that there was a way off the treadmill.

The next morning, without Isidore the firebrand, we continued our girl talk over breakfast. They talked of women, usually traders, who'd built tower blocks and fine houses in Cotonou and Porto Novo. Many tales of women starting with a fish stall in the market and little by little . . . I impressed them, for a time, when they asked how I lived. Then I caused a silence when I said I had no children.

So, a lot of big talk, but I was a loser after all.

'It is my choice,' I tried, to win them back.

They looked dubious.

Marie sounded worried for me. 'Husbands are one thing, madame, but children are why God put us on this earth.'

I decided against contradicting God.

The two women drifted away.

We remained friendly while I stayed there, but never again got into a feminist fever.

A little girl sat at the end of the *auberge* drive selling oranges. She was wearing a pair of pants on her head, as if it was a perfectly good hat. She waved to me, I waved back – 'Nice hat.'

She picked up her tray of oranges and ran towards us.

'Look,' Isidore said. 'Now you've done it. The way you wave, people think you're calling them. Don't waggle your hand about like that to say hello; just hold it up, still.'

Because of my bad waving style, I had to buy four oranges. The pant-headed child peeled a single spiral of peel off each of them with an over-sharpened razor blade in a matter of seconds. Children in Benin always seemed to be doing something skilful involving implements London children would hospitalize themselves with.

The girl was about six years old. By the time she was ten she could be sent to the home of a distant relative in Cotonou to work as a maid. Or for a small fee, her parents could let her go to an agency employing maids – she could end up in Lagos, Gabon, Ivory Coast . . . It could take her years to earn enough to come home. If she was paid at all. If she wasn't on one of the horrifying reports of these children who died in transit, usually by truck, and were simply thrown wherever it was convenient to throw a dead body.

Crops failed, disease killed, droughts came – parents thought their child might starve at home, and that being sent away was an opportunity for life. In fact, despite occasional hysterical reports in the foreign media, the majority of the children who went away to do maid work ended up with a better life than they'd have had at home. There was no need for the parents to have to make these dreadful choices. In one year, $70,000,000 of foreign-aid money given to Kérékou's government had gone missing. Maybe it had helped the French build the roads.

The intensive labour required for the farming of maize, vegetables and cotton in the Borgou had led to the construction of innumerable tiny villages – a village every half mile. Although most of the people were Bariba, there were also the tall, broad built, lighter-skinned Dendi. The Dendi men had three descending scars down one cheek – this showed they'd fought a lion and won. The Bariba had scars that went across the cheek horizontally – one for an elder son, several for younger brothers.

The Fon didn't scar their faces but often scarred their bodies.

The marks were religious rather than tribal. Usually they protected a child from human-wrought evil. Sometimes they prevented the divinities taking a child away, showing the divinities that the child belonged to someone and was needed.

Isidore decided that in all of Benin it was the people of the Borgou who had the most children. 'But then,' he sighed, 'it is the least modern part. I think it will never be modern.'

The lives we passed in the villages were ancient. Women pounded wooden mortars with wooden pestles and crushed shea nuts between stones. Shea butter was used in the north instead of palm oil. Patches of red pepper and manioc were spread on the tarmac at the road verges, an ideal flat surface for drying the product as well as advertising its availability. Men bundled sticks at the roadside to sell as firewood. Or carried blackened sacks on their heads into the village market, filled with newly made charcoal. Charcoal bought food; freshly grown produce was sold to buy charcoal. People went to market and back by foot, several times a day around the key mealtime hours. In addition to marketing or preparing goods for market, women had to fetch water at least four times a day. In the dry season they often had to walk a mile to find a deep-water pump.

With their giant cattle and swarms of goats, the Borgou verges were noticeably more roamed by the Fulani nomads. There was a particular bright royal blue the Fulani men wore, usually as a long robe, with wide-brimmed straw hats on their heads. 'Peul blue', Isidore called it – he tended to use the French name for the nomads. Peul blue was a colour that told you these were people who often roamed far from water in harsh red and yellow lands, creating their own refreshing splash for the eyes with their clothes.

As is the case with most of the world's nomads, they were a highly decorative people. The men wore earrings, round ones or long silver dangling ones. They frequently had facial tattoos, silver bracelets and walked their tall thin walk across the land, bright streaks of colour visible for miles. The women wore strings upon strings of beads round their waists, armfuls of bracelets and beaded necklaces from chest to chin. Their eyes were kohl rimmed, they wore lipstick – sometimes their faces had delicate blue tattoos, some-times they dotted flower shapes on their cheeks with bright-coloured nail varnish. Their hair bloomed with scarves and beaded braids. Extra strips of beads might be tied on to the ends of their hair – some of the younger girls had strings of small plastic toys plaited in. There were little twists of beaded hair that hung down in front of their ears, or there'd be long curls by their ears reminiscent of Hassidic Jews. Their tall rangy bodies were swathed in the brightest of *pagne*. One in five of them had the lanky shape of catwalk models – put Naomi Campbell among them and she'd be the small dumpy girl they were sorry for. But they weren't models; they hung out in gangs at roadsides and markets selling vegetables and cheese.

We liked the round, creamy cheese, white- or red-rinded. Nor-mal people in Benin used it in cooking, chopped up instead of meat – Isidore and I would eat it by the greedy fistful when we found it. If we found cheese we felt fearless, we could adventure for hours and need no dinner.

I was intrigued by the dazzling Fulani; Isidore was reluctant to involve himself with them but I wore him down.

'They can be big thieves, these people – you have to watch them. They move around all the time so they can't be caught and punished. I think when you talk to them they won't be very interesting. They're just simple people. In a few hours we'll reach Karimama, on the border with Niger, it's thick with Peuls up there, so we'll see.'

Isidore was more interested in the Dendi who dominated Kari-mama, and he went hunting round the central square of Karimama for someone who could find him a Dendi king.

We found a king's house, but no king. There was a shy giant of a Dendi Mayor, who talked to us by a thicket of quinine trees bordering the house that was now used for public meetings. He explained that at the time the last King of Karimama died, Kérékou's revolution was in full modernizing frenzy, trying to do away with tribal kings. So they didn't enthrone a new king in case he was imprisoned, or worse.

The people had got into the habit of sharing the Dendi King of

Malanville. The Mayor reported to him because the Malanville King was far too old to travel. There were discussions going on about reinstating the monarchy at Karimama but people had come to like the mayoral system; a mayor was elected for five years by five representatives from each of the major villages around Karimama, and this was found to be a very fair way to run things.

There was a lull in the conversation. Isidore had little interest in secular government. I commented on the quinine trees – were they used as medicine? They were. The French had an idea that it was good to plant quinine trees near villages, but, of course, there was a good reason why Africans left quinine trees out in the bush where they belonged.

'We knew the medicine,' the Mayor said. 'But they're not a good tree. There's not much shade from them. See, over there, I used to have mango trees, lots of fruit and shade. Now these things have poisoned them. They poison other trees, they grow fast. They have seeds that the birds spread. Look at them . . .' He pointed at a clump of saplings near him. 'I'm sure these weren't here last week. Wretched things. Also, their roots are strong and break up walls. Once you've got quinine trees you soon won't have anything else.'

As if unable to bear the sight of the pushy quinine trees any longer, he stood and offered to show us the main sights of Karimama.

As I walked beside him, barely coming up to his broad shoulders, I remarked that the Dendi people were very tall.

'It's true,' he laughed. 'Originally, hundreds of years ago, we came from Mali. In Mali you'll see they're like us. Big, big people. Mostly Karimama is Dendi. There are some Fon around who sell *sodadi*; we don't make that drink here, we have no palms. And there are some people who came from Burkina about a hundred years ago. Sonheu people. They named Karimama. They ran away from a war and their soldiers came to take them back but they said, "No, this is our home now, a place of peace." The Dendi helped them and defended them and they stayed. So it's their name, Karimama, Place of Peace.'

'And Peul?' Isidore asked. 'I had the impression there were many Peul but I don't see them.'

'Yes there are Peul but they have their own settlement about a mile away. They're nice people but who could live with them? All those animals getting in people's maize . . . Ah, now, here's our maternity hospital, and there's our elementary school . . .'

Isidore interrupted to ask about the price of maize.

The big Mayor laughed. 'Even if I wasn't the Mayor I would tell you Karimama has the best maize in the Borgou. It isn't a market day but call at any house and you'll be sure to find a bargain.'

Isidore beamed. 'Excellent, let's look for Peuls and then buy maize.' Like we were off to paint the town forty shades of red.

The Mayor pointed away from the village. 'The Fulani are down there. See how you get on for yourselves, I don't really have the right to introduce you to their community. You know how odd they are.'

A mile further, where the land became more open and tree-sparse, we found a dozen Fulani women pounding millet in a field. Isidore approached them politely, speaking French. They stopped work and hovered, like they'd bolt if he made any wrong move.

The first of them to break the freeze and speak was a beautiful pregnant woman sitting to one side of the group. Isidore laughed and replied, not in French. They had a long conversation, slightly flirty from Isidore, coolly amused from the pregnant goddess.

'She speaks Fon. She used to work in Ouidah,' he told me.

She addressed her sisters, they relaxed. They laughed when Isidore asked if I could take their photograph – they were working, their hair wasn't done, they looked terrible, how could I want their photo?

It was hard work, banging wooden poles on to piles of millet to de-husk it, scooping it into metal bowls, sieving it, pouring it into other bowls . . . The pounding itself shook the earth like heavy-bass dance music. They'd forcefully drop the pole, it would bounce up and be caught, then dropped again. They pounded in rhythm, occasionally bursting into pounding songs. They finally agreed I could take their photograph if Isidore helped with the pounding.

He threw himself into this women's work with great relish,

provoking screams of laughter and applause. Then they all pounded together, Isidore getting quite giggly and skittish among the perspiring Fulani beauties. He was particularly giggly and skittish when he glanced over at the pregnant beauty. She'd asked me not to take her photograph; it wasn't proper when someone was pregnant. Then she said if we'd like to see the village we could go with her – she wanted to go home to rest; she'd only been out to chat with her friends a while.

She took us to a young man weeding a field. He spoke good French and was to show us round the village. Isidore watched her go.

'Imagine, this will be her fourth child.'

I supposed she was in her late twenties. And actually I could imagine – she was one of those lucky women who had the svelte grace, long eyelashes and bone structure that kept them beautiful forever.

Isidore was still watching her go.

'Ah, Isidore. I lost my heart in Karimama.'

He flustered gruffly. 'She's a nice woman. Come, this man will show us their village.'

The field the man had been working had maize planted as orderly as if it had been done with a ruler and tweezers. The village was so clean, you'd think they all rushed out and scrubbed it with toothbrushes every hour. There were no piles of rubbish, no flies, no animal leavings . . . No animals.

We discovered that the Fulani kept their animals away from where they lived. There were pens at the edge of the village for young, pregnant or sick animals but the whole impression that the Fulani roamed with their herds all the time was wrong. They were only semi-nomadic. They might take the herds away for months to pasture them, but they had settled communities. Drought, war or persecution might make everyone move on, but usually it was the men with the animals who took it in turns to do the moving.

One time, they'd been an expanding, powerful Moslem empire, spreading across West Africa. As the empire broke up, they'd kept shifting because of waves of retaliation. There were still waves of persecution of them, in Guinea, Senegal, Sierra Leone . . . When countries became unhappy and unstable, the slightly different, rootless people were very pogrom prone.

I asked our guide, Ali, if the Fulani always lived separately.

'It's easier that way. People like the Dendi are always making a fuss, suspecting us of stealing and accusing Peul animals of trampling their maize and so on. It's easier to keep away. Our children mix at school, as adults we have Dendi, Fon, Bariba friends, but when we live in their communities, we fall out. It's no fault on either side, really. But we are different and we don't want to blend in.'

They looked different and they weren't really connected to the place they lived. They were connected to other Fulani, all over West Africa. They had patterns of movement that didn't recognize national boundaries. If there was a drought in Mali or Burkina, those Fulani would come into Benin or Nigeria with their cattle and then go back when there was news of rain, so they didn't overgraze their neighbours. Frontiers did cause problems but sometimes exceptions were made for the Fulani, or they bribed their way through.

The people in the village, simply called Quartier Peul, were quiet and reserved. Ali tried not to get caught looking but he was intrigued by my *batture* blue eyes. Isidore always said that my hair and eyes made me look 'too white' in a way that sounded like I was unpleasantly freakish. Ali admitted that they had their own word for us, '*tubac*'.

'In Gambia and Senegal, white people are called *tubab*,' I told him.

'You know words from places where Fulani travel among us, especially a word for a new thing, fairly new thing.'

Ever the self-appointed school inspector, Isidore wanted to know why he saw so many Peul children herding animals, didn't any of them go to school? Ali said plenty went to school, and – a little sharply – pointed out that it was currently the school holidays.

We passed a mechanical pump set in a wide stone trough, where women were washing *pagne*, laughing and jostling as they slapped wet colourful cloth on stone.

'Ah.' Ali smiled. 'Women, see how they laugh at their work? Men don't have time to laugh like that when we're working. All our work on this earth is for the women, just to look after the women. They get fat while we get thin.' But it was said with wistful fondness. I could see Isidore getting equally wistful and fond over the water-shiny, splashing women.

I asked, making Isidore squint at me, what would happen if a Fon wanted to marry a Peul woman.

'If he is a good man, why not? More likely a Bariba because they are also Moslem. It happens. Not often. The man would normally give the girl's parents some cattle, but if he is from outside perhaps some money. But never a lot of cattle or money – the elders speak against large dowries because it is like selling the daughters.'

It was a bright clear day in the bright clean village that seemed almost laid out as a Fulani themepark. The only animals I saw were little birds with red, red bellies pecking under tidy shrubs. As we came to the edge of the village, by the perfectly ordered fields there was another pump, where a line of women waited to collect water, all carrying identical bowls.

This was a deep-water pump, essential in the dry season. But used for drinking and cooking anyway because the water was better. People paid 50 francs for every big basin of water. This way there was always money in a fund so the pump could be fixed quickly when it broke down – these deep pumps were notorious for breaking down.

'Is that why they all have the same bowls?' I asked.

'I don't know why they've all picked the same colour, they must have decided to make it a fashion. But the bowls should be the same size.'

'This village is so well organized,' Isidore marvelled. 'And the people must be very honest to keep such a system running.'

Ali remained perfectly pleasant, just a flicker of irritation in his eyes hinted he knew the stereotype that was being dented in Isidore's mind. 'Of course they're honest. Look at your car out here in the fields. Perfectly safe. You could leave it out here for a week and it would be safe.'

Isidore nodded, keen not to have offended. 'When I get back to Cotonou, I'll tell people the Peul up here aren't what they think. They live in the ideal community. Like a paradise.'

Ali looked . . . patient.

Isidore abandoned trying to dig himself out of the hole. 'Where does this road go if we continue, another village?'

'This road?' Ali laughed. 'You continue along this road and you will fall in the River Niger.'

'I left my heart in Karimama,' I repeated as we drove away and Isidore looked mistily to where the women had been with their pounding sticks, all gone now.

'Stop that,' he said. 'Or I'll leave you here with your Peuls.'

'You liked them too.'

'I am amazed by them. One of the things people say against the Peuls is that they are dirty. That's because we always see them in the bush with their animals – people don't know their homes. It goes to show: find out for yourself, don't listen to what people say.' Then he raised his hands off the steering wheel for a moment, as if delivering his revelation to a congregation on the bonnet. 'That's why you Europeans travel. It seems like it has no purpose, but it's to learn for yourselves. Ah, of course.'

We found maize at a good price with a Dendi woman in the main town, so that was some of the shopping done. Not that it was done in any shop-and-go kind of way. There was extensive bargaining, examining, sieving, shifting from bowls to plastic sacks . . . Two big sacks. If those children of Isidore's had onions on top of this, why, they'd be thinking it was Christmas.

There were several fierce-looking little girls around the maize compound, all with tight stumpy plaits sticking out of their heads, making them look permanently startled, or Medusa-like when angry. The Medusa came yelling out of one junior miss when she got into a fight with a little boy. He picked the fight by running up and taking a piece of cloth out of her hand, but she soon made mincemeat of him – punching, biting, kicking, strangling, ready to throw him in the bush. Shrieking mothers pulled them apart, one holding out a *pagne* as a shield between them, bullfighter-style.

'Go away now, before he sees where you go,' she told the little girl. The little girl sauntered off, yelling some taunt back at the boy.

Isidore whistled his amazement. 'Look at that, girls are stronger than boys.'

Another fierce small female with sticky-out plaits snapped indignantly at him. 'Of course.'

The mother, folding her feinting *pagne*, laughed. 'We're all stronger. Stronger means nothing on this earth.'

Maize dealing continued peacefully for a few moments, then the scowling little boy set out as if to go hunting for the girl. Isidore jumped up and barred his way.

'Where are you going? Are you going to fight your sister again? You can't. You haven't the strength.'

The little boy burst into humiliated tears, made all the more pitiful by the ferocious Dendi lion-fighting scars down either side of his face. He ran off howling, wretched with shame. The little girls laughed to see such fun.

Isidore watched the boy go and sighed for him.

13
Joie de Vivre

Despite pleas from the staff and offers of cut rates, Isidore declined the lodgings at the idyllic *auberge* and spent his nights somewhere else in the town. Only in emergencies did he stay where I did. Sometimes he stayed with relatives, sometimes in cheap hostels, insisting he preferred this as it saved me money. But I think what he really needed was to finish work for the day, to be who he was when I wasn't there.

I had other company. I lolled about in the *auberge* restaurant with the staff, watching telly. A rare treat, as in Kandi it only broadcast for a few hours a day. There was a Yoruba theatre group doing a play; Marie translated the action.

A woman had a dead child, she was sure witchcraft had killed it. They went to a *gri-gri* man who said, 'No one killed your child, God gives and God takes away.' The woman couldn't accept this. She went to a second *gri-gri* man, who prayed and revived the child. We then went to a scene with the woman's family at dinner, celebrating the revival of the baby. Then a third *gri-gri* man appeared, who envied and wished evil to the master of the house – killing the baby with witchery had failed, so this time he was going to send the master mad, send him running naked in the marketplaces. The actor made great extended play of pulling off his shirt, shoes, roaring and rolling on the ground – a tremendous performance of madness, drawing applause from all in the *auberge* restaurant. With much comic struggle, the family tied the madman up and took him to the first *gri-gri* man. He said he could cure the madman if they left him in his house for a month. The ill-wishing sorcerer, with pantomime-villain cursing, left, frustrated and defeated.

I thought there'd be a second part, but that was it. That was the story. The broadcasting time was over, the television went to grey and we settled to discuss the play. Nobody understood my question: but what did it mean? There wouldn't have been time to explain anyway, because Jacob, who usually said little, suddenly went berserk. From silently leaning on the bar counter he started roaring at us.

'You see the sorcery in Benin! The work of the Devil! Satan is here and we encourage him. I thank God I'm saved. I fall on my knees every hour and thank God I have been washed in the blood of the lamb and I'm free from the Devil and his manifestations in this country . . .' It went on a bit longer than this, with a lot of blood and lambs. We all stared open-mouthed, except Christophe, who picked up a magazine and read it carefully.

There was more crying to the rafters about the end being nigh and lambs, then Jacob pointed at Hassan, who was wiping down the tables – 'And you, you Moslems you want to kill us all! In the end the Moslems will kill the Christians and the Lord Jesus will have to save us from you. We see it happening in Nigeria. Blood and blood!'

Hassan folded up his cleaning cloth and went to sit with Christophe.

'I'm not Nigerian,' he said mildly, and started reading over Christophe's shoulder.

I had the impression he wasn't put out because this wasn't the first outburst of this kind from Jacob and it wasn't worth getting involved. I came to the same conclusion and gathered my belongings to go to bed. Isidore had told me to get an early night . . .

'Madame, listen to me, you're an educated person, you must not waste your soul. You must let Jesus save you.'

'How do you know I'm not saved?' I said, provoking a titter from the others.

'I hope you are, madame. I would hate to go to heaven and not see you there. The world will soon burn, you must all go there with me. Christophe, do you not care? Christophe?'

Christophe looked up from his magazine with pretended surprise. 'Oh, are you talking to me? I thought you were addressing the nation.'

Jacob was slightly thrown by this. He tried a new tack.

'Don't you know there's too much sorcery here? It was brought here by the French, Satan came across the sea. My own father was killed by sorcery. He campaigned for Soglo in ninety-six and he was poisoned by the sorcerers in our village. I've seen sorcery with my own eyes.' He crumpled as if he was going to start sobbing. 'I've seen the sorcery. It will destroy us if we're not saved.' He slumped, staring straight ahead like he was watching a sudden descent of lambs.

Marie, sorry for him now, said, 'I believe in Jesus; He protects us, Jacob.'

'Yes,' Amiée said. 'Whenever I come across sorcery I'm only afraid for a short time, because Jesus is with me.'

Not having Jesus with me, I thought I should check. 'So you've seen a lot of sorcery?'

'Oh yes,' Marie said apologetically. 'In our villages it still happens quite often.'

Jacob leapt alert, pointing at her. 'Quite often? All the time. It's a stain across this land like the shadow of Satan himself! I praise God that I've been saved by God, that the blood of the sweet lamb . . .'

I went to bed.

★

Jacob was subdued and efficient in the morning. Not a lamb crossed his lips. I don't know if he'd a drink taken the night before or simply the spirits had taken him, but I was glad to hear no more about it.

'Born-again Christian,' Isidore sneered. 'I hate the way they go on. The world won't end tomorrow so we should do our work.'

His work for the morning was to keep me calm when I saw signs along the Malanville road warning of elephants crossing. Who cared if the park was closed – we were going to drive smack into an elephant at any moment.

'There's no point hanging out the window looking all the time,' Isidore said. 'They won't be behind the hedge. The elephants will be away far off in the park now.'

'Why are all these signs here, then?'

'I don't know.' He sighed patiently. 'Probably to excite the foreigners.'

A hundred and five kilometres to Malanville and not one elephant behind a hedge.

Close to the Niger border, Malanville felt very different, much more Islamic, people dressed in veils saying '*Salaam aleikum*'. For the first time, I saw Islamic women in the full Saudi-style chador.

The very old King of Malanville was hardly bigger than a shoe, sitting wrapped in a blanket on a day bed under an awning. His grandson, in a Sherringham football shirt, assured us that although the King was a bit sick he loved to see foreigners, so it really was fine to disturb him.

The King was a Dendi. He said he didn't know what the Mayor of Karimama was doing talking about origins in Mali. The Dendi came into Benin from Niger at the beginning of the twentieth century, refugees from a war. Some returned, some remained.

'I think he meant hundreds of years before that.'

'He's a young man. What does he know about hundreds of years ago? I was born in nineteen twenty-one and I don't know.'

This made the King eighty. He did look it. But as if there was some doubt about his age, he told the grandson to bring his documents from the house. In a woman's white patent-leather clutch bag was the King's identity card; his date of birth was written 'around 1921' – that is, he or his parents wouldn't have had an exact date to give to the French authorities. His occupation was marked as 'farmer'. He said that generally the Dendi were hunters and farmers. No, Malanville wasn't the Dendi name, they didn't have a name for the town. The name Malanville came from 'Malan', the name of the Frenchman who'd made the first European map of the area. The old King coughed, his whole body shivering, and he went in to his white bag for more papers, muttering something in Dendi.

'My grandfather apologizes; he used to speak good French but he's forgotten it now.'

The King had learnt French in the army. He'd been conscripted by the French and sent to Casablanca in 1945. He showed us his French army papers. He said Casablanca was interesting, they'd done a lot of marching and training, but then it was 1946, the war was all over and they were sent home. The King wanted his grandson to have his photograph taken with me. We exchanged addresses and Isidore wished the King better health. He didn't really look like better was an option.

Although the King had escaped harm in the war, there were West Africans who fared less well. In World War One, the French mobilized 211,000 Africans to the Western Front; 24,762 were recorded killed and many more disappeared. In World War Two, the African troops were sent into Europe late because they'd been defending the allied cause in Africa. But on our next visit we met an eighty-year-old who'd had considerable experience with the Germans, far away from Africa.

This was a much more sprightly eighty-year-old and Isidore was as excited about seeing him as a *yovo* seeing an elephant.

'You will find him marvellous. I have a small envelope of money for him from his son who drives taxis with me in Cotonou. We all went on a hunting trip together with some men from Denmark; the old man is a retired ranger in the forest, he knows how to hunt

very well. You'd never believe he was eighty. He hunted with us
for five days in the bush, always ahead of us younger men, scouting,
then he'd make fires and organize the camp in the evening; really
he's all *kif-kif*.'

Isidore insisted that *kif-kif* was French for someone bouncingly
healthy and full of beans. In that case, this was certainly a *kif-kif vieux*.

A short, turtle-faced man, he didn't stop telling stories, chasing
children to bring us cold drinks and acting out every word of his
yarns with vigour and love of life.

When he first left school he'd gone to work in a French cotton
plantation, so he'd been quite glad to be conscripted into the army
in 1945. They were given boots and a uniform and put on a boat
at Cotonou to take them to France.

'This was an immense boat —' he stretched out his arms — 'almost
a kilometre long. We went to Marseilles where we did some
training. They showed us guns but it was mostly marching. Then,
just when we were ready, the war was over. They took us to the
Bordeaux region, where the bombed towns needed rebuilding.
They were using German prisoners of war to do this. These men
needed guarding. I was left with two other Beninois to look after
twenty-five German prisoners, who were to rebuild a street of
houses and part of a hospital. The French army bosses went off and
left us to it. Now, I could see those Germans weren't going to
work hard or co-operate with a black corporal, only five foot three.
I was a youngster, these were men in their thirties, big yellow-haired
Germans who'd been in battle. I could see when the French left
they were starting to laugh at us Beninois. I said to them they were
free to try escaping if they wanted, but they were far from Bordeaux
and even further from home. And if I found them trying to escape,
I'd have to shoot them in the back, and I didn't want to do that.
So what would be better all round was if they just got the building
done. Well, the Germans, they muttered and shifted around . . .'

Kif-Kif Vieux acted out muttering, shifting Germans, making a
very funny guttural noise that sounded exactly like disaffected
German.

'I could see I needed to make it clearer to them. I got one of my men to search out a map of the world from our office, a globe. I set it in front of the Germans. I said, "I want you to understand, we are all prisoners of war here. You can't leave, and nor can I." I showed them where Dahomey was. I said there I had my parents, my family and obligations and I wanted to get back there as fast as possible. "But," I said to them, "the French won't let me go until this building work is done. Because I am a prisoner far from home, like you. The sooner we do our job here, the sooner all of us are free men again."'

The Germans said nothing to him but they worked hard. When the French officer came through he was amazed to see so much progress. He'd asked Kif-Kif Vieux how he'd done it. He'd shrugged and said that it was simply a question of knowing how to talk to people.

When his job was done in France, they brought the West African soldiers back in a ship to Dakar in Senegal. 'Then they took us on lorries through Senegal, Mali, Burkina, Niger and finally for me the military camp at Parakou. They asked me if I wanted to stay in the army. I said no thank you, and walked out of there quickly. I trained to work as a forest ranger and that's always been my work. In the forest, I'm a free man.'

He was heroically his own man. He was polite to me but making a big fuss of Isidore – I was just a tourist; Isidore was his son's friend. A friend trusted enough to be sent with a money envelope. It was Isidore who Kif-Kif Vieux wanted to tell the great adventure he'd had since they last met. But I so wanted it to be me. Kif-Kif Vieux was just one of those people – you wanted it to be you that he liked best.

Kif-Kif Vieux, a devout Moslem, had been given a tremendous gift by his sons – a trip to Mecca. I think it was important that his glee, his appreciation of every detail, was passed on to his sons by Isidore.

He said he had photographs and he could describe the whole pilgrimage from soup to fruit. He explained what you had to do on the pilgrimage. He described the vastness of the crowd taking the seven turns round the Kabala, how you had to be careful not to fall or you could get trampled to death by the constantly oncoming people. He showed how this could happen, playing both the fallen person and the tramplers.

Even the administration of the pilgrimage fascinated him. You had your special clothes, your own group, your own guide – and on your arm you had a plastic card attached to you showing your name and where you were staying. 'Now remember, this place is huge, full of people from all over the world, if you got lost you'd be finished. Except there are police everywhere, like flies. If you get lost you go to a policeman, bow to him – no point talking to him, he won't understand you – so you show him the card on your arm and he whistles to a taxi. He reads what's on your arm to the taxi driver, the driver takes you, you pay, all done. Clever people. And rich! Such buildings, a mosque with walls covered in gold, tarmacked roads everywhere . . . But all around, all I saw was desert, so the thing I asked myself was how do these people eat? What do they grow? Where's their food? So when I asked I was amazed to learn that all their food comes from other countries, all of it.'

As our visit ended he took us out into his courtyard and picked up a grain of sand between his fingers. 'Not so much of that is out of place on the streets of Mecca.'

His own courtyard was all in well-ordered place, with fruit trees and a cote of white doves. He showed us his hunting dogs and an extension he was building.

'My sons are helping me buy the cement, so by next month my house will be the size of a Saudi palace.'

A grown-up daughter was in the courtyard playing with a baby in a basin of water. Kif-Kif Vieux crowed delightedly at the baby boy. 'Ah, you're in your boat, sir, right as rain in your boat.'

The *joie de vivre* of Kif-Kif Vieux infected us; we yelped and jumped around taking photographs of each other on the bridge that marked the border with Niger. Until a policeman ran up to us and told us to stop.

'I've got a queue of people at the barrier here, you can't just run across the bridge like that – you're lucky no one shot you.'

I explained that I didn't want to run across the bridge, I just wanted a photograph of myself standing in the middle of the River Niger.

'Why?'

'I've never been here before.'

'Well, don't go any further. You see that rivet? That's the mid-point – go past that and I'll tell someone to shoot you. Otherwise help yourself – it is a very nice view, isn't it?' He looked across the vast floodplain, with red-rock mountains behind it. 'I see it every day but it's really not bad.'

I thought about the map of the world and how far I was from my family and obligations, looking at a not bad view from the River Niger, and got overexcited all over again.

We found onions and dried yams at a good price in Malanville market. We already had maize. The boot was full of vegetables, all we needed to find was Peul cheese and some eggs and Isidore would be Father of the Year.

'Sometimes, it's hard. I earn money and think I'd like this shirt, these shoes, but the boys are there eating everything, needing football outfits or books for school. But they won't be there forever, will they? I don't want them saying, "Oh, my father didn't do this for me, didn't do that." That would be a waste of sons.'

I assured him I'd never seen any evidence of son wastage. I wondered, as we'd glided into the arena of personal discussion, if I would hear about the marriage now. Why had that gone to wastage? But Isidore was pulling off the road, shouting at a woman on a bicycle. Tied to the back she had a basket of fat hens – they were an exceptionally good price.

'What do you think? Should I buy one and take it back to Cotonou? Will it last?'

Cotonou was at least four days away. Even if we kept taking it out of the hot car and putting it in hotel fridges, it would be putrid. What was he thinking of?

'Of course it won't last.'

'No? OK.' He waved the woman away.

I didn't understand why I was suddenly the meat-preserving expert. Perhaps there'd been too much excitement with Kif-Kif Vieux and the river and cheap onions – he'd peaked and gone into one of his floundering depressions and I'd have to be wearing the brain for a while.

At a small village market down the road was a woman with acres of eggs. But they weren't a good price. Isidore walked away, disappointed.

'Really, there aren't as many bargains to be had up here as I thought there would be.' He looked back towards Malanville yearningly. 'Those chickens were good, though. A very good price.'

'But Isidore, in two days, a day, it would be stinking.'

He looked a bit pouty. 'It wouldn't. I'd put it in the back in a cardboard box.'

Cardboard box?

'Then in the evening, I'd put it on a little piece of string and keep it with me where I stay.'

Right, I could probably drive the Peugeot – I'd just get him to give me the keys, gently put him in the passenger seat and find a doctor.

'The nightwatchman could keep it out the back, give it some maize and water.'

Maize and . . . This was a live pet we'd be getting. I told him what I'd thought.

'Dead? Oh, no wonder you made that face. No, I'd have it on a string, look after it, get it fat to take home.'

I felt terrible. 'Shall we go back?'

He laughed. 'No. Now I see the picture, car full of vegetables and a chicken on a string, all we'd need is some extra luggage and a goat tied to the roof to have you looking like a bush dweller. What a shameful way to treat my passenger.'

'I'd love to look like a bush dweller. Next chicken we see, we're having it.'

He smiled. 'Never mind, one day I'll come and visit you in

London. I'll bring you yams, onions and a string with a fat chicken on. I can put it in a box during the plane journey – they won't mind, will they?'

'Go ahead. See what they do to you.'

He laughed. 'Really, I am from the bush, but I would love to try that just to see the faces at the European airport. Eh? Look at this African with his chicken on a string.'

We took a walk round the egg village, as it was a quiet, mango-shaded place with people who seemed very happy to let us stretch our legs and look at their lives.

'Nago people,' Isidore said. 'I can hear them. Little villages of Nago turn up everywhere.'

We startled some children playing horses with manes of coloured paper stuck to sticks. Then we had a cantering entourage. 'Boy or girl? Boy or girl?' they kept asking me. When I said girl they didn't look convinced.

'It's the trousers,' Isidore said. 'They don't understand that. And the boots. To us those are boy's boots. Well, for men working in the bush, really.'

I made a face at him and took my cavalry escort off to look at a pale-blue house, painted with chameleons and dancing people. A little girl came over from a group of women and children preparing maize under a mango tree. She crossed her arm over her chest and bowed to me, then Isidore, while saying '*Bonjour*'.

'That's very polite,' Isidore said. 'You see, children from good homes do that when approaching their elders. You don't see it so much now.'

The little girl told us she was twelve, her name was Rachida, she'd learnt French in school. She was almost shaking with fear but, behind her, mother and aunties urged her to get on with it and find out what we wanted.

This was all a bit unfair on Rachida, as Isidore spoke Nago and could have explained himself perfectly, but he did like to play spies.

I told her I was interested in the decorations on the house – were they there for a reason? It was her father's house; her brother liked to paint pictures and father had allowed him to decorate the house.

Isidore started cross-examining her. She said her father was a tailor and had some fields although he paid people to work them for him, also he sold petrol. This busy man had two wives, one with eleven children, one with ten. Twenty-one in total. But then she said the children weren't all alive. Of the eleven, six were dead. Of the ten, four were dead.

There was some heckling from the women under the tree.

'They want to know what she's found out,' Isidore whispered. 'They're annoyed she's found out nothing.'

To Rachida he said, 'We'll be going to Cotonou in a few days. We'll take you with us – what do you think about that?'

She said, 'My father isn't here.'

Isidore exaggeratedly shook his head. 'What a pity, otherwise we'd take you.'

It turned out that an eavesdropping auntie understood French perfectly. 'That one, you can have her, I'm giving her to you. Take her away.'

Translating and raucous laughter under the tree. Rachida smiled at us, looking hopeful. Then her mother said something to her. Her face fell and she ran inside her painted house, sobbing.

'What did her mother say?'

'She said, "You're too black – you can't go away with them, you wouldn't look right."'

'That was mean.'

'It wasn't mean. Her mother doesn't want her imagining she can leave with strangers. Her mother was protecting her.'

I still thought the mother was mean. But, whether she was the eleven- or ten-birth mother, she might have good reason to have a mean streak.

When someone in our culture numbers their children they don't mention children who've died. We say how many are alive, that's it. Maybe if you've known someone for a long time they might mention there was another child that died.

Isidore thought this was cold. He said if a woman carried a baby into the world she remembered it, even if it died. If two women went in to maternity together and only one had a child that lived, the one with the dead child would see the living child and always think, 'Ah, mine would be that age now.'

Our culture did feel cold. We didn't have so many dead children but we didn't actually cherish life enough, just for itself, for a tiny breath, a short two-day, two-month, two-year miracle. No one counted their dead children. In our culture we had to get over it, move on.

The Western rationalism I believed in had no rituals to deal with pain and loss, just the arrogance contained in the notion that pain went away with wishing. There were no dances to summon the dead, no shrines to revere the spirits of children too sick to survive – our dead had to disappear and leave us looking into the void, only our willpower for comfort.

Isidore thought Africans were idiots to have so many children. I didn't think they were.

Africans kept on having children because they never knew how many of them would live to be adults. They had children because when everywhere you looked there were babies, toddlers – running, tumbling, weird-acting, sticks-into-horses giggling children – there was your joy. If you saw a child everywhere you looked, one of them would do something, in some ludicrous baby-gaited way, that lifted the hard day for you.

There was an advertisement on Benin television for a contraceptive pill. The pill cost money. The couple in the advert, the light-skinned couple, had one light-skinned child in their Western-style home, with their shiny Mercedes in the drive. Those, then, were the rules – you swapped life for stuff. You swapped joy for order.

When I got home it would take me weeks to get used to London's streets again. I thought it was the weather, the complication of European life – but it was the absence of children from our lives. Our carefully counted indoor children didn't breathe life and fun into every street, weren't under every tree in every village. To have order and possessions, and because we were terrified of our children coming to any harm, we'd suffocated their presence in our lives.

We never looked out the window and saw skipping, rolling, crawling reason for life; the continuum. The sense that nothing began and ended in one person.

I walked around London, where no one had stumps and goitres and few people had more mouths than they could feed because we'd polished up our lives, made them safe, by minimizing life. Despite everything that had been done to Africa, the people kept believing that the will to life was never wasted.

The things our world did get right were things we could do with money. African children died almost entirely because of poverty. As money wasn't coming, there was combatable evil: witchcraft.

I wanted to show Isidore why there were no witches, but I couldn't. Every time he said witch, I said, no, here's the rational explanation. We were both only talking. I had no non-witch to show him; he had no witch to show me.

Isidore said children died because of two kinds of witchcraft. The first kind came from an ordinary man consumed with envy.

'If I have a good wife, good fields and healthy children and my neighbour's crops don't do well and his wife can't have children, well, first he might ruin my crops; he'll drink a special tea and piss it out over my maize at night.'

Maize was particularly susceptible to this kind of attack and in a day or so the whole field would rot.

'Or, he'll do *gri-gri* and kill one of my children. It will take sick and die in a matter of days in a terrible fever. And sadness will have been introduced to my household.'

My version of the story went: meningitis.

'The other way children die is pure witchcraft. One of the reasons old men learn to be strong in *gri-gri* is to protect the family from the old women, from the grandmothers. The grandmothers join a local congregation of witches. This gives them money, good fields – all kinds of wishes are granted for them. In return they have an obligation to provide the congregation with a child from their family. For cannibalism. And once they've tasted the flesh of children they can't stop.'

I groaned. 'Why is it always old women?'

'I don't know. Sometimes it's men but men don't have internal changes in age. Often when this happens to women it turns their insides sour; this affects their mind. Anyway, for their meetings at night the witches turn into vultures and sit in iriko trees. So when a child dies suddenly, the night before you will always have heard a lot of vultures. And as soon as the child is dead if you go to the old women's houses, you'll find meat in all their cooking pots. It will look like deer or tree rat they're cooking. They turn it into this so it looks harmless, but really it's the child they're eating.'

Although you might have cannibal grandmothers down the road, the situation was not as hopeless as, say . . . the chance of getting a village child with meningitis into intensive care fast enough. I became convinced the real and final way to kill witches was with money. Isidore worked very hard at his own methods to keep them out of his life.

'I collect a lot of *gri-gri* from my father to protect my children and my house. They are very well protected. If a witch, as a vulture, tries to land on a protected house it drops dead. You have to get all the vulture's body, every feather, put it in a pot and burn it, then pound it until it's nothing but black powder. Then you make scars on the body of the youngest child, put in the powder and the witch will die.'

'Did you do this to Lucien?'

'Yes, he's the youngest. I couldn't rest if I thought I hadn't done everything I could to protect them. What if I neglected one thing and the children got sick? And remember, I have my car, my work with whites. This provokes envy. It's not me the envious would hurt. All protection is for the children. And I know witchcraft happens for a fact. In Cove, the man who was the boss of my taxi firm had a lot of *gri-gri* against witchcraft in his house. One night I was there with him, helping him do the books. We heard a vulture. My boss said, "Let's go outside." Sure enough, the vulture fell dead in the courtyard. I wanted to burn it; the boss wanted to wait and see who it flushed out.'

In the morning, next door's grandmother came round with a

feeble story about wanting a bird feather to clean wax out of her ears. The boss called up all the next-door family, who'd had three children die.

'Then my boss went to set fire to the bird and the old woman screamed out, "No, no, just give me a feather first!" Because, of course, with a feather missing, her witch spirit in the bird couldn't be killed. This made the neighbour and his wife realize the truth: "So it's you, grandmother, that killed our dead children, it's you that's a witch. Set fire to the bird!" And at that moment as the bird burnt, the old woman screamed and fell dead at our feet. You see, Annie, how I know all this from my own experience?'

Hmm. I spotted some Peul women with cheese at the roadside. It was expensive but I persuaded Isidore it would be my present to the children. The cheese was fastened to the windscreen wipers in plastic bags. This was the correct way to travel with it – the soft cheese stayed fresh, didn't smell out the car, and developed a protective crust.

Isidore didn't want me turning up at the hotel in Cotonou with his shopping all over my luggage, so he asked if I'd mind if we stopped at his house first to drop it off.

A child hanging around in his road saw the car and screamed, 'It's your dad!'

The car had barely parked. Lucien was out first. He grabbed open the car door and threw himself across Isidore's lap.

'*Papa!*'

Antoine was close behind, and jumped on top of his brother. They hugged Isidore and sobbed into his neck with delight, until Isidore became shy and manly about the fuss and his own closeness to tears. He said flatly, 'Come on, come on, get some bowls from the house, we have things to take inside.'

Reluctantly they climbed off him.

A crowd of neighbouring children had come out of the darkness to see what gave.

'It's our dad!' Lucien squealed, dancing in front of them. 'It's our dad!'

'Come here,' Isidore said gruffly. 'Dancing like a madman! Where are the bowls I asked for?'

Antoine wasn't getting bowls either – he was attached to Isidore, dragging along, arms locked round his waist.

Isidore laughed. 'What can I do to get some obedience here?'

Not much. Now every child in the neighbourhood was out dancing and clapping with Lucien as he sang out, 'It's our dad!'

14

Never Have Sex without
a Mat Under You

I had noticed that the statute of limitations on my spell for a house in Bloomsbury had long expired. Perhaps the divinities might relent, as I tried to lose my simplistic trick-or-treat notions of what vodou was. Would they appreciate that this wasn't easy? I never saw the same kind of ceremony twice, I could keep no track at all of the immense number of divinities, and when I asked Isidore what was the difference between vodou and *gri-gri*, he said: 'What do you mean? Both are true.'

When we did manage to communicate, answers sprawled, tangled and shape-shifted. Because vodou was like that. Vodou was the spiritual extension of practical, day-to-day magic and healing. The *gri-gri* man, often improperly called a witchdoctor, was not the same as a vodou priest, a *vodounon*, although the same person might perform both functions. The spirits of the dead or the power of supernatural entities could intervene in life, if approached correctly, and would thwart enemies, bestow success, improve crops, protect from witchcraft, cure ailments, and, of course, mediate in gynaecological distress. But sometimes a few correctly applied leaves were all you needed.

Where the *vodounon* and *gri-gri* man were one person, there was the priest and doctor in one. Both used traditional forms of divination to find out what ailed you, if there wasn't an immediately apparent physical cause. Some concentrated more on their religious calling, some more on their ability to heal – a matter of preference, acquired knowledge and aptitude.

Vodou was not Devil worship, witchcraft or about sticking pins in dolls.

In Haiti, Papa Doc deliberately made vodou sinister, using it as part of his system of fear to control people. Doll sticking was a witchcraft, practised in one Afro-American community of New Orleans. Somehow, Hollywood horror writers got hold of the relatively obscure practice, and suddenly that was all we knew about vodou. In fact, vodou was the antidote to doll sticking – if someone stuck a pin in your doll, you would go to the vodou priest to have the spiritual power to be safe from the curse and to the *gri-gri* man to be physically protected and healed.

Gri-gri, magic, could be good or bad. Vodou priests and healers needed to know the dark side of the supernatural to save their people from it – just as Catholic priests would need to know the type of thing their devil was likely to be capable of. If a vodou priest or a *gri-gri* man used his powers to do harm, he'd crossed over and become a witch, excommunicated himself from the forces of good.

It could be hard to tell good from bad among the priests. Isidore said that because I had no knowledge, I should use my instincts. I should sense when someone was a con artist, a manipulator or plain crazy. Isidore believed part of the faith was a quest to find the well-meaning, thoughtful and prayerful practitioners to help you. If they felt right, their practices would be effective.

If I wanted to find bad vodou practice, I did it by not listening carefully to Isidore. Whenever I was doing something I that thought would be a good experience, and it all seemed to be going terribly wrong, I would remember that he'd usually made some warning noises.

'I wouldn't bother with her,' was the unambivalent warning noise he made about Josephine, the priestess, but I was too caught up with the idea that this was a woman – how could she be all bad? I imagined a wise old lady, a refreshing change from Isidore's male priests and their fears of female draining.

Josephine had a sign up on the main road though Dassa Zoumé, just past the Virgin's shrine. It advertised her as a vodou priestess and traditional healer, with a medicine show-list of ailments she could cure. But in large, top-of-the-bill writing was advertised: PROTECTIONS FROM WITCHCRAFT AND CURES FOR MADNESS.

The priestess was an adept of the Atinagli cult, a rural divinity with a reputation for wildness in the ceremonies that Isidore pronounced 'unnecessary'. Her highly painted compound was full of young men – all bleary or overexcited, the effects of *sodadi* and kola nuts respectively. Shaven-headed Josephine was young, midtwenties, dressed in a simple *pagne* and wearing very few ornaments; only a leather-bound *gri-gri* talisman on one arm. She had a plumpness that made her seem mumsy, until she started eyeing me up and down like she might fight me.

What did I want? If I wanted her photograph it cost £10. She looked like she'd be handier in a brawl than me so I was very polite, said I was simply interested in talking to her about her temple. She looked bored, shrugged and led us into the temple, taking a bowl of something to drink with her and putting a kola nut in her mouth.

The walls were covered in red paint-dots and blue handprints. There were flags and cloth drapes, and the focal point, by the back wall on a raised stone platform, was three indistinct carvings, about four foot high, covered in oil and feathers. There was disconcerting smeary debris all around the floor.

Josephine sat on a carved stool, telling us to sit on a wooden bench opposite her. Some of the young men and a cowed-looking older man came and crouched at one side of the gloomy room.

Josephine's face was very striking, high cheekbones and kohl-rimmed eyes. She used her eyes a lot, widening them and rolling them in a way I'd have advised her not to if she didn't want to look like some dreadful Hollywood stereotype of a vodou priestess. But she felt it worked for her . . .

Although a few minutes' acquaintance with Josephine made me feel she wasn't too stable, I was curious about her advertised cures for madness. What forms of madness did she treat?

'All of them – didn't you see my sign, can't you read? All forms.' She answered questions like a boxer about to go into the ring, psyching herself to punch something at any minute. As she drank out of her bowl, I expected her to spit and get towelled down by the boys. But they just crouched, looking awkward.

The eye-popping and pugnacious Josephine might not have been the ideal place to seek ancient psychiatric secrets, but I persisted with what I'd decided to find out from her.

I asked if she knew the causes of madness.

'I know all the causes. Sometimes the brain gets overheated, sometimes circumstances cause it, sometimes it's other people. Other people by their behaviour, or by witchcraft.'

What did she think of modern methods of curing madness, of trying to cure it with a pill?

'In your hospitals? They can't cure the madness we have here. Some things they can do but they don't understand the traditional Africa. Even things they learn to cure in schools, I know how to cure better than them. I could give you so many examples . . . But these doctors in the hospitals, they should study with someone like me.'

There was no chance of questions now; she was on a self-aggrandizing roll.

'I can give you many, many examples. Serious physical illness, too. Once they had a child in the hospital at Parakou who came from here. They were going to operate on him. I was consulted by the family. I said, "Bring the child to me, don't let them operate." By the time the hospital doctors came here to argue with me, I'd cured the child. They went away looking stupid. They don't know what things are caused by witchcraft. I know how to track down all kinds of witchcraft. I'm the strongest in this area for catching witches – ask anyone.'

She barked an order at one of the men. He came back with a large, handsomely framed colour photograph.

'Look,' she said. 'That's a photograph of the spirit with a witch.'

It was a picture of Josephine in an outfit, looking ferocious, with some poor old woman by the scruff of the neck.

Josephine, in her spirit form, had white paint on her cheeks, a leather band round her head, necklaces, bandoliers of bullets, beads and cowries, a raffia skirt, plenty more leather and beads round her ankles and wrists and she was brandishing a painted cudgel. She looked amazing. She looked as if she'd had this perfectly focused photo staged, as an advert for her trade.

I'd imagined witch catching was a more fast and frenzied moment, no time to get everybody so exactly posed for a shot. But even if it wasn't an authentic action picture it still made me shudder. This bullying young girl could be out there like an Abigail, accusing anyone who'd crossed her.

I asked what the witch in the photograph had done. Made a child sick. What had happened to her? The spirit had driven her away from the village.

Josephine widened her eyes and narrowed them at me.

'You understand that's not me in the photographs. It's the spirit with a witch.'

I said I understood.

'I'm the most powerful priest and healer in this whole district – ask anyone. The men in my family always did this, including my father, but I've surpassed them. I'm far more powerful than all the priests in my family. My own father is scared of me now – ask anyone. Here's my uncle, ask him if my father's scared of me or not.'

She pointed to the older man. He just looked worried.

Then, bored with bragging, she said, 'If you wait fifteen minutes I can go and bring out the spirit for you. You can take a photograph for fifty pounds. If you pay a hundred pounds I'll let you make a cassette of me saying incantations. But you can't resell them or I'll know, even if you're far across the world, I'll know and you'll be sorry you did it.'

I declined the offer. There was a very loud argument with Isidore in Fon. She was demanding £50 for her time anyway.

'Give her two pounds. Let's go.'

I did as he said, taking his cue to move fast as she came out after me, balling up the notes, throwing them on the ground and screaming.

'Two pounds? I'm the most powerful in this whole district. Don't think I can't send something after you. I wouldn't get in a car with her if I were you! What I send after her will follow her on her whole journey!'

The young men had followed her out and stood around looking confused. The old man bent down and picked up the money.

'Oh no,' Isidore said flatly. 'Now we'll have a crash.'

'You think so?'

He laughed as he sped away. 'Her? She's nothing. She's an idiot. A lot of the people in that cult are a bit mad. She can't cure anything or do anything. You saw how my father is, quiet. If you know how to ride a bicycle you just get on it and ride. You don't stand beside it shouting about how well you can ride a bicycle.'

A shame Josephine had let the girls' cycling team down so badly. Particularly as the outfit she was wearing when she was the spirit was exactly that of the Amazon warriors of Dahomey.

The last of the Amazons had died in the 1940s. There was still a well-maintained Amazon temple at Abomey where women of the royal household came to do ceremonies, learn the war dances and remember the spirits of these women warriors.

An early-twentieth-century French legionnaire who fought against the Amazons reported that they were crack shots and terrifying. If they ran out of ammunition they'd use their fists, their feet, their teeth . . . He reported that they chanted and screamed while they fought and always stank of alcohol.

There were even more hysterical reports about the Amazons,

usually from the English. Talk of lesbian orgies, filed teeth and self-performed abortions to keep in fighting fettle. They also became completely confused with the Amazons of ancient Greece, chroniclers claiming the Dahomey women warriors cut off one of their breasts. They didn't.

The first female warriors were used by King Akgba in the late seventeenth century. He had extended wars with the Yoruba, the Nago, the Mahi . . . There was a chronic shortage of manpower. He needed everyone who wasn't pregnant to be fighting. It wasn't such a great leap of imagination to put women into combat. Women worked in the fields, hunted, did building work – there wasn't much physical labour they didn't do. It was only with the arrival of the Europeans that the Dahomey kings realized it was in any way unusual to have female soldiers.

Being an Amazon was more like joining an order of nuns. They had very strict rules of behaviour and male soldiers weren't allowed to touch them. They had male commanders and by the time of Gbehanzin there were many who preferred wearing European-style military uniform to the kind of outfit Josephine wore. They trained exactly the same way as the men and hard drinking before a battle was widespread among both sexes at the time of Gbehanzin, when it was becoming obvious all was lost. He'd have lost a lot sooner without the Amazons.

The Amazons of Dahomey were one of the few female combat armies that were fact, not legend.

In case Josephine had disappointed me too much, Isidore offered me an alternative: 'There are many Fon in an area of Parakou where my sister lives and they have a temple similar to that woman's. You can be initiated if you like. I was initiated into their temple; it's interesting but I dropped out. They're very noisy and their rules are too complicated for me. I think noise in these matters is unnecessary, but they're not like Josephine – they're nice simple people. What do you think? Do you want to see the tron temple?'

'Tron?' Was this some modern cult, the divinity in a computer game?

'Tron is the Togo word for vodou. Some Togo people started this temple, there's another in Cotonou. "Tron" just means "vodou" in Mina. The priest here is from Abomey. Also, Mamiwata is at this temple, a female divinity with a fish body. You'll like her.'

I could tell when we reached the Fon quarter. Children scooting out yelling '*Yovo*!' As we parked up, nearby children started a hand-clapping game, singing the *yovo* chant: '*Yovo, yovo, bonsoir, comment ça va, ça va très bien, merci, yovo yovo, bonsoir . . .*' and on, indefinitely, to an 'eenie meanie minie mo'-type tune. I'd heard it often and something about the way children sang it made it seem to rhyme. Isidore said it had been around for years – children had sung it, clapped and skipped to it when he was a child, when there might not be a *yovo* sighted for weeks on end.

The tron temple was in the corner of a courtyard full of contented-looking women of all ages, cooking, hairdressing and gossiping.

'The priest here is very good at helping women,' Isidore said. 'Women like this temple because he advises them very nicely about things that worry them.'

The three women who went in to fetch the priest came out laughing with him, clearly very fond of the well-fed, smiling old man in his voluminous cream robes. He had very badly dyed black hair and eyebrows, which made him hard to take seriously. He was friendly but too oily, too determined to charm me. He said he could happily explain the temple to me but it would be much easier if I was initiated. Then I could see everything that they did. I'd see how vodou could help even *yovos*.

He claimed he had several *yovo* members of his temple, one he'd helped get a hotel business in France off the ground. Why, that Frenchman was coming back next week, to give the temple a gift of 200 francs for all the help he'd had.

Me, too – he could give me success in business, a good husband, if I needed one, children . . . 'You *yovos*, you have your witchcraft, your aeroplanes and ships that sail underwater. But we too have powers you can use.'

I thought this was fake naïvety. Pleasant and welcoming though he was, his operation was not going to be a profound religious experience.

What was an experience was looking at Theodore, his twenty-one-year-old assistant, a minor god of handsomeness. Theodore would conduct the initiation ceremony with me, with the priest's supervision – it was a tiring business and hard for the old man to do alone.

The priest said: 'She can give us ten pounds to buy the things needed for the initiation and come back tomorrow morning.'

'What things?' Isidore squinted at them.

'Well we'll need to buy her a white *pagne* to wear – she can't wear *yovo* clothes. There are candles, kola nuts, perfumes, rum, talcum powder . . . my son, you must know the things needed. And of course there is a donation to the temple included in this.'

Isidore grunted. It was up to me.

I was being gazed at with such kind concern by Theodore that I could see exactly why he was chosen to be a fisher of souls. He was not only all biceps and handsomeness – he had a way of making you feel like he really cared about you, only you, just by some melty trick he did with his eyes. If I lived round the corner I'd have been in here with my worries all the time.

If Groucho Marx had been there he'd have said: 'I wouldn't want to join any vodou temple that would have me as a member.'

Isidore said: 'You know if they initiate people just like that it is a very simple, ordinary temple, nothing special.'

'But it will be an experience.'

'Up to you.'

Driving back to the hotel, Isidore saw the elderly gardener boss of the Hôtel Belle Vue in Natitingou. We stopped to say hello. He was waiting for his wife, who was in a shop built from corrugated iron. It sold computers. His wife had a complaint about some software they'd sold her. Well, they'd need every divinity they knew to help them if they'd tried to rip her off with some dodgy

Nigerian forgery. This woman, Françoise, was one of the true present-day Amazons of Benin. Fought her way up from the farm, selling vegetables in the market, now had two children at university, a hotel, a souvenir shop and was forever corresponding with people by email, learning about the world from the Internet and plotting to sell African souvenirs in cyberspace. The husband did whatever she decided they were doing. So did her hotel guests.

The first time I stayed at the Belle Vue I'd only heard her husband speak of her in reverential tones; she'd been away on business. The second time, she was there and took charge of me almost as soon as she introduced herself.

I was talking to Isidore about an extensive and flashy orphanage on the road into Natitingou that I wanted to visit. Françoise was suddenly beside me.

'Excuse me for interrupting, madame, but do you work for a charity?'

'No, I'm writing a book on Benin.' Something about her immediately told me not to try lying.

'Well, you know that orphanage is very well funded – it's run by SOS, they have places everywhere, they have plenty of money, they are world renowned. If you wanted to write about something in Benin to move people's hearts, if you wanted to write something useful, I can show you something.'

She took me to meet her friend, a former civil servant who, with his wife and daughter and a dozen volunteer staff, had started a school for the blind. He went out in his little car, round all the villages of the Atakora region, looking for blind children. He had thirty children now, girls and boys, in a building he'd constructed with some help from the American embassy. They had no state aid, relying instead on people like Françoise, who'd furnished the living quarters with sheets, old furniture and crockery from her hotel. Françoise had made the expensive French hotel in Natitingou hand over their old sheets and crockery. She'd made the French buy food and presents for the children at Christmas. Françoise made anyone she spoke to do something for her friend and his school.

Some of the children were born blind, but there was blindness caused by untreated infections and a hereditary disease prevalent in some tribes of the region. A blind child was a lost child to the parents. They couldn't work, couldn't play – they were left sitting indoors, no one sure what to do with them.

The parents resisted letting them go to live at the blind school, afraid it would cost them money. They also thought it was pointless: the child was blind, how could they learn anything? The teacher would make an agreement with them – he'd bring them to visit the child in three months' time and they'd see for themselves. That was always his proudest moment, the parents' faces when they saw their child could do so much for themselves – weaving, cooking, washing and feeding themselves, using white sticks and their other senses to get around. They'd see that their child had become a different person, confident, able to cope with life. When the parents came back in two years and saw the child reading and writing Braille, teaching the practical skills to the smaller children . . . they thought it was a miracle.

He talked so positively about the school I was shocked when I drove down with Isidore to visit it. I understood why Françoise was so ferocious in her efforts to help.

It was on a piece of waste ground, no shade trees, just bleak, army-barrack-style sheds. There were only four Braille machines. There was nothing beyond basic beds, chairs and tables in the accommodation. It needed money. That was all.

You could see which children had been there a while – they were noisy, confident and understood how to do remarkable things, like following the sound of people's voices to know where they were wanted. The new arrivals were thinner, quieter, more confused and nervous.

There was a little boy who'd only arrived two days ago. He sat in a doorway, his head at an odd angle, very frightened. Another child brought him over to meet me. He was stick thin, covered in scabs, a wretchedly neglected-looking child. There were voices all around him he didn't recognize; he was petrified. I put my hands carefully on his shoulders to try and reassure him. He was shaking with fear – it was as if I'd caught a little bird in my hands and I could feel its fluttery heart beating. I rubbed his back for a while, and this slowed the frantic heartbeat. He stopped trembling.

'He will be all right,' the teacher said. 'He's been very neglected, but look, he'll be like them in three months.'

A group of plump, rowdy children were at the side of a building, washing themselves with buckets and basins, splashing and leaping, roaring with laughter.

The teacher took over the back rubbing when I left. Never mind the great beyond, he was someone who gave you faith in human nature.

When we drove away from the patched together school, the feeling of how the world must have seemed for the trembling boy swept through me and I started sobbing. No use to anyone but it gave Isidore quite a turn.

If Françoise had been in the car she'd have said, 'What are you crying for, you silly girl?'

Françoise had been to London, Paris, Brussels . . . but her favourite city was Lagos.

'I love it, it's so dangerous. I love big dangerous cities, always having to be on the *qui vive*. I'm sure you love your London, but to me, I'm afraid, it was sleepy.'

I said, 'I hear New York's very dangerous.'

She laughed a big laugh. 'I shall go there, then – are there men with guns and knives?'

'I believe so.'

'Good. I love that. Walking around fast, thinking, "Just let them try it!"'

So, whatever Françoise wanted in the computer shop in Parakou, she'd got it.

She told me the blind school was still struggling pitifully but a German charity was giving them some more Braille machines.

'And you, what are you doing?'

'Oh, you know, exploring Parakou.'

I just knew if I told her I was messing around joining vodou cults for the experience she'd have given me a slap and sent me to scrub out the blind school if I needed an experience.

Mamiwata, the mermaid painted on the temple of tron, was a good divinity for the girls. She was water, she was life, she was associated with Isis, Eve, Hera, the first woman, the mother of all. She had a massive following, from her origins in Nigeria to the Caribbean and United States. She was a fortune teller, healer and protector.

The temple I was joining was under the Mamiwata spirit but the altar was dedicated to her male spirit, Dangbe the serpent. Although Dangbe was also known as Mamiwata's husband, this temple had an altar to the Dangbe spirit's wife, Confo.

One of the essential preparations for a proper initiation to a Mamiwata temple was a ceremonial bath. Nobody offered me any kind of bath, but I was newly washed and wearing presentable underwear because I'd remembered in time that there'd been talk of a ceremonial white *pagne*. I thought some of the temple women might be with me when I changed and didn't want to be shamed by some of the well-travelled underwear shreds in my suitcase. A good decision, because the one-eyed main woman of the temple approached me with the white *pagne* and told me to take off my T-shirt so she could dress me, right there on the temple steps with half the Fon and Mina community, of both sexes, hanging around.

Isidore could see I was getting bashful as the woman tugged my T-shirt and flapped the *pagne* at me.

'Can you take her somewhere private? They don't like to show their breasts,' he whispered.

The one-eyed woman snorted scornfully and pinged my bra straps. 'She's wearing a bra, what's the problem?' and gave a determined yank at my T-shirt.

So I was there in front of the crowd in my second-best bra, having a *pagne* tied round me with no more fuss than if they were putting a new hat on me. I was allowed to keep my skirt on underneath – thighs were the parts of a woman's anatomy that couldn't be displayed in a public courtyard without scaring the horses.

The old priest arrived, his dyed eyebrows seemingly badly slept in and all brushed up the wrong way. Theodore, the young priest, in ceremonial outfit of white trousers and a white sleeveless shirt, didn't look any wrong way at all.

They showed me a dark room to the left of the main temple entrance. This was the room for Bangele, the protector of the divinity. Before entering the main temple I had to kneel with the priest and Theodore. Theodore threw a kola nut on the ground. It split. I was given a piece to eat. The taste reminded me of an accidental eating of privet leaves as a child.

'If it didn't split it is Bangele saying you can't come in,' Theodore said, in husky French.

There was further bowing and tapping on the ground to do before we could go in. We were followed by four drummers, Isidore, six women and a boy child who refused to leave his mother. A shoving, giggling group of women and girls gathered outside the door to watch.

The white-painted temple had mermaids, snakes and ladies dancing on the walls, all framed by flower paintings.

To one side was Confo's altar. She was definitely a girlie girl. All the things she liked were piled on a table: powder puffs, tins of talcum powder, pieces of lace, bottles of eau-de-Cologne, candles, fancy jars and pots, make-up, mirrors, and yellow-haired Barbie-type dolls. Confo spent a great deal of time making herself beautiful, I was told, but she had an important role as peacemaker, especially between fighting women.

The priest sat with Isidore by Confo's altar. The women and musicians loaded themselves on to benches at the other side. Theodore led me to a stone seat in front of what looked like a large, white-tiled fireplace. When I looked into the fire and up the chimney, I saw it was more like an attractive atrium. It was open at the top, sun streaming in on a gigantic pile of kola nuts, glistening with water. There was some refreshing greenery where the kola nuts had sprouted. Pushed into the centre of the pile was a metal *assin*, a sceptre-shaped portable altar representing an ancestor's spirit.

Theodore sat opposite me and showed me the things he'd bought for me to give to the *vodou*: candles, kola nuts, eau-de-Cologne, talcum powder, rum and matches. He tapped a stone mortar resting in front of the tiled fireplace, threw four kola on the ground and studied their configuration. It was good. We could begin. He poured eau-de-Cologne over my hands He poured eau-de-Cologne into a bowl of kola nuts then picked out three. He held them in the palm of his hand and chanted prayers over them, then touched them to my head, chanting more prayers. I had to hold these three nuts in the fingers of my left hand. This didn't feel a natural or comfortable way to be holding small slippery things, but I would have plenty of time to get used to it.

The drummers began. Singing, clapping and chanting began. The old priest called out occasionally – this was to summon the divinity.

In turns, the women got up to dance. The one-eyed lady was the best, her whole upper body rippling, twisting – just as you figured out what way she was moving, she'd move in a different way.

Every quarter of an hour or so, Theodore would cast four kola on the tiles, study them and say no, the spirit wasn't ready to come out.

The dancing, drumming, asking-and-refusal routine went on for over an hour. I'd gone way beyond any kind of pain threshold in my nut-clamping fingers and was feeling uncharacteristically compelled to get up and join the dancing, but while the other women partied I was stuck, kneeling by the altar, clamping nuts.

Finally the spirit said yes. Isidore was told to take his shirt off out of respect for the spirit. This obviously irritated him. Well, why shouldn't he strip off? I'd had to show my bra to half of Parakou.

Theodore took the three kola from my aching fingers and asked me to write my name in an exercise book. He threw the kola and marked the way they fell with a set of dots under my name. He then dipped the kola in a little font of mud inside the fireplace, put them to my forehead, inner elbows and at two places on my back, repeating prayers as he did this, five times. He washed the kola in eau-de-Cologne, threw two into the altar pile, prayed over one and gave this to me to eat, like a Communion wafer, put on my tongue with his left hand.

Now I was in, I had to get up and dance. I felt caught up in the mood, and revelled in a sense that I was dancing like the temple women – with rhythm and vigorous lack of inhibition.

The priest had allowed Isidore to take photographs of my initiated moment. A friend back home screamed with laughter when he saw them. 'Even if you couldn't see the colour of your skin you'd know you were the white person.' He shook his head. 'You look so . . . white.'

I did. All spiky, mincy limbed and uptight. You couldn't see my feet in the photo but you'd swear I must have my handbag down there.

The people in the temple, however, had been very polite about cheering and clapping for my dance. When it was finished I had to sit outside on the steps while the one-eyed woman, with a little help from Isidore, told me what I was now obligated to do and not allowed to do.

On Saturday or Sunday, if I was in Benin I should attend a ceremony at a tron temple. I wasn't allowed to eat pig or flat fish or shrimps or a white rooster. I wasn't allowed to drink gin or eat kola nuts on a Monday or Friday. If I was in the shower, I wasn't allowed to answer anyone who called me unless I was sure they were an initiate, otherwise they might be a witch. I wasn't allowed to make love on the ground without a mat under me. I wasn't allowed to tell anyone about the things I wasn't allowed to do . . .

Theodore led me into the dark side-room; Isidore followed to help translate. The drummers came too and crammed themselves into a back corner of the small room. The one-eyed woman asked me for a pound – she needed to get a small hen to sacrifice for me. I was distracted by the blood on the walls of the dark room and didn't think anything about what she'd said she needed the money for.

Theodore said he could do a ceremony for me, now I was

initiated, to see what my problems were and what kind of protection
I would need.

Four more kolas were washed in eau-de-Cologne. I had to hold
them in the fingers of my left hand.

'Stand, please,' Theodore said, as the woman came back with a
very small white rooster. Theodore took it by the feet, bashed me
about the head with it, ran it down one side of my body, back to
my head and down the other side. Then he smacked it on my back
and chest. The rooster was even less at ease about all this than I
was, squawking, flapping – I was sure I'd get pecked to ribbons,
but Theodore was moving fast.

After the last rooster thwack, Theodore pulled out a penknife
and cut its throat. The knife wasn't sharp so there was more a
sawing action than a clean slice. The profusely bleeding beast was
swung by its feet over a blackened altar where my four kola had
now been placed on four mushroom-shaped stone stands. At the
centre of the altar was a square hole, with a chain leading down
into it. I hoped they wouldn't pull up whatever was down there.
The rooster's blood was dripped down the hole. Then, Theodore
threw the still convulsing bird on the ground, where it writhed,
splattering blood wide.

I could feel Isidore flinch when the rooster hit the ground. I
didn't feel flinchy; I think I'd gone into a kola-nut- and drumming-
induced stupor. I watched the gory convulsing demise of the rooster
with vague curiosity.

'He'll look at the blood,' Isidore said. 'That's how he can tell
your fortune.'

Theodore wasn't happy with the blood trails and said he needed
more information. A second rooster was paid for.

'It's not only I don't know enough,' Theodore said. 'I see you
have a lot of things against you in life. I want to be sure what I
give you is our full protection. I want to hold you safe in both
hands.'

His anxious Bambi eyes looked into mine. I suddenly understood
why people all over the world lost their minds and fortunes to
religious cults. If the charismatic charm of people like Theodore

drew you in, you wanted to stay in, for any moment of their attention you could have.

My second rooster was much better, much more blood came out of it, right up the walls and sprinkling my feet.

Theodore said that now he'd seen the second rooster, he knew his instincts had been right: I had a world of trouble in my life.

One of the drummers was ordered to do some rooster house-work, wiping up each bird's blood with its own body and putting them to one side of the altar. Theodore moved the kola nuts off the altar and put two in the open breast of each bird, so they looked like some obscure gourmet dish ready for roasting.

Theodore had drawn more dots under my name – whatever they meant it wasn't good.

He sat me down and looked into my eyes. 'You live in fear, don't you? You're right to do so, until now. I can protect you and take away all the fear.'

The older priest had come in to sit behind me. I don't think Theodore had noticed him, he was so carried away with saving me – and with what may have been a little extra-curricular notion of his own.

'The best thing to make you safe is if I come to where you live. I can see what in your house is against you, cast out the evil myself. This is what we'll do; I'll come back with you to your house and make you safe.'

'Excuse me for interrupting,' Isidore said scornfully. 'But do you have a passport? Do you have five hundred pounds for your flight to her house, or is she supposed to pay for that?'

The priest laughed. 'Theodore, you can't go to *yovotome* [white land] just like that.'

Theodore looked hurt, foolish and very young. To justify himself he showed the exercise book to the priest.

'Ah,' said the priest. 'I see what you mean. You'll have to make something very powerful here for her to take back with her. But you in *yovotome*, I don't think so.'

Big worldly men, he and Isidore guffawed excessively.

★

The priest told Theodore to make a list. I was to come back when I had bought the things on the list. He handed the list to Isidore, who kept a poker-blank face and said, 'Fine. I'll explain it to her later.'

Then, perhaps to reiterate how much I needed to come back, Theodore said that my main trouble was people I'd trusted who'd let me down. These people were against me and ruining things for me. Theodore watched me very carefully all the time, the way good fortune-tellers do, to see when they're hitting a nerve to follow it.

Curiously, there was suddenly a lot of talk about a big expensive thing I wanted to buy. Did I want to buy a house? Well I mustn't, not yet, even if I had the money, because I needed to clear the enemies out of my life.

So maybe this was why the other spirits hadn't given me the house yet, because they knew it would all go wrong for me. And once Theodore had sorted it, I'd be packing for Bloomsbury.

Theodore, priest, drummers, one-eyed woman and the girls from the compound all saw me off affectionately. I was to get my shopping and come back in a week.

They were affectionate, Isidore said, because they hoped to make a great football of money out of me.

'This list,' he explained to me over dinner. 'Even the President doesn't need this expensive level of protection. We don't want to insult them, so tomorrow we'll go and say you have a problem with your family and have to fly home early.' He handed me the shopping list. 'I promise you: no one's life is in this much danger.'

We made my excuses; the priest was egregiously understanding. Theodore was a cold, shrugging, completely different youth to the one who'd practically hypnotized me and come home with me. I felt ridiculously wounded that he switched off all the concern when he heard it wasn't going to be worth his while.

On my shopping list were: candles, a hundred kola nuts, perfume, matches, a needle, talcum powder, an arrow, a fish hook, two metres of lace, two metres of plain white cloth, kohl, seven chickens, and black, red and white leather pouches and thongs to make the containers for the protection. Also I had to get a bullet, a cat and a dog.

Isidore said they'd be wanting at least £50 on top for the ceremony. And tips.

'You mustn't worry. It's rubbish. You're fine in your life, you don't need it.'

Silly question: 'What were they going to do with the cat and the dog?'

'Well you saw what they did with the chicken . . .'

I didn't mean to become a Yoruba queen but these things happen. It was the only way we were going to get to see the divinities in the Dassa Zoumé hills, up behind the Virgin Mary, so it had to be done.

Isidore was hoping to avoid the King of Dassa, having heard tales of his slipperiness from other drivers, so he first tried an alternative route to the divinities, through the *gri-gri* union.

A friend of his father's tended a small Sakpata fetish in the Dassa hills, not important enough for the pushy King to involve himself in. When we arrived the priest was working in his fields in old clothes.

'Ah, welcome. Just let me go and wash my feet and I'll take you to my shrine.'

He came back wearing a white robe with black spots for his role in the service of the smallpox *vodou*.

We walked across fields and up a wooded hill, to find a small clump of rocks with bowls of oil and candles round them. The priest said prayers for our journey and Isidore's family.

Then Isidore asked, 'Can you tell her how she can know a real healer from a fake?'

'Ah,' the priest said. 'Results is one way. Also they should be registered with our association.'

He showed me a card, like a driving licence. His name and photo-graph, under the heading, 'Member of the Union of Traditional

Healers, Benin'. Folding pages at the back showed a renewal stamp for every year since 1992.

'We started this at that time to discourage the fakes.'

They had meetings every so often, shared knowledge and a committee decided on renewals – any report of bad practice and they could be struck off.

Despite union clout, he told us that his friend, a fellow Fon, who was the chief religious elder at the King's court, wouldn't be able to take us to the important *vodou* without the King's permission.

'The palace is at the start of the way up there. The King has subjects living along the path who would report to him that strangers had been up. The King . . .' He sighed. 'He likes money too much. It's a pity.'

The King had what I'd call a mid-range palace, big but not too fancy, although he had a recent-model four-wheel drive parked at the back. Isidore played his game of pretending not to understand the local language, Nago, so he could find out what the King was up to.

The King didn't like the look of Isidore, either, addressing everything to me and glowering if Isidore spoke. The King was also blatantly flirty with me, regardless of a wife circulating the throne room with drinks. I told him Isidore was my husband to make him back off.

There was much summoning of elders, including the Fon religious elder, who was quiet, watchfully withdrawn. When they were all assembled, the King had a long discussion with them in Nago. He then made two announcements to me in French. One, that I was to be taken to see the *vodou*; and two, that the following day there would be a celebration of my visit, during which I was to be made a member of the royal household. The King switched to Nago again and the elders responded to what he said with enthusiasm. Except the Fon elder, who smiled weakly at Isidore.

The King had a side room where he called me to a private audience. He looked put out when Isidore followed. The King said he was sorry but it was the elders who had demanded that I should be made a member of the royal household, as I had paid them the honour of a visit. The King was happy with this but unfortunately these things cost money. He had none. Could I help him with a contribution to this ceremony, as it would make his subjects so happy and he hated to let them down when they asked for something? And I would enjoy it immensely. I would be a Nago Yoruba queen, beloved of the people; I could build a house on the palace land . . . Oh, and he was sorry to mention it but there was also a small fee to pay to visit the *vodou*, for the upkeep of the temple.

He put the temple-upkeep money with the celebration money, in his pocket.

Isidore, who'd understood what was said in Nago, told me that the King had lied. The elders hadn't asked for any ceremonies, coronations or feasts. They'd simply asked the King who I was. The King had told them that he wanted to make me a queen, with feasting at his own expense. The amount of money the King had asked me for was enough for an extremely lavish feast, but Isidore expected there'd be local beer and a cheap meal – the King would keep the excess. It was up to me, but the King would be planning to trick yet more money out of me – was it worth it? I decided it probably was.

The Fon elder who escorted us up the winding path to the *vodou* was a gentle man who also understood everything the King was up to. He apologized to Isidore – the King shouldn't have charged a fee to visit the *vodou*. I could see Isidore liked him, and there was long chatting in Fon as we walked through woods and over mountain streams.

From the shrine I had a clear view out over what was to be my royal domain of red mountains, green fields and the rusty tin roofs of Dassa town. So far it had cost me £30 to see this view, but I've seen less attractive things for more money.

Surrounded by small stones representing sacred twins, the main shrine was Ougon, the god of iron and war. A five-foot square of curvy stone circled by the skulls of sacrificed animals. The shrine

was special because the representation had been brought here from
Ife, the holy city in Nigeria, hundreds of years ago, by migrating
Yoruba who wanted to bring their religion with them. Students of
vodou from Haiti and America often came to visit this important
site. That's why the King liked to control the visitors. Isidore and
the Fon elder agreed that the foreigners who came from America
were often very holy people, priests and priestesses – pilgrims who
shouldn't be exploited. But the King was the King.

I couldn't quite believe the extent of the ceremony to make me a
member of the Dassa royal household. Even the local paper was
there. All the elders, the Mayor, about 150 people in best robes,
drummers, singers, dancers . . .

I was taken to a back room and put into a *pagne*. This time the
women said a bra looked terrible; I needed bare shoulders. There
was a lot of unabashed sniggering at my pants and my flat chest
while I was stripped and wrapped. I made a three-time fuss that I
didn't think the *pagne* was fastened tight enough. I didn't like these
women and didn't trust them not to be setting me up. The King's
wife joined the women and started whispering in Nago, confirming
my impression that the King's winky fuss over me had set the girls'
claws on edge and they might just send me out badly wrapped.

As we processed out, a young male acolyte of the King's was
lurking in the corridor looking flustered. I noticed the large knot-
holes in the changing-room door and was very sharp with him
when he told me I should remember to give a present to the women
who had dressed me.

'At the end,' I said. 'I'm busy now.'

I was busy. I had to go through the throne room with a new group
of senior women who clicked their fingers and dropped water in
front of me as I went out to the crowded clearing behind the palace.

The King was on a throne, and I had to kneel in front of him.
He said a great deal in Nago. Then I had to follow a conga line of
dancing women shaking cowry-covered gourds, round the clearing
and then back to kneel before the King, who smelt a little boozy
for this early in the day.

I knew this co-option into the royal household wouldn't involve anything too intimately unpleasant with the King – Isidore would have eaten his own Peugeot rather than allow such a situation to arise – but it seemed to me this was a very large-scale ceremony for someone who'd just turned up on the palace doorstep. What would I have to do in return? Giving the King some beer money couldn't be all there was to it.

Individual women danced before the King. A senior woman pulled me up for a solo dance. I felt a bit shy in front of the King, the gathering crowd and the snapping news photographer. I did my best white-girl shimmy for as long as I could stand it. The King developed the unabashed leer of a fat businessman in a lap-dancing bar. I stopped dancing, head-to-foot flushed with embarrassment.

The King applauded and told me to kneel again. He made a speech in Nago. Then he had a batik bag and a cardboard folder brought to him by the male acolyte.

From the bag he first brought out strings of red stone beads. He put beads round my neck and wrists. Then he gave me my crown. A little white 'kiss me quick' hat. I thought this was something they'd found down the back of a cupboard and said, 'Oh give her that, tell her it's a crown.' But it was new and the King showed me my royal name printed on the front: 'Princess Iyolode'. It had been made specially for me. As had the contents of the folder. A certificate with the royal seal, telling the world I was Princesse Iyolode, a queen of the Yoruba Nago Royal Household of the Kingdom of the Forty-One Hills of Dassa Zoumé. I suddenly lost any cynicism and felt very moved. This was a real thing, trouble had been gone to . . .

The King wanted me to make a speech to the people, in English if I liked. I thanked everyone, told them how kind they were.

'Say more, say more,' the King urged.

I was a bit stuck now. I blethered a while about the loveliness of Dassa Zoumé, how honoured I was, how kind they were . . .

I noticed Isidore at the back of the crowd, muttering with the Mayor and missing my big moment.

The King made a speech in Nago. Everyone looked bored. It occurred to me that they'd looked fairly bored all along.

There was a final song from the gourd-shaking women. I heard the word '*oyimbo*', Yoruba for 'white', in the lyrics.

The King made another speech, in French, saying that I was the first white person who had ever been given this honour, how much I would always be cherished in my second home, Dassa Zoumé.

There was lukewarm applause. Apparently it was all over. I could go back to the palace and change.

The women in the changing room were drinking gourds of maize beer and talking about me in Nago. I heard '*oyimbo*' in a sneery tone once too often to want to give them a very nice present, but thought I should in case there was hair pulling.

Isidore was in the throne room muttering to some elders in Nago. I noticed that the nice Fon elder of the day before still hadn't put in an appearance. The King's Peeping Tom acolyte came out and asked me if I had a gift for the King. Isidore pulled me aside and handed me an envelope.

'I've put ten pounds in here. That's it. Don't give him any more. Pay me back later. It's more than he deserves.'

'I think he went to quite a lot of trouble, actually, all those people, a certificate . . .'

Isidore shrugged. 'If you want to give him more, it's your money.'

The acolyte told me I could come through to the King's private room. He looked a bit panicked when Isidore followed, bringing an elder with him. The King saw the elder and looked fit to behead someone.

'We don't need you!' he shouted.

The elder scuttled away.

The King was all smiles at me.

'These old men, they get confused,' he said. Then he was terribly gushing, how he hoped I'd enjoyed myself, when would I be back? How serious he was that we were now true friends . . .

I handed over the envelope. The King looked in it in a way that ensured the acolyte couldn't see the contents.

'Five pounds, very kind,' the King said.

Isidore said something sharp in Nago. The King glared at him, the acolyte looked shocked and Isidore was telling me to leave.

There was a hasty goodbye to elders tucking into fish and maize dumplings and suddenly the new queen was gone.

Isidore drove right out of town without a word of explanation. He was seething. The mysteriousness of it all got on my nerves.

'Listen, it wasn't right to drag me out like that. I've got a hat, beads, a certificate, he'd got all those people gathered. I think it was money well spent. You'd no right to drag me out like that and make me look ungrateful.'

He said nothing for a long time. Then sighed.

'You know what happened at the end? I said in Nago, "Did you look in the envelope properly?" So two things happened, his assistant saw the King had lied and the King saw I spoke Nago.' He sighed again. 'I know you're pleased with it all, but really, the King is a big liar. First, he told the people he paid for the feast. As I predicted, poor food and local beer – so he kept half the money. Second, from the start he told the elders, then the people, and he even told the Mayor, that he had contacted you and brought you here. That you were a rich person who was going to build a maternity hospital for the people. This is what the Mayor asked me about. Don't worry, the Mayor didn't blame you – the King has lied like this before.'

Having a very poor-quality character, the maternity hospital wasn't my first worry.

'So . . . I'm not a queen?'

'You are a queen, you have your certificate, your hat and your beads. You are a queen,' Isidore said in the patronizing tone of voice I deserved.

Too many minutes later I realized what I should have asked first.

'What happens in a year and the people notice there's no maternity hospital?'

'When the people start to ask, the King will spread a rumour about what a typical white you are, full of promises and letting everyone down. It's easy to blame a white, people know what they're like.'

And so the new queen folded away her ceremonial *pagne*, her beads, her crown and her certificate, put them in her suitcase and knew she would probably not be going to the royal ball at Dassa Zoumé again.

My sudden searing backache wasn't sorcery sent by Josephine or the King of Dassa. It was just what Isidore called 'the feebleness of age'. I'd been playing tiddlywinks with some children at a roadside, bending too low, standing up too fast. The healer we were visiting in Bohicon was a good union man, someone Isidore trusted, so if I did need treatment we were in the right place.

The healer's flower- and fruit-tree-filled garden had all kinds of divinities, god of iron, twins, god of lightning . . . His house was white painted with black spots for the smallpox divinity, Sakpata.

In contrast to Josephine, this quiet, charismatic old man was a great believer in Western medicine. He said he knew herbs and plants and how to address the gods, but how could he take out an appendix? He could sometimes save children from smallpox but he had no medicine to give children to make sure they never caught smallpox. There was no conflict: the gods had sent the medicines of white people to be used in Africa; the ancient and new should embrace each other.

He said traditional methods were good for matters to do with women, and for curing infections and maladies of the soul, not big diseases. I asked him what he meant by maladies of the soul. Madness, the various forms of madness.

Isidore said this priest was excellent on madness. A friend of his who worked in the brewery had gone so crazy he had to be tied up and brought here. He stayed in the priest's house and in two months he was completely cured.

I believed that. The place and the priest would be very soothing to someone who'd had a brewery-related frenzy. For maladies of the soul a kindly traditional healer would be better than half the forms of newly dreamt-up therapy practised in the West.

Suddenly the priest asked me what was wrong with my back.

'How do you know there's something wrong with my back?'

'You've been holding it and making a pained face when you move.' He laughed. 'We have common sense, we African healers, you know, it's not all magic.'

Isidore wanted him to make me an ointment to show how good African medicine was.

The priest asked me what had happened, and shook his head. 'She has no need to be buying ointments, she just needs to lie flat at night, no pillow, and it will go away. And if you're driving back to Cotonou, you should adjust the car. Let me show you.'

The magic man adjusted the car seat so I could fully recline and take pressure off my back. He brought his wife out to see and they both held their backs they were laughing so much, as I was driven off, waving to them from my horizontal position.

This ludicrous mode of travel fixed my back in a couple of days. We fixed the King of Dassa by writing to the local paper about why there would be no point printing a story about the new maternity hospital.

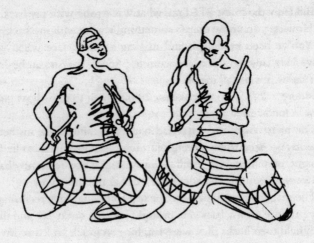

15

Catching the Detective

'Do not attempt to leave your room between the hours of eleven and six. There are unsupervised wolf dogs on the premises at this time. If there is an emergency please ring the bell by the door for someone to come from the house. This is a matter of your security.'

There was a fine thing to see, on a very small-typed notice on the back of your hotel-room door, at ten to eleven. I hadn't been planning to cavort out of my room in the night, but a more visible warning about 'wolf dogs' would have been helpful.

Every window in my room had bars inside and corrugated iron outside the glass. Every time I tried to settle to airless sleep, I thought I heard snuffling noises outside the door. I had a little chat with myself; there was no way the wolf dogs could get in the bolted metal door. Did it say 'wolf dogs with oxyacetylene torches loose in the yard'? No. And there was no mention of wolf dogs with burrowing equipment, ability to make themselves credit-card thin and squeeze themselves . . .

But I took no chances. When I wanted to leave my room at eight in the morning, I rang the emergency bell until a receptionist appeared.

'I wanted to check the dogs had gone,' I said, peering out, door open less than dog size.

'They go at six,' the receptionist said, irritated. 'Didn't you read the notice?'

If I hadn't read it I might have slept a great deal better. If I hadn't a head full of Isidore's stories about the frightening sorcerous bandits who roamed this district of Mono I might have slept better. Between the wolf dogs and hearing a bang on the corrugated-iron window – probably a bird but in the night definitely a bandit – I was glad he told me there might be another hotel on the Togo border.

'But I don't think a good detective should be scared of dogs,' Isidore smirked at me with my puffy eyes and unslept hair.

'Wolf dogs.'

'That just means big dogs. And as for bandits, didn't I tell you the man we're going to see ended the bandit problem?'

Davi, pronounced like the diminutive of the English boy's name, had ended the problem. His methods were a little different from Sherlock Holmes, Poirot or even your thief-roughing *NYPD Blue* types. Davi the detective investigated crime in the region, apprehended the guilty parties and set fire to them.

We were about to complete our own detective work on the kings of Dahomey, but detective Davi was on our route and it would be a shame to miss him.

Or not.

The flat Mono district, on the route to Togo, was fertile and reasonably prosperous. Its bandit problems continued with the much poorer people of Togo making runs over the border to thieve, but the bandit sorcerer gang that had terrorized the region in the unstable seventies had led to the emergence of Davi as a local hero and national legend.

The most terrible bandit was called Zanou. There'd have been no point getting wolf dogs and banging metal to your windows –

no matter how securely a house was locked up, he would use sorcery and his gang would get in. His gang would take everything in the house, rape wives in front of their husbands, daughters in front of fathers – and kill anyone who moved against them. Before they left, as their sinister calling card, they would shave the heads of everyone in the house.

The police could never find Zanou; some local vigilantes tracked him down but couldn't kill him because he was protected by massive sorcery. People lived in fear.

Brought up a farmer, Davi left the troubled region as a young man and travelled far away. Nobody knows where he went to find a *gri-gri* more powerful than any ever seen in Africa. Some said India, some said China. But years later, in the early 1980s, he came home.

One of the difficulties with catching the bandits was they were numerous, living in the community – the worst of them could be the apparently average man next door. Davi began walking around the communities of Mono and using his foreign power he could point at someone and say, 'You. You're a bandit. I know you.'

My guess is he just searched for the wealthier-looking people without shaved heads.

Davi gathered up a civilian militia of young men and captured more and more bandits. Those who hadn't killed anyone he let go with a beating and a warning. Lying was no good; he could tell those who had killed by using his sorcery. If they'd killed, he and his men tied them up, hauled them into the public squares and burnt them.

To find the evil and elusive Zanou, Davi turned himself into an ant to listen at a bandit's house, and from what they said he figured out where Zanou would be. He turned back into himself for travel, and then became an ant again so Zanou wouldn't see him approach. But, having powerful magic himself, Zanou could sense the presence of another sorcerer, even one disguised as an ant.

Zanou fled his hideout, ran into a village, saw a woman and turned himself into a baby inside her stomach. An ordinary person would have thought they were seeing a pregnant woman but Davi cried out to her stomach, 'I know you're in there – get out!'

In the shape of a lizard, Zanou ran out of the woman's vagina and into the forest. Davi turned himself into a bigger, faster lizard, caught Zanou and as lizards they fought. At the end of the fight, their forms changed back to men and people saw Davi, with his hands round Zanou's throat about to kill him. Zanou was weeping and shouting to be rescued. Davi tied him up. He said, 'I won't strangle you. You have to die in front of the people.' So there was another public burning.

Soon there wasn't an unburnt bandit in the province. Davi was contacted by Kérékou, who said, 'Well done, but enough with the public burnings. I'm sending some workers to build you a prison, just put the bandits in there and I'll send soldiers to take them back to Cotonou.'

Davi obviously decided that Kérékou was a bit soft, and carried on with his own methods. If he thought his prisoners were killers he'd tie them down in the cement courtyard of the prison in the full heat of the day and let them burn to death slowly.

'Visitors to Davi are supposed to have a letter of permission from the Minister of the Interior. But I don't think this will apply to a foreigner like you,' Isidore said as we drove deeper into Mono. 'I think Davi will be pleased to know a foreigner has heard of him.'

I thought this might be some kind of bet hedging from Isidore. After all, he hadn't shown me any kind of a witch and there was an ant-turning element to Davi that made me doubt his existence. Yet when we stopped in a market to ask a petrol seller if we were on the right road to Davi's, he said yes, yes, about five miles down on our left. We'd see a sign for a German medical clinic; Davi was a mile down the track past that.

'Except I happen to know he's not in at the moment,' the petrol seller said. 'I just saw his Mercedes drive off thataway.'

So this was a real person that people could see driving a car. Maybe it would be better than the witches.

In Davi's courtyard there was a statue of him, so I could see the type of outfit one wore for bandit burning. It was a sort of

Che Guevara-type composite revolutionary-about-town ensemble, with bandoliers of cartridges crossing his chest, along with strings of *gri-gri* talismans and cowry shells. There were amulet-bearing thongs around the neck, wrists and arms. Combat trousers, a military cap at a jaunty angle, and a machine gun held loosely in one hand completed the outfit. He was short, stocky, with an open, easygoing face but I felt there'd be other qualities in his eyes if you saw him for real.

Davi was an Adja, the dominant people of the region. The Adja had been the first subjects of the kings of Dahomey and were closely related to the Fon. Isidore said they had a reputation in history for being tough. They generally didn't do anything tough now, except if they worked for Davi.

Plenty of malevolent youths were hanging around the compound, which was much more of a plain but prosperous farmhouse than the stockade I'd expected. Some of the youths sprawled on a row of wooden benches under a tree, some leant in the shade of buildings. They wore mixed Western and local clothing and didn't seem to be armed. They looked like they were trying to be very cool about our presence but were actually edgy and suspicious. I tried to look as flameproof as I could.

A tall, maudlin man came out of the main house, very surprised to see us. He said he was Davi's bodyguard – Davi wouldn't be coming back until after dark. Isidore's story was that I was a tourist who'd read stories about Davi and wanted to meet him.

The bodyguard was a mostly menacing type you'd want for a bodyguard, but he became very giggly and skittish if I met his gaze for too long. Isidore pleaded ignorance when we were asked for our letter from the Minister of the Interior – we were just travellers, it was a spur-of-the-moment thing . . . Bodyguard looked very put out and said sulkily, 'You should have a letter. Go to the *Sous-Préfet* and get a letter, he's only down the road.'

As quite large youths were drawing closer to hear what was going on, I was all for leaping in the car and getting any letters I was told to get. Isidore wasn't so easily intimidated.

'You're the bodyguard. Can't we make an appointment through

you?' This was very foolhardy – being slightly mocking and infuriat-ingly persistent all in one sentence.

The bodyguard looked thunderous, folded his arms and said: 'No!'

I thought he'd be less likely to thump me. 'Sir, if we could make an appointment, then we'll get a letter of permission, wouldn't that be the best way?'

Skidding away from my eyes before he lost his composure again, the bodyguard grunted – 'It's not normal' – and stomped off into the house.

I thought it was all over, but Isidore felt he'd gone to fetch someone.

Probably someone with a gun.

Attempts to menace were being ruined for the malevolent youths by gathering clumps of awed children who kept asking them questions about me and needing their tumbledown trousers adjusted.

I had expected a more *Heart of Darkness* domestic set-up. Not shrunken heads exactly, but more the kind of thing Western reporters and literature had told me to expect in the home-decorating choices of sorcerer-militia leaders. This was an ordinary farming compound, a mile from a German charity clinic, sur-rounded by what Isidore pronounced as excellent maize fields.

The bodyguard came back with a young man all dressed in canary yellow, carrying a clipboard. Davi's secretary. He drew us away from the bodyguard and menacers and, after smiling pleasantries, asked us what we really wanted. What did we need Davi to do? What was our real problem?

We assured him we weren't victims of horrendous crimes. He seemed quite happy with the curious-tourists story. 'Look, it is unusual to see Davi informally, but write down your names and where you're from – I'll explain to him you have no problems, simply want to talk. Then I suggest you come back at six-thirty tomorrow morning, so if he wants to talk to you before he goes out, he will.'

I wrote on the clipboard and slipped the secretary the £2 Isidore advised would get us in for sure. 'Shall I give something to the bodyguard?' I whispered.

'No. He's a bit mad. You couldn't buy him.'

The secretary seemed optimistic. The bodyguard listened to what had been arranged, glowering or simpering according to whether I caught his eye or not. The menacers completely lost face by joining the kids yelling, '*Yovo, yovo, au revoir!*'

The hotel, without wolf dogs, that Isidore had decided to move me to looked promising and after his inspection he emerged very pleased with himself. 'Why didn't I think of this one first? You'll love it.'

It was small and flowery pretty. My first-floor room had a balcony with a long-range view of hills and a close-in view of a roadside market.

'Look, you can sit and write, watch the people – perfect for you.'

I always felt a little catch in my heart when I realized how much I'd sunk into Isidore's mind.

He said he didn't want to eat in my hotel because they served very small fish. We found a place with big fish that was also a brothel. Isidore denied this, said that the crowd of overdressed girls round the terrace were simply meeting there to socialize. I think if he admitted he'd brought me to a brothel he'd have felt he had to deprive himself of big fish for the sake of propriety. But I saw men arrive, go upstairs with a girl and come down tucking their shirts in. Could have been a laundry service.

Mono may have had a lurid upstairs life but it wasn't worldly. More than half the population had never been as far as Cotonou, and only a scattering had seen the two Germans at the charity clinic. We were told this by a young doctor we met in a medical centre on the edge of the Mono bush. He'd been away to train, in Cotonou and Lagos, and thought he'd come home to his backwater to save everyone and show the traditional healers a thing or two about modern medicine.

If the locals could be persuaded to trust his clinic at all, his main problem was that his modern treatments and medicines cost more

than traditional treatments. Gradually he'd learnt that not all traditional healers were charlatans and not all their treatments were
nonsense. For instance, the system of scarring patients to administer
the remedy – this put the remedy into the bloodstream fast, just
like an injection. It was remarkable how the scars never became
infected, because the healers knew so many natural antiseptics.
Often he would make a diagnosis and a healer would give him an
ancient remedy that worked. Although they'd never part with their
secret about what their recipe for the remedy was.

Sometimes they were wrong. They didn't understand malaria,
for instance. Most people had some form of malaria, occasionally
manifesting itself in fevers or weakening the immune system, giving
rise to shortlived opportunist diseases. The healers would cure the
short-term symptoms, but the doctor was working hard to convince
them that what was needed was malaria prevention. The Germans
up the road were specializing in malaria treatment and prevention;
they depended on this doctor to persuade patients to go to them.

'So I live in two worlds out here. If I'd stuck to my training and
chased the healers out of my medical centre, for one thing I'd have
very few patients. And for another I'd have lost access to an ancient,
low-cost dispensary. Mono has trusted the healers a long time and
the world outside is mysterious and fills the people with suspicion.'

The market was full of children who didn't know if I was a girl or
a boy, big fish or fowl. There were women shouting things like,
'Look at that, I've never seen one in real life!'

The people in the Mono village were so unaccustomed to
yovos they not only couldn't determine my sex, they also couldn't
determine my age, by a very long chalk.

A family resting under a tree – father, mother and several children
– were obviously talking about me. Isidore translated. The children
were asking if I was a boy or girl. The mother said: 'That's a girl.'

The father considered a moment and said: 'Yes, a girl, a very
young girl, probably only about ten years old.'

The mother scoffed: 'Don't be ridiculous, how can she be only
ten and be that tall?'

Father put her in her place. 'Listen, they grow very tall, you'd be amazed – even at ten they can be that tall.'

As I looked back the whole family were watching me, amazed.

They were several yards away but it was still a pleasing mistake to hear about when you're over thirty-five. Isidore tried to stop me showing off about it all evening. 'They don't know white people's faces. They don't know how to read them. They just see white, not shapes and wrinkles.'

'Oh, unlike you who can see the wreckage.'

'You don't look ten.'

I made pathetic attempts to prove him wrong by telling children who wanted to know girl or boy, where from, what age and so on as they followed us around that I was ten. Not one of them baulked.

Tired of my vanity, Isidore talked about the Adja people, how in general they did very little *gri-gri*. Their problem was machetes. In Benin these were called *coup-coup* – cut-cuts. The men drank too much *sodadi* when their fields were done and got into fights; they didn't punch or fight with sticks, they pulled out their machete and went wild. A few moments after hearing this, a gang of thirty schoolchildren came round the corner, all swinging machetes as big as their arms and shouting raucously.

Some of the children had very sharp and dangerous-looking hoes instead of machetes. It was the first week of school. The first week in the countryside schools was spent cleaning and weeding the overgrown playgrounds and buildings.

But still, very small children wielding cut-cuts did worry me – if they hadn't seen a *yovo* and took fright, like Isidore's small relative, I could get a lot worse than a stick in the face. I quickly steered Isidore across the road, pretending I had an urgent need to look at an egg stall.

We finished letting me show off my youthfulness round the market and wandered back to the car. A giant man, naked, was leaning on our bonnet, peering transfixed at the interior. He didn't look dangerous, just very strange. All the same, we decided we'd rather take a bit more of a walk around than tackle him.

'I hope I don't see my wife,' Isidore murmured as we walked. 'Then in some ways I hope I do. Serve her right.'

'You mean she'd think you were with me?'

'Sorry. But I did mean that. I know she lives somewhere in Mono now.'

'You miss her?'

'No.'

He sat down at the market bar, ordered drinks for us. He fidgeted with the foil on his beer bottle for a long time. Then he looked out across the market and sighed.

'When I married her she agreed with me, that we would only have the children we could afford. But after our first two, she always asked for more. I wasn't a wealthy man, you've seen where I live. But she persisted, even her mother came to talk to me, angry at me. She said how dare I take her daughter as a wife when I was too poor to have children. It wasn't that. I wanted to live a sensible life. My wife forgot about children for a while, she said she wanted to have a market stall. I spent my savings to get her things to sell. And she did ladies' hair.' He drank some of his beer, talking faster now, angrier. 'She was making money that she always spent on herself – clothes, shoes. So this was a new thing to argue about. The situation deteriorated. Then one night I came home and the house was empty. Television, clothes, furniture, radio, fridge, pictures off the wall, all gone. But what stopped my heart was for a moment I thought she'd taken Lucien and Antoine. But, thank Jesus, she'd left them with a neighbour.'

The neighbour told him that as soon as he'd gone to work, his wife brought the children round, saying she had to do some hairdressing work and would be gone all day. Later the neighbour had to walk to market, passing Isidore's house. The wife was there with her brothers from Abomey, loading a truck, emptying the house.

The neighbour was afraid of the wife and didn't intervene. She hurried back to her own home, saying nothing to Lucien and Antoine, waiting for Isidore to come back.

As soon as he was given the news, Isidore left the neighbour's house and drove to Abomey. At first his wife's family pretended she wasn't there, that they knew nothing. But Isidore ignored them, searched the compound and found all his furniture hidden in a rear building.

'I told the mother, if my wife wanted to leave, that was fine but she couldn't take these things away from the children. I told her I knew my wife was nearby and she should fetch her – we could discuss the ending of the marriage and get it over with. Sure enough, in five minutes she came back with my wife, her brothers and her grandfather. All my wife kept insisting was that to keep the furniture was her right. I said keep it, go away, live your life. She didn't even ask if the children were upset. To this day she's made no attempt to see Lucien and Antoine. She knows me, she knows I would let her visit them, for their sakes.' He rubbed his face as if to wake himself out of a bad dream. 'Bit by bit, I'm getting nice things in the house again. That's why I always make you wait outside; I used to have good armchairs, a television . . . now there are plain wooden chairs and only a radio. I can't invite you to a house like that.'

'Invite me, see if I care about chairs.'

He smiled at me, thought a moment before he decided I was probably telling the truth. 'Anyway, she married a man from Mono, has other children, she's forgotten us.'

She'd been gone five years.

If she'd gone off to have a career or something I might have looked to see her side of it, but she sounded like a right little . . . 'She swapped those boys for furniture.'

'Yes. Her dowry for the new husband, I expect. I don't understand it. She has other children but those were her first. That's why my boys are still a bit odd, you know, very nervous. I like my work, I love travelling around finding things out, but the boys, you can imagine why they hate me to be out of their sight.'

It's our dad, it's our dad.

Isidore finished his drink, stared at the glass. 'If she could be just a little as unhappy as me and the boys were those first months.' He looked up, smiled slightly. 'Ah, but my father advised me, remembering it will poison me. So when it comes in my mind, I put it out.'

'OK, we won't talk about it any more.'

We sat a while, having more drinks, watching people, saying 'girl', 'ten', to kids who asked. I went to pay the bill, he protested: 'No. Let me do this like we're just friends, not boss and driver. It's a strange thing to have happened, but I feel you are my proper friend.'

Walking back, I couldn't answer any more girl-or-boy questions because I was close to tears. Isidore, on the other hand, became quite chipper, telling me he'd actually employed the giant madman to guard the car.

'Yes, he's a bit peculiar but he's good at his work. He did have a uniform but he won't wear it, so he can't serve dinner to guests because he won't wear his trousers.' He fished a small coin out of his pocket. 'Here is his salary, I'll send him home. It may surprise you to learn his home is in the madhouse.'

The poor giant was in exactly the same position, still watching the inside of the car for sudden seat movements. It took him a while to register that we'd arrived. Isidore handed him his salary. He put it on top of a leaf full of peanuts someone had put on the car bonnet for him. Then he picked up the leaf, peanuts and money, and held the bundle to his upper arm as if stopping a wound with it.

His entire torso and arms were covered in tiny deep scars. Isidore said they were probably from *gri-gri* to try and cure him.

'But there are some people in Togo . . . the men cut each other with knives, little cuts like that for some kind of initiation ceremony. I don't know, big and black-black like that, he looks more like someone from Mali or Burkina, who knows what they do. If he was from here, those would be cuts from *gri-gri*.'

'No point asking him, I suppose?'

'Why not? Go ahead. You ask.'

Something about the way he still had his hand in the wound-staunching position, staring, head tilted to the sky – I couldn't think how to phrase the question.

*

It was great to be up just after dawn. There was mist over low-lying fields, the air was cold and clean, people were just opening their doors, starting fires. I waited for Isidore at the front of the silent hotel – for the first time in Benin I had to jump around to keep warm.

I was up even earlier than necessary. I'd be totally alert for the meeting with Davi. If he tried turning me into an ant, I'd be ready for him.

Women drawing water and washing babies along the track to Davi's were very surprised to see me come bowling along out of the morning mists. We nearly ran over the bodyguard, who was suddenly standing in the middle of the road looking very big and very ferocious.

We were just at the edge of Davi's compound, and there was another road out of it ahead of us. I'd a feeling the bodyguard had stepped in the road to stop us in case we'd seen his master just disappear down the other road and tried to follow him. The bodyguard made us park and went to fetch the secretary, who – surprise surprise – told us Davi had just gone: hadn't we met his blue Mercedes on the road, how odd . . .

He said Davi was very busy, but if we could get a letter from a government minister and call back in a few days . . .

It seemed obvious that Davi had flown the coop to avoid us and would always have flown no matter how many government letters we came back with.

The secretary remained gushingly friendly, suggesting we call in on our way back from Togo. When would that be? Two days, but that would be ideal. We could see the *Sous-Préfet* today, get our letter and call back in two days.

Isidore was becoming irritated with the secretary and his gush. I felt nervous as the menacers in their pyjamas started to meander out, scratching themselves and staring. Isidore started raised-voice talk about how the King of Abomey had seen me, the King of Nikki had his horsemen out for me . . . Generally making it clear that I was used to being made welcome in far higher places than Chez Slipper of the Burnt Bandit Yard.

The secretary was unimpressed, regretful. 'Really, if you see the *Sous-Préfet*, he can arrange your visit.'

I thought it was a very bad omen that, as we were leaving, a man with a baby-size coffin strapped to the back of his bike cycled through the yard. Isidore was so incensed with the secretary that he didn't notice. The bodyguard and the menacers were distracted by the coffin, wandering off to see which baby was dead.

Fortunately they were out of striking range when Isidore had a go at the secretary in a sudden burst of angry Adja, then slammed the car door on further gush and roughly accelerated us away.

I was ready to give up, but Isidore swung the car straight into the drive of the *Sous-Préfet*, demanding that a startled and disconcertingly bearded lady at the front desk make us an immediate appointment.

The *Sous-Préfet* hadn't arrived at his office but we were given chairs by his door to wait for him. A queue of chairs began to form – a dozen other people behind us.

While we were waiting, I reflected on the nature of the man we'd been hounding in a bush paparazzi sort of way. This was someone so scary that even Kérékou had asked nicely if he'd mind not torching the populace. And instead of getting angry when Davi continued burning and torturing, Kérékou made him an honorary colonel.

I found it more soothing to hear Isidore explain what a *Sous-Préfet* did for a living. Quite a lot. He administrated public works, drains, school buildings, market repairs . . . He sorted out land disputes, inheritance disputes . . . He was a sort of small-claims court and town councillor. The bearded lady seemed to be his only assistant and the queue of chairs was getting longer.

The *Sous-Préfet* arrived; he was a smartly dressed man of about thirty-five, rushing but affable. We were shown straight into his office with apologies for the wait.

I think at first he imagined I might be something good – a worker from a charity project, a nice German wanting to build another clinic, something to make a change and give an inspiring start to the hectic day ahead.

His desk was piled yards high with papers and thick, dull-looking files.

'That looks like a lot of work,' I commented as we took our seats.

He looked at the piles wearily. 'It is, but also I don't have a filing cabinet.'

From hopeful and interested, I could see the *Sous-Préfet*'s face slam down into disbelief as Isidore told our tale.

Isidore said I'd heard about Davi and wanted to visit him; Davi's secretary told us we had to get a letter of appointment from the *Sous-Préfet* so that in two days' time when I . . .

The *Sous-Préfet* interrupted quietly, tautly polite. Now looking at us as if we were something he needed to handle with caution because we had a strong whiff of insanity about us.

'Could you first perhaps introduce yourselves, tell me who you are?'

The *Sous-Préfet* wrote down our names, very slowly, then Isidore said that he was my driver and I taught Comparative Literature at London University – this was something we'd devised as a ridiculous new cover over yesterday's big-fish dinner. I chipped in with my part of the lie: how I wanted to research African life as a background to my teaching on African literature . . . I stopped myself because I sounded such a tosser and because it was written all over the *Sous-Préfet*'s intelligent face that he thought 'tosser' and 'liar'. And, probably, 'journalist'.

Whatever I was, it was all bad, but he maintained his quiet politeness. 'I don't know what you think there is to see. Davi . . . he's just a person like the rest of us. Just someone who lives here, was born here. We don't have some kind of extraterrestrial out in the bush for you to see.'

I wanted the earth to swallow me up.

Isidore was still trying: 'She just heard the stories and was curious to meet him.'

Somewhere in his eyes, the *Sous-Préfet* was whacking his pile of papers off his desk, picking up the heaviest file and smacking me round the head with it – but he kept a reasonable tone.

'Well, you know, I am the *Sous-Préfet* for a very large district. As you noticed, there is a lot of work here. So making appointments for people to see someone who is just another citizen here, like every other citizen, is actually not my job.'

I tried to make it clear that this situation wasn't entirely my responsibility: 'Davi's secretary told us we had to see you.'

The *Sous-Préfet*'s hands flailed in exasperation. 'What on earth has his appointment book to do with me?'

To try and look halfway bright, I said: 'So they just said that to get rid of us?'

Just a hint of irritated sarcasm. 'Probably, that would be the case.' He tried to return to a pleasanter tone; achieved vaguely threatening. 'Look, like I say, he doesn't have horns, he's just a private citizen with a right to privacy so, to a certain extent, like any other private citizen, he's entitled to the protection of the state from intrusion into his life and property. So, my advice is to leave him alone. If he doesn't want to see you, that's his business and you should leave him alone. Listen, all those stories about him, that's all a long time ago and I'd rather not have them brought back into people's perception of us here. Personally I don't believe a word of the things told about him. Journalists made those things up to sell papers.'

The way he said 'journalists', long, drawn-out and looking me in the eye, I knew that's what he thought I was. I made a far-too-late last-ditch attempt to stop him thinking I was a moron as well as a liar.

'I don't believe the stories either,' I said. 'But I was curious to find out what the truth was about him, what provoked such stories.'

'Nothing provoked them. Journalists seize on a tiny thing and make up the rest. How could such stories be true?'

I apologized for taking up his time. He bade us a stony farewell. Almost slammed the door behind us.

We fled to the big-fish brothel for breakfast. I'd started to find it quite funny. I'd been spending far too much time trying to live

Isidore's version of the world and had suddenly cracked my forehead against the real world. Did you want to see the *Sous-Préfet*? Yes, I'd like to meet a man who sets fire to people and turns himself into a lizard, please . . .

Isidore was subdued, thinking our mission had failed. He was pleased I was laughing. 'You don't mind not seeing Davi?'

'That *Sous-Préfet*'s face when he realized what we wanted . . . We mustn't try and see Davi on the way back.'

'No,' Isidore agreed. 'I think if the *Sous-Préfet* even saw us in his town again he'd lose his mind. You know what I think? I think he's a bit afraid of Davi.'

Afraid of Davi and faced with the potential nightmare of a foreigner getting Davi riled.

In a recent human rights report on Benin, Kérékou got good marks for general attempts to create a fair judiciary. Bad marks for food and hygiene conditions in his prisons. And particularly bad marks for not sorting out a vigilante group in the Mono province, notorious for torturing and publicly burning alleged wrongdoers.

The witch was real. An ordinary citizen.

Kérékou had asked once and wasn't going to ask again. Davi was a folk hero; if Kérékou moved against him all hell could break loose. It had happened in the Congo, in Sierra Leone – folk-hero sorcerers with guns in the woods were better left to go about their bizarre business. Or next thing you knew, they had a coked-up boy army who thought bullets couldn't kill them on the edge of the capital city. In his new democratic phase, what Kérékou had learnt best was pragmatism.

The Togo border was only a couple of kilometres from Davi town. We stopped for petrol before leaving everyone in peace.

A madman, a small stocky one but telltale naked and muttering to himself, was walking our way.

'Look,' Isidore said. 'Here's your friend.'

'It's you,' I said. 'You attract them.'

'No,' Isidore said. 'The *Sous-Préfet* said to him, "You think you're mad? Go look on the Togo road and you'll see what mad is."'

At the frontier there were forms to fill in in triplicate, forms to be copied into ledgers, and men in no apparent uniform worked at all this busily and slowly. Then Isidore gave them a pound. They smiled, stamped everything, and told me I could go.

The Togo frontier was much more official-looking. Half a dozen high buildings in contrast to Benin's three men in one corrugated-iron hut. There were gangs of men in military uniforms, gangs of police with guns and no question of smiling or making up your own rules. Inches into it, you knew this was a tough country.

Isidore had to go off to a big building with two aggressive policemen. He said they wanted to check his car papers but it did look more like he was under arrest.

I was left at a desk under a tree with a middle-aged sergeant and a hulking young corporal who looked as though he enjoyed giving people a good kicking.

'Visa? We don't do visas here,' he snarled at me. 'Who told you that?'

'The people over in Benin.'

'Benin's got nothing to do with us.' The corporal glared at me then interrupted the sergeant, who had started to say something. 'You should phone Benin and tell them to do things like we told them.'

The sergeant nodded and did nothing. He hadn't the same uniform as the corporal, and his rank obviously gave him only the most cautious authority over whatever force the corporal belonged to. But he did make so bold as to offer me a seat and say apologetically, 'You may as well rest, madame, this might take a while.'

We breathed easy a moment as the corporal went off to bully some small men on bicycles who were coming in through the thatched arch of the pedestrian entrance rather than the metal vehicle gates. The sergeant glanced vaguely through my passport.

'There won't be a problem. It will just take a while.'

The corporal stomped over again and snatched my passport, making a big show of scowling at every page. Meanwhile Isidore was all done and dusted, back and asking what the problem was. The corporal started cross-examining Isidore about what business he had asking. Tactfully the sergeant sent the corporal to fetch something. Isidore gave the sergeant some money, which he pocketed fast.

'There shouldn't be a problem.' The sergeant smiled. 'I just need to check the price for a visa for . . . English?'

'Yes.'

He smiled, relaxing. 'Ah, yes, how is your Queen Margaret?'

'Elizabeth.'

'Oh. Who is Margaret? They say she's iron-hearted or something.'

'She used to be our Prime Minister.'

'Ah. I'm confused. Elizabeth is the Queen, Margaret was the woman with the yellow hair. Yes, Queen Elizabeth. And she has a husband who doesn't take the throne from her. I think her husband's afraid of her. Has she any sons?'

'Three.'

'Three? Why don't they take the throne from her? She must be strong to scare them so much. I never understood, how is it she has a husband and he isn't the King?'

I tried to explain the succession of the British monarchy to the best of my ability. The sergeant looked astounded; Isidore was hot, fanning himself and looked like he was losing the will to live.

The corporal brought back a dog-eared document in a plastic folder. A list of the countries of the world and prices of visas required – could we find England, *Angleterre*, *Grande-Bretagne*? Nowhere. The sergeant read the cover of the passport. Europe, of course! No, there was no such thing.

Then, the sergeant pointed to United Kingdom on the passport. That's what we needed to look for! He scanned his list and triumphantly offered me . . . Uruguay.

There was some fuss with women and goats and bicycles jammed in the pedestrian entrance. The sergeant went to untangle them, handing me the list to check for myself. The corporal put my passport in his breast pocket, which I found slightly intimidating. Isidore wanted to look at the list and the corporal wouldn't let him, so he went off to kick at his car tyres to avoid an incident.

I read the list, word by word. Finally I saw it – French, of course, *le Royaume-Uni* – all very well to be smirky about people who didn't know their Uruguay from their elbow but I'd been too dense to think of looking for the French name for Britain on a French-language list.

Everyone was happy that it turned out to be me that was stupid. So they now knew I had to pay £10 for an entry visa – but obviously it couldn't be over just like that; they had to go and photocopy some forms in the main building, they had to find someone senior to countersign the forms but he might have gone to town . . . Isidore pulled at his head, making madman's hair tufts, but in another hour we were through.

I had a copy of the British Foreign Office advice on Togo. Fortunately we weren't going to Lomé, where apparently you'd be murdered the minute you got out of your bed. But even the countryside was aleap with bandits, kidnappers . . . Visitors should never drive alone or stop in remote areas. Isidore had assured me he met many white people who'd come into Benin from Togo on holidays and business and not one of them showed any sign of being dead. Nor had they complained of another Foreign Office warning – that there were fake police checkpoints set up on country roads by cut-throats and thieves.

The road to Tado was lined with teak forest – thin, densely planted trees with big leaves that made an unnerving clattering sound. Isidore remarked on the lack of villages. Even in the remotest forests of Benin you had a sense of life going on, nomads ambling around – this place felt quiet, too quiet.

'Of course it's very poor here, many of the people will be in Benin working in bars and restaurants. I hope we can leave before dark, though, I don't want to drive through this forest at night.'

Show Me the Magic

'Don't say that.'
'I'm just saying it makes me nervous.'
'Don't.'

Unfortunately, Isidore asked the Tado town drunk the way to the old palace. A rum-smelling, wild-eyed man who wanted to get in the car to escort us. Isidore sped off in the direction the man had indicated.

'Good riddance. Why did I stop and ask him? Drunk evil man with a head like a donkey.'

He did have a long-bearded, donkey-type head. I asked Isidore why he said evil.

'I could feel his evil spirit as soon as he came near me. Damn, here's the palace, he'll catch up with us.'

It had to be the palace – big metal gates, high, painted walls, pictures of panthers. A teenage boy in a pink T-shirt had just started telling us we needed to see the elders but he could run and get them for us . . . when the drunk man ran up, shouting at the boy angrily. The boy backed away from the car.

Now he came near I could feel something off the drunk man. I wouldn't have called it an evil spirit, but there was something very creepy about him. Just a feeling. No more evidence to it than evil spirit.

The drunk said he knew the elder we needed to see – he'd get him – but could we give him £2 to buy anything nice the elder might want for coming?

'If the elder wants anything we'll give it to him when he comes.' Isidore was leaning away from the window, but this was more from fear of the stink of spirits than evil spirits.

'No, it's much better if I take the elder a few nice things in advance.'

'What sort of nice things?'

The drunk then started talking to Isidore in another language. Isidore answered in French, saying we weren't paying anything in advance for meetings with people we hadn't seen. The drunk talked more urgently, cajolingly in the language. Isidore replied harshly in the same language, then called the boy in the pink T-shirt to fetch the elder. The boy ran, the drunk ran after him.

'Oh, that man,' Isidore groaned. 'You know what he said in Mina? He said, "Come on, you know these whites have money, you can persuade her to give me two pounds. Instead of taking her side, you should help your brothers." So I said to him, "This isn't some white, this is my sister and mother in life and who are you?"' He sighed. 'I wish I hadn't spoken to him; now we're stuck with him.'

'How did he know you spoke Mina?'

'He didn't know. He was just trying it. Maybe the elder's a priest and won't be afraid to get rid of him.'

The elder didn't seem to be a priest. He seemed very irritated to have the drunk dogging his footsteps, but wasn't casting him off.

The elder was about sixty, dressed in dapper lemon and blue cotton, as if for a summer golf game. He had a wide, middle-aged man in a blue robe with him, who he introduced as the palace guardian. The metal gates were opened and we drove into a vast overgrown courtyard.

This place was as big as Abomey Palace Museum. It looked as though an attempt had been made to stop it completely merging with the forest but it was like finding the Secret Garden.

'Here we are.' Isidore stretched out his arms. 'Where the kings of Dahomey originated.'

The elder smiled at his excitement. 'I think you're a Fon.'

'I'm not a Fon,' I said. 'And I'm very excited too.'

'Then we must make it an excellent visit for you. Is that your camera? Please, take photographs.'

The walls were painted in black and white reliefs in a different style to the art at Abomey – more naturalistic, simpler. There were no gory images; there were animals, there were kings on horseback, forests and birds.

The dapper elder explained that the two large empty buildings were the royal reception rooms. They had applied for a grant to an international organization to turn them into a museum. At the moment the plans to open the palace to the public couldn't go

ahead because the King had died two months ago. It would be a
year before the new King was installed and ambitions to revitalize
the palace could continue.

The elder said we could find out more if we visited his uncle,
who was a bit too old to walk down to the palace – would we
mind?

We followed him and the guardian. The drunk tagged along,
loudly moaning that I'd promised him £2 for fetching the elder.
Why had I tricked him? How could I be so cruel, he was a poor
man.

'Ignore him,' Isidore said.

The uncle had an iron-god shrine in his courtyard – a palm-oil-
scorched mound with pieces of old car stuck in it. As we'd now
entered private property, we'd managed to shake off the drunk at
the gate.

Uncle, I was told, was a hundred and ten years old. He was very
alert, if a mite feeble in the leg and walking area. All his skin seemed
to be a scrunch of wrinkles but his eyes were clear and he had every
tooth but one middle-front pair.

Uncle had two wives and eight children. He told us one of his
sons had two wives and fourteen children – this was too much. He
didn't understand the greed to have children that had come upon
people. In the ancestors' days they didn't make children with their
wives in a crazy way. They would go to wives at their fertile time,
have a couple of children with them and then that would be that.
They had some slave girls for pleasure but they didn't go having
official children with official wives to a point where there were far
too many to share the inheritance. Also, the ancestors were warriors
and believed time spent with women took your strength.

Isidore grinned. 'He's a hundred and ten. He's very wise and he
agrees with me that having too many children is crazy.'

I was bored with the children argument. There were more
important things to find out. 'What do you eat to live to be a
hundred and ten?'

Everyone laughed at my question. Uncle said, 'Oh, nothing, I
eat plants, sometimes meat.'

There had to be more to it than that, if he really was a hundred and ten. Although he could have passed for a lad of eighty any day. 'I expect you don't smoke.'

'I smoke and I drink. But bear in mind, I smoke fresh tobacco leaves I grow in my own fields. I drink distilled palm wine from my own trees. What kills you people is sugar, the sugar added to your drinks. And your kind of smoking is bad because they add chemicals. Normally tobacco is just a harmless vegetable.'

Now we'd discovered the key to long life, it was time to get to business. The elder said that he would explain the history to save his uncle's energy, but that he liked to have his uncle present to check all the facts, seeing as he was a hundred and ten and knew many facts.

The elder and his uncle didn't give me the panther story, but they did tell me something that wasn't accurate. They said their ancestors came to Tado in the thirteenth century from far in the northeast, from the Sudan, and may originally have been Egyptians.

Mali, to the northeast, was called Sudan when it was a French colony. I suspect the French may have encouraged the confusion about various Sudans and the notion that the kings of Dahomey were Egyptians, to imply they were Arab, not African. There were similar rumours about many African civilizations. The more Europeans could imply that anything complex going on was to do with non-Africans, the easier it was to dismiss Africans as lesser beings.

In fact, the men who came to install themselves at Tado in the thirteenth century were breakaway princes from a Yoruba empire, to the near northeast of Tado. Everyone was African.

It seems very arrogant to be telling you that an elder sitting in his hometown didn't know its history, but slavery and colonialism had shredded the tradition of oral history that was kept at Tado to ill-matched fragments. What was significant was that through the centuries of slavery, colonialism and dispersal, a clear knowledge that there was a rich history of African civilization was determinedly maintained. Told and told, by old men to young men. The details

weren't as important as the reiteration down the dislocated genera-
tions that no one had just been hanging around in the bush when
the Europeans arrived; the progress of African civilizations had
been interrupted by the Europeans. It hadn't always been as it was
now, and there was a legacy of memory to reassure that things
could change again.

The uncle brought out a box of letters, airmail letters. Some very
old, some recent. These were from Martinique. From former slaves
who had traced their ancestry back to the royal house of Tado.
Some had even visited. Uncle pointed at the dapper elder: 'And
one of them, you would say he was his twin.'

'Gbehanzin was sent to Martinique,' Isidore said.

'That's right. One of our correspondents is his direct descendant.
So a cousin to us. In Martinique. And of course, the new Gbehanzin
looks very like us.'

Which Gbehanzin was this?

The one in Abomey, they said. The present traditional King of
Dahomey, who had been enthroned a couple of years ago. After
the trouble with Agon Agonli.

Horrified to find himself confused, Isidore got to the bottom of
this. The rotund king we'd met was a descendant of the puppet
King, Agon Agonli, installed by the French after the exile of
Gbehanzin. Now that all the kings were reinstated, there had been
considerable dispute about who should take over at Abomey.

'That's why they were funny about the enthronement ceremony,
you remember, when you asked?' Isidore shook his head. 'I'm
Beninois; why didn't I know this?'

'Ah, it's politics.' The dapper elder smiled. 'Agon Agonli was a
friend to Soglo. Kérékou has given everything to Gbehanzin.
Perhaps among the Fon they still prefer the secondary line. But
Gbehanzin is the King of Dahomey.'

Gbehanzin, the new, was a clever, middle-aged and modern man
quite entitled to call himself the King of Dahomey. When we
tracked him down, a few days after our revelation at Tado, he was

welcoming and informative. He pleasantly explained that Agon Agonli had made a lot of trouble for him, but that Agon Agonli had been allowed to remain as the King of Abomey, not Dahomey.

When I told Gbehanzin I'd been to Tado he looked impressed.

'So you are very interested. Oh yes, they're still out there. And I'm here. This is a living tradition.'

Perhaps by the time we'd tracked down the living Gbehanzin I'd developed king fatigue. I loved the fact that he was there, descendant of a legend, obviously a powerful and wealthy man in his modern, two-storey palace down the road from the ruins of the original Gbehanzin compound. And he clearly resembled the poor stragglers in Tado. But their sense of their history seemed more moving than his educated assurance of his place in the world. He had phones, he travelled, he'd been on the Eurostar . . . He wouldn't have collected and preserved letters from Martinique with careful awe.

In Tado the airmail letters were carefully replaced in their box by their keepers.

'My uncle hopes to go Martinique himself one day.' Dapper elder smiled.

Uncle laughed. 'They say I'm too old to try an aeroplane, what do you think?'

I said, 'I don't think there's an age limit.'

The uncle said I was a very nice person and should be shown to the sacred forest. He summoned a teenage grandson to help show the way.

The drunk was waiting for us at the gate with the teenager in the pink T-shirt. They joined the entourage along with the shy grandson and the guardian of the palace. The drunk immediately demanded the £2 he claimed I'd promised him. The pink-shirt teenager said if anyone was owed money it was him. The dapper elder looked stressed and walked ahead with me, saying quietly: 'I apologize if people are bothering you for money. They're very poor people here. They forget how to behave.'

I said it didn't bother me at all. He perked up. 'So how is your Queen? She must be very old now.'

'She's about seventy, I think. Her mother is still alive, too – she's over a hundred years old.'

'The one who was married to George? Still alive?'

I don't know what it was with the Togolese and British royalty . . . I could see that the elder was bursting with further royal questions but we'd come to the next stage in the Tado pilgrimage.

More elders, this time under an awning with grandsons, a central blind elder swathed in white.

'The blind man is the guardian of the sacred forest, we need his permission to enter. And he needs a gift,' the grandson told me.

I gave some money to the blind man. I'd also given money to the uncle. Now the drunk complained loudly in our wake. 'She deliberately gives money to others to mock me – I helped her and she won't give me the money she promised. I'm a poor man. Look at her, with her camera and Nike shoes, and she didn't even give me anything to eat.'

I gave him £2 and told him to go away and leave me alone. But he pocketed the money and continued to follow along.

Isidore whispered to me that I shouldn't do or say anything else to drive him off. 'I'm serious, Annie. I don't want his evil spirit following us on our journey. And if he goes now he'll go and slash our tyres or something.'

We reached a crossroads and the dapper elder suddenly excused himself. He had a problem and had to go to his house. The guardian of the palace would bring us to his house to say goodbye once we had seen the forest. He raced away. I thought he'd been taken ill.

Isidore told me it was all to do with the drunk man; the elder was embarrassed beyond belief and feared further scenes over money at the end of the tour. If there was trouble, the guardian would protect us, but the elder would rather not be shamed on the sidelines.

A long walk through the forest, the guardian occasionally carping at the drunk and the drunk continually trying to walk next to me, Isidore bravely making a moving shield of himself. A clearing where there were three foot-high stones in the ground, cylindrical, round-ended. Two were the same size, one was very small. The same formation of stones was outside the royal palace of Allada by the statue of the first king of their dynasty.

The palace guardian explained. These stones represented a king, his wife and the wife's purchases. A king of the eighteenth century. The king and his wife had gone on a journey, during which the wife had bought some things at a market. When they came to the edge of the forest, they realized that slavers had come to their kingdom and were taking their people. So that they weren't taken, the king turned himself, the wife and her purchases into stone. After many years, the stone king restored himself and his wife to life, and he started the kingdom again.

So presumably he just hid out in the forest. And what happened to the shopping?

That was the end of the tour. The stones representing the ancestors were the thing to see. Isidore said there were probably other secrets in the forest to do with religious matters that I couldn't see. But I was happy with the stones. Seeing the same symbols in Allada, letters from Martinique, the returned Gbehanzin . . . It was a like a circle of resistance.

My personal circle of resistance to the drunk and his attempts to talk to me finally succeeded. As we left the forest he suddenly sloped off.

'Needs a drink,' Isidore said. 'Good riddance.'

Only the palace guardian came with us to the dapper elder's compound. It was full of flower trees, happy kids, busy women. There was a small building at the edge of the compound, with paintings of children on it, children sitting together, holding hands.

'This is a shrine to Tohosou, divinity of malformed children,' the guardian said. 'It's very important to the royal house of Tado. They had many of these children in the family. They must be cherished.'

Isidore suddenly grinned and talked to the guardian in Adja. The guardian, almost imperceptibly, nodded.

'What's happening?' I asked.

'You'll find out something soon,' Isidore said. 'You'll like it.'

★

The elder was pleased to see us, had water brought for us, wanting us to relax in his sparsely furnished room. He seemed like a man desperate for good conversation. First there was a rapid return to the British royal family. Then there was the political trouble in the Ivory Coast, then the problems of drugs among the youth.

'Even out here in the bush they're getting drugs. Half of my children have gone to work in Benin – it's a better place for the young; they need work or else . . . Well, you've seen the people here, drinking, drugs.' He changed the subject. Where were we going next on our journey? Where else had I travelled?

He kept us talking for close on an hour, thoroughly enjoying whatever we told him. He seemed like an unhappy person who was having a good time for a change. I enjoyed it for him, but I did wonder, where was the thing I would like?

The elder eventually said he should let us go, so we wouldn't be driving after dark. He had one last thing he needed to know: 'I hope you don't mind, but I have a question for you young people who've been to school: does Aids exist?'

I was thrown for a moment. I felt like I'd been handed a very big responsibility. I told him everything I knew.

The elder absorbed what I said. He looked very shocked. 'Thank you,' he said. 'I'd heard about it but wasn't sure it was true.'

'How lucky to have intelligent visitors,' the guardian said.

Isidore smiled at the guardian, then said to the elder, 'Sir, may I ask you something? Would you write your address and name for us? So she knows.'

The elder smiled. 'I was going to do that. You understand it is a time of mourning and I shouldn't speak of these things but I can write it.'

He wrote his name: Gabriel Prince à Adja Tado.

I understood. 'You're going to be the new King?'

The prince smiled and turned his head away.

The guardian said, 'He isn't allowed to talk of it in the time of mourning.'

The prince took us to our car. 'When you come back,' he said, 'I hope you find us in happier times.'

*

Isidore didn't lift his hands from the steering wheel, racing me to Abomey to find the new Gbehanzin.

'When we see the living Gbehanzin, you will have the whole thing. Beginning to end.'

The circle complete. Right back to an original panther king, dressed for golf.

16

One Flew Over the Vulture's Nest

Claude was a nice new friend we'd made in Cotonou. But now we'd gone and lost him.

As we went on a hunt for him, Isidore had an inspiration. 'I bet if we find someone at his house they'll tell us he's at the hospital.'

'What, you've had some kind of *gri-gri* premonition he's had an accident?'

'No, it's his wife, she'll be having a baby – you remember, when we met her? She's pregnant.'

'Oh. I thought she was just a big girl.'

'I thought observing was your job?'

Sure enough, Claude's neighbours told us he had left with his wife at four in the morning and hadn't been home for thirty-six hours. There were complications with his wife's labour.

We were both worried about him. Claude was the sort of person you didn't want to be unhappy because a damper put on his exuberant oddness would be awful to see.

I was proud that Isidore was so taken with Claude; it was unusual for me to have sought out and befriended someone who didn't turn out to be some kind of rogue or maniac who I'd need rescuing from.

I'd been buying Claude's work by the acre until it suddenly occurred to me that the woman in the market profiting from my enthusiasm might be able to introduce me. She sold cards, postcards, envelopes and T-shirts hand-painted by Claude. They were simple silhouette paintings, touched with colour, not a stroke out of place. The elongated figures of men in fields, women carrying babies and water jars, boatmen at Ganvié or herdsmen with animals seemed abstract – but at a distance, on a hot afternoon, people did look exactly how they appeared in Claude's work. 'Matchstick' figures, Claude called them. This was it: if Lowry had painted in Africa, he'd have painted like Claude.

The market woman and I were just working out how to arrange a meeting, when what seemed to be an old man on a moped, an old leather cowboy hat rammed over his eyes, skidded up to the stall. Here was Claude, come to replenish the stock. The instant he took off the headgear you saw he wasn't old at all; he looked what he was, twenty-five and full of weird beans.

He darted through traffic while we followed in the car. He thought the best reward for my enthusiasm was for me to see where he worked, see the paintings done where I could sit comfortably and talk, rather than bellowing at him over traffic and market uproar.

It turned out that Claude lived round the corner from Isidore in a family compound of brothers and cousins. Rented property, Isidore observed. They were very much the same kind of people, up from the villages working hard to make good in the city. Open, friendly, decent, without a big back in sight.

Claude's parents were Togolese migrants. The painting was in the family, taught by the father to the two of five sons who'd showed aptitude and interest. The father had been an orphan, rescued from begging in the bush by a kind painter who'd taught him the craft. If I looked around Cotonou, I'd see other cards, wall hangings, murals . . . These could be by the brother or father.

'There are rules and ways of doing it. Like your old European painters, they had apprentices all learning to paint in the same way. But anyone who knows the paintings would know, for instance, what was by my father and what was by me. You see these bushy trees? I invented that, that is my innovation. We learn the style but people develop in their own way.'

It paid, but not enough. There was no possibility of teaching art – the nearest art school was in the Ivory Coast and Benin's schools thought sport was a more important subject to put on the timetable. Claude subsidized his painting income by coaching football at local schools. His father had worked as a cartographer in local government after he came to Cotonou, and before that he'd driven trucks. He'd preferred the truck driving, as it enabled him to travel, see things and sell his paintings in new markets.

Claude's studio was a table in one of his two rooms. He took off his shirt and put on the stripy apron he wore for work – this was his wife's idea, as she had threatened to divorce him after a week if she had to keep washing paint out of his clothes.

'I'm doing a big card, so you can see the strokes. Also, I want you to see it's really me that does these paintings, I don't sell them at double the price for the real artist.'

By coincidence, as Claude began painting at his heavy wood table in front of the window, an unusually cloudy sky cleared so the sun poured in.

'He's all lit up,' Isidore said. 'Do you see? Not just the sun – as he starts to work he's happy.'

Claude smiled. 'Very true. I can do this for hours. Ah, really, my father gave us a great inheritance. As he taught us he said it probably wouldn't make us rich but it would give us infinite pleasure in being alive.'

Working with a very thin brush, Claude chatted while he continued making deft strokes, first the outlines in black. It was a little like watching an elegant version of those 'guess what it is' paintings

Rolf Harris used to do on children's programmes. Disconnected strokes, what would they be? Then you saw heads, legs, trees . . . While one black painting dried, Claude would usually begin the black work on a second painting; today he spent the drying time organizing a young cousin to fetch us cold drinks and introducing his wife, who came in from the courtyard, shy and escaping quickly.

'She is my only wife. Always. My father had too many.' He shouted into the back room where his wife had disappeared. 'But look at her, so pretty, no other wives for me.'

She said something in Mina.

'She's saying she won't come out again now I've embarrassed her.' Claude beamed with fond thoughts of her. 'I knew I would marry her from primary school; she's my friend.'

He moved on to use white paint, which created a shadow of the black. Then tiny details in colour: dress fabric, leaves, jewellery on silhouette wrists. In twenty minutes, I had a painting of women going to market, passing houses and trees.

I wanted Claude to do some paintings for me to take home as presents. I wouldn't need them for a week but I firmed up the prices and left a deposit so he knew where he stood. I wouldn't be one of those foreigners he had to argue with in front of people, like a Swiss woman at the Sheraton who had photocopied his work and resold it: 'I argued with her in front of people and made her ashamed, but I think she still does it.'

I felt sorry for the people who'd bought from the Swiss woman. The pleasure in buying a little bag of Claude's cards in the market was running your hand across them and realizing that each one was hand-done.

The photocopying Swiss woman led me to ask what he thought of . . . Picasso, for example.

'Ah, my father used to talk about Picasso a lot. He's a rascal, a big rascal, my father said. But he copied everyone. My father said he would go to other artists' studios in Paris to see what they were doing and take their ideas. But he did them in his own way, so we can't say he had no talent. Ah, we know him here, a big rascal. But when I looked at his pictures in a book once, I thought he had a very good mind. When I have time, I want to try some of his ideas.'

Claude said the style of painting he did was called Poto Poto painting; he didn't know what this meant but he thought the whole tradition originated in the Congo. He suspected that it meant 'shadows' in some Congo language, but he was just guessing.

Later, on the off-chance, I consulted the Internet for him. Poto Poto was the name of a district of Brazzaville in Zaïre/Congo, where a Frenchman had set up an art school in the 1950s to encourage traditional African art, particularly the silhouette paintings he saw people use to decorate their homes. His free school also taught sculpture, marketing, and the traditions of European art, but its particular work was in formalizing the tradition of silhouette painting. The influence of the Frenchman had been quite odd. He was determined to maintain Poto Poto painting as a pure tradition – for this reason the subject matter could never include anything modern: cars, skyscrapers, motorbikes . . .

What Claude liked most about my report was that the man who'd adopted and taught his father had probably been educated at the famous backstreet school in Brazzaville. 'My father always said the paintings had to be of traditional subjects, real African things, so that tells us, doesn't it.'

Once we knew that Claude was only temporarily lost to us, while his wife had her baby, we could go where we were going. That Claude would resurface to cheer up Isidore after the experience I was about to put him through was more important than either of us imagined.

Isidore had occasionally pointed out Cotonou's psychiatric hospital, on the edge of town, ironically close to the beach where he'd lived as a child with his mad uncle. There were buildings all round the hospital now, but once there'd only been forest. Then, the patients would come out for walks with their nurses, two by two, through the forest and along the beach; they wore khaki suits and looked very sad. They didn't wear suits any more, though, and they didn't do their two-by-two walks. Isidore didn't know what they did, but we thought I might as well try to find someone inside to answer my question: what did they do with someone who'd been sent mad by witchcraft?

Ignace, the chief psychiatric nurse, was a similar type of man to the traditional healers Isidore liked – quiet, kindly with something about him that inspired trust. I told Ignace that I had no training in his subject, just an interest.

'A writer, of course you're interested. Good.'

He said it would be easier for me to see what he did by following him around, asking questions and seeing for myself. I could talk to the patients for myself, draw my own conclusions about the hospital.

The hospital was a collection of small buildings scattered round an extensive garden. I did know enough to recognize the heavy tread of Largactil and Diazepam when I saw it. The hospital garden was like walking into the film set of *Suddenly Last Summer*. This was a garden of slow-moving, vague people, shuffling through their cure in a Tennessee Williams play. They were sedated but still flamboyantly peculiar.

A young woman all in pink with very pink lips and a netted pink pillbox hat rushed up anxiously to Ignace as he walked in with me.

'Who is she? She looks like a doll I've seen; she's a doll I've seen.'

'She's a visitor from Europe,' Ignace said. The woman accepted this for a moment but it was clear she didn't think it was a good enough answer.

In the centre of the garden, Ignace had his office and treatment room. There was a stable-style door he said he only closed when he was treating someone who didn't want to be interrupted, but even then he tended to leave the top half open so the patients could see he was there.

'So I'll leave it open, if you don't mind – they become anxious if they can't come and find me.'

Anxious, the woman in pink appeared in the doorway. She spoke very loudly, like a child calling out from the back of the class.

'Excuse me. Excuse me, but I have seen a doll like her.'

Ignace considered this for a moment. 'Perhaps the doll came from the same country as this visitor.'

'They all look like dolls?' She was a bit frightened about this.

'Where are you from, madame?' Ignace asked me.

'From England.'

The woman stared at me. 'And you all have the heads of dolls?'

'No. I think they made the dolls to look like them,' Ignace ventured.

She stared at me a moment, then laughed – she'd got it. 'They copy your heads for the dolls. They copy your heads.'

Happy now, she went back into the garden shouting that she knew why I had a doll's head to whoever else was interested.

Ignace smiled. 'If we try to see what they're seeing, then we can communicate. Now, I have some students from the university coming soon. They have to report on case studies they've been doing; you can see the sort of problems we have. There's a small number doing psychiatry at the university – mostly they do straight medicine. Psychiatry is . . . It seems like a luxury compared to the need for straight medicine. We may have more this term; the university is still sorting itself out. There's a problem with students who would normally go to the Ivory Coast but because of the trouble there we have to find places here. Also, there were universities in Burkina and Niger but they closed down because of lack of money, so Benin is fast becoming the educational centre for the Francophone countries.' He beamed enthusiastically. 'I'm hoping in the new influx I can benefit and find more who want to study psychiatry.'

While we waited for the students he told me the hospital's history, occasionally interrupted by patients at the door wanting to know if their visitors were still coming, if they could go to the shops with their supervisor, if it was true they had to eat lunch even when they didn't want to . . .

Ignace always addressed the patients respectfully, '*vous*' not '*tu*' even for the teenagers. He called them all by name and, for the moment they were talking to him, he acted as if they were the only patient in the place. I felt that half the reason for their fretting at the door with questions wasn't for the answers – they liked the way he spoke to them; it assured them of their importance in the world where they were more usually dismissed as crazies. Some just put their head in the door to check he'd arrived for work. Ignace was in his office: all was right with the world in the Tennessee Williams garden.

In the colonial days, the hospital had been a private institution for ex-pats gone strange. Then it had been a state institution, run on very 'lock 'em up' lines, for the criminally insane. Now the criminally insane were in the prison system and, since the late seventies, the hospital had been rebuilt on more soothing and attractive lines – and tried to cure the troubled.

There was some government funding for the hospital but never enough. People were brought by their friends or relatives. Relatives were better because Ignace liked to involve the family in the treatment, to help them understand that they might have had responsibilities in the illness and they could help in the cure. Each patient needed someone to stay with them to do their cooking, shopping, supervise their medication – to keep them sorted out on a practical level. It also helped that people unused to being away from their community had a familiar person with them and weren't troubled by the added problems of homesickness and isolation.

Food was provided free, as were medicines if the patient really couldn't afford to pay; there was, of course, no charge for the treatment. Patients could come daily as outpatients, or pay £2 a night for a shared room, £3 for a private room. The hospital took anyone, except pregnant women or people under sixteen. There was another hospital in the north, but this one was the facility for the entire southern region as far as Parakou.

Ignace had to move us to the side of the room as the students arrived. There were five female students, one male; all looked to be in their early twenties. Studying something regarded as a luxury, they did all look well-to-do for students.

They were just settling with their notepads when a smartly dressed man carrying a briefcase came in and said, 'I'm just off to my conference at Government House.'

Ignace nodded, said he would talk to him later.

'Good morning, students.' The man smiled at them. 'Nice to see you. Work hard.' And he hurried away.

'He seems better,' one of the students commented.

'Hmm.' Ignace looked dubious. 'He was screaming and carrying on till nine o'clock last night. I prefer him when he thinks he's my boss. We'll see how he is tonight. It's the thought of night that sets him off. He's a patient who would interest you –' he looked at me. 'He thinks witches will take him in the night. I haven't really treated him for that yet, I've just been giving him something to make him sleep, but we'll address it little by little. Anyway . . .'

The students began their presentations and Isidore, who'd been almost silent since our arrival, seemed to be having a turn. He covered his face. Then, after the first student had been talking a while, he excused himself and dashed from the room. I didn't know what to do.

Ignace said gently: 'Some people find this a hard place to visit.'

The student was making a report on a patient who was a Fon, so perhaps it was as well that Isidore was absent for what Ignace said next. The student had found it hard to get the man to talk to him, so he couldn't make a proper report. Ignace asked if he knew the man's race and family history.

'He's a Fon, from Abomey. He's one of nine children. His father had three wives. A niece is with him as his caretaker so I have this information from her, that's all.'

'Talk more to the niece,' Ignace suggested. 'You have a lot of clues there. The Fon have a lot of problems, particularly around Abomey as they intermarry too closely. Also they are polygamous; polygamy causes a lot of trauma and unhappiness for people in childhood. Arguments and distress. The Fon believe in witchcraft – they have many malevolent people in their communities who prey on these fears.'

'The patient was brought here after he'd been drinking for a long time; he said a spell had been put on his house and he wouldn't go in.'

'Hmm. The alcohol here is very strong, quickly producing

hallucinations. For the moment talk to the niece for more family history and treat the patient with Diazepam for his alcoholism.'

Ignace was spelling out these things for my benefit. Alcohol and witchcraft seemed to be involved in all but one of the cases. All but one of the patients was Fon. There was a Yoruba from Dassa. But Ignace always wanted to know if someone was a Fon before he started hearing more. He was Fon himself; he knew the territory.

What emerged was that every patient the students talked about had been taken to traditional healers before the hospital was tried. Every patient's family had been advised that witchcraft was the problem.

Ignace sighed. 'I find it isn't hard to explain to the patient that they're not bewitched. The hard part is convincing those around them.'

When they finished their presentations, Ignace talked to the students about the importance of involving caring family members in the treatment. They had to be convinced that this was simply an illness, not necessarily permanent, not a source of shame. It was also *never* witchcraft. But people lived in a belief system; you couldn't say 'There's no such thing as witchcraft', or the door would be closed. You could make them believe that, in this instance, it was simply an illness. That the family member they thought was lost could be restored to their place in society. Ignace finished with a heartfelt inspiration for his students. 'You're entering a profession that is seldom followed and little understood in this country, but you should be very proud of what you've chosen to do. Mental illness touches so many people, and if you succeed in curing only one person in your career, restoring a person to their rightful place in society, only one, then you have succeeded.'

He made me want to rush out and retrain in psychiatry immediately. The students left enthused. I needed to go and check on Isidore.

He was sitting with an old man, the gatekeeper. The old man had a slightly tilted demeanour which made me think that he was a former – or current – patient. He was gentle but definite, consulting lists, telling some patients they couldn't go out, telling others they could go out but they could only be half an hour. Telling another she could come in if she wanted but Ignace wasn't expecting her for three days . . .

'I'm sorry,' Isidore said. 'I had to come out. Luckily this man said, "Sit down, have some water." He said I shouldn't worry, some people can't stay in there. I didn't expect I couldn't cope. I can wait as long as you like; don't ask me to go back in there.'

I apologized to him.

I'd been very thick-skinned. Madness had ruined his life. I was no expert, but I'd come to the hospital with far more information than Isidore had.

He said he felt very bad – in a place like this he should be beside me, just in case . . .

'There's nothing that worries me, honestly.'

'I'm sorry, Annie. Everyone has something they can't cope with. For you it was the blind children made you cry. For me, seeing so many people so mad, it made me cry. Take as long as you like, but I'll have to wait here.'

'He'll be all right with me.' The tilty gatekeeper put a hand on Isidore's shoulder. 'You go on back.'

I took a watchful walk through the Tennessee Williams garden. I couldn't see the horror that confronted Isidore. The strangely muted people were so obviously cared for, to the best standard that Ignace and his boss could muster. Patients worked in vegetable gardens; some were repairing a building, with a lot of Laurel and Hardy feet-in-buckets confusion but enjoying themselves nonetheless. Some lay in the shade, staring, hopeless. But I thought the hospital was the best it could be.

Ignace was studying papers in his office.

'Is your friend all right? He's Fon, isn't he?'

I said yes to both questions.

'I'm a Fon. That's why I chose this career. There are social factors with us that cause a lot of unnecessary unhappiness. And you get old devils out in the villages who know all about what's happening to a person, know every detail of their situation, so they can prey on their fear. If someone's at the very edge of stress and find a bad *gri-gri* in their house, it terrifies them, sends them over the edge. Come, here's a young man you should meet.'

He was young, eighteen. He was very bleary from tablets but answered clearly Ignace's question about witchcraft.

'Yes, me and my family, we thought it was a witch but it's an illness.'

'Is that better, for it to be an illness?'

'It's in my hands. I can make myself well with tablets and keeping calm, never drinking alcohol. This kind of thing. It's in my own hands. What else do you want to know?'

'That's what I wanted to know, thank you.'

'Right, only we're building a new dormitory here. I'm the only patient who has some building experience so I can't leave them.'

He went away, with his life in his own hands.

I asked Ignace why people were always reported as running mad in the markets, why they were always naked in the markets.

He smiled. 'Yes, they do say that, don't they. The men, yes, they do go naked. I don't know what that is. Whereas the women do the opposite, they overdress and decorate themselves excessively. I think people want to manifest things. What would they do in your culture to ask for help? Suicide attempts, don't they do that a lot in the West? Now, I have two patients to see. Think of something when you see these people. There is no concept of dysfunctional family here. People always think their problems are recent – loss of a job, bad husband – the idea that childhood affects later life isn't understood here. People love their children but they aren't careful of their feelings. They think madness falls on someone. It's hard to make them see that it has built and built.'

A mother and her teenage son came in. He seemed very hyper, very loud, but whatever was wrong with him he exuded an endearing, jovial warmth. I'd seen him wandering about the place earlier,

giving a new arrival directions to the dispensary, then helping with
the dormitory building, showing another patient how not to get
paint all up their arm.

His mother looked tired. She was half the size of the big rowdy
son and, despite what Ignace had said about dysfunctional families
and lack of understanding, she seemed to have a lioness determination that her son could be put right. Guillaume, the son, wanted
to know where my husband was.

I didn't understand the question. The mother answered quickly.
'Her husband is outside.'

'Outside? He should be in here. Ignace, why is her husband
outside? He's supposed to stay with her.'

'He'll be back in a minute,' Ignace said, smiling at me.

'But she should know to stay with her supervisor.'

'He'll be back,' the mother said, with an apologetic glance at
me.

Guillaume seemed to think this was a very rum do and told me
sternly, 'You should stay here in the office with Ignace until your
husband comes back.'

I told him I would.

Then Guillaume forgot about me; he had troubles of his own.
'My mother just told me I had to stay here another five days – I
thought I could leave tonight. What's happening?'

Ignace smiled at him calmly. 'We're friends, aren't we,
Guillaume?'

'Yes, but I have to leave tonight.'

'It's a long journey. I'd like you and your mother to rest first.'

'For five days?'

'Are you unhappy here?'

'No, I like it here but my mother wants to go home. She misses
the other children.'

'Your mother is happy. I don't know why you're worried; you'll
go home very soon. Were you helping on the new dormitory?'

'Yes, we're painting it. But my mother wants to go home.'

Taking her cue, mother said, 'I would like to see the dormitory
finished. When other patients come here, we can think to ourselves

we helped make the new nice dormitory for them. Let's stay till it's finished.'

For his mother's sake, Guillaume decided he would stay. But as for me . . .

'Ignace, do you want me to call her husband, or can she sit in here?'

'She can sit here till he comes.'

Ignace said Guillaume could get himself worked up into a frenzy of anxiety about nothing but today's crisis seemed to have passed. 'The reason he's staying is I know I haven't balanced his medication right yet. But we're getting there.' He smiled. 'Besides, he's kind of fun.'

'He obviously thinks I'm in big trouble.'

'Yes, that's interesting. Most of the other patients are assuming a white person must be a doctor.'

A large family group came in with a middle-aged man. He was very slow because of his medication. He looked fifty; he was only thirty. His family had completely written him off and Ignace had worked hard to persuade them to come.

The patient was a mess of shame and misery. For my benefit Ignace asked his aunt a question. What was he like as a child?

'As a child?' She looked baffled. 'He was a child.'

In Britain, America, even people who couldn't read and write understood how to answer that question. Although the language of psychiatry and therapy we'd all gleaned didn't seem to make us happier, or healthier. Just helped us have names for our problems and places to lay the blame.

The man told his life story very slowly and painfully. It made me loathe the family sitting round him.

He'd been working in Niger, sending home good money. He had a wife and child. But he was helping all the family. He came home on a holiday to find his wife had died of cholera. No one had told him. They hadn't wanted him to lose his job. He'd refused to return to Niger, wanting to spend time with the child. But the child was sick, too, and died in a matter of weeks. He couldn't bear it, but he was persuaded that he must help the family – he was the only one with qualifications for a good job. He took another job, miles from home, in Kandi. He knew no one up there and didn't feel like making new friends. He'd started to drink in the evenings to ease his loneliness. This got out of hand and he was sacked. For two years he lived in a community in Ouémé where they made *sodadi*, doing odd jobs down there. He could stay drunk all day. He drank himself so crazy that eventually his family was summoned. They took him to a traditional healer who said someone had done *gri-gri* against him because he'd made such good money in Niger.

'But it wasn't *gri-gri*,' the man said, glaring at his family. 'It was that terrible things happened and no one thought I would feel anything about it. I'm sorry I let my family down. But you sent me away.'

His younger sister seemed to see his life too clearly. She started crying. 'I'm sorry,' she said. 'I am sorry.'

The man looked at Ignace. 'That's enough,' he said. 'It's too much for them.'

The man went away and Ignace told the family how much better he was. 'You see, he stopped it for your sakes. He wants to return to his place as your protector but you need to wait until he's ready. In the meantime behave as if he has an illness, you understand me? He's weak but he'll get better if you don't expect too much.'

Apart from the crying sister, who seemed to understand, the rest of the family went out complaining about how long the cure was taking – and, whatever Ignace said, they didn't see much improvement.

I asked Ignace what he thought would happen.

He sighed. 'Actually what he needs is a life without that family, without the *sodadi*, and he needs a new wife. That's all. And that won't happen, will it?'

Ignace dealt calmly with a helterskelter of bizarre requests as he walked me to the gate. Guillaume appeared out of nowhere, his little mother panting behind him.

'Where's she going?'

'She's leaving now.'

'Alone?'

'No,' his mother told him. 'Her husband will take her home.'

'She's allowed home? She just got here. Ignace, is this right?'

I went with Isidore to a restaurant near the fishing beach. It was a haunt for the more entrenched French ex-pats. Long-term absence from France had made them cling to their nationality. They were having a *pétanque* tournament, drinking red wine, twirling handle-bar moustaches, and generally behaving like pantomime French-men. They were being thrashed in the game by the Beninois owner and staff of the bar.

The *clip-clip* noise of the game, the sea breezes and laughing shouts of '*Oh là là!*' seemed to help soothe Isidore's traumatized state. He told me there had been a particular thing that made him bolt from the room.

'Where I was sitting, I could see out the door. There was a boy, well, he was about twenty. I realized I knew him. Not well, but he lives in my area, he has a moped he takes to the same mechanic as I take my car. He was there, just outside, filthy. He was playing with himself in his trousers. Then someone gave him a bowl of soup. He drank some. Then he urinated in the bowl and drank it. And all the time he was looking at me, I knew he recognized me. I had to go.'

Isidore could see that Ignace could possibly help people get better, but not in serious cases like this one. I found myself resorting to something Ignace said he used in desperation – telling Isidore that psychiatry was stronger than witchcraft.

'It's not,' Isidore said. 'He was an ordinary man, out on his moped, suddenly he's worse than an animal. That doesn't happen without witchcraft.'

Dedicated and determined though Ignace might have been, I couldn't promise Isidore that I knew for a fact his neighbour would be all right. Psychiatry was not saving the world it came from.

'It's amazing how much people can break and still get mended,' was my final fluffy argument.

'Not if a witch has their soul.'

★

Claude had the biggest baby boy in the entire world, his brother told us at the gate.

'How big?' I asked.

'I don't know.' He grinned. 'But you know how Claude is.'

The baby weighed five kilos and Claude was wild with excitement and the adrenaline of exhaustion.

The baby had to be delivered by Caesarean section after his wife had a terrible labour, but she was fine, the baby was fine and Claude couldn't stop talking.

'Oh, that place. Women, what they go through. All the screaming, I never expected such screaming – we never heard that in the villages, did we? My wife was screaming, screaming. I was crying. I did this to her. I thought the hospital was the right thing. My mother told me it was bad there, I should take her back to the village where she wouldn't be surrounded by cold white tiles and strangers.'

Isidore agreed with him. He'd done exactly the same as Claude, thought that Cotonou hospital, all bright and modern, would be the best place. But the women did scream in there. He'd never heard screaming in the villages, either.

The doctor we'd met in Mono told us that when he'd first gone back to work in his community, one of the major conflicts he had with the traditional healers was over childbirth. But twice he'd yelled at families who'd refused to let him send a woman to hospital for a Caesarean and twice a traditional healer had delivered the seemingly impossible babies, with barely a murmur of pain from the women. His conclusion was that he was a young doctor and traditional healers had delivered babies for decades, using centuries-old knowledge. They knew how to do it better. No magic, nothing up their sleeves – they simply had more experience.

Isidore told Claude, 'Hospitals make the women frightened. Once they're frightened it all goes wrong.'

'But the trouble with the villages . . .' Claude sighed. 'There's the witchcraft.'

Isidore gave me a look as if to say, 'See, not just me.'

'You mean witches will kill babies?' I asked, knowing the answer.

'Yes, yes,' Claude said. 'There's too much trouble with witches out there. Oh, but my poor wife. What women go through. My mother and my wife's mother kept telling me to go home, that it wasn't my place to be there. But now I know, oh, really, now I know how much women should be respected.'

He suddenly hit a mental slump, all the strength had finally gone from his vocal cords. 'Ah,' he said, 'let me get you some drinks.'

And he sat motionless staring out the door, stupefied with exhaustion. Isidore sent a small Claude nephew to the shop for sugary drinks.

We took over the talking because Claude's brother wanted to know where we'd been, what we'd seen. Claude settled back in his painting chair, happy to let something that wasn't screaming in the labour ward go into his ears. An oversweetened drink and tales of the Peugeot's meanderings revived him.

'Truly, there are things in Benin. When my son is grown enough, I'm going to do like this: I'll get a little car and go all round every road in Benin, show him all the wonderful secrets here. Me and my wife and my son. I'd like us to see the world.' Suddenly he remembered there was plenty of excitement to be had at home and jumped to his feet. 'Wait, wait till you see this, Annie, you'll like it very much.'

He showed us the crib he'd bought for the baby, with a matching basket for all the baby's belongings. It was somehow very Claude, frilled with lace, lined with a baby-rabbit print.

'My wife hasn't seen this yet. I got my sister to line it all in the rabbit cloth – you can imagine, when I saw this rabbit cloth in the market . . . ! And see, here are some little wheels I bought; my brother's going to solder on the wheels. Then she can push out here, back and forth, see, out she goes with the baby, and easily, back in she comes . . .'

Sometime in between all the rabbit cloth and the panic at the hospital, Claude had done me some beautiful paintings.

I was leaving soon. I wasn't going to see the biggest baby in the world. But Isidore was going to call in: 'When you leave it will cheer me up to see him with it.' He laughed. 'Imagine how he's going to be with it. It would make a stone laugh.'

17

Don't Leave Your Dead
Cat Behind You

'Good morning. Sleep well, madame? No animals in the room?'

Boniface, the giant, slow-moving night receptionist had to say this every time he saw me. In a while, he'd check that there were no animals in my breakfast; if I went to the pool he'd ask me if that was animal free; he'd tell Isidore to check there were no animals in the car . . . With shy glee, Boniface had his joke about me and he'd created an entire album of improvisations on its theme. And he'd spread it all round the Hôtel de la Plage for others to make amused enquiries about the presence of animals.

This was now my identity in the hotel. I was the completely insane *yovo* who'd had a bad dream of animals and run the corridors naked looking for someone to save her. I'd have preferred my identity to be that of the very wise, beautiful or kind *yovo*, but . . . at least I must also have been considered the *yovo* with a sense of humour, because it was fine for everyone to do the animals joke at my expense, all the time.

I hadn't actually been naked; I had a towel round me on the night of the incident, officer. But I just know that had I been spreading the story for weeks, the towel would have got smaller and smaller. The towel in question, Exhibit A, was large enough for decency but not really large enough for dignity. Not when worn by a shaking, panting, high-pitched gabbling person appearing in the middle of reception, hair on end, at two in the morning.

Too much thinking about witches before bed, too much sun, insufficient attention to napping and possibly a dining experiment with tree-rat bolognaise were my pleas of mitigation. Also, the political situation in the Ivory Coast.

A panic among the moneyed of the Ivory Coast had led to a temporary exodus into Benin, filling the hotels and leaving nothing available for me but a shabby ground-floor room next to the back pool-cleaning sheds. Everyone had been very apologetic; it would be just the one night in the neglected underbelly of the hotel.

I'd heard a scratchy sound somewhere in a corner of the room just before I fell asleep. I decided it would be nothing.

The scratchy sound combined with rich ingredients to make me wake up convinced there was some beast at the end of the bed. When I was sure I was awake, I knew there really was a noise from the floor at the end of the bed. Common sense prevailed for a moment: it would be cockroaches. They were available as big as your pillow in Benin, and I'd become very flippant about them. If I turned on the light, they'd go.

They didn't go. The noise was far too much to be any kind of insect. And there were two of them. One was running about under the bed, the other was crashing around in a carrier bag on top of my suitcase. Rats. One running, one fighting a carrier bag to death in its sabre-toothed maw. That's what it would be. I grabbed the towel off the bed. Leapt for the door to avoid an ankle lunge from the under-bed beast and pelted down the corridor.

Boniface, dozing at the desk, was awaked by a woman yelping: 'Sir, sir, help me there is an animals in my room. An animals.' All French grammar gone with my dignity.

He smiled benignly and, with the polite, patient tone Ignace used for his agitated patients, he said: 'Animals, madame? What sort of animals?'

He was already on his feet, ready to help, but not as poised for battle as I thought he would need to be.

'Big animals, under the bed and in a carrier bag, it's somethings quite big.'

'Oh dear,' he said and just managed to hide a smile under an expression of earnest concern.

As we walked towards the room of death, I couldn't get the infantile quiver out of my voice. 'Sorry to disturb you, I didn't know what to do.'

'That's what I'm here for – any problems, I'm here.'

He pushed back the bedroom door slowly. As he'd suspected, there were no rampaging panthers with machetes.

He had his flashlight, looked under the bed. Nothing. He looked at the end of the bed, nothing. In the wardrobe, down the side of the wardrobe – every possible bear-hiding cranny. He kept a very straight face.

'Madame, I think they've gone.'

I pointed a quivering finger at the carrier bag on the suitcase. 'It's hiding in there.'

He opened the carrier bag, looked inside for a very long time, then bravely plunged his hand in and brought out . . . my toothbrush and shampoo.

Suddenly I felt very awake.

'I'm sure I didn't imagine it.'

'Of course not. Something disturbed you, but it has gone. The thing is, you've been all upset now, so you won't sleep easy in here. I'll move you to the room opposite. It was supposed to be taken but the people didn't show up.'

In his great arms, he picked up all my belongings in a swoop and transferred them across the corridor. After thoroughly checking inside wardrobes and under beds for danger, he took his leave.

'Thanks,' I said. 'Sorry to make such a fuss.'

'Not at all. I'm just glad to see you've calmed down. Now, sleep well. Any more problems, you know where I am.'

★

In the morning, Isidore was at reception with Boniface and a clutch of waiters. Boniface was doing something that looked suspiciously like an imitation of a woman clutching a towel round herself. Isidore looked long-suffering and weary. It was all very well for Boniface; Isidore had to put up with this kind of thing all day.

Boniface stopped and smiled kindly when he saw me. 'Ah, madame. I was just explaining why your room had changed.'

'What do you mean, "animals"?' Isidore wasn't going to indulge my nonsense. 'What sort of animals?'

'Something big got in the room.'

'Big imagination,' Isidore said.

Boniface was a much nicer person than Isidore and said, 'Well, we'll move you up to the first floor today, so you needn't worry any more.'

Isidore wasn't having me encouraged like that. 'I don't see what kind of animal you think could have got in your room.'

'I've been considering that,' said Arnaud, the head waiter. 'When a cockroach gets in a carrier bag they make a terrible noise, just terrible.' He did a rather disturbing imitation of a clawing cockroach trapped in a bag, not something the Ivoirians coming down to breakfast expected to see the normally po-faced elderly Arnaud doing with accompanying sound effect: 'Crack–crack–crack Waaah. Was it like that, madame?'

As he'd done claws–waving antenna and flailing legs, I said yes, it was exactly like that – in case he did the extraordinary performance again and the Ivoirians called an exorcist.

'Of course that's all it was.' Isidore tutted at me. 'Running about in towels and no shoes . . . you're lucky you didn't have an accident of the feet.'

I ignored him and again thanked Boniface the hero.

'Ah, it's night time, madame, it plays tricks.' He glowed with benevolence. 'I know too well.'

I couldn't imagine what night terror would shake Boniface's six-foot-six solid sense. Isidore looked at him with scathing impatience and hurried me out into the day's business.

Long after the event there was still a round of animals joshing to be entered into before I could settle to write on the terrace. As I did this in school exercise books, easy to squash into bags, I think it contributed to a suspicion among hotel staff that I wasn't quite the age I should be in my mind. But if I was sitting quietly with my pens and books I wasn't doing anyone any harm, or likely to do myself any harm, so I was left in peace until Isidore arrived to take over responsibility for me.

Someone may have been telling the animals story to a new staff member, so that the strange Nigerian who approached me knew to say, 'Excuse me, sister, I hear you're English. I'm from Nigeria, doing some work here in the customs office. I'm going to sit by you and talk to you.'

Before I could say 'I'm waiting for someone' he was sitting and talking.

'Good, you have friends here – maybe you can recommend me to them. I'm looking for patrons who need aquariums. I design aquariums. I can draw one for you and you can recommend me. Do you know the hotel manager here? You can connect me with him; they need a beautiful aquarium in the restaurant.'

For a start, the manager was a shadowy figure, keeping to back offices and occasional staff-terrorizing runs around the building. He had better things to do than acquaint himself with guests, particularly the odder type of *yovo*.

'I don't know the manager,' I said.

'But you know people here – you can tell them about my aquariums. These are beautiful aquariums, with goldfish.'

'I'm going to London in two days. I can't help you.'

'London, even better. Then you can do business with me. I sell mobile phones in Nigeria. I need someone to buy them secondhand in London for me.'

'Why? Our mobile phones don't work in West Africa.'

He grumbled at me. 'Yes, yes they do. The Erikson model fours can work in Nigeria with minor alterations. I'm a cellular-phone engineer. I know how to do the alterations.'

He showed me some sort of identity card, very quickly.

'See, that's me. So you buy them, send them to me. I can sell

them for a profit and split that with you. It'll be very nice. Give me
your address and we can do business.'

A used-mobile-phone dealership with an aquarium-designing
customs officer didn't seem like steady work. 'I'm really not interested in doing business, thank you.'

'But you must be. It's an excellent plan, you'll find yourself very
rich.'

Presumably, I'd also find I'd been born that very morning.

I carried on with my pens and books, ignoring him.

He watched me a while, then gave an exaggerated laugh. 'You
are funny. You're not interested in being rich. Funny. But we will
be friends. I will give you my address, you will give me yours. You
are a Christian, yes?'

'No.'

He was astounded. 'What is your religion?'

'None.'

'What, no religion? You don't believe in God above?'

I said no, hoping brutal heathenism would finally drive him off.

'But, you are a human being, yes?'

I conceded that I had always been under the impression that I
was a human being, yes.

'So how did you come in this world?'

'From my parents.'

'Who put them in this world?'

'Their parents.'

Again the forced laugh, now with belly clutching. 'You are
funny. "Their parents." You are very funny. I work in a church
just behind the hotel here. You can come with me and see that
God exists.'

He'd pointed in the direction of the Fagin's Den fishing shanty.

'I'm not interested.' I was sure I said this with finality.

'Not interested to see that God exists?'

'No.'

'What is your name?'

'Annie.'

'Anne?'

Yeah, whatever.

'You know the name Anne is in the Bible.'

'Yes, I do know. She's the mother of Mary. Now look, I'm sorry, but I really am . . .'

I was cut short by a huge pantomime of laughter and gasping incredulity. 'You say you have no interest in religion but you know the name of the mother of Jesus? You are funny. We will be friends. You can help me, you will come with me to the church and we will be together.'

The whole thing was spiralling into too much madness. I put on a loud voice that couldn't possibly be funny.

'Look, I am very busy here. Please stop talking to me. I'm sorry, but you have to go, I have too much work to do here.'

Arnaud sidled out of the restaurant to see what was wrong with me now. The Nigerian smiled weakly and drifted away to whatever surrealist school of con trickery he'd come from.

If he had been a genuine aquarium designer, shown me impressive drawings and an extensive portfolio, that wouldn't have surprised me. I was always meeting people seething with talent, pursuing creative dreams despite getting stuck in a limbo of poverty and lack of opportunity. They did their thing anyway, just for the infinite pleasure Claude's father believed in.

There was a twenty-year-old called Philippe, living in a village outside Cotonou, who'd left school at fourteen to work as an apprentice in an electrical repair shop and now ran a community radio station from bathroom-sized premises at the back of the village hall. The day I came by, they'd been an hour late getting on the air because a chicken had jumped in the transmitter and knocked it off the roof.

Philippe ran the whole thing with his mate, MC Dassa, and anyone else who was around for roof-climbing, transmitter-rewiring assistance. The small studio was equipped with all the necessary, made from whatever worked. The headphones were two ear-size half-gourds, with a strip of bamboo arched between them. The microphone stand was wood, as was the control panel and its switches, wired up to an assortment of old speakers and cassette players. There was no electricity in the village, so the entire broadcasting enterprise ran off a car battery.

Almost as soon as I arrived, Philippe coaxed me into taking a seat behind the microphone to explain myself and take part in a phone-in. The only other phone in the village was a pay phone in the bar down the road, so there were some very slurry callers, a lot of excited shouting and long silences, with Philippe patiently explaining to callers that their phone might work better if they pressed the 'speak' button when they spoke.

With all his articulate confidence, I'd imagined Philippe must be the local rich boy with a hobby, but he had made this career for himself from imagination and gourds. What had driven him was seeing health pamphlets being distributed by a charity in the village, with warnings about meningitis. He realized this was well intentioned but hopeless – people couldn't read. He went to the Mayor with his idea. The Mayor said: 'I can give you a room and my blessing, the rest is up to you.'

Somehow it got going. Central government fretted at them, then embraced the idea. The main motivation, to broadcast health and nutritional information, was still at the heart of a wide range of broadcasts. The current campaigns were to get children injected against cholera, encourage the use of mosquito nets and to warn people off fake antibiotics manufactured in Nigeria and sold in the markets – there was nothing in the tablets but chalk.

Information was linked with music, chat, local news and interviews with anyone not local who happened to be passing. Programmes were in Fon, Mina and French. There was farming advice, there were religious broadcasts and teachers came in to give educational talks. The radio station, Esperance FM, stayed on the air as long as the battery held out.

Philippe still supported himself doing electrical repairs for a shop in Cotonou. He hoped his village would have electricity one day, and he hoped for a proper high transmitter, free from chicken interference. Apart from that, he was a young man basking in the infinite pleasure of his achievement.

★

Alihonou, a young artist in Porto Novo, wanted a lot more. He charged into government offices confronting ministers and he complained in the newspapers – Benin wasn't doing enough for its artists. I asked him if the government was making much effort on anyone's behalf.

'Football,' he told me. 'Too ridiculous. But the government makes an effort in football. They think it will make them popular. If Nigeria and Cameroon can be in the World Cup why can't Benin? Because we're too small and poor to develop a great football team. Our team is amateur, rubbish. But arts and crafts, that's our strength. We're historically artists and artisans. There's artists everywhere in Benin.'

There were. People sculpting, building strange cubist follies at the roadside, painting murals . . . Or making water pots in the woods. But Alihonou read, he told me – he knew what international artists got paid. He wouldn't be selling to tourists. He was an artist, not a souvenir maker.

Alihonou was in his mid-twenties and had already secured himself exhibitions in the foyers of foreign embassies and had his paintings sent to galleries in Germany and Paris – now he was working on America.

Alihonou was not going to be happy with enough money to buy rabbit cloth for a baby crib. More than money, he wanted African artists to be seen properly, not as makers of ethnic gewgaws to slot into interior-design plans.

Luckily, Alihonou was a very good painter. He mixed gouache and oils with local materials – soil, raffia, sacking, pieces of leather – to make abstracts perfectly evocative of the colours and textures of Benin. Slashes of blue broke up the burnt earths; materials were layered so deep on the canvas they reflected the historical tradition of bas-relief. Some canvases had geometric segments slashed out of them – angry, modern references to Dahomian appliqué. One slashed painting with layers of unidentifiable fragments piled on to it was called *Wasted Things*. It had tiny symbols in the middle. 'That's Fon,' Isidore said. 'It means "Learn to read".'

*

Meanwhile most people were more interested in football. It was the final of Euro 2000. French *yovos* were roaring round the television in the hotel bar. The staff watched the television in reception. I was on one of the reception armchairs, having become a sort of retarded pet for the staff.

A waiter suggested, very quietly, that perhaps the Beninois should want Italy to win Euro 2000, not France.

Arnaud thought this was petty – what did they know about Italians?

'The Italians never had a colony,' suggested Sylvian, the day receptionist.

'It's a football match, shout for the best players,' Arnaud grouched at him.

France scored. An African player. Sylvian was now arguing with a room cleaner about whether Ethiopia had been an Italian colony or simply invaded. There was a murmur of complaints against the French from junior waiters. Arnaud glared at them as if they should all be fired.

'Watch the game. It's a game.'

Another last-minute goal for France: they were going to win. The answer to the supporter crisis rumbled quietly out of Boniface.

'Those goal scorers for France, they're all Africans.'

Arnaud looked like he might jump up and kiss the wise giant's face. 'Yes, yes. And their great Zidane. He's what, Algerian? Moroccan? North African. This team winning the European championship is an African team!'

He beamed at his waiters. They saw the light. The European championship had been won by Africans. The loyalty crisis was resolved with wonderful timing, just as a boisterous Frenchman banged through the reception doors.

'We won! Come in the bar, I'm buying everyone a drink, we won!' he crowed.

The Frenchman banged out again. The staff decided that it would be a fine idea to go through to the bar and toast the winners.

'We can toast France,' Sylvian laughed. 'And know we mean us!'

*

Boniface stayed to mind the store. Isidore had been reading a newspaper with his back to the television.

'Is it over, then? Can we go to dinner?'

'Isn't it interesting about the French team?'

'What's interesting? The French can't do anything without Africans? Oh, big surprise.'

I took him out for his dinner before he burst a head gasket. Isidore had no time to worry about football – now I'd be eating late, I'd a busy day ahead and what if my dinner disagreed with me and I started some half-naked insanity in the night to make me the talk of the terrace all over again?

My sleep was disturbed, this time by music. I didn't mind the music so much as one of those terrible DJs who kept stopping the music to yell: 'Good evening, Cotonou, are you having a good time?'

Everyone would scream that they were, yet for some reason he'd have to ask again straight away and then ten minutes later check again.

I thought there must be a party outside by the pool, so presumably I could leave it to one of the French guests to ring down and complain about the noise – no point me soiling my reputation for having a sense of humour. I was very surprised that there was equipment in the hotel efficient enough to make that much noise.

Next morning, the French were staggering about the terrace in a very bad way. They all had hangovers from football celebrations anyway and then the noise . . . Till four in the morning, one man complained. I must have been made of deafer stuff because I'd slept long before that.

The music hadn't been anything to do with the hotel. Boniface showed me a leaflet about what they'd thought was a fancy restaurant and apartment block going up behind the hotel. Cheekily, at the eleventh hour, these leaflets had been put out advertising 'The Biggest Disco in Africa. Music till five, five nights a week'.

'Oh no,' I sympathized. 'This could be a disaster for the hotel.'

Boniface shrugged. 'The manager is sorting it.'

Funnily enough, The Biggest Disco in Africa never played loud music again. It became an overspacious restaurant. What the owners hadn't reckoned with, in their sneakiness and cheekiness, was that the hotel was owned by the government. A few phone calls and it wasn't bleary-eyed Frenchmen complaining, it was Kérékou's soldiers on the doorstep telling them to keep the noise down.

While the French sat around looking ill and the live-in staff crawled dozily from table to table, I was annoying everyone – chattering cheerfully to Isidore about what a lovely breezy day it was, and look what the people on the beach were doing, wasn't it great . . . ?

The breeze had brought out kite fliers; men with home-made coloured kites stood at the sea borders absorbed in the meditative pleasure of their hobby. Then a gang of kids came along and started doing acrobatics on the sand: human pyramids, perfect cartwheels, backflips, high double-somersaults – Olga Korbut-level midair japes. Anywhere else, you would think it had to be a troupe of professionals having an open-air rehearsal. But here . . . Isidore confirmed it: just kids, mucking about.

His own kids were in the car, not jumping or springing in any way. They always took a while to relax out of shyness. I'd sing and chat and generally disport myself like a fool till their silence snapped and they'd twitter questions and opinions in their tiny voices.

They'd come out with us a couple of times, and they weren't exactly hard to please – a trip to the airport to meet me from the plane was a day out. Isidore worked himself ragged to see that his cherished boys had everything they needed – pleasure jaunts were something there was seldom the time or money for.

As usual, Antoine and Lucien were scrubbed shiny and ironed crisp. They had their church outfits on: shirts, ties and little tiepins with pictures of the Sacred Heart. Antoine liked to carry a lot of pens and put his hands in his pockets to show he was really quite a big fellow. Lucien was much softer and, once shyness left him, he liked to be hugged by any available adult.

At first it looked as though the excitement of our excursion might have to be just in being out, not in the place itself. We left the main road, down a dirt track and into a large, neglected car park. We had to pay at the entry gates, and ahead of us there seemed to be a many-years-overgrown bombed city. Near us was a man offering himself as a guide; we thought we'd better take him along as we had no idea what we were seeing.

Leading us away from the bombed view, the guide showed us an attractive bar and small hotel, maintained and in use. Then he led us down a formally flower-bordered path and through a trimmed hedge to an artificial lake. A lake the size of Hendon.

There was a wide-ended jetty – here, the guide explained, people could have parties.

A couple of pedalos were stranded on an artificial beach and all the lake surrounds were grassed in what must have been a massive turf-laying operation.

'People can come here to have picnics, just pay the entrance and enjoy their day,' the guide enthused.

Down another path, another lake. This one was surrounded by weeds and covered in green slime. A few rowing boats mouldered on the banks. This lake was for fishing.

Up a slope and we came to a Hilton-sized hotel, Olympic-sized outdoor pool, a totally deserted dust-filled shopping mall and all kinds of neglected bordering hedges and picnic bowers.

'Only the outdoor pool here is ready. Inside the tall building is an indoor pool and a conference centre. These shops and the main hotel, they aren't finished yet. The owner has had a problem raising the money. But we make a living from what's here.' The guide didn't seem to be registering how dumbfounded we were. The children were looking politely bored.

Another trek to some extensive foundations overlooking the sea. These were to be self-catering apartments. Then, finally something for the boys. A funfair. All attractions but the central rusting roundabout were covered in plastic sheeting. The guide shouted for the roundabout man; Antoine and Lucien climbed aboard. Antoine not such a grown-up fellow that he wasn't chirruping with glee to be in a small red aeroplane, while Lucien chose a silver motorbike. It was the equivalent of five pence a go. I had no small change, so Isidore went off to the bar to find some. Meanwhile the roundabout did its round and slowed. I gave the roundabout man a note equivalent to fifty pence and told him to keep the machinery going. I'd suddenly remembered that childhood dreaming of how wonderful it would be for roundabout rides never to end.

I thought Isidore would berate me for being so indulgent, and that it would all be my fault when the boys were sick as dogs, but luckily he was distracted with his own find.

'Something very strange in the bar,' he whispered. 'I shouldn't tell you but it's full of prostitutes. They wanted to know if I'd come for them. Apparently men from Porto Novo with a bit of money come out here for this. And there are four mysterious Frenchmen in the hotel; they never go out but they use the bar and the girls.'

What were they doing out here in this beached white elephant? And what was the story of the white elephant anyway? Isidore thought we'd pal up with the guide a bit more to get the full story. Meanwhile, what was I doing to his children . . . ?

We passed through more overgrown acres, studded with rusting construction equipment and semi-finished or empty buildings. The guide had forgotten what half of them were supposed to be for. He said that the owner had started the place eight years ago and the finish date was uncertain. One morning the builders were gone. The owner said he'd fired them but six months had passed and there was no sign of a new firm.

The staff employed in the finished sections still had their wages. Visitors came at weekends, just enough. The project had gone too far to close down but, as Isidore suggested, the owner hadn't really thought how unlikely it would be he'd ever see a profit. It was way over the top. Foreigners didn't come to Benin for this kind of thing, and rich Africans could get the real thing abroad.

The guide told us the owner was a politician. He had been in government before Kérékou's '72 revolution – very corrupt, very rich. Kérékou had chased him away. He'd lived in Switzerland until Soglo allowed him back, and that's when he'd started the grandiose folly. Now that Kérékou had returned in a more pragmatic frame of mind he'd let the owner stay in Benin, in exchange for some political funding. Perhaps backhanders to Kérékou had left the owner too cash light to resume his African Disneyland; perhaps the scam behind financing it had collapsed with the change of government.

We hiked another hike and came to another living section of the folly, the zoo. Lucien and Antoine brightened nearly as much as they had at the funfair.

A lanky Bariba zookeeper welcomed us.

'Oh good,' he said. 'Children is what we are here for.'

He currently had a clientele that were definitely not children.

In a big enclosure were five baby chimpanzees, all called Michael. With them were the four mysterious Frenchmen, who all looked like they had just that morning escaped from a high-security jail. The Frenchmen were larking about with the Michaels, showing them somersaults, karate moves, dances. The animals copied them with uncanny accuracy. Training them to courier cocaine would possibly be the next step.

'Ah, the Frenchmen are here playing with the Michaels all day,' the guide said. 'They never go out. Straight after breakfast, they come here. They love to see our Michaels.'

They didn't like to see me so much. Their gambolling with the Michaels was halted, they scowled and muttered among themselves. I tried to look as much like a top CIA girl after drug barons as I could with a Michael pulling at my hair and another one clamping itself to my back.

We all had a good go of the Michaels then the Bariba moved us on. The Frenchmen stopped muttering and went back to their animal training.

There were crocodiles to see, and baboons, antelopes, vultures, hawks, a hyena . . . Soon they hoped to have giraffes. The Michaels had rather stolen the show with their too-human personalities, but Frank the lion put on a good second billing of roaring at us and ripping into some animal intestines for a mid-morning snack. The guide showed us Frank's discarded metal feeding bowl, with great claw gouges right through it. There were two layers of metal fencing round Frank, but Lucien and I weren't going nose-pressed close like Isidore and Antoine. As Lucien said: fences break.

The Bariba clearly loved his job and his animals. For his sake and the guide's, I hoped that day trippers, prostitutes and muttering Frenchmen did keep the place ticking over. I couldn't see who would be coming to make it all operational and thriving, but if that did happen a peculiar magic would be lost, no more of the feeling that we were scavenging in a lost city dreamt up by J. G. Ballard.

Kérékou's communist revolution had encouraged some good intentions. In the 1970s he'd given the nod to a rich African-American who'd founded an agricultural college in Porto Novo. The education was specifically geared to village farming life. Someone from a village with a college diploma might end up driving a taxi or back working in the village fields anyway – this college gave them a qualification they could take back to their village and use.

Having traced his own origins to somewhere on the Nigeria-Benin borders, the American founder liked the anti-imperialist stance Kérékou was taking and offered him Project Songhai. The name was taken from the once powerful West African empire of Songhai.

Students came from all over West Africa. As well as climatology, soil studies and the usual stuff of agricultural courses, there were experiments using animal waste to power village pumps, and solar-power experiments and all manner of recycling experiments. Water hyacinth were planted to purify water; stronger, more nutritious vegetable strains were developed; better ways of protecting gardens from pests were investigated. The simplest things were taught – like locking your chickens up so they grew fat instead of developing the cyclist's sinew common to village chickens.

Using all the fresh produce grown in the college, Project Songhai was also a great place to eat. A tour of the college had taught me that methane gas from recycled excrement was used to power all the cooking stoves in the establishment, but the public restaurant still served excellent meals. So I'd made myself forget about the fuel.

To supplement their funds, students took visitors and school trips round the college. As we'd already done the tour, Antoine and Lucien were tagged on to the end of a school group and sent off into the greenery to learn.

I didn't know if it would be that interesting for them, but they came back an hour later very excited about nearly being pecked by turkeys and extremely taken with the concept of recycling.

'You put the old pig pooh, any pooh will do but mostly here it's pig pooh, you put the pooh . . .' Lucien bellowed over his post-tour juice.

'Yes, yes,' Isidore interrupted. 'We've seen it, stop saying "pooh".'

Lucien looked momentarily crushed.

Then with an irrepressible beam he said, very loudly, 'Even chicken or people pooh.'

'Some children,' Isidore narrowed his eyes at him, 'are lucky I don't take them up to the pooh pit and drop them in.'

The children fell about, too full of hysteria and sugary fruit juice now to be taken home; they'd have to be exhausted with sea air and a long walk.

On the drive back to Cotonou there was a lot of giggling and whispering about pooh from the back of the car until Isidore shouted, 'The next person who says "pooh" gets out and walks home!'

It had to be done: 'Pooh!' I yelled. Lucien, Antoine and I screamed with laughter all the way to the beach. Isidore said he very much regretted ever laying eyes on me.

Not really.

While the children were on the pooh tour he'd asked, if I had the time or money, if I could remember to send out *friperie*, secondhand clothes for the children. Any kind of clothes with English tags on them were very thrilling for them as well as useful.

After asking, he sighed. 'Sorry, there's always something I have to ask for. One day, and this is one of the things I'll be working and praying for, I'd like to have a house you and your friends can come to stay in. I'd like you to come as a guest, so our friendship is properly balanced, not always me asking.' He smiled. 'But in the meantime . . .'

Then he looked sad. I thought he'd finished talking and I didn't know if I could find something consoling enough to say. But he had a story for me: 'You know among the Fon we have a lot of respect for the animal the cat. Because it's clever and asks for nothing during its life. If a cat is killed on the road, we move it to the side of the road and put some leaves on it. Then, everyone who happens to walk past has to drop some leaves or earth on the cat, until finally it's completely covered and can rest in peace.' He paused a respectful moment for the cat. 'And then, there are people we call dead cats, who always have to be given things. That's me. Whatever leaves you can remember to drop on me . . .' He smiled without brightness. 'You might be gone a long time now, so don't forget you left your dead cat behind.'

He didn't see that I'd already been given a world of things by him. I'd always been asking.

I got in his taxi – he took responsibility for me. Now I had to figure out what responsibility for him I could take . . . There was no plan, I just knew I had a cat-covering job.

I'd got in his taxi, no idea where it would take me, and through prancing horses, witches, spells, crying over blind children, car breakdowns and arguments, Isidore had emerged, out there in Benin, in his *gri-gri*-threaded car, a new fact of my life.

At the far end of the fishing beach the Celestine Christians in their white robes were walking slowly with incense burners and singing a tuneful hymn that the breeze snatched away to give to the waves.

Three lines of fishermen hauled their nets, made soft focus by the sea spray glistening in the evening sun. Isidore collected razor-fish shells; he liked to clean them, polish them and use them to decorate his house.

We tried to taunt a fat crab out of its shell with palm fronds. It disappeared into a hole. Antoine and Isidore dug after it with frantic hand scoops, saying it would make a fine tea, but all they managed to do was cover me and Lucien in sand.

The heat and the digging drove Isidore up the beach to rest under a shade tree. 'Walk where I can see you,' he told us.

The boys didn't know the game of building castles at the sea's edge and trying to channel water to stop them being washed away. We played it for half an hour, working very hard and screaming dances of rage when a rogue wave would simply crash down and destroy our creation.

'We're making castles to drown,' Lucien squeaked excitedly when Isidore came strolling back to tell us the catch was almost in.

'That's useful,' Isidore said. 'Come on, there's a lot of fish. It's been a hot day, you see, it's brought them to the surface.'

Women and children were pouring down the beach now. A toddler in a too big shirt trotted past us bowling a saucepan lid with a stick for his toy. A cavalry of sisters followed him on stick-and-paper horses.

There was a big glistening catch being stomped up the shore. I watched with the boys. Isidore watched me. Then he looked away, pretending to be interested in the fish because he was getting upset. This early-evening scene – sweat, celebration, sea spray and palms in the heat haze – was the first image of Benin that came into my mind. And it was something I watched with him every goodbye day.

Waves crashed, everything was blue and bright and yellow. Lucien and Antoine were scattering sand in a romping castle-build. Women sang, children danced and somersaulted round the catch. Isidore called me to the water's edge to show me a fat blob of jelly on the sand.

'A jellyfish?'

'No. No. Look inside, can you see?'

Through the cloudy white flesh I could see a star shape inside. A starfish.

'You see the star. When it dries the jelly goes and you're left with the star.'

I wanted to take it with me. Could we put it in a plastic bag so I could take it home?

'You can't take it, it would rot.'

I really wanted a starfish.

'Well, you can try. But it's better if you leave it where it is, let the sun bake it. Then later you come back and you see what it is, waiting for you all beautiful on the sand.'